THE FIRST HUNDRED YEARS OF MIKHAIL BAKHTIN

THE FIRST HUNDRED YEARS
OF MIKHAIL BAKHTIN

Caryl Emerson

PRINCETON UNIVERSITY PRESS   PRINCETON, NEW JERSEY

Copyright © 1997 by Princeton University Press
Published by Princeton University Press, 41 William Street,
Princeton, New Jersey 08540
In the United Kingdom: Princeton University Press,
Chichester, West Sussex
All Rights Reserved

Third printing, and first paperback printing, 2000

Paperback ISBN 0-691-05049-X

The Library of Congress has cataloged the cloth edition of
this book as follows

Emerson, Caryl.
The first hundred years of Mikhail Bakhtin / Caryl Emerson.
p.   cm.
Includes bibliographical references and index.
ISBN 0-691-06976-X (cl : alk. paper)
1. Bakhtin, M. M. (Mikhail Mikhaïlovich), 1895–1975.
2. Criticism—Russia (Federation)—History.   I. Title.
PG2947.B3E49   1997
801'.95'092—dc21   97-12451

This book has been composed in Galliard

The paper used in this publication meets the
minimum requirements of ANSI/NISO Z39.48-1992
(R1997) (*Permanence of Paper*)

http://pup.princeton.edu

Printed in the United States of America

3   5   7   9   10   8   6   4

In his time, Chesterton divided humankind into three large categories: *simply people, intellectuals,* and *poets. Simply people* are able to feel but they are not able to express their feelings; *intellectuals* are able to despise to perfection the feelings of the *simply people,* to ridicule them and to root out those same feelings in themselves; but the poets, in contrast, are granted the ability to express adequately what everyone feels but what no one can say. According to this classification, Bakhtin belongs in the ranks of the poets.

(*Sergei Averintsev, "Lichnost' i talant uchenogo"*)

Contents

Acknowledgments

A PARADOXICAL tension exists between Bakhtin's celebration of dialogic and carnival relations and his own modest, reluctant, self-effacing practice of them. He wrote very few personal letters and disliked the genre (whereas the "monolithically monologic" Leo Tolstoy exchanged literally thousands of letters and exposed himself at every turn); he avoided the telephone and was made acutely uncomfortable by formal interviews; he left no diary or written memoirs whereby others could piece together his life. He rarely spoke on his own initiative about his personal experiences. In a group, apparently, he favored restraint and "single-voiced" behavior: the role of featured speaker or of bemused and tolerant listener. Even with close friends he remained on formal terms of address. His style in the classroom—if we are to credit reminiscences by his former students— was that of an impassioned, authoritative lecturer before whom others sat silent and in awe; in seminars he remained very much the leader, never functioning as therapist in the guise of pedagogue. Talking about feelings was not his strong suit. For Bakhtin, who prided himself on his philo- sophical rigor, interrelations within the world of the text came first; to revoice its ideas in one's own intonation and to assume a responsible position toward those ideas was, in his opinion, a sufficiently challenging and delicate task. The emotions and anxieties that fill our own immediate lives (lived in what Bakhtin called the realm of "Small Time") should be visited upon that text only with the greatest humility and self-discipline.

Nor did Bakhtin make a fetish out of that category of academic dia- logue we call "scholarly apparatus." The first major essay he prepared for print contained only the scantiest documentation. As he put the matter dismissively in his opening paragraph—in what was, for a junior scholar, an astonishingly cavalier tone—excessive footnoting was unnecessary for the competent reader, and for the incompetent reader, useless. He never entered debates over his own work in print, which, as this study shall demonstrate, routinely received harsh reviews. Physically crippled for the second half of his life, the mature Bakhtin was increasingly immobile, ill, and (voluntarily or no) reclusive. One woman from Kustanai (the region in Kazakhstan where the Bakhtins were exiled in the early 1930s) does recall, however, a younger Mikhail Mikhailovich, pacing back and forth in the small office where he was employed as a bookkeeper, talking to himself.

Clearly Bakhtin's most important dialogues were with ideas. He read *in* them before he felt compelled to share *of* them. Most often these ideas were attached to specific personalities (living or deceased); on occasion, we must suppose, Bakhtin altered his own adamant opinions by submitting them to others' judgment. But given the pace of change around him—he lived through every major Soviet cataclysm—Bakhtin changed his mind and his topics with exceptional slowness. At the end of his life he returned, his lexicon scarcely altered, to the questions of his youth. He remained stubbornly a man of the book. And he valued, above all, two things that twentieth-century life (and certainly the postmodernist climate) has lost affection for: *depth* and *duration*. Both are required, he felt, if we are to develop the ability or the desire to linger over something long enough to know it; this lingering was the first prerequisite for "aesthetic love." Most of the time, as far as we can tell, Bakhtin lived in the category he called "Great Time."

These virtues of Bakhtin's method could not be reflected in the present book. As with all cults built up around reticent, private persons who have become valuable commodities, the Bakhtin industry has known its share of gossip, turf wars, unsubstantiated rumor, dialogue in bad faith, nostalgic fantasy, and willful misreadings. These "cultic" judgments, coexisting alongside superior scholarly commentary produced under often appalling conditions, are part of the fabric of this project. The image of the man and his thought that results is of course of my own assembling, everywhere subjected to the pressure of my paraphrase and selection of materials. But the basic inspiration for this image was the Russian community of scholars, and what I have taken to be its most fruitful lines of thinking on Bakhtin up to the centenary Jubilee in 1995. As such, this study owes a huge debt to a large number of Russian colleagues, credited in a cumbersome apparatus. Of them, I owe special gratitude to Vitaly Makhlin, Konstantin Isupov, Sergei Averintsev, Oleg Osovsky, Natalia Bonetskaia, Mikhail Ryklin, Igor Solomadin, Mikhail Girshman, Nikolai Pan'kov, Vladimir Turbin, Alexei Lalo, Leonid Batkin, Liudmila Gogotishvili, Elena Volkova, Mikhail Gasparov—and, of course, the three founding Bakhtinians to whom we are indebted for the initial preservation of Bakhtin's word: Sergei Bocharov, Vadim Kozhinov, and Georgii Gachev.

In this country my debts are also profound. The work of Michael Holquist and Katerina Clark, authors of the pathbreaking 1984 biography *Mikhail Bakhtin* and pioneers in the editing, translating, and explicating of Bakhtin's texts in English, remains foundational to the field. Clinton Gardner organized "Bakhtin sessions" in connection with meetings of his Transnational Vladimir Solovyov Society from 1993 to the present, which facilitated Western interaction with Russian Bakhtin scholarship at a crucial moment in the interaction of our two academic worlds. Several dozen Princeton students, graduate and undergraduate, startled me with their insightful "outsiderly" perceptions about Bakhtin in our seminars on his work, and I thank them for this experience. The intellectual support of the following colleagues has been especially helpful: David Bethea, Natalia Reed, Thomas Pavel, Alexandar Mihailovic, Donald Fanger, Deborah Haynes, Gary Saul Morson, Robert Louis Jackson, Richard Taruskin, William Mills Todd, Amy Mandelker, Mikhail Epstein, Brian Poole, Anna Tavis, Clare Cavanagh, Randall Poole, Robin Feuer Miller, and Charles Townsend (to whose wisdom I owe the initial insight, in the afterword, on Bakhtin and competitive sports). Thomas Cunningham provided the index and indispensable technical expertise. Princeton University Press, and especially the intelligent midwifery of Mary Murrell, Molan Chun Goldstein, and Rita Bernhard, made the final stages of fixing the text in print a consummate pleasure. My parents, husband, and larger family have graciously put up with this unendable project, absolving and sustaining its author for longer than any of us wish to remember. A special dialogue of the threshold was born within a highly irritable chronotope, which began with the line: "Bakhtin doubtless had something to say about that too, but I do not want to know it."

This book is dedicated to the lifesaving notion that no matter how our efforts or words may weigh in on the scales of Bakhtin's Great (or even Small) Time, all is not yet said, done, lost.

Abbreviations

A&A 90	*Art and Answerability: Early Philosophical Essays by M. M. Bakhtin.* Edited by Michael Holquist and Vadim Liapunov. Translation and notes by Vadim Liapunov. Austin: University of Texas Press, 1990. Contains "Author and Hero in Aesthetic Activity" ("A&H").
Bakhtinologiia 95	*Bakhtinologiia: Issledovaniia, perevody, publikatsii* [Bakhtinology: Research, translations, publications]. Edited by K. G. Isupov et al. Sankt-Peterburg: Aleteiia, 1995.
B sb I 90	*Bakhtinskii sbornik I* [Bakhtin anthology]. Edited by D. Kujundzić and V. L. Makhlin. Moscow: Lit. Inst. im. Gor'kogo (Moskovskii gosudarstvennyi pedagogicheskii universitet [Moscow State Pedagogical University], or MGPU), 1990.
B sb II 91	*Bakhtinskii sbornik II: Bakhtin mezhdu Rossiei i zapadom.* [Bakhtin anthology II: Bakhtin between Russia and the West]. Moscow: "Kollektiv avtorov" [Authors' collective], 1991.
B sb III 97	*Bakhtinskii sbornik III.* Edited by K. G. Isupov, V. L. Makhlin and O. E. Osovskii. Moscow: Labirint, 1997.
DKKh, no. 1 (92); *DKKh, no. 1(2) (93)*; *DKKh, nos. 2–3 (93)*; etc.	*Dialog Karnaval Khronotop.* General editor, N. A. Pan'kov. Vitebskii pedinstitut, Vitebsk, Belarus'. Maiden issue, 1992; last issue incorporated into this study: no. 2 (1996).
DI	*The Dialogic Imagination. Four Essays by M. M. Bakhtin.* Edited by Michael Holquist. Translated by Caryl Emerson and Michael Holquist. Austin: University of Texas Press, 1981. Contains the major essays in M. M. Bakhtin, *Voprosy litera-*

tury i estetiki: Issledovaniia raznykh let [Questions of literature and aesthetics: Research from various years]. Moscow: Khudozhestvennaia literatura, 1975.

Est MMB i sov 89 *Estetika M. M. Bakhtina i sovremennost'* [The aesthetics of M. M. Bakhtin and the present day]. Edited by A. F. Eremeev et al. Sixty theses prepared for the first Bakhtin lecture series, 16–19 October 1989, Saransk, by the Department of Aesthetics, Mordovia State University, 1989.

Fil MMB i etika 92 *Filosofiia M. M. Bakhtina i etika sovremennogo mira* [The philosophy of M. M. Bakhtin and the ethics of the contemporary world]. Edited by R. I. Aleksandrova and O. V. Breikin. Saransk: Izdatel'stvo Mordovskogo universiteta [Publishing House of Mordovia State University], 1992.

MB: FP 90 *Mikhail Bakhtin: Filosofiia postupka* [Mikhail Bakhtin: The philosophy of the act]. Edited by V. L. Makhlin. In the Znanie series "Filosofiia i zhizn'," no. 6 (1990).

MMB: ENS 92 *M. M. Bakhtin: Esteticheskoe nasledie i sovremennost'* [M. M. Bakhtin: His aesthetic legacy and the present day]. Edited by A. F. Eremeev et at. 2 vols. Saransk: Izdatel'stvo Mordovskogo universiteta, 1992.

MMB i fil kul XX, 1 (91); *M. M. Bakhtin i filosofskaia kul'tura XX*
MMB i fil kul XX, 2 (91) *veka: Problemy Bakhtinologii* [M. M. Bakhtin and philosophical culture of the twentieth century: Problems of Bakhtinology]. Edited by K. G. Isupov. 2 vols. Rossiiskii gosudarstvennyi pedagogicheskii universitet imeni A. I. Gertsena; Izdatel'stvo "Obrazovanie," Kul'turnyi fond SSSR, S.-Peterburgskoe otdelenie Bakhtinskogo obshchestva; S-Peterburgskii fond shkoly; Maloe gosudarstvennoe nauchnoproizvodstvennoe predpriiatie "Vnedrenie."

MMB i gum mysh I (95); *MMB i gum mysh II (95)*	*M. M. Bakhtin i gumanitarnoe myshlenie na poroge XXI veka* [M. M. Bakhtin and thinking in the humanities on the threshold of the twenty-first century]. Edited by N. I. Voronina et al. 2 vols. Precis from the Third Saransk International Bakhtin Readings, October 1995.
MMB i met 91	*M. M. Bakhtin i metodologiia sovremennogo gumanitarnogo znaniia* [M. M. Bakhtin and methodology in the humanities today]. Theses of talks by participants of the second Saransk lecture series, 28–30 January 1991. Izdatel'stvo Mordovskogo universiteta. Saransk, 1991.
MMB i PGN 94	*M. M. Bakhtin i perspektivy gumanitarnykh nauk* [M. M. Bakhtin and future perspectives for the humanities]. Materials from the Bakhtin conference held at the Russian State University of the Humanities, 1–3 February 1993. Edited by V. L. Makhlin. 1994. Prilozhenie k zhurnalu *Dialog Karnaval Khronotop*. Seriia *Sobytie v nauke*. Izdatel' N. A. Pan'kov. Vitebsk, Belarus', 1994. Publication realized with the financial help of the fund "Kul'turnaia initsiativa" in cooperation with the Saint Dmitry Orthodox Brotherhood, Vitebsk.
MMB kak filosof 92	*M. M. Bakhtin kak filosof* [M. M. Bakhtin as philosopher]. Edited by L. A. Gogotishvili and P. S. Gurevich. Institut filosofii, Rossiiskaia Akademiia nauk. Moscow: Nauka, 1992.
MMB: PNN 92	*M. M. Bakhtin: Problemy nauchnogo naslediia* [M. M. Bakhtin: Problems of the scholarly legacy]. Edited by S. S. Konkin et al. Saransk: Izdatel'stvo Mordovskogo universiteta, 1992.
MMB: ss 5 (96)	M. M. Bakhtin: Sobranie sochinenii v 7-i tomakh [Collected works in seven volumes], 1996–. Vol. 5 (Works of the 1940s to the beginning of the 1960s).

Moscow: Russkie slovari, 1966. General
editor, Sergei Bocharov.

MMB v S 89
*Mikhail Mikhailovich Bakhtin v Saranske:
Ocherk zhizni i deiatel'nosti* [Mikhail
Mikhailovich Bakhtin in Saransk: A
sketch of his life and activity]. Edited by
G. B. Karpunov et al. Izdatel'stvo Sara-
tovskogo universiteta, 1989.

MMB v zerk 95
M. M. Bakhtin v zerkale kritiki [M. M.
Bakhtin in the mirror of criticism]. Edited by T. G. Yurchenko. Moscow: Labirint, 1995.

NLO
Novoe literaturnoe obozrenie [New literary
review]. Edited by Irina Prokhorova.
Moscow.

PDP
Mikhail Bakhtin, *Problems of Dostoevsky's
Poetics* [1963]. Edited and translated by
Caryl Emerson. Minneapolis: University
of Minnesota Press, 1984.

Prob p&ist lit 73
*Problemy poetiki i istorii literatury (sbornik
statei)* [Problems of poetics and the history of literature (a collection of essays)].
Edited by S. S. Konkin et al. Festschrift
for Bakhtin's seventy-fifth birthday. Saransk: Mordovskii gosudarstvennyi universitet, 1973.

Prob n nasl MMB 85
*Problemy nauchnogo naslediia M. M. Bakh-
tina* [Problems of M. M. Bakhtin's
scholarly legacy]. Edited by S. S. Konkin
et al. Festschrift for Bakhtin's ninetieth
birthday. Saransk: Mordovskii gosudarstvennyi universitet, 1985.

SpG
M. M. Bakhtin, *Speech Genres and Other
Late Essays.* Translated by Vern W.
McGee. Austin: University of Texas
Press, 1986.

TPA
M. M. Bakhtin, *Toward a Philosophy of the
Act.* Translation and notes by Vadim
Liapunov. Austin: University of Texas
Press, 1993.

THE FIRST HUNDRED YEARS OF MIKHAIL BAKHTIN

East Meets West in the Ex-USSR

WHO WAS Mikhail Bakhtin? As the centennial year drew near, generated its promised mass of material and then receded, this question appeared ever more complicated. Although the restoration of lost or suppressed biographies has long been routine in postcommunist Russia, the obstacles to understanding Bakhtin's life are not the usual Soviet ones. This matter was addressed on the brink of the Jubilee year, in the December 1994 issue of the journal *Voprosy filosofii* [Questions of philosophy], by I. N. Fridman.[1] Bakhtinian terminology has been fashionable now for twenty-five years, Fridman notes; in fact, Bakhtin's name is already somewhere between a classic and a cliché. But no clear sense of his intellectual place in the history of Russian thought has yet emerged. Similarly confused cults had accompanied other post-Stalinist rehabilitations—of the great film theorist Eisenstein, for example, or the persecuted philosopher Aleksei Losev—but in those cases, the reasons for the obscurity were more straightforward: savage times, tyranny, disobedient genius targeted by the state and duly punished. Once the tyrant dies, sooner or later the records are unsealed and the lives are filled in. However shamefully delayed, eventually a slot is found for the thinker in Russian cultural history.

But with Bakhtin, nothing of that sort has happened. Although his life was indeed darkened by politics, we cannot blame political suppression for the lacunae in his biography—nor would Bakhtin, who was completely alien to a victim mentality, ever wish us to do so. We are now free to fill his life in, and yet, Fridman writes, "Bakhtin remains homeless and unattached. It is unclear where he came from (the philosophical tradition that nourished him is yet to be clarified), where or how he lived (there is still no biography in Russian),[2] or even who, in fact, he is (it turns out that Kanaev, Medvedev, and Voloshinov are also Bakhtin). Such a state of affairs is most auspicious for the growth of scholarly rumors." Fridman is

---

[1] I. N. Fridman, "Karnaval v odinochku." *Voprosy filosofii*, no. 12 (1994): 79–89. Quotations are on page 79.

[2] By 1994, this was not strictly true. The authoritative 1984 Clark-Holquist biography, which had long circulated among Russian scholars in unofficial translation, was supplemented in 1993 by a documentary biography authored by two of Bakhtin's colleagues, a father-and-daughter team at the University of Saransk; see S. S. Konkin and L. S. Konkina, *Mikhail Bakhtin (Stranitsy zhizni i tvorchestva)* (Saransk: Mordovskoe knizhnoe izdatel'stvo, 1993). The Konkin biography itself played into the legacy wars over Bakhtin; see chapter 1 of the present study, pages 58–59.

certainly correct. The appeal of a "homeless and unattached Bakhtin," unfinalized in the spirit of the novels he so loved, a thinker who appears not to have needed the secure points of reference that the rest of us require, has given rise on Russian soil to some paradoxical portraits. Two will suffice. Their composite features will become leitmotifs in the chapters that follow.

The first is by Vitaly Makhlin, professor at Moscow State Pedagogical University, host of the 1995 International Centennial Conference, and a central figure in the Bakhtin industry of the capital.[3] The essay, which appeared in 1992 in an anthology entitled *M. M. Bakhtin as Philosopher* published by the Institute of Philosophy of the Russian Academy of Sciences, deals with Bakhtin's legacy in the context of Western postmodernism. Makhlin asks how we might explain the "grotesquely anachronistic 'influence' of Bakhtin's thought, which ripened at the beginning of the century, in the West of the postmodernist epoch." The contours of his philosophy coincide with no major twentieth-century movement. Bakhtin was—and Makhlin enumerates—a non-Marxist, non-Formalist, non-Freudian, non-Structuralist, nonexistentialist, noncollectivist, nonutopian, nontheologian; "in a word, a non-modernist." Makhlin then surmises that Bakhtin's popularity today owes something to the fact that modernism, with its hierarchical and universalizing impulses, was at base monologic, whereas the postmodern temperament finds something congenial in Bakhtin's insistence on noncoincidence, incompatibility, and otherness [*drugost'*]. But Makhlin admits that the *bakhtinskii boom* of the 1980s and 1990s must have been motivated by more than the appeal of fragmentation and centrifugal energy, by then a commonplace. For Bakhtin is no postmodernist either. In fact, rather the contrary is true. As Makhlin concludes in his later and lengthier review essay "Bakhtin and the West" in *Voprosy filosofii* (1993), critics either get Bakhtin wrong from the start by equating the carnival impulse with political resistance, *ressentiment*, or ethical relativism (all of them, in Makhlin's view, "alternative monologisms"); or else they find, to their dismay, that the inner contradictions and unsatisfying aspects of "postmodernist theory" are most perfectly highlighted when we attempt to integrate Bakhtinian ideas into them or to explicate Bakhtin through them.[4]

The second portrait—by far the more eccentric—is also constructed out of what Bakhtin is not. Its author, the culturologist and literary historian Georgii Gachev, is one of the most colorful senior Bakhtin hands in

[3] V. L. Makhlin, "Nasledie M. M. Bakhtina v kontekste zapadnogo postmodernizma," in *MMB kak filosof 92*, 206–20, esp. 206, 209–10, 219.

[4] V. L. Makhlin, "Bakhtin i Zapad (opyt obzornoi orientatsii)," *Voprosy filosofii*, no. 3 (1993): 134–50, esp. 135–37.

the capital. At the Bakhtin panel of an international conference on Russian philosophy held in Moscow in March 1993, he delighted and appalled the audience with a spirited refutation of almost all the papers (Russian as well as foreign) that had been delivered on the subject of the friend of his youth, Mikhail Mikhailovich.[5] There is altogether too much sober scholarly talk about who Bakhtin is or what he could do, Gachev insisted. Better that we concentrate on what he could *not* do, on those aspects of reality that his particular angle of vision walled out. Bakhtin had no feeling for, nor knowledge of, the natural world; no living Eros (Gachev is among those disciples convinced that Bakhtin never consummated his marriage); no children; no dogs (only cats, Gachev obscurely remarked, "mystical and untrustworthy"); no daylight. "They sat around the table all night and smoked and talked, smoked and talked." In the process, Bakhtin destroyed the vertical dimension; everything was sublimated and spread out flat along a loving, horizontal "I-thou" axis where the ever present possibility of benevolent communication among equals supplanted—or at least kept at bay—the anxieties that would later define the bleaker landscapes of Western existentialism. In place of God, Bakhtin deified the everyday interlocutor. A creature made neither for prayer nor for parenting, he reigned in a world of philosophical conversations carried out over endless tea and cigarettes in small rooms in the dead of night. Bakhtin was a *mezhdusoboinik* (a "just-between-you-and-me-nik"). For him, the intimate voice and the chamber space was all. Gachev implied that such thinkers, or talkers, can be the source of brilliant isolated insights about literature and much spiritual uplift for their audiences— but they cannot be taught in school, cannot themselves form "schools," and are rarely forthcoming with a reliable methodology or an easily applicable theory. Such academic and institutional matters, sooner or later, require discipline, organization, verification procedures, and some constraining hierarchies.

To be sure, negative theology of this sort (defining a revered object by what it is *not* so as to respect its power or impenetrability) has a place in all mystifications and cults. As regards his own person, Bakhtin contributed to this state of affairs. He rarely spoke of himself and kept most contemporary schools of thought at a bemused distance; his tendency was to look at the world, discern two unacceptable poles functioning in it, and then posit an idea or method that would mediate or dissolve the opposition. He was always careful, however, to distinguish between the

[5] Transnational Institute East-West Conference on "Russian Philosophy and the Russia of Today," Moscow, 15–19 March 1993, cosponsored by the Institute of Philosophy of the Russian Academy of Sciences and the Humanities Research Center (PUT') in Moscow; panel on Bakhtin, 16 March 1993.

strength and importance of an idea, its internal coherence and ability to influence other ideas productively, and what he considered the much smaller importance of his own attitude toward it (an exemplary instance being his attitude toward Freud).[6] According to Sergei Bocharov, a close friend and disciple, Bakhtin considered himself neither a religious thinker nor a philosopher in the professional sense ("I was carried away by the Marburg school," Bakhtin remarked; "that says it all."). In Bakhtin's view, philosophy was a strict science—and much of what passed for Russian philosophy was, in his opinion, mere "thought mongering" [*svobodnoe myslitel'stvo*].[7] As this study will show, however, philosophizing, in the loose interdisciplinary sense, is precisely what many of Bakhtin's most ardent followers consider his most valuable contribution to scholarship. The local task of water-tight literary theory or a satisfyingly whole explication of artistic texts and authors had never been Bakhtin's primary concern. He tended, rather, to invoke literature as illustration of his principles or strategies for living and thinking.

During an interview held in the spring of 1973, the Mayakovsky scholar Viktor Duvakin asked the aged Bakhtin: "So [in the 1920s] you were more of a philosopher than a philologist?" "More of a philosopher," Bakhtin answered promptly. "And such have I remained until the present day. I am a philosopher. A thinker."[8] By Bakhtin's own testimony, then, his certified profession (philology, the academic field of linguistics and

---

[6] According to oral testimony at the end of his life (see n. 8), Bakhtin admired Freud as a great innovator, an "otkryvatel'" or one who opened up new worlds, whose work unfortunately had "no serious continuation on Russian soil"; but when pushed toward a personal assessment, Bakhtin admitted that with his Kantian orientation he found the Freudian approach "alien to him." "[Freud] did not exercise a direct, unmediated influence on me," Bakhtin remarked. "But all the same, there was a great deal that was not direct, that was rather more general; like every discovery of something new, even though one is not directly studying that new thing, all the same it has in some way broadened the world, enriched me with something." "Razgovory s Bakhtinym [Vaginov i drugie]," *Chelovek*, no. 4 (1994): 188–89.

[7] See the portrait in S. G. Bocharov, "Ob odnom razgovore i vokrug nego" [About and around a certain conversation], *NLO*, no 2 (1993): 70–89. Quoted material is on page 81. The essay has appeared in English, abridged and with some imprecisions, as Sergey Bocharov, "Conversations with Bakhtin," trans. Stephen Blackwell and Vadim Liapunov, *PMLA* 105, no. 5 (October 1994): 1009–24. There the term *svobodnoe myslitel'stvo* is rendered "unconstrained philosophizing" (1019).

[8] Overall, Duvakin taped eighteen hours of conversations and reminiscences with Bakhtin in February and March 1973. Selections from the transcript of these tapes have been serialized in the journal *Chelovek*, 1993–95, and were published in book form in 1996 (see ch. 1, nn. 1, 2). For the discussion referred to above, see "Razgovory s Bakhtinym: Sem'ia i gody ucheniia" [Conversations with Bakhtin: Family and student years], *Chelovek*, no. 4 (1993): 136–52, esp. 152.

literary scholarship) served him somewhat as a refuge and cover. He never disowned his work on Dostoevsky or Rabelais. But in the early 1960s he remarked to Sergei Bocharov ("with a grimace," Bocharov tells us) that much of what he had written on Dostoevsky remained "mere literary criticism . . . and there must be a way out to other worlds."[9] What might those worlds have been toward which Bakhtin was striving? The present study will suggest some possible answers to that question, as it examines the shifting boundaries and paradoxes in Bakhtin's reconstituted Russian image now that he has passed his hundredth year.

This project was prompted by several factors. On a world scale, of course, there was the collapse of the Soviet Union and the concomitant explosion of enthusiasm among Russian intellectuals for reclaiming, re-complicating, and "de-ideologizing" their recent cultural heritage. There was also the temptation to sum up the work of a world-class thinker during his centenary Jubilee; the Russian Bakhtin boom generated dozens of lecture series, monographs, pathbreaking essays, conference volumes, and specialized periodicals, all still virtually untranslated. And then there was my private conviction, after twenty years' work with these texts, that the person and philosophy of Mikhail Bakhtin could serve as an excellent test case and foil for Russia's "postcommunist postmodern-ism"—a postmodernism that is now being realized and evaluated along lines quite different from those followed by late-twentieth-century theo-ries of culture in the West.

Before we embark on Bakhtin, however, it might be helpful to the nonspecialist if this reclamation project were placed in some context and its major difficulties mapped out, for the political and literary culture that had shaped Bakhtin throughout his creative life is no longer intact. By the mid-1990s the unspoken codes that had conditioned Bakhtin's genres of self-expression had changed beyond recognition. The end of Soviet Communism was only the most recent parameter. For six centu-ries the ideal of centralized control had officially held sway in Russia (an ideal indifferently implemented in some eras and in others with vicious efficiency); Russia's cultural life was then freed of state supervision almost overnight. The nation became legally pluralist. Writers, philosophers, and religious thinkers, banned or crippled under Soviet rule, were revived enthusiastically and then risked becoming illegible in the space of several years. Such creative diversity and attenuated memory was exhilarating—but it was accompanied by an understandable anxiety. The new freedom, although it did serve to open Russia up, also created generation and liter-acy gaps more profound than at any time in modern Russian history—

---

[9] Bocharov, "Ob odnom razgovore i vokrug nego," 72 n. 7.

except, perhaps, during the reforming decades of Peter the Great. America has been a poor reader of this shift. Raised on Cold War slogans, many assumed that Communism had been merely an obstacle, not a worldview with its own languages, rationales, rewards, and economies. Once the obstacle of Communism had fallen away (or so many thought), Russian culture would begin to see clearly, get back on our track, and endorse values that made sense to us.

That this convergence is not likely to occur rapidly and easily—if at all—had become clear by the mid-1990s. The present study is designed as a contribution to that sobering discovery. For it is my conviction that Russian twentieth-century thinkers, and especially those of Bakhtin's stature who have been widely and successfully translated, stand to lose a great deal if detached wholly from their original contexts. The focus of this book, then, is Bakhtin's reception by his own culture—undertaken by an outsider to that culture. My outsideness brings both losses and benefits. Inevitably a non-Russian will assess evidence and assign value differently than natives and eyewitnesses. Russians researching their own past, for example, have been powerfully tempted to see residents of that prior oppressive regime as either martyrs or collaborators. Bakhtin was neither. He was a *survivor*. And in order to survive, both morally and physically (that is, in order to avoid causing harm to others and avoid sacrificing himself to no purpose), he had mastered certain protective skills and evasive tactics. It is unlikely that students of Bakhtin's life and work will ever know definitively to what extent these survivor skills deformed, or informed, his major ideas and texts. But interested parties, both East and West, should make an effort not to forget the pressures— and at times the exaltations—of working for one's whole life within such a language environment.

Here, then, are the major "classical" features of that rapidly changing environment. For most of Russian culture (from the tenth through the twentieth century), the printed word was viewed as sacred, and it was, in varying degrees, unfree. To outwit the unfree authoritarian word, numerous strategies were developed in the nineteenth century—among them "Aesopian language," a hermeneutic device perfected by Russia's radical intelligentsia. Designed to work under combat conditions, Aesopianism assumes that the world is allegory, that no one speaks or writes straight, and that every officially public or published text (by definition, censored) has a "more honest," multilayered, hidden subtext that only insiders can decode. Ever since the birth of modern Russian literature in the eighteenth century, Russia's greatest writers have been alert to the dangers of Aesopian thinking and at the same time fatally drawn to indulge in it. In the words of two prominent American students of Russian contemporary culture, Russian literary language was "the antithesis of 'plain-speak'; instead, it was a kind of culturally institutionalized and revered 'oblique-speak.' "[10]

Aesopian language and the prerequisites for reading it correctly would be mere academic chatter, a glass-bead game, were it not that literature and criticism has always filled a wider slot in Russian culture than has its equivalent discipline in the United States. In successive Russian empires, omnipresent censorship of real-world events tended to make literature the best refuge of honest ideas—and for at least the last 150 years, progressive Russian readers were trained to see nonfictional referents beneath every fictional surface. This was a very mixed blessing. Not only were writers taken as prophets (and often proved to be very poor ones), but those who interpreted literary art—the critics—assigned themselves an altogether inflated task.[11] The "nurturing critic" became a mainstay and lodestar of Russian nineteenth-century intellectual life. As one such critic put the case confidently in 1870: "All our artists would wander off along various paths, were it not for the critic-journalists who show them the way. Who guided our novelists—Turgenev, Dostoevsky, Goncharov . . .? They were guided by Belinsky, Dobrolyubov, Pisarev [contemporary radical or nihilist critics]. Novelists merely collect the firewood and stoke the engine of life, but the critic-journalist is the driver."[12]

This situation might appear to mimic the politically correct American campuses of the 1990s, except for one thing. Russian literary critics, as a rule, have not been seen as residents of a self-contained academic caste on the margins of society, whose operating procedures are parodied by outsiders from the "real world" to the amusement (and disdain) of the general public. On the contrary, Russian literature *was* the real world, and

---

[10] Nancy Condee and Vladimir Padunov, "Pair-a-dice Lost: The Socialist Gamble, Market Determinism, and Compulsory Postmodernism," paper delivered at the third meeting of the Working Group on Contemporary Russian Culture, Moscow, 15–19 June 1992.

[11] The best discussion of this phenomenon remains Donald Fanger, "Conflicting Imperatives in the Model of the Russian Writer: The Case of Tertz/Sinyavsky," in Gary Saul Morson, ed., *Literature and History: Theoretical Problems and Russian Case Studies* (Stanford: Stanford University Press, 1986), 111–24. Fanger opens with several lapidary utterances by Russian writers and bureaucrats on the status of the word, including the nineteenth-century Minister of Public Education Uvarov ("Among the rights of the Russian subject, the right to address the public in writing is not included"); Trotsky ("Reality began to live a second life in Russia, in both the realistic novel and comedy"); and Pasternak ("A book is a squarish chunk of hot, smoking conscience—and nothing else!") (111–12). "Russian writers have always worked with relation to a large imperative—cognitive, social, and ethical," Fanger remarks. "Whether they have proclaimed, accepted, resisted or rejected it, a considerable part of the meaning and importance of their writing has derived directly from that relation" (113).

[12] Nikolai Shelgunov, "Dvoedushie esteticheskogo konservatizma" [The two-facedness of aesthetic conservatism], in *Delo*, no. 10 (October 1870), cited in Charles Moser, *Esthetics as Nightmare* (Princeton, N.J.: Princeton University Press, 1989), 29.

Russian readers were raised to expect that literary criticism would provide the key to it. Critics assumed that their work would have important societal repercussions. When Maxim Gorky laid down the Socialist-Realist "rules" for creative literature in the Stalinist 1930s, and when Mikhail Bakhtin, then in political exile in Kazakhstan, wrote hundreds of pages that refuted those rules by invoking as exemplary different genres and different authors, both men were acting wholly within the tradition of Russian literary culture. For unlike America in much of its modern phase, literary accomplishment and criticism in Russia has mattered. You could get arrested and killed for it; thus educated society revered its poets and considered literary progress to be a bellwether of its own.

Such a fate for literary artists and critics has long proved both discomfiting and dazzling to free-world watchers of Russian culture. As David Remnick described this dilemma: "None [of the Western writers who visited Russia during the Communist period] were foolish enough, of course, to want to trade places with their mythic counterparts, but there invariably came a moment when a Western writer found himself wondering, painfully, why democracy necessarily meant a marginal place for serious writing and totalitarianism an impossibly exalted one."[13] It was this special status granted to writing and to writers that lost its official support—and its officially sanctioned torment—in the Russian Press Law of August 1990.[14] That law abolished Glavlit, the censorship agency whose approval stamp had to be present on everything with printed words on it; of equal importance, the statute legalized the whole idea of "autonomous publishing." Before 1990 a publishing venture or periodical in Russia had to be an "organ" of some other official body: the Writer's Union, a government ministry, an academic institution, the Communist Party. After that date, it become legally possible to register officially as independent, a move that would have been an absolute oxymoron under the old, that is, the Communist, regime. In place of the old polarity—in which the nauseating bland mush of official documents was answered by the often hysterical righteousness of underground dissident prose—one could hear the beginnings of a shared, neutral civic language. Thus Aesopian language began to have a rival in the public sphere, and lawful public discourse began to emerge that, for the first time in recorded Russian history, did not require the prior assumption of a lie. These developments were enormously healthy for the growth of civic consciousness. But so novel an attitude toward the printed word had its inevitably dislocating effects.

---

[13] David Remnick, "Exit the Saints" [Letter from Moscow], *New Yorker*, 18 July 1994, 50–60, esp. 50.

[14] For this story see Jamey Gambrell, "Moscow: The Front Page," in *The New York Review of Books*, 8 October 1992, 56–62.

Held captive, the word was believed to contain the truth. Once freed, it was supposed to work miracles. Instead of this miracle, language began to devolve into the same loose and indifferent thing that we in the West have long known the commercially public word to be.

The end of state censorship brought other paradigm shifts. There was the unhappy loss to literature of all those disciplines that, in more oppressive times, had invaded fiction because they had not been free to constitute themselves as professionally autonomous fields of study. "In Russia, criticism always played the role of an absent philosophy, sociology, culturology," one contemporary critic remarked, in a forum entitled "Critics on Criticism" that appeared in *Voprosy literatury* at the end of 1996.[15] "It was higher than ideology, higher than the censorship, because it dealt with great literature. In Russia, criticism is a reflex toward life, not toward the text. But life is too ambivalent, huge, diverse, and thus criticism deals with literature as a mediated form of life's mode of existence. The way a physicist needs an ideal gas for theoretical constructs." Freedom put an end to literature as the ideal laboratory science. When philosophy, theology, economics, politics returned to their rightful homes—that is, when Russians gained the right to talk openly of God, idealism, real-life murderers and state swindlers—there was less need to invoke the names of such literary heroes (or antiheroes) as Raskolnikov, Chichikov, a Russian Lady Macbeth. What, many wondered, would be left to literature, except the naked, free, and now devalued word?

Then there was the oft-heard, more practical complaint from professionals that "the literary process had disappeared." By this people meant that all sense of proper sequence or organic evolution in the production of literature had died out. And indeed, with the collapse of government controls and the return of Russian émigré literature to its homeland, everything appeared at once: the Gospels, the Talmud, Nabokov, Solzhenitsyn, Franz Kafka, Henry Miller, Samuel Beckett, James Joyce, the Marquis de Sade. Literary texts, stripped of their original contexts and genesis, were crammed into a sort of supersaturated space. In a culture accustomed to a great deal of regimentation from above and a quasi-religious mission attached to literature from below, this overload temporarily paralyzed writers and disoriented their readers. It resembled Bakhtinian carnival—but with this difference: there was no promise of any reimposition of the hierarchy, nothing stable in the background that might reassert traditional order and thus guarantee participants the recurring pleasure of violating it. As one young hopeful put it to me: How can the ordinary writer hope to compete "with Christ crawling out the win-

---

[15] "Kritiki o kritike," in *Voprosy literatury* (November–December 1996): 3–57, esp. 40. The critic is Dmitrii Bykov.

dow and Lolita walking in the door?" Clearly the time and need for Aesopian language had passed. But passed on to what?

This study will sample Bakhtin's role in this dizzying shift from centripetal Marxism-Leninism to the centrifugal currents of neo-humanism, neo-nationalism, and postmodernism. The émigré literary critic Mikhail Epstein provided early guidelines for understanding the transition in his 1991 essay entitled "After the Future: On the New Consciousness in Literature."[16] In previous eras, Epstein notes, literature—both official and unofficial—tended to be distributed in categories of pro- and anti-, "our own" versus "outsiders" [*svoi* versus *chuzhoi*]. After the collapse of Communism, however, things were suddenly no longer *anti-* but simply *post-*. Without the certainty of a single totalizing standard that one could either endorse or resist, it became much more difficult to get one's bearings. Epstein sketches a terrain where, once the old politicized binaries began to soften, Bakhtin's dispersive, centrifugal values, his carnival grotesque, his delight in authors who design their heroes to resist and outgrow their worlds, would have manifest relevance and appeal.

Epstein suggests that during those protracted years of collapse the great Hegelian plot (*plot* in all senses of the word) was thoroughly discredited in his homeland. The linear trajectory that Communism fixed for a culture or for a life—cradle-to-grave welfare, cradle-to-grave slogans, all of which sealed up the present and handed it over to a radiant future—went down in defeat, and with it, the very idea of epic plots and heroic leaps into tomorrow. Progressive sequence itself had become suspect, wherever it might be found. The immediate result was a flurry of new literary movements and sensitivities that favored modesty, fragmentation, interruption, residue, parts of things rather than purported wholes: phenomenalism, conceptualism, the rear- as opposed to the avant-garde, necro-realism, the metaphysics of garbage. This overtly postmodernist agenda glorified transitoriness and deadpan parody; it advocated a special style of writing whose aim, Epstein writes, was "not to proclaim but to stutter." Although a certain minimal metonymy might keep objects in a holding pattern, "there is no center in the city of the text, . . . it consists entirely of outskirts." As he develops this idea further: "Even belonging to a definite genre, like having a set number of pages, could be perceived as the guard towers of an aesthetic Gulag, where the prisoners are to be distributed by zones and strut about with numbers on their backs. Smashed into hundreds of dully glimmering prisms, the spec-

---

[16] Mikhail Epstein, "After the Future: On the New Consciousness in Literature," in *South Atlantic Quarterly* 90, no. 2 (Spring 1991): 409–44. Quoted material is on pages 434 and 436. In this article Epstein also notes the "supersaturation of literary space" and the disappearance of the literary process mentioned above.

ter of postcommunism wanders over the most recent prose: the backbone of history—the plot—has been broken up into a multitude of vertebrae . . . The century is ending. In place of a hard-pawed and relentless predator, there are tender bugs that flash in different directions. . ."

The search in Russia for alternative literary models took place, then, against an almost Kafkaesque background of radical experimentation and decay. In its initial stage, verbal messages collapsed into visual ones; the literary market was flooded with how-to manuals, pornographic literature, videos, comic books. Powerful "postmodernist" forces seemed to be de-verbalizing culture, making it blunt, immediate, non-contemplative, non-Aesopian. But equally powerful forces in Russian culture continued to work against a full embrace of the postmodernist spirit. (As another émigré scholar, Dmitry Khanin, has noted with some irritation, the postmodernist mood of "jovial pessimism" and "ahistorical, inconsistent, and generally confounding claims about history lying in ruins" at times appeared brazenly to take credit for the fact "that the Berlin Wall *actually is in ruins.*")[17] "Of course, the interval of play did its deed," the critic Irina Rodnianskaia acknowledged in the journal *Novy mir* in 1993. "It did a good job of emancipating authors who had become overly serious. . . . [But] how they broke their spears over the so-called instructive principle of Russian literature! How many head-spinning turns were accomplished . . . to make the Russian classics, which taught 'truth' rather than 'play,' into the guilty parties in all our historical misfortunes!"[18] While welcoming the new pluralism, Rodnianskaia warned that the turn away from the "instructional" classics could give rise to graver dangers: cults, totalitarian sects, facile national myths, the loss of the concrete human being as a measure for art, flight into an irresponsible, unauthored, "abstract-utopian space."

By 1996 "the postmodern condition" had lost its shock value and become itself a platitude. For many commentators, focus had shifted to the reasons that Russian critics found it difficult to take this noisy international phenomenon with the sustained seriousness of Western theorists. Surveys and critical samplings of the major thinkers (French, German, American) had become routine in the Russian press but were performed

---

[17] Dmitry Khanin (a Moscow-trained aesthetician, later at Colgate University), "The Postmodern Posture," in *Philosophy and Literature* 14 (1990): 239–47, esp. 241, 240. For a bewildered discourse on the continued appeal of Marxist worldviews in the West, see also Khanin's later piece, "Will Aesthetics Be the Last Stronghold of Marxism?" *Philosophy and Literature* 16 (1992): 266–78.

[18] Irina Rodnianskaia, "Plaster Wind: On Philosophical Intoxication in Current Letters," in "What Ails Russian Letters Today?" *Russian Studies in Literature* (Summer 1995): 5–44, esp. 8–9, 23–24 (originally appeared as "Gipsovyi veter" in *Novyi mir* 12 (1993): 215–31 [translation adjusted]).

somewhat dryly, without excitement.[19] One senior scholar, Nikolai Anastasiev, summed up the Russian mainstream position in an issue of *Voprosy literatury* (Summer 1996) in the following way:

> Postmodernism, briefly put, is a revolt against any hierarchy, a war of the outskirts against a center which should not exist, a war of freedom against authority, of the act against metaphysics, of practical experience against any form of knowledge that strives to generalize that experience in any way. . . . in sum, if postmodernism affirms anything, it affirms absolute freedom and an equivalent boundless toleration, for the sake of which it is willing to sacrifice even itself. This is splendid, and for us—people raised under a totalitarian regime, for us, captives for so many years to every sort of ideological cliché, . . . for us, such a position should be especially close and compatible. But here an extremely unpleasant circumstance presents itself. The irreproachable pluralists and liberals unexpectedly reveal a hidden, yet still manifest tendency toward aggression and even toward that same intellectual terror against which they direct all their inspired battle. This is noticeable even in the democratic West [references follow to Paul de Man and Lyotard] . . . The quest of postmodernism is a quest for failure.[20]

Mikhail Epstein has taken the case further. It was no coincidence, he argues, that in Russia a postmodernist fad followed so hard upon the demise of communism.[21] The two ideologies have much in common. Both celebrate "hyperreality"—similacra behind which there is no autonomous reality—and perpetuate themselves through citation, eclectic borrowing, cultural recycling, oxymorons, and (when a cutting edge is required) violent and absolute negation of all other possible positions. In both, the line between elite and popular culture is erased. Both are suspicious of any claims to free will or self-determination on the part of the individual subject. In Epstein's view, the only major difference between the postmodernist spirit and bombastic, overripe Soviet ideology is that the latter did not play or laugh (it is here, of course, that Bakhtin's carnival corrective proves so subversive). "Communism," Epstein writes, "is postmodernism with a modernist face that still wears the expression of ominous seriousness. . . . In the 1970s and 1980s, when intellectuals in

---

[19] See, for example, V. Kuritsyn, "K sitsuatsii postmodernizma," in *NLO*, no. 11 (1995): 197–23. Kuritsyn isolates four characteristics of postmodernism: replacement of vertical hierarchies by the horizontal and a rejection of linearity and binary oppositions; the "virtuality" of the world and "doubled presence"; "otherwiseness," the interface and intertextuality; and attention to context, marginal practices and genres, and crises of authorship.

[20] N. Anastasiev, "'U slov dolgoe ekho,'" *Voprosy literatury* (July–August 1996): 3–30. Quoted material is on pages 6–7; the final two sentences are on page 30.

[21] Mikhail Epstein, "Postmodernism, Communism, and Sots-Art," in Marina Balina, Nancy Condee, and Evgeny Dobrenko, eds., *Endquote: Sots-Art and the Dilemma of Post-Soviet Literature* (Evanston, Ill.: Northwestern University Press, forthcoming).

the West were still deadly serious in their left or right sympathies/antipathies, when they still defended the truth of their modernist heritage and fought for various projects for the rational reshaping of the world, in Russia a postmodern reevaluation of all values, a conceptualist game with all known ideological and cultural codes, was already in full swing." Can it surprise us that our novelty strikes Russian intellectuals today as impossibly familiar and old?

In the realm of cultural criticism, post-Soviet Russian intellectuals are anything but naive. They have benefited from the invigorating effects of delayed reception and ideological "backwardness." In a situation that recalls the imperial, cosmopolitan Russian eighteenth and early nineteenth centuries, when upper-class Russians read and spoke every European language because no one yet translated them, the highly educated urban elite in Russia today finds perfectly natural a cynicism toward all received dogma that the American scholarly community can only dimly appreciate. And thus the newest ideas of the past several decades, which have generated true believers in the countries of their origin, are released into Russian academic discourse already accompanied by their own parodies and trenchant critiques.[22] The best of Russia's "postcommunist literary theorists" combine Structuralism, post-Structuralist skepticism and "play," a rich store of resurrected spiritual values, and an impeccable knowledge of the canon; in addition, they are still able to draw on the familiar privilege of cultural leadership that Russian readers have long granted, almost by reflex, to their critics.

[22] The debunking phase set in early. "The word 'postmodernism' remarkably quickly lost its seductive glimmer of originality in our criticism," O. V. Vainshtein remarked during a 1993 roundtable on "Postmodernism and Culture." "Under the sign of postmodernism not only can one put on performances or write poetry but also cook pancakes, wear extravagant outfits, make love and quarrel, and recruit as one's predecessor any author one likes from the pantheon of world culture: the Marquis de Sade, Sasha Chornyi, Saint Augustine. Despite the manifest triviality of this widespread term, the concept itself paradoxically remains in the highest degree foggy and indeterminate . . . What is important [to postmodernism] is not depth or intensity but sliding over the surface, an extensive choosing among various signifiers. Profoundly postmodernist in this sense is the image of rapidly flipping through television channels with the help of a remote-control switch, during which the viewer's pleasure consists largely in the very process of pressing the buttons—an activity which gives a pleasant feeling of power over the picture on the screen, and in the sphere of visual aesthetics promises unexpected montage effects." Other scholars in the forum speculated on reasons for Russian impatience with postmodernist production: a general nervousness toward -isms (8); a long-standing preference for realism in art (although no longer "socialist") (7); a reluctance to endorse "the total insincerity of events and texts" (13). However, some participants did admit the value of viewing art as an open, dispersible event—even though the feeling was widespread that deconstruction would remain foreign to Russian sensibilities, which were better attuned to structuralism or to ethical criticism. "Postmodernizm i kul'tura: Materialy 'kruglogo stola,' in *Voprosy filosofii*, no. 3 (1993): 3–16. The quote is on pages 3–4.

Watching the domestic Russian scene from the diaspora, Epstein himself quickly moved beyond *post-*. His whimsical pronouncements began to suggest the wholesale replacement of linear time with the more generous image of coexistent options in space. "Posthumanism, postcommunism, postmodernism—the river of time has entered an ocean and lost its fluency altogether," he remarked in an interview in 1993.[23] "The concept of postmodernism is beginning to sound absurd. . . . Instead of such a proliferation of posts, I would suggest defining the current epoch as 'proto.' 'Before the next' is a more appropriate definition of uncertainty than 'after the last.'" Epstein proposes that we call this new, more positive cultural attitude "proteism": "Utopians have taught us to fear the future, even though it is presented as an inevitable paradise. In order to overcome utopianism, it's not enough to be anti-utopian or even postutopian; one has to restore one's love of the future, not as a promised State, but as a state of promise, as expectation without determination."

To live in a "state of promise," where we expect something productive of the world but are not determined by that product, might be said to sum up Bakhtin's vision of healthy literary consciousness and the healthy self. As one St. Petersburg scholar expressed the matter at the Third International Bakhtin Readings in Saransk (October 1995) in a paper entitled "Bakhtin as a way out of contemporary crises in the philosophy of culture":

The philosophy of postmodernism—of poststructuralism, deconstruction, hermeneutics—contributed a great deal toward destroying the old "classical" picture of the world, which resembled a system, an ordered whole. Postmodernists have demonstrated the fundamental ambivalence of culture, the absence within it of a single code, the fluidity and mutually transformative quality of all its elements. But to see in culture merely a field of play and transformation of meanings, to reveal the role of latent factors—of silence and of absence—is not enough. Constructive motion is also necessary. Without it, the philosopher of culture remains in the position of a photographer who holds in his hands a negative and does not know how to turn it into a positive. The most fruitful [way out of the crisis] has been that of M. M. Bakhtin. . . . Bakhtin's main methodological innovation was a transition from dialectics to dialogue. But this transition turns out to be not that simple; in order to accomplish it, one must learn how to listen. . . . the method Bakhtin proposed for studying culture was not visual, but auditory. One can not just see a culture, one has to be able to hear it.[24]

[23] "Postcommunist Postmodernism—An Interview with Mikhail Epstein," conducted by Ellen E. Berry, Kent Johnson, Anesa Miller-Pogacar, *Common Knowledge* 2, no. 3 (Winter 1993): 103–18, esp. 117–18.

[24] V. V. Prozerskii, "Krizis sovremennoi filosofii kul'tury. Dialogika M. M. Bakhtina kak put' vykhoda iz krizisa," in *MMB i gum mysh II (95)*: 134–35.

This image of Bakhtin as "one who listens," and thus as one who can restore a dialogic core to a moribund dialectic, presents a peculiar challenge. On one plane, we are rapidly losing the literacy necessary to understand Bakhtin's generation; the fears and pressures that shaped his life have largely dissolved, and thus the feel of his life, the Aesopian texture of his "survivorly" writings, will become increasingly remote. His patient ear is an anachronism in a world increasingly impatient, deafened, visually stimulated. In another sense, however, Bakhtin is quite at home in the contemporary climate. He is an optimistic *proteist* in precisely Epstein's understanding of the word; we need only recall his famous passage in *Problems of Dostoevsky's Poetics*, where he assures us that "nothing conclusive has yet taken place in the world, the ultimate word of the world and about the world has not yet been spoken, the world is open and free, everything is still in the future and will always be in the future."[25] Bakhtin offers something for every camp. Neo-humanists detect in him a liberal spirit and a patron saint of the new plurality and *tolerantnost'*; philosophers of religion have discovered a "vertical hierarchy" in his thought and a commitment to absolute values; Russian nationalists locate his roots in Orthodox spirituality. Even nostalgic Marxist-Leninists, disillusioned by Russia's postcommunist slide into chaos, have found reassurance in the fact that the corruption and disintegration of daily life has also been named by Bakhtin, incorporated into a model, and thus rendered transitory and manageable—for do not these ugly everyday phenomena recall the "debasings" and "decrownings" of carnival?[26] With Bakhtin's help, it seemed, one could get outside any disaster and analyze it. In this plethora of literary and sociocultural philosophies, only one group appears to remain beyond the pull of Bakhtin's categories: Russian converts to hard-core deconstruction. Unlike many of their colleagues in the West, they tend to find in Bakhtin—who did not acknowledge a void anywhere—an ungrateful, intractable, and uninteresting presence.

Let us pursue this final incompatibility. Western ways are everywhere

---

[25] Bakhtin, *PDP*, 166.

[26] V. V. Prokin, a scholar from Perm, remarked at the 1995 Saransk Readings that the Soviet-era faith in spiritual progress and socially responsible literary achievement had given way to world decay, mass commercial manipulation, disinformation, the political lie, "a new counter-ideological reworking of minds and hearts"—but this sorry fact only further justifies the placement of "the powerful intellectual figure of Bakhtin at the very center of contemporary Russia, or more precisely, of all civilization. . . . The anti-Soviet and anti-socialist revolution in Russia and in other countries includes significant elements of 'carnivalization,' the radical debasing of national, patriotic, and moral values traditional for the USSR, [replacing them with] ideals of grotesque ridicule 'from above' and 'from below' of authorities and heroes from all ranks and spheres, the laughing-down of tsars and leaders, the turning inside out of all systems of coordinates for measuring and assessing every type of idea and act" (V. V. Prokin, "Sotsial'naia filosofiia M. M. Bakhtina i sovremennost'," in *MMB i gum mysh I (95)*: 118–22, esp. 119–20).

mimicked on Russian streets and in Russian classrooms of the 1990s. It might be helpful, therefore, to note what aspects of our various post-modernisms have been absent, or present only in very weakened form, in the post-Soviet context. What has tended not to be there? First and most understandable, there is little enthusiasm among intellectuals for *neo-Marxism* in any form. Although "Gorbachev nostalgia" was still a factor at the beginning of the decade—the fantasy of a cleaner, more responsible Marxist socialism as an alternative to dirty politicking, a crime-ridden economy, and the disappearance of shared cultural values—and although more orthodox communism made a comeback as well, most Russian academics of my acquaintance continue to find remarkable the existence of, say, a Fredric Jameson or Terry Eagleton, productive scholars who have demonstrated considerable skill in building careers for themselves within their respective bourgeois establishments, who nevertheless in good conscience appear to take Marx and Engels seriously. In economic and political matters, that pair are simply charlatans in the eyes of Russians who have lived through seventy years of their applied science. On questions of art the verdict is kinder: those two men were well-read nineteenth-century European intellectuals and thus not wholly dismissed. But that the debased Leninist and Trotskyite versions of Marxist aesthetics can still command attention in Britain, France, and the United States at the end of the twentieth century is an almost impossible fact to communicate to our Russian colleagues.

This credibility gap was felt with some acuteness during the Fifth International Bakhtin Conference—held in Manchester, England, in July 1991—the first that could boast a respectable showing of delegates from Bakhtin's own homeland. In a Russian review of that conference and the volume of essays that issued from it ("Bakhtin: Carnival and Other Subjects"), the Saransk scholar Oleg Osovsky remarked on some reasons for this failure to connect.[27] In part it was caused by "the language barrier, since the majority of Western Bakhtinians are not Slavists"; in part it was owing to the "clash of different academic cultures, at times confusing but exceptionally fruitful"; but "most serious . . . was the non-coincidence of our fundamental postulates about the nature and aims of theoretical research as a whole and Bakhtinistics in particular" (172). With some justification and to varying degrees, the non-Russian delegates, many of them politically left-wing, were upset when their post-Soviet colleagues gave them to believe that for "professional and ethnic reasons they were

[27] O. E. Osovskii, "Karnaval'nye siuzhety Manchestera" (Bakhtin: Carnival and other subjects; Amsterdam-Atlanta [1993], 303 pp.), in *DKKh, no. 4 (95):* 171–77, esp. 172–73. The volume is edited by David Shepherd, who currently directs the Bakhtin Centre in Sheffield, England.

doomed to an untrue perception and image of Bakhtin and his ideas." The Russian delegates, supported by the occasional old-fashioned North American Slavist, could not understand how "any connections could exist" between the idiosyncratic, individualizing Bakhtin and the conformist, group-driven, "absolutely discredited discourses" of Marxism and feminism. This mutual incomprehension is likely to persist until Soviet Communism passes from living memory. Bring up the likelihood of any benevolent Marxist-Leninist influence on culture in the twenty-first century, especially in a society that is free to select other starting points, and Russian academics simply laugh in disbelief.

What other postmodernist moves have passed the Russians by? Despite a flurry of attention in the journals and a multitude of textbooks designed to introduce postmodernism into Russian schools, two other fashionable ideas have not caught on in the post-Soviet era: the *death of the author* and the *disappearance of the subject* (tenacious metaphors made famous by Roland Barthes and Michel Foucault). This is so not only because Russians have a long tradition of dead—really dead, that is, murdered—authors and disappeared subjects; they also have an altogether more protective, some would say obsessive, relationship with their literary canon. Even in those agitated decades when Russian nihilists or Futurist poets insisted that "boots were more important than Shakespeare" and that "Pushkin, Dostoevsky, and Tolstoy must be dumped overboard off the ship of modernity," the very aggressiveness of the manifesto was testimony to its being the flip side of a cult. For too long, as I have suggested, Russian literature has been the real world—and when other identities begin to slip, Russians tend to recite all their Pushkin by heart. To this day (although who knows how long the practice will survive), schoolchildren are raised on a diet of memorized classics. Such intimacy is not easily cast off. In fact, Russian culture has been more prone to constructing creator cults (what one scholar has called, affectionately, "icon envy")[28] than to suffering an anxiety of influence.

What, finally, can we say of the whole *multiculturalism* movement in the West, what we call "postcolonial studies," and the various academic groups pressuring to make the marginal more central? Here, too, Russian

---

[28] Gregory Freidin, "By the Walls of Church and State: Literature's Authority in Russia's Modern Tradition," *The Russian Review* 52 (April 1992): 149–65, esp. 162. In his opening pages Freidin makes the intriguing claim that Russia, as a "weaker neighboring nation," was "forced to compete with countries that had greatly benefited from the scientific revolution, rationalization of polity, and concomitant social development," and from Russia's disadvantaged perspective "the historically singular Western way tended to look like a set of normative principles with a claim to universal validity" (150). Freidin's point is that *Russia*, not the West, is the global norm—a point we in the West should not forget, for it helps to explain why Russia's inferiority complex periodically erupts into messianic fervor.

scholars are frequently confused and dismayed. What comes to their minds, of course, are the ubiquitous propaganda campaigns and grandiose political posters proclaiming "*Mir i druzhba*," "Peace and Friendship," that littered Russian public space during the Stalinist years and then the Brezhnev stagnation—symbolizing, with an expanse of grinning, black and brown "natives" in comic book style, Soviet imperial pretensions to save other cultures they barely understood, often deeply resented, and could scarcely afford to take on. This delicate topic was raised by Vladimir Maliavin, Russian Orientalist and culturologist, at a 1992 conference, held at Dartmouth College, on the Renewal of Russian spiritual life. In a paper entitled "Russia Facing East and West," Maliavin suggested that the transition to pluralism and a free market has been difficult for Russians because, despite the opening of borders and dissolving of boundaries, Russia is fated to remain superficially the land of "unrealized Americanism."[29] It is a nation drawn to see salvation in Western procedures but one that remains unable to embody them. In Maliavin's opinion, the reasons for this are linked to traditional Russian ways of addressing human inadequacy. In Russia, he notes, wrongdoing has been perceived as moral sin, as an act to be continually foregrounded, pondered, repented. But such behavior has not necessarily been viewed as bad policy, as an event or an attitude to be confronted and modified for pragmatic reasons. On the contrary, "being in sin" is an interesting and tolerated state, quickly forgiven, often compassionately indulged.[30] Sinners might transcend the sin or be transfigured by it, but most viably on an abstract or symbolic plane; payment is not cast in the prosaic terms of a legal code or compensation to the victim or a compromise settlement. As Maliavin explains in a later essay, "Russia Between East and West: A Third Way?" (1996), the most enduring psychological trait of the Russian people has been repentance for sin followed by a cosmic receptivity to *all* sides.[31] "The elevating force of repentance freed up in Russia the

---

[29] Vladimir Maliavin, "Russia Facing East and West," The Transnational Institute Conference on "The Renewal of Russian Spiritual Life," held at Dartmouth College, Hanover, New Hampshire, 8–11 July 1992, with cooperation from the Institute of Philosophy of the Russian Academy of Sciences, PUT' in Moscow, and the "Open Christianity" movement in St. Petersburg.

[30] Other Russian culturologists have made similar observations about the paralyzing effects of religiously based moralism on the development of a Russian civil society; see esp. Mikhail Yampolskii, "Iznasilovanie pokaianiem" [Rape by means of repentance], *Literaturnoe obozrenie*, no. 8 (1991): 89–96. Yampolsky argues that the reflex of indiscriminate repentance during the perestroika years actually prolonged totalitarian structures: when all are guilty for everything endlessly, then no single person takes responsibility for any individual act nor believes that he or she can influence its course.

[31] V. Maliavin, *Rossiia mezhdu Vostokom i Zapadom: Tretii put'?*, INOE (Moscow: Khrestomatiia novogo rossiiskogo samoznaniia, 1996), in the series "Rossiia kak ideia," esp. 16.

immense energy of selfless devotion, gave palpable form to the moral principle in a human being," he concludes, but the practical results of this cultural impulse in the civic sphere have been sobering. Traditionally Russian culture has denigrated comfortable, nonheroic, and "Philistine" values in favor of the extremes of the moral spectrum—and has tended in equal measure to "rejoice in the spiritual exploit and sympathize endlessly with human feebleness." To the extent that Maliavin is correct, Bakhtin's "first philosophy" of a modest "architectonics of the act" provides a corrective to this national trait.

In contrast to Russian fascination with sin and compassionate forgiveness, one of the telltale signs of the Western philosophical tradition, Maliavin asserts, is a rational, aggressive, rather cold-blooded *attack on itself.* In this reflex to idealize the other—what we might call the illusion of the "tender barbarian," from Tacitus to Rousseau—one can see a trademark of Western thought: to be radically critical of its own contributions to world culture and to assume that true virtue can be found only somewhere else, usually in a more "primitive" place.[32] Maliavin intimates that recent fads in the United States for deconstruction, anticolonialism, multiculturalism, making the marginal central, all reflect the same automatized gesture of the American intellectual today: "If it comes from us, if it is authored by us, then it must be meaningless, out of control, corrupted or corrupting." Here again, Bakhtin offers his own world-weary, postimperialist Russian intellectuals (and perhaps our theorists as well) a plausible alternative to the ennobled savage syndrome. Bakhtin is a moral philosopher and culturologist, not a multiculturalist. Utterly unsentimental about cultural difference, on guard against the illusion that to act ethically we need only decide to despise the time and place we personally occupy in the world, and convinced that we cannot (in any case) shed our accumulated selves and still remain responsible agents in the world, Bakhtin has no patience with generalized guilt or abdicated positions.

In short, Bakhtinians and ex-Soviet intellectuals of Vladimir Maliavin's cast of mind are not sympathetic toward the justice-and-equality argument that fuels much multicultural work in the West. In part their suspicion stems from the conviction that this is Western social philosophy at its weakest: patronizing and idealistic toward poorly understood cultures (the other), and casually contemptuous toward that which it knows best and answers for most directly (the self). In part it might be because Soviet Communism also justified itself by such ecumenical mottoes—and brought in its wake massive inequality, universal impoverishment, and a monstrous legacy of flattening out cultural particulars, both good and evil. What many Russians tend to see in multiculturalism as an ideology,

---

[32] For an elegantly argued Western statement of Maliavin's position, see John M. Ellis, "The Origins of PC," in *The Chronicle of Higher Education* (15 January 1992), B1–2.

then, is not its desire for justice and equality but its fascination with *power*. And here, of course, Russian cultural survivors are real connoisseurs. They are totally fed up with power, and with the way power-centered thinking can rob literature (or any cultural act) of its essence. For some time now, Russian intellectuals have been experiencing a general and very sensible revulsion against politicized group-think—which, after all, had brought them to the edge of an abyss. They argue that there is no greater honor than to be genuinely marginal, out of the way, not part of a powerful institution, your own person, alive.

Just such a "centrifugal," out-of-the-way person was Mikhail Bakhtin. As shall become clear, Bakhtin's outlook on the world was most definitely "politically incorrect"—by the standards of his time as well as our own. From his earliest youth on, he was suspicious of organized political activity and shunned the mass event. In March 1917 he already mourned the end of the monarchy, attended no political meetings, and sat home reading his books before burning them for fuel during the ghastly winter months of the Civil War. Being, as he put it, "utterly apolitical," he despaired at the onset of a noisy, maximalist regime that brutalized the human act and cheapened the word.[33] It could be argued, in fact, that the most enduring lesson Bakhtin offered his Soviet era was this: Do not conflate the ethical with the political. Not, of course, because politics has no ethical dimension, but for the time-honored reason that the ethical realm, if politicized, is prevented from functioning as an autonomous *check* on the political. Viewed in this way, Bakhtin's ethical position could be seen as an alternative both to the moral neutrality of the Formalists and to the overtly political commitment of the Marxists.

Curiously—and of some relevance to the present study—not only Bakhtin's writings but also his lived experience have become for many Russians a prototype of *a*political integrity and spiritual purity. As Elena Volkova, philosophy professor at Moscow State University, noted in 1990, Bakhtin founded no coherent school of thought, for "to become a true follower of Bakhtin" one cannot merely develop his ideas but must repeat his "moral deed—and this is not within everyone's power to do."[34] What was this "moral deed"? In part it was his boldness in posing, from within his corrupt and bloody epoch, such wondrous concepts as "aesthetic love," "participatory autonomy," laughter as liberation from terror, and personal death as a gift of wholeness to the other. In part, surely, it was surviving arrest, exile, and re-integration during the Stalinist period

---

[33] See Bakhtin's reminiscences about the revolutions of 1917 in "Razgovory s Bakhtinym: Nevel'. Vitebsk." *Chelovek*, nos. 4–6 (1993): 158–72, esp. 159–61.

[34] E. V. Volkova, "Estetika M. M. Bakhtina," in *Znanie* no. 12 (December 1990); "Estetika" series, Moscow, 64 pp., esp. 7 and 8.

without compromising himself or endangering others, without hungering after higher professional rank or a Lenin Prize, and without giving in to the vanities of victimhood ("Never," Volkova writes, "is there the slightest hint that his own fate, as a human being and a scholar, kept him from expressing his ideas"). Many have found irresistible Bakhtin's apparently instinctive disgust at official hierarchy and at defensive, protective attitudes toward one's professional domain. (In the Duvakin interviews of 1973, reminiscing about his gifted and wholly nonconformist friend, the concert pianist Maria Yudina, Bakhtin remarked that her most wonderful trait, which others mistakenly viewed as eccentricity, was her continual straining "toward something higher that could not be fit into the frame of any profession, any professionalism . . . not poetry, or music, or philosophy. . . . She was a person who was absolutely not official. . . . Like me, by the way; I too cannot endure any crass officialness [*ofitsial'shchina*].")[35] Surely Bakhtin's reluctance to attach any special significance to his own lived biography has played a role in others' eagerness to canonize him. But in the half-decade since Volkova's comment, of equal importance to Bakhtin's image in this saint-building culture has been an enhanced understanding of what constitutes ethically acceptable survival.

As more archival material becomes available on Bakhtin's "officially public" years—primarily his quarter-century at Mordovia State Teachers' College in Saransk—the nature of his "moral deed" becomes clearer. Bakhtin considered himself a philosopher, although he made his living as a teacher of literature. "Literary scholarship," he is reputed to have said, "is an interim profession; [when practicing it] one must be either an artist or a philosopher" in order to "invest oneself wholly," to "devote one's entire soul."[36] Bakhtin's special talent on this interim ground was perfect pitch as regards the realness of an addressee; within that context, he made words *work for him*. He was willing, if conditions required it, to work up a lecture on "The Language and Style of Literary Works in the Light of I. V. Stalin's Linguistic Studies" and "Applying the Teachings of I. V. Stalin on Language to Questions of Literary Scholarship" (Bakhtin delivered both in October 1950, in his capacity as chair of a Foreign Literature Department); such words and genres did not carry authentic meaning and, more important, had no specific addressees. But Bakhtin would not use words to disadvantage or disable concrete, identifiable others—which, in his official position, meant that he would not check up on the content of his colleagues' courses nor insist on a unified program

---

[35] "Razgovory s Bakhtinym: Mariia Veniaminovna Yudina," *Chelovek*, no. 1 (1995): 165, 169.

[36] Reminiscence of Vadim Kozhinov, cited by I. V. Kliueva (Saransk), in her "Fenomen Bakhtina i kul'turnaia missiia filosofa," in *MMB i gum mysh II (95)*: 66–69, esp. 67. Additional page references in text.

for the department. He hoped that this practice would slide by un-noticed. Evidence suggests that if rebuked for it, however, Bakhtin de-fended his behavior.

An intriguing glimpse into this ethical balancing act was provided in 1996, when the report of an official, two-week government inspection of Bakhtin's academic department carried out in March 1951 was exhumed from the Saransk archives and published.[37] At the time, the faculty of Foreign Literature at the teachers' college consisted of two members: Bakhtin and one young female assistant. The commission praised Bakh-tin's hard work, the scope of his courses, the above-mentioned public papers on Stalin, and Bakhtin's "masterful lecturing style" and "lively and emotional" delivery (69). But the department was also reprimanded on seventeen counts, several of which applied directly to Comrade Bakhtin. He did not sufficiently control the curriculum; he settled matters in the department through informal discussions (*besedy*) with his one junior col-league rather than through a formal meeting with resolutions fixed in minutes and procedures; he had not implemented the guidelines from the Ministry of Higher Education (they had not yet reached the prov-inces); he routinely failed to sum up his two-hour lectures with "well-focused conclusions emphasizing the ideological content of the lecture, including the class profile of the writer and his work, its evaluation by the classics of Marxism-Leninism" (74). He had not visited a single lecture by his assistant, Comrade Estifeeva, during her first half-year of teaching and apparently did not monitor her materials. On a practical daily level, as teacher and administrator, Bakhtin clearly had no talent for hierarchy and no special interest in exercising authority.

In fact, the impression we receive from all Bakhtin's work, and from his personal behavior, is that *power*—whether understood as prerogatives embedded in an institution, in official rank, or as rights won and then concentrated in a besieged self—has little to do with knowledge, free-dom, literary insight, and spiritual growth. Bakhtin had neither the public manner nor the physical vigor to fight power in melodramatic ways. His temperament was not that of a testifier or witness. He worked largely

---

[37] "Arkhivnye materialy o prepodavatel'skoi rabote M. M. Bakhtina v Mordovskom ped-institute," ed. and with an introduction by V. B. Estifeeva (the junior colleague in the department at the time of the government review), in *DKKh, no. 1 (96)*: 63–78. The commission recorded the response of the faculty members to its reprimands. When crit-icized for his methodology (supervision of practicums), for example, the report notes that "the chair of the department M. M. Bakhtin held to an incorrect point of view, that such questions [of methodology in the delivering of lectures] did not properly belong to the purview of the department, since in his opinion a lecture was a strictly individual phenome-non and it could not be reduced to any template provided by the department" (67). Addi-tional page references in text.

with attitudes and responses, not with policies or events. Among the matters for which he was reproached in 1952 by the Academic Council of his teachers' college was a lecture, delivered at a local conference commemorating Stalin's birthday, on the topic of art—which Bakhtin interpreted as "the fruit of our great longing for a better future" (77, 78). While this position was not quite reactionary (the triumph of Communism did, after all, glint through it), still there was a mournful feel to the phrase. It was noted in the official minutes that the lecture by Comrade Bakhtin contained a "mistaken notion of art," an "idealistic, mistaken notion expressed by pessimism: it dooms people to passivity and does not emphasize a struggle for what is progressive."

The Academic Council was not wholly wrong. As I shall attempt to show in the chapters that follow, Bakhtin was indeed "pessimistic" as regards progress achieved through struggles of that sort. His position, for all its overt Christian motifs and its obvious Kantian origins, recalls the intensely difficult, contemplative, minimalist ethical program of those Hellenistic philosophers—Stoics, Skeptics, Epicureans—who must have been part of his undergraduate classics major at Petrograd University. There, in the ancient world after the Age of Socrates, we might seek the fundamentals of what Volkova called Bakhtin's "moral deed." Those Greek thinkers also lived during an era when the polis was in disarray; as Epicurus preached, a man would do well to fashion an upright and inconspicuous life for himself out of the conventions of his time, since heroic martyrdom of Socrates's sort would not register on a diffuse and corrupt body politic. An individual's primary moral responsibility was personal integrity realized through a withdrawal from public life (Epicurus and his Garden), a commonsensical acceptance of death, and, to whatever extent possible, the removal of pain. For several thousand years, such philosophy has been belittled for its selfishness and lack of social conscience. Bakhtin's resonance with it, I suggest, is one index of his distance from mainstream Russian revolutionary activism.[38] This facet,

[38] Although a connection between Bakhtin and this wing of Hellenistic philosophy has not been pursued by Russian Bakhtinians—nor by Russian classicists, who, like their academic counterparts in the West, remain wary of Bakhtin's incursions into their philological territory—the integrity of Bakhtin's life, as well as the values he celebrates in the novel, are surprisingly compatible with the philosophy of mature Stoicism. For a modern survey of these thinkers, with abundant citations that suggest intriguing points of contact with Bakhtin's lived and preached philosophy, see R. W. Sharples, *Stoics, Epicureans and Sceptics: An Introduction to Hellenistic Philosophy* (London: Routledge, 1996), esp. ch. 5, "How Can I Be Happy?" and ch. 6, "What about Other People?" It is not accidental, I believe, that Martha Nussbaum, arguably the most prolific American theorist of "the nineteenth-century novel as ethical philosophy by other means," devoted a lengthy study to just these philosophers; see Martha C. Nussbaum, *The Therapy of Desire: Theory and Practice in Hellenistic Ethics* (Princeton, N.J.: Princeton University Press, 1994). I thank R. Bracht Branham for

too, has entered contemporary portraits of Bakhtin. "Philosophy is a special sort of chosenness, a sort of spiritual aristocratism," one scholar remarked in her centennial tribute. "Not by chance does one sense in Bakhtin a great respect for the nobility."[39] Paradoxically, this aristocratic and disengaged image (at first denounced, then secretly admired, then openly exalted) is one of the shadowy constants in Communist Russia's reception of Bakhtin.

In the Soviet Union, then, that most politically harassed and harangued of modern states, Bakhtin counseled his compatriots (with the necessary Aesopian tact) to begin their search for agency and personhood elsewhere, not with political consciousness. Such a stance on power and individuality is so alien to our era's most prominent postmodernist analysts—prolific thinkers like Foucault, Lyotard, and Bataille—that it takes some effort to assimilate it. For Bakhtin starts on quite other ground: with the assumption (not, of course, original with him) that genuine knowledge and enablement can begin only when my "I" consults another "I" and then returns to its own place, humbled and enhanced. In its curiosity and charity, this model is immensely attractive, especially as a counterweight to some of the shrill excesses of cultural politics familiar in the West. It is possible, however, that such a reading of Bakhtin—although true to the man and spiritually irresistible—is, in the Russian context, as much part of the problem as it is part of the solution. For one could argue that in Russia, a nation whose history has been so very deficient in happy political experience, a pragmatic working-out of responsible and differentiated power relations should be the first priority of the day. In this respect, Bakhtin shares perhaps too much with his friendly rival and frequent negative example, the Christian anarchist Leo Tolstoy.

The present book is in two parts. The first is chronological: a selective account of recent, and then more distant, reception of Bakhtin's work in his homeland. Part 2 is thematic, presenting three areas where recent Russian—and, on occasion, non-Russian—rethinkings of Bakhtin as philosopher have been especially provocative: polyphony and dialogism (largely as they relate to Dostoevsky); carnival and the problem of open-endedness (of both bodies and time); and "outsideness" as an imperative in ethics as well as artistic form. In a brief afterword, I speculate on the future shape of Bakhtin studies—as Bakhtin's *inonauka*, "scholarship [or science] in some other way," becomes an established field of inquiry.

---

his comments on notions of the moral life amid a decaying polis (see R. Bracht Branham and Marie-Odile Goulet-Cazé, eds., *The Cynics* [Berkeley: University of California Press, 1996]).

[39] I. V. Kliueva, "Fenomen Bakhtina i kul'turnaia missiia filosofa," in *MMB i gum mysh II (95):* 66–69, esp. 68.

Bakhtinian method is not modest: it will tell you how to teach, write, live, talk, think.

An auxiliary goal of this study is to consider potential roles for the cultural critic. Is a national tradition best served by intellectuals who provide a mirror, an apology, or a skeptical corrective to their culture's most stereotyped and unforgiving extreme? The question is not a trivial one, for over the past ten years Russians have been subjecting their own radical intelligentsia, the pride of previous regimes, to a blistering self-critique. Cultural critics, once revered as national prophets, are being held responsible for the absence on Russian soil of a "normal life"—the shorthand phrase Russians apply to societies that appear to get by without heroics, horrendous sacrifices, and Promethean goals.[40] Alongside this reevaluation of the revolutionary mystique has been a parallel campaign to demystify, and perhaps even dismantle, that most oppressive and distorting of binary oppositions for organizing Russian culture: "East versus West," or worse, "a virtuous, victimized Russia versus the rest of the hostile world."

Here Bakhtin studies, with their vigorous cosmopolitan base, have proved to be a useful test site. In an overview of the Moscow Centennial Conference, one participant remarked on the unfortunate administrative decision to register all Russian delegates with white name tags, non-Russians with yellow ones.[41] "By this innocent gesture," she notes, "a sharp distinction was drawn between ours and not-ours, one which, we must presume, had not entered into the organizers' plans." And why, she asks, do we continue to divide Bakhtin studies into "Western" and "Russian" wings at all? There is now as much diversity in the one as in the other. An intellectual spectrum stretching from traditional philology to postmodernist fantasy can be found in both—and Russian scholars are no less "national" for being so diverse. The old Cold War lumping practices can

[40] See, for example, the lengthy article entitled "Komu sluzhat intellektualy?" [Whom do intellectuals serve?], in *Rossisskie vesti*, 22 July and 30 July 1994, by the political theorist Aleksei Kiva: "Normal development, without revolutionary shocks, is in practice always tragic for the intelligentsia. . . . The syndrome is that age-old Russian idealism, utopianism . . . and a certain detachment from life; in intelligentsial heads, meanwhile, all sorts of schemes for ideal social constructs are hatching . . . ideal democracy, ideal government"; Bolshevism, too, "was based on the principle of a non-acceptance of reality." Kiva continues: [The intelligentsia is governed by] "the syndrome of the untranscended slave, or, what sounds more euphonious, the Russian serf. A slave does not know the Golden Mean." And he concludes: "So whom does the Russian intelligentsia serve? 1) its own age-old errors; 2) its own mythic, messianic, predetermined mission; 3) routine 'great shocks'; 4) its own corporate interests; 5) the social command; 6) its own money-pouch; 7) society; 8) no one at all; 9) its own demise."

[41] Irina Balabanova, "Beloe & Joltoie: Sed'maia mezhdunarodnaia bakhtinskaia konferentsiia," in *NLO* 15 (1995): 428–30, esp. 429, 430.

only perpetuate that "morose and short-sighted opposition Russia/West ('white'/'yellow,' ours/not-ours)." In a retrospective statement on the Moscow conference in a mid-1996 issue of *Voprosy literatury*, Vitaly Makhlin concurred.[42] For all the language barriers and differences in ideological experience, the primary divide had ceased to be "Russia versus the West." More significant tensions could now be registered, Makhlin writes: those caused by a shift in generations (the "founders" who knew Bakhtin personally and are known for their reminiscences about him, and then scholars a decade or more younger, who apply his thought); and by the rift between literary scholarship and philosophy, each speaking its own professional language and each side acting at times "as if 'the other' did not exist, as if 'the other' were occupied with an uninteresting and manifestly useless matter."

In a word, well into the first post-Soviet decade it is probably time to stop reinforcing the Brezhnev-era fiction of "East versus West" in the cultural landscape of the ex-USSR. Those categories were never unitary, and they are already eroded beyond repair. Bereft of the cruder forms of Aesopian language, Russian thinkers are now freer than ever before in living memory to make judgments that are empirical and autonomous rather than politically reactive; they need no longer view outsiders through a "for and against" or "good and evil" lens. Russia can return to the values of hybridization, amalgamation, *in*clusivity—always, it could be argued, her native strengths as a country located at the crossroads of so many cultures. These are Bakhtin's strengths as well. For against the unsettled backdrop of Russia at the century's end, how much richer, more frightening, and more interesting do her own great thinkers appear.

---

[42] V. Makhlin, "Bakhtin i sovremennoe literaturovedenie," *Voprosy literatury* (May–June 1996): 65–67, esp. 67.

Part I

Бахтиноведение, Бахтинистика, Бахтинология
BAKHTIN STUDIES, BAKHTINISTICS,
BAKHTINOLOGY

CHAPTER 1

The Russians Reclaim Bakhtin, 1975 to the Jubilee

As PART OF the opening plenary session at the Bakhtin Centennial Conference in Moscow in June 1995, delegates were treated to "the living word of Mikhail Bakhtin." Thus had the event been listed in the program—and the playing of this scratchy stretch of conversation taped in the early spring of 1973, between the sixty-four-year-old Soviet literature specialist Viktor Duvakin and the ailing, seventy-eight-year-old Bakhtin, was at once intimate and majestically solemn, almost to the point of awkwardness.[1] Our host institution, Moscow State Pedagogical University, had decked out the stage of its main auditorium with baskets of flowers and a huge commemorative portrait. The living word of Bakhtin intensified this nostalgic spirit.

Bakhtin died two years after this interview; Duvakin himself died in 1982. An accomplished Mayakovsky scholar, Duvakin had begun his ambitious oral history project on early Soviet culture in 1966, after Moscow State University stripped him of his right to teach in retaliation for his support of a former student, Andrei Sinyavsky, at the time on trial for literary treason. In fifteen subsequent years of devoted work, Duvakin recorded more than six hundred conversations with three hundred persons. His six meetings with Bakhtin, eighteen hours in all, took place in Bakhtin's Moscow apartment in February and March 1973. Bakhtin had been widowed fourteen months earlier. The loss of his wife—they had been inseparable—had clearly been traumatic: photographs indicate that Bakhtin lost half his body weight in two years, and during the sessions with Duvakin he revealed acute embarrassment when, apparently for the first time in his life, his powerful memory began to fail him. Profoundly out of touch with the present, the discussions breathe the spirit of a wholly other epoch. They open on recollections of childhood (Bakhtin was born into a large, close, materially comfortable banker's family), con-

---

[1] V. D. Duvakin (1909–1982) was of the proper age and academic status to put his septuagenarian interviewees at ease; the published transcripts indicate a flexible, decentered questioning style that appears to have stimulated the often fragile and finicky subjects to maximum recall. See the précis by V. F. Teider (Moscow State University), "Zhivoe slovo M. M. Bakhtina," in *Proceedings of the Seventh International Bakhtin Conference*, Moscow State Pedagogical University, 26–30 June 1995, Book 2, 304–7. See also the portrait of Duvakin by V. Radzishevskii ("Beskonechnyi Viktor Dmitrievich . . .") in *Besedy V. D. Duvakina s M. M. Bakhtinym*, 10–14 (see n. 2, below).

tinue with Bakhtin's university years during World War I (where he was a fastidious, somewhat reclusive student), go on to discuss the revolutions of 1917 in the capital (Bakhtin opposed them both), and end with portraits of close friends and fellow scholars in the outlying towns of Nevel, Vitebsk, and then Soviet Leningrad, mostly from the 1920s. "You've given me a splendid portrait," Duvakin remarked appreciatively at the end of the sixth and final session. "Do you plan to write your memoirs?" "Certainly not," Bakhtin answered. "What sort of memoirs could I possibly have?"

Throughout 1993–95 a transcript of these taped interviews was serialized in the Russian journal *Chelovek*, with some delicate content edited out but scrupulously preserving their meandering shape (the fully restored and annotated text appeared in book form in 1996).[2] Despite its published status, the librarian-archivist V. F. Teider, in charge of presenting the conference delegates with a brief segment, spoke anxiously for half an hour about the propriety of broadcasting this "conversation" to a large hall full of strangers, when "Mikhail Mikhailovich, a very old man, was speaking informally with a colleague in a domestic setting"—and all his lapses of memory, slips of the tongue, shufflings, distractions caused by the cat and deep drags on his cigarette were so very audible. (These archivists, raised in a climate of reverence toward their cultural heroes, were faced with a very Western-style dilemma: when the ikon becomes a human being, the traits that make it accessible are also what make it imperfect.) As a public product of the Soviet era, the recording was indeed extraordinary. In the segment we heard (the final minutes of the final session) it was immediately apparent that this was genuine dialogue, with speech tics, coughs, and digressions intact—in itself memorable under a regime where most "interviews" were staged in advance and then cleansed. Equally unexpected, Bakhtin was present in a mode not often

---

[2] For the six conversations in seven edited installments, see "Razgovory s Bakhtinym," in *Chelovek*, no. 4 (1993): 136–53 ("Sem'ia i gody ucheniia"); no. 5 (1993): 131–43 ("Peterburg. Universitet"); nos. 4–6 (1993): 158–73 ("Nevel, Vitebsk"); no. 3 (1994): 169–82 ("Salony i kruzhki"); no. 4 (1994): 178–89 ("Vaginov i drugie"); no. 6 (1994): 154–72 ("Mariia Veniaminovna Yudina"); and no. 1 (1995): 156–76 ("Mariia Veniaminovna Yudina" [cont.]). Quotes in the text are from *Chelovek*, no. 1 (1995): 173, 176. Fully transcribed at three hundred pages, the text of the interviews was published as *Besedy V. D. Duvakina s M. M. Bakhtinym*, edited and prepared by members of the professional library staff of Moscow State University, V. B. Kuznetsova, M. V. Radzishevskaia, and V. F. Teider, with brief essays by S. G. Bocharov, V. V. Radzishevskii, and V. V. Kozhinov (Moscow: Progress, 1996). The text is being translated and annotated by Brian Poole for University of Texas Press. The actual tapes contain inconsistencies, evasions, and sophisticated storytelling techniques that the edited portions printed in *Chelovek* specifically mask. Whereas Bakhtin was apparently scrupulously honest—and generous—in his recollections of others, he tended to fib with regard to himself.

in evidence in his novel-centered written texts, namely, as a connoisseur of poetry.

With only ten minutes of tape time left, Duvakin suggested to Mikhail Mikhailovich that he read (which for Russians means, recite) some verse. Bakhtin demurred ("It should have been before . . . then I had a voice . . . I did that so endlessly long ago"); he hesitated, mumbled something to himself, and then, in quick succession, recited in a vigorous and resonant voice the Russian lyric "Night" by Afanasy Fet, followed by the dedication to Goethe's *Faust* in German, a short poem by Rilke—"Mir zur Feier"—and then, in French, in a single exultant breath, Baudelaire's "La mort des amants." He launched into several lengthy passages from Pushkin but broke off. "There simply aren't the words to thank you, Mikhail Mikhailovich," Duvakin said, switching off the machine. "But there's nothing to thank me for," Bakhtin said. "*Izvinite menya, chto ya tak neskladno vse vremya*" [Excuse me for having been so incoherent all this time].

Russians in the audience took Bakhtin's love of poetry for granted, as they did the fact that cultured people carry several languages and literary traditions around in their heads. Western delegates, who often had trouble following the crackling Russian on tape, watched the Russians listening. It was a moment to remember. Through memoirs recorded in the 1970s about the distant 1910s and 1920s, our Russian counterparts in the 1990s were living in to Bakhtin's multilingual, still thoroughly Europeanized world. Those fifty hateful, shameful Stalinist and Brezhnevite years in between had simply dropped away. Miraculously, Bakhtin was simultaneously a survivor and a *pre*-Bolshevik.

This striving of the Russians to recuperate a less tainted part of their own past was felt strongly during the five days of conferencing that followed. The foreigners' presentations tended to be at the theoretical cutting edge and "outside" Bakhtin's lived experience; several were recognizably postmodernist, some were feminist and deconstructive in their approach, quite a few were critical of Bakhtin's formulations. Others were imaginative expansions of his thought into genre theory, translation practice, and the visual arts. We outsiders, it seemed, were forever grasping a small amount of Bakhtin and then applying it to concerns within our own fields of expertise. For the majority of Russian delegates, in contrast, *Bakhtin himself* was the field. A large portion of their papers were archival, pedagogical, closely argued philosophical investigation, at times simply reverent paraphrase. Textological problems were cleared up, details of Bakhtin's biography filled in. Enticing paradoxes from within Bakhtin's own thought—for example, those two oxymorons so beloved by Bakhtin, "autonomous communion" and "open wholeness"—were lovingly scrutinized. If the Russians were at times burdened by reverence toward their source and made somewhat timid by it (such are conventional reflexes at a Russian jubilee), then the scholars from abroad, in turn, were often obliged to pay for the virtues of our creative imagination by getting the simplest things wrong, and by an unseemly scrambling after facts and documents with which to validate our "outsiderly" ideas.

But validation was itself one of the issues that divided us. In America and Europe we have long been comfortable with the revisionist hypothesis that historical narrative is a "construct," that historical sources might turn out to be merely "stories," and that individual interpretation is our natural birthright. Such ideas, after all, cost us very little to entertain. Our cultures permit professional humanists to live in an academic environment with considerable security and few constraints; imagination is rewarded, the future is open, and past political events quickly crowd one another out and are forgotten. Russian scholars of the 1990s, who still keenly remember state censorship and for whom yesterday's history books were not cultural constructs but simply lies, are understandably concerned lest such corrosion of potentially knowable facts be carried too far or into too many disciplines. This aspect of Western academic practice makes the best of them apprehensive.

For much is at stake. Sociologists concur that until the 1990s the Soviets were probably the most "reading people" in the world. Printed texts and their heroic genesis were a serious matter, not to be treated casually or undone by a pun or current trend. At the 1995 Bakhtin Conference I was struck, as foreign academics so often are in that country, by the sense that for its own communicants Russian culture is such a huge, rich, beloved, and intimately familiar homeland that—despite Bakhtin's well-advertised passion for multiple boundaries and "outsideness"—Russians hardly *need* the outside. Their papers at the panel sessions were saturated with unidentified quotes to Russian and world classics (it would have been an insult to the audience to identify them); these scraps of poetry and literary lore were the common denominators of a tightly knit profession. Their literary canon is still largely unquestioned and intact. By and large, the Russian delegates listening raptly to Bakhtin's voice in that hall in June 1995 were uninterested in a hermeneutics of suspicion. It became clear at the Jubilee, with its participants from twenty different countries, that the stage had long been set for a new Bakhtin—but he was coming into focus in his homeland according to the same familiar, reverent rules.

As suggested in the introduction to this study, the Russian intellectual establishment observes our "crises in criticism" and "culture wars" with a mix of amusement, intense curiosity, and dismay. Bakhtin's legacy has been claimed by all sides. On what ground will the Russian- and English-speaking worlds come together? The task of the present chapter is historical in the simplest sense: to provide some chronological background to

the posthumous reclamation of Bakhtin in his homeland, a rich and diffuse process that has developed in several stages over the past twenty
years.

THE THREE WORLDS OF MIKHAIL BAKHTIN

To orient ourselves in these debates over the legacy, it might be helpful
at the outset to offer a brief capsule of the three major concepts that
Bakhtin developed during his long life.[3] The first might be called *prosaics*,
his starting point for a theory of novelistic prose. In such prose—with its
voracious incorporation of genres and its proliferation of voices—Bakhtin
detected a type of energy that was likely to create more options (and thus
produce more freedom) than could ever be realized in the hierarchically
arranged genres of a classical poetics. A prosaic worldview, I hasten to
add, does not reject poetry as an art form. Bakhtin first made that dismissive rhetorical gesture in his essays of the mid-1930s, when the spirit
of poetry and epic functioned for him briefly (if colorfully) as the bad boy
and discredited alternative to his beloved novel—which, at the time, was
well on its way to becoming for Bakhtin the world's only freedom-bear-
ing literary form. The remarks he made in that context are no index of his
appreciation of poets or poems. Bakhtin knew poetry well, loved it
deeply, lectured on it continually—but rarely chose to analyze poetic
worlds professionally or on their own terms.[4] The challenge of the prosaic
world came to occupy him wholly; it was so much more difficult to discover the rules that prose lives by.

Prosaic reality is the very opposite of, say, the compositional constraints
of a sonnet, or of conspiracy-theory thinking, or a five-year plan. At their
ideal extreme, those structures all assume concrete parameters, a fixed set
of options, an effective ending point, and—in the case of the latter two
examples—a mean, lean world full of efficient agents. Prosaic thinking, in

---

[3] These three global concepts are discussed at length, although with somewhat different
content and emphasis than they receive here, in Gary Saul Morson and Caryl Emerson,
Mikhail Bakhtin: Creation of a Prosaics (Stanford: Stanford University Press, 1990), esp.
part 1, ch. 1.

[4] When he did analyze a poem—as in his close reading of Pushkin's 1830 lyric
"Razluka"—Bakhtin's interest lies in voice zones and points of view, not in technical pros-
ody. In Bakhtin's reading, the various rough drafts of the lyric's opening lines ("For the
shores of your native land, you abandoned this foreign region") indicate how sensitive
Pushkin was to the "*svoi/chuzhoi*" distinction ("what is one's own" versus "what is someone else's"); the woman addressed in the poem is introduced as speaking from an already
displaced *chuzhoi* position and quitting it to return to herself/her own home. In general,
Bakhtin considered such a shift essential for any consciousness of the self to emerge. See
"Author and Hero in Aesthetic Activity" in *A&A 90*, 211–31, esp. 211–17.

contrast, is more predicated on slack, asymmetry, unexpected interruption, variety, distraction. This is not to suggest that a prosaic world is necessarily careless or anarchic. Patches of order most definitely exist in it. But such patches, Bakhtin would have us believe, are rarely simply "discovered": they are not essences but rather evidence of hard uphill work and complex pressures, at best holding patterns, the result of continual compromise and negotiation among several competing voices or worldviews.[5] On the whole, prosaic order—or prosaic harmony—is accretive and temporary. It values slow, open processes, and it rewards those who are successful at developing, over time, flexible, particularized, nonrepeating relations among differentiated parts. Such relations, Bakhtin felt, are more fundamental to human experience than are systems, dialectics, or rules. The literary form that best expresses prosaic values in art (and, as Bakhtin saw it, in our lives as well) is, of course, the novel. Not surprisingly, Bakhtin spent a good part of his life studying novels.

The second concept crucial to Bakhtin's universe is *dialogue*—or, as he first argued this position in the 1929 Dostoevsky book, the double-voiced "dialogic word." By dialogue, Bakhtin meant more than mere talk. What interested him was not so much the social fact of several people exchanging words with one another in a room as it was the idea that each word contains within itself diverse, discriminating, often contradictory "talking" components. The more often a word is used in speech acts, the more contexts it accumulates and the more its meanings proliferate. Utterances do not forget. And by their very nature, they *resist unity and homogenization*—two states that Bakhtin, a close student of biology, considered akin to death.[6] Understood in this way, dialogue becomes a model of the creative process. It assumes that the healthy growth of any consciousness depends on its continual interaction with other voices, personalities, or worldviews. Although the youthful Bakhtin experimented with metaphors taken from other aesthetic media (music, visual imagery, sculpture), by the end of the 1920s—and most forcefully in the Dostoevsky book—he had come to believe that the toughest, most elastic and trustworthy medium in which to store and share other people's worldviews was words.

***

[5] For a fine extension of this principle, see the discussion of prosaic "threshold chronotopes" in Lisa Eckstrom, "Moral Perception and the Chronotope: The Case of Henry James," in Amy Mandelker, ed., *Bakhtin in Contexts across the Disciplines* (Evanston, Ill.: Northwestern University Press, 1995): 99–116.

[6] In an interview with two Polish correspondents granted near the end of his life, when asked to sum up the achievements of Dostoevsky and the polyphonic novel, Bakhtin remarked: "In general I think that any closure, even the closure of a great work of art, smells a bit of death." See Mikhail Bakhtin, "O polifonichnosti romanov Dostoevskogo," in Vittorio Strada, ed., *Rossiia/Russia*, vol. 2 (Torino, 1975): 189–98, esp. 193.

In addition to prosaics and dialogue, Bakhtin also endorsed a third virtue, what he called "*nezavershennost'*," *unfinalizability*. In an unfinalized world, everything (even a bad thing) can change (even if only a little)—and in the process, it gives birth to something new. This new thing, simply because it is different and increases our repertory of responses to the world, is, by definition, positive. Bakhtin had little patience with people who did not wish to increase their options in life, and he insisted that human potential, even if unrealized, was always real. It is, of course, under the hopeful rubric of "unfinalizability" that carnival enters Bakhtin's thought. The grotesque body functions for him (somewhat paradoxically) as a sign of the *materialization of openness*. Under carnival conditions, a human body is valuable not so much for its ability to talk but for its ability to incorporate other bodies, to swallow up an outside thing or leak some inside thing out—to serve, in short, as a conduit between a human organism and the world of natural, cyclical processes that provide it with unexpected potentials. For Bakhtin, these exchanges (quite counterintuitively, one could argue) always lead to fertilization and growth. True to its foundations in folklore and myth, the carnival economy is rooted in a fairy-tale world of miracle harvests and utopian plenitude.

The fullest exposition of the carnival worldview is found in Bakhtin's book on Rabelais, defended as a doctoral dissertation in 1946. But carnival is present as a loophole and an inspiration throughout Bakhtin's work. In 1963 he inserted into the revised Dostoevsky book an entirely new sixty-page chapter on the role of carnivalization and menippean satire in the development of the polyphonic novel. Nikolai Gogol's fictional worlds, it turns out, are largely carnival. Alexander Pushkin's great works of drama and narrative prose are also "carnivalized."[7] Clearly the idea remained dear to Bakhtin—and apparently he considered it no threat to dialogue nor to the rigors of religious faith. Bakhtin's right-hand man for the final ten years, Vladimir Turbin, remembers Bakhtin saying in Saransk (in a delighted whisper): "And the Gospels are carnival too!"[8]

Psychologically, carnival has much to recommend it. In the hungry, godless 1930s, faith in an unfinalized, always potentially bigger, freer, and better nourished future must have been an immensely attractive countercosmos to the disappeared pluralism and phantom prosperity of the Stalinist years. As a working principle, of course, carnival could never be the basis for a responsible politics, just as "unfinalizability" cannot.

---

[7] See Bakhtin, *PDP*, 159: "In addition to Gogol, mention must be made here of the huge influence exercised on Dostoevsky by the most carnivalized works of Pushkin: *Boris Godunov*, the *Tales of Belkin*, *Little Tragedies*, and *Queen of Spades*."

[8] See V. N. Turbin, "Iz neopublikovannogo o M. M. Bakhtine (I)," in *Filosofskie nauki*, no. 1 (1995): 235–43, esp. 243.

But as noted in the introduction to this study, Bakhtin was not a political thinker. His concepts of dialogue and polyphony, like his concept of carnival, are free of all constraining (and defining) codes, hierarchies, one-way conversions, prohibitions, subversions that really subvert or compulsions that really compel—in fact, free of everything associated with the practice and distribution of power. This alone should give us pause when considering his image of Dostoevsky, a writer in whom the sense of power relations was cruelly and excruciatingly precise.

Prosaics, dialogue, and unfinalizability are concepts isolated not by Russians but by Americans working on Bakhtin. Indeed, up until the Gorbachev years (1985–91), most of the large-scale writing on Bakhtin had taken place outside Russia. Monographs and biographies appeared here, not there. Starting in Canada in the early 1980s, meetings of the International Bakhtin Society were held throughout the Western and Central European world (Italy, Israel, Croatia, and Serbia)—but without Soviet delegates. As mentioned earlier, this awkward absence of scholars from Bakhtin's homeland was remedied only in the summer of 1991, at the Fifth International Bakhtin Conference in Manchester, England. Given the traditionally high visibility and status of Russian literary criticism within its own culture, it is not surprising that Russian academics were embarrassed—although surely not to blame—for contributing so little to the international boom that followed immediately upon the master's death in 1975.[9]

Bakhtin's reemergence in Russia is best understood, however, not against the background of our appropriations but in the context of the larger drama within Soviet culture during Communism's twilight decades. From the early 1950s on, Russian literature underwent, albeit fitfully, a process of de-Stalinization. Perhaps less well known is the parallel

---

[9] Distributing credit for "resurrecting Bakhtin from obscurity" has become a sore point on Russian soil, and many native *bakhtinisty* resist an apologetic stance vis-à-vis the West. As one aging colleague of Bakhtin's at the University of Saransk remarked petulantly in 1992: "One should talk about the continuation, not the *beginning*, of large-scale work; one must not ignore what has been done and imagine oneself a Robinson Crusoe on an uninhabited island at a time when no small number of roads have already been laid down, where there are other markers of human activity, where there are even human beings." A. F. Eremeev, "Ot 'sobytiia'—k 'so-bytiiu'" [From 'event' to 'co-being'], in *MMB: ENS 92*, 19. Eremeev's chief domestic target is Vitaly Makhlin, who opened his sixty-page pamphlet on Bakhtin's early ethical philosophy (1990) with the following "embarrassed" statement: "The life and work of Mikhail Mikhailovich Bakhtin . . . has been little studied, and is even less familiar to the general reader. In the West, monographs alone on Bakhtin numbered ten in the 1980s, and in our homeland there was not a single one; Soviet citizens have not participated in the colloquia of the 'International Bakhtin Society' . . . we must make sense out of all this without resorting to the usual explanations and rhetorical accusations." V. L. Makhlin, *MB:FP 90*, 3.

movement among Soviet literary professionals to de-Stalinize the traditional "conscience of Russian culture": literary criticism and theory.[10] In
this process, the Bakhtin revival played a significant role. A brief survey of
the major ebbs and flows of this movement will set the stage.

THE POST-STALINIST REVIVAL OF THE RUSSIAN LITERARY PROFESSION

By Stalin's death in 1953, literary studies (like most areas of intellectual
pursuit in the Soviet Union) were shackled and terrorized. Over the next
thirty years efforts were made to rehabilitate the profession along several
lines.[11] At first, literary debates centered around what Russians called "the
struggle between physicists and lyricists." On one side were the gifted,
somewhat heretical "physicists": young, high-tech linguists who advocated cybernetics, computer modeling, machine translation, and impersonal quantification as the coming future of literary science. On the other
side were the "lyricists," old-fashioned Marxist-Leninist humanists who
insisted that the worst abuses of Socialist Realism had been venial, not
mortal, sins; they clung to the hope that the "party method" for literature could be cleansed of its Stalinist perversions and returned to its ideal
mission, which was to reflect the human being whole within a humane
society. The "physicists" considered this goal hopelessly utopian. As history had cruelly shown, human-centered methodologies—by virtue of
their very softness—were dangerously open to distortion by outside
forces, especially in a society where art mattered so centrally and ideological regulation was the norm. One of the original "physicists," Dmitri
Segal, has strenuously insisted on just this point in his memoirs on the
period: that the Structuralist approach to literature, far from being a scientistic straitjacket for ideas and values, was widely perceived at the time
as liberationist.[12] In Russia, he argued, the malleable, ethical component

---

[10] The battle for the rights of creative literature was carried out largely in the journalistic
press, beginning with Vladimir Pomerantsev's famous article "On Sincerity in Literature"
that appeared in *Novy mir* in 1953. My discussion in this chapter will be limited to the
strictly professional side of the reclamation: the evolution, within the academy, of more
flexible, pluralistic *theories* of literature and culture.

[11] The fullest account we have of this "academic" process, albeit partial to the Structuralist side of the debate, is Peter Seyffert, *Soviet Literary Structuralism: Background, Debate,
Issues* (Columbus, Ohio: Slavica, 1985). Proceeding literally month by month and article by
article (with large translated inserts of actual texts), Seyffert traces the local disputes and
evolving professional positions of dozens of Soviet literary scholars.

[12] "The semiotic method is the most appropriate for demonstrating the artificiality of all
normative, ideological, and ethnocentric categories created by man," Dmitrii Segal wrote in
1993, in his memoirs of the 1960s. "That is why semiotics had such influence precisely in

in cultural criticism had always been too easily subsumed by an absolutist politics. Only an objective methodology like cybernetics (and later, semiotics) was equipped to demonstrate the conditioned nature of cultural value and competent to urge individual thought toward its "search for universal inner freedom." Scholars trained in this discipline were thus able to resist the "iron laws of history"—as well as other politically imposed paradigms and death-dealing myths—without risk of a collapse into nihilism or trivial relativism. The key to honest scholarship in the humanities, Segal reasoned, lay in a dispassionate "semiotic historicism," that is, in the *reconstruction* (not the imposition) of norms.

Segal's defense of a "dispassionate semiotics," initially invoked against Marxist-Leninist literary practice and then refurbished as a bulwark against the excesses of Bakhtin's dialogism, is a recurring theme of the present study. With the opening moves in that momentous debate brewing, a major symposium on semiotics was held in Moscow in 1962. Arguing for a methodology in the humanities that was specifically *nauchnyi* (the Russian word means both "scientific" and "scholarly," but assumes stricter standards for falsifiability than is usually required of humanist criticism in the American academy), the "physicists" took their inspiration from Hjelmslev's universal semiotic law, which taught that for every process there is a corresponding system by which that process can be analyzed. The old-style humanists came under attack for their subjectivity, their reluctance to abstract and codify, and their refusal to relinquish their obsession with "things" in favor of the more universal category of *functions*.

Anyone acquainted with the history of literary criticism in America will recognize here the familiar tension in the humanities between soft and hard methodologies. But in the Russian context there was an additional, extremely important subtext. That subtext, which constitutes the second important post-Stalinist "direction" in the rehabilitation of the literary profession, was the fate of Russian Formalist criticism. Russian Formalism, in spirit and doctrine somewhat akin to our later New Criticism but aligned with Russian Futurism and thus much more receptive to technology, had flourished in the experimental climate of the early 1920s. Its most aggressive spokesman, Viktor Shklovsky, had stunned traditional literary critics at the time with his call for the autonomy of the literary

---

the Soviet Union and in the countries of the former socialist camp. There the destructive power of those forces was especially strong. . . . The discovery that the 'iron laws of history,' critical and Socialist Realism, and even many 'historical facts' were only semiotic codes liberated us from the yoke of the communist dictatorship." See Dmitrii Segal, "'Et in Arcadia ego' vernulsia: Nasledie Moskovsko-Tartuskoi semiotiki segodnia," in *NLO*, no. 3 (1993): 30–40, esp. 31–32.

function, a downplaying of content, and a simplification (even an elimination) of complex, ethically marked authorial sentiment. In the interests of professionalizing the practice of literary scholarship, he had proposed a "scientific" vocabulary of mechanical devices and defamiliarization that focused attention on art as something separate from life. Formalism as a movement was cut short when Stalinist controls were extended to literature after 1929; its advocates had been more or less banned in the Soviet Union ever since. But in the early 1960s several events made it again possible for Russians to draw officially on this rich heritage.

First was the reappearance, on the Russian scene, of Roman Jakobson. This great paradigmatic Formalist, who had emigrated from the Soviet state to Prague in the early 1920s and later established himself in the bourgeois West as the century's best-known structural linguist, became a rallying point for Russian literary scholars of the "physicist" persuasion. After Jakobson's visit to Moscow in 1956, his works became selectively available in his homeland. To be sure, the Old Guard "lyricists" hastened to discredit the celebrated émigré—pointing out that the very concept of "literary autonomy" was non-Marxist, indifferent to history, and dismissive of class struggle; in a less ideological vein, they complained that excessive quantification of critical method would undermine the integrity of the literary personality. Where in Russian Formalism, they asked, could one find love, intuition, social justice, the humanistic horizon of art? What about those aspects of literature that simply could not be "segmented" and systematized? The battle lines were drawn.

This two-camp configuration was soon complicated—and skillfully mediated—by the pathbreaking achievements of the Moscow-Tartu school of semiotics. Centered in Soviet Estonia, this gifted scholarly collective has since become famous in the West through the work of Boris Uspensky and especially the late Yuri Lotman. At the time of its formation in 1961, its members (many of them "physicists" by temperament) were united by little more than the desire to break out of a dead, cliché-ridden past. As Boris Egorov, a scholar of Lotman's circle in Tartu and later Petersburg and a legendary storyteller of Russian literary follies, wrote much later in his memoirs: "The party-minded orthodox were still dubious about Structuralism, and we were afraid that the new term *semiotics* would provoke even more fears. We began to reason by [Saltykov-] Shchedrin's Aesopian principle: 'How might all this be expressed more obscurely?' Then the Moscow mathematician V[ladimir] A. Uspensky invented a splendid term, *secondary modeling systems*. Clever, and incomprehensible."[13]

The ruse worked, but these creative, highly productive thinkers soon

---

[13] B. F. Egorov, "U istokov Tartuskoi shkoly," in *NLO*, no. 8 (1994): 78–98, esp. 97.

made of it much more than a ruse. The Tartu semioticians were "specifiers" and "segmenters," completely at home with quantification; in this sense their origins can be traced to the Formalists of the 1920s. But important differences obtain between them and hard-core early Formalism (as well as the more technically oriented Structuralists of a later day). The Tartu scholars were quantifiers who had been raised in a socialist ethos, however disfigured by Soviet practice. Not surprisingly, they insisted from the start that any sensible Structuralist approach to art also attend to thematic and social dimensions, that is, to authentic communication between real people within a cultural continuum. Thus, while retaining a certain mechanical *nauchnyi* vocabulary and a fondness for binary constructs, they came in time to focus less on internally autonomous systems of *signs* (as these signs functioned, say, within a work of art or within a series of artworks) and more on the dynamic interplay of *codes*— that is, complex bundles of behavioral signs that provide the ground rules for personal honor, exchange of goods and values, and the reciprocal trust binding individuals within a society. This approach eventually gave rise to an impressive body of work on cultural and behavioral semiotics, both purely theoretical and (in the case of Lotman's superb studies of Karamzin and Pushkin, as well as his work on the Romantic canon), biographical. For all its reliance on models and codes, then, and for all its fierce eclecticism and independence, the research of the Tartu school seemed to many Russians of the 1960s and 1970s reassuringly close to familiar Marxist-humanist concerns, both in its search for a materialist aesthetics and in its careful attention to sociohistorical questions. It promised the rigor of Formalism without any embarrassing neglect of content or social responsibility—that is, it promised "Structuralism with a human face."

How does this changing landscape for literary criticism in the academy relate to the fate of Mikhail Bakhtin in his homeland? By the mid-1960s Bakhtin was in poor health and in his final decade. He had become famous. His "rediscovery" is now the stuff of legend: in the late 1950s several graduate students from Moscow's prestigious Gorky Institute of World Literature (among them Vadim Kozhinov and Sergei Bocharov, later to become Bakhtin's literary executors) happened upon Bakhtin's 1929 book on Dostoevsky. They assumed that its author—like the authors of so many valuable pre-Stalinist things—had long ago perished. Their shock and delight was considerable, then, when they discovered that Bakhtin was still alive and even in academic harness, teaching Russian and world literature at a teacher's college in the provincial city of Saransk. The Gorky Institute group made numerous pilgrimages to Saransk throughout the 1960s, begged the kindly, ever phlegmatic Bakhtin to rework his Dostoevsky book for a new edition, helped him to get his dissertation on Rabelais out of the files and into print, eased him through many disillusioned moments, and fostered, through their personal devotion, the initial phase of the Bakhtin cult. Surely to his own great surprise, Bakhtin witnessed the reshaping of himself from a marginalized, invalided intellectual, a former political exile teaching in the provinces, into a vigorous mainstream academic—and then into a celebrity with a burgeoning world reputation.

In 1970 the leading Soviet literary journal *Novy Mir* sought Bakhtin's advice on the current state of literary criticism. Indirectly, the probe was also intended to elicit this senior scholar's opinion on the "lyricists versus physicists" debate. Cautious and sanguine as ever, Bakhtin saw potential in both approaches. He singled out for praise Yuri Lotman and the eminent medievalist Dmitri Likhachev, but at the same time he noted that the "specifiers" (that is, the Formalist-leaning critics) were often negligent of literature's larger ties with the history of culture. "Narrow specification," Bakhtin remarked, "is alien to the best traditions of our scholarship."[14] Clearly he associated "narrow specialization" and specification—recall his defense of the eccentric, passionate, "unofficial" Maria Yudina—with a narrowness of soul, contrary to the spirit of philosophy and fatal to those who would grasp the workings of genuine creativity. He recognized in Lotman's early work the very best that a "physicist" could offer the humanities.

Such evenhandedness in the debate was both characteristic and prudent of Bakhtin—for his own person was soon to become yet another route of "reclamation" explored by the new generation of Soviet literary critics. But much in this appropriation still confounds us. How did this theorist of the novel, this patron saint of open dialogue and openly rebellious carnival, who never evinced any interest in Marxism and who spoke categorically against Structuralism and its fondness for codes, come to offer all post-Stalinist parties something to their ideological taste?

The story is an intricate one. The initial Russian rediscovery of Bakhtin, which occurred while he was still alive, remained for some time binary along the familiar lines. The Gorky Institute group was not without its own agenda. Politically Vadim Kozhinov began to evolve into a neo-nationalist, ostentatiously Russian Orthodox in religious orientation while remaining in aesthetic matters an ambitious, conservative "lyricist." In 1965 Kozhinov published an essay entitled "Is a Structural Poetics Possible?" that attacked the entire idea of a linguistic-based methodology for literary studies. To give authority to his views, he evoked those friends

---

[14] Bakhtin's contribution to the *Novy Mir* literary roundtable is available in Bakhtin, *SpG*, 1–7. For Bakhtin's letter in larger context, see Seyffert, *Soviet Literary Structuralism*, 295–300.

and colleagues of Bakhtin, until recently under ban, who had written against Formalism in the 1920s.[15] With this move, Kozhinov began the practice—soon to become endemic—of selectively deploying the writings of Bakhtin and his circle, culled from archives available solely to him and other select disciples, in the struggle against the "physicists" and the Tartu school.

The Tartu semioticians rose to the challenge. By that time several of their members had become enthusiastic about Bakhtin's work, too, and began to claim him as an honored predecessor in the field of "meta-linguistics." In spirit, they pointed out, Bakhtin is not so anti-Formalist. He was, after all, a technician, a generator of typologies, a thinker who had always resisted the simple "reflection theory" of literary analysis in favor of more complex theories of cultural refraction. Like the Formalists, he celebrates craftsmanship and analysis; he constructs his literary theory not out of subjective categories such as genius or intuition but out of concretely observable devices (his "dominant" just happens to be a hero's consciousness rather than a work's literariness). He had specifically limited his Dostoevsky book to a discussion of the formal functioning of ideas and words in the polyphonic novel, disregarding the suspicious ideology or content that fill them.[16] In sum, the Tartu scholars insisted that Bakhtin, despite all the nonquantifiable aspects of his thought, was still a "scientist"—and to be scientific, *nauchnyi*, did not mean to dehumanize or de-historicize. Scientific criticism is dehumanized, Lotman intimated archly, only when it repeats itself, stuffs itself with stock phrases, and labels writers reactionary or progressive according to preestablished criteria.

By the time of Bakhtin's *Novy mir* letter (1970), the success of Soviet semiotics was attracting world attention. It had a journal, *Trudy po znakovym sistemam* [Studies on semiotic systems] and its own annual summer workshops. In 1973 the Tartu school devoted an issue of *Trudy* to Bakhtin in honor of his seventy-fifth birthday; its lead article, an address delivered by Vyacheslav Ivanov in 1970, made Bakhtin embarrassingly central to a vast number of intellectual enterprises, from struc-

---

[15] See Seyffert, *Soviet Literary Structuralism*, 204–8. As his mentors, Kozhinov most often mentioned Voloshinov (not yet republished) and the classics Vinogradov and Vinokur. Kozhinov's complaint was the familiar "humanist" case against linguistics, but with a Formalist bent: why diminish literary science by reducing the laws of literature to the (simpler and more predictable) laws of language? Should we not find precise analytic devices that apply to *literary* structures?

[16] These several points—embedded in a critique of "material aesthetics" that is only partly contra Formalism—are indeed made by Bakhtin in his 1924 essay "The Problem of Content, Material, and Form in a Verbal Work of Art," first published in Russian only in 1975. See the translation by Kenneth Brostrom in Bakhtin, *A&A 90*, 257–325.

tural anthropology to Eisenstein's filmmaking.[17] Over the next decade, the Tartu Structuralists devoted much space in their journals to tidying up Bakhtin's unruly ideas. They attempted, for example, to draw boundaries between shapeless, open, real-life dialogues and the highly organized dialogic relations that obtain in art (a line Bakhtin refused to draw), adding discrete levels of structure across whose boundaries "coding" and "recoding" could take place.[18] This ideological annexation did not pass unnoticed. To many skeptics it seemed that such an effort to stratify polyphony into discrete layers eviscerated Bakhtin's critical method.[19] Under semiotic conditions, it was pointed out, analysis is limited to the residue (what Bakhtin referred to as the "sclerotic deposits") of a dialogic exchange—and thus it obscures the main thing, the human impulse that gave rise to the dialogue and the human potential that might result from it. Any attempt to remove this dialogic aura—what Epstein would later call the sense of "living in a state of promise"—was to remove everything that was indispensable to the model. Were the semioticians really recuperating and explicating Bakhtin or were they transforming him into something else? The question is not trivial. For although good reasons can be found for desiring more preciseness in Bakhtin's thought, his entire phenomenology and discursive cast of mind appear to resist it.

In fact the very ideas of modeling and coding were causing considerable backlash among more traditional Russian critics, now rallying to re-enter the fray. This group included both the Marxist-Leninist brand of official "lyricist" as well as the neo-nationalist, mystical-religious brotherhood that had begun to cluster around the aging and now seriously ailing Bakhtin. As a forum for their views, the nationalists founded a counter-

[17] See *Trudy po znakovym sistemam* 6 (Tartu) (1973); and esp. Vyach. Vs. Ivanov, "Znachenie idei M. M. Bakhtina o znake, vyskazyvanii i dialoge dlia sovremennoi semiotiki," 5–144. Translated as Vyacheslav Ivanov, "The Significance of the Ideas of M. M. Bakhtin about Sign, Utterance, and Dialogue for Modern Semiotics," in Henryk Baran, ed., *Semiotics and Structuralism* (White Plains, N.Y.: International Arts and Sciences Press, 1967), 310–67.

[18] See, for example, P. Kh. Torop, "Simul'tannost' i dialogizm v poetike Dostoevskogo," in *Trudy po znakovym sistemam* 17 (1984): 138–58.

[19] For a model rebuttal of this Tartu School "extension" of Bakhtin's thought, see the penetrating review by I. R. Titunik, "Bachtin and Soviet Semiotics (A Case Study: Boris Uspenskij's *Poetika Kompozicii*), in *Russian Literature* 10 (1981): 1–16. "Neither Bachtin nor Vološinov, in any of their studies of which Uspenskij made use, ever operated via a system of discrete levels of structure," Titunik observes. "Indeed, both argued against just the sort of abstracting that would be needed to produce such a system" (5). See also Michael Holquist, *Dialogism: Bakhtin and His World* (London: Routledge, 1990), 85–86, on the Tartu school's distinction between literature and life as one of *quality* of internal verbal organization, rather than Bakhtin's criterion of *quantity* or density of the ordering, a continuum more "gradualist and historical."

or antisemiotic journal, *Kontekst,* in the early 1970s. With or without Bakhtin's knowledge and consent, the editors of *Kontekst*—who were also the guardians of Bakhtin's chaotic, uncatalogued literary estate— began dribbling bits of his early and late unpublished manuscripts into print. Naturally they favored those parts where Bakhtin's distaste of fixed codes and mechanical modeling combined with quasi-mystical, although often Aesopian, references to Christianity. (In their reading, for example, the brief but provocative comments on Christ that Bakhtin ascribes to Dostoevsky in his book on that writer—Christ as the model for a free, dialogically oriented consciousness—become by extension Bakhtin's own personal convictions.) Meanwhile, potshots at the quantifiers continued. The politics of *Kontekst* became so inflexible and obscurantist that in 1982 even *Pravda,* a paper not known for its pluralism, reprimanded the journal's editorial board for intolerance. At the time a quip circulated in Moscow: "Bakhtin in the context of *Kontekst* is a bad joke."

Which side had the sounder claim? Taken as a whole, it must be said, Bakhtin's extant writings lend more support to an anti-Structuralist view. In the early 1920s Bakhtin argued vehemently against abstraction and systems building of all sorts (what he called "theoretism"); similar sentiments are reflected in the notebook jottings of his final half-decade. "Semiotics deals primarily with the transmission of ready-made communication using a ready-made code," he noted in 1970–71, in a passage that has since been much quoted. "A context is potentially unfinalized; a code must be finalized. A code is only a technical means of transmitting information, it does not have cognitive, creative significance. A code is a deliberately established, killed context."[20] To be sure, we should not make too much of this startling remark, a casual private jotting of Bakhtin's whose implications he nowhere works out. But it is also, of course, not true; codes can be cognitively and creatively significant to an enormous degree. For whatever reason, during fifty years of scholarly activity Bakhtin chose not to deepen or make more sophisticated his understanding of signs, codes, and their interaction with more inchoate human material—as so many contemporary semioticians and socio-ethnographers (including Yuri Lotman himself) have done.[21] *Znak,* "sign," remained for

---

[20] "From Notes Made in 1970–71," in *SpG,* 147.

[21] See Allen Reid, "Who Is Lotman and Why Is Bakhtin Saying Those Nasty Things about Him?" in *Discours Social/Social Discourse* 3, nos. 1 & 2 (1990): 325–38. According to Reid, Bakhtin flattens out Lotman's theory of coding: he reduces to mere mechanical "internal recoding" even those instances of complex, "external multiple recoding" that Lotman intended—as far back as the 1960s—to be flexible in ways fully compatible with Bakhtin's requirements for an interaction of contexts. For a more temperate discussion, see P. Grzhibek [Grzybek], "Bakhtinskaia semiotika i Moskovsko-tartuskaia shkola," in M. L. Gasparov et al., eds., *Lotmanovskii sbornik,* no. 1 (Moscow: ITs-Garant, 1995): 240–59. It

Bakhtin the rather crude, binary Saussurean instrument that had been criticized by his circle in the 1920s.

As we shall see in chapter 5 of this study, Bakhtin's reluctance to ac-knowledge the creativity of codes left a profound mark on his mature understanding of form. For it is noteworthy, I think, that Bakhtin never seriously entertained the ways in which a personality—and especially the poetic (not the prosaic) personality living in a highly "convention-driven" era—might actually be weakened and made more desperate by endlessly renegotiable dialogue; nor, conversely, how such a personality might become *more* creative, more capable of initiative and honorable activity, when confronted with the challenge of manipulating many vig-orous codes. For this reason, one might argue, Lotman became a great Pushkinist, whereas Bakhtin, although not without his own wisdom on the Russian Romantic era, tended to "read backward" from his beloved Dostoevskian novel into earlier periods of literature, even those periods governed by manifestly different dominants.[22]

The static, somewhat archaic role Bakhtin allotted to signs and codes could well be connected with the larger difficulty he had with any nu-anced discussion of authority. In his work, authority most often functions as a dull and impoverishing force: as centripetality, as the grim monolith of officialdom opposed to sunny carnival, as the dead epic. Authoritative political power [*vlast'*, *avtoritet*] was heavy, simple, homogenous, one-sidedly "serious"—and it was bureaucratic, always pressing down from above on something more valuable and vulnerable than itself. We might even say that for Bakhtin (as for many of his marked generation), *vlast'*, institutionalized political power, appears to have been a distanced, some-what demonized "untouchable," not without its fascination but better exiled from the kingdom than dispassionately explored. There was no flex to it. And not surprisingly, to counter such an unforgiving force Bakhtin

---

is tempting to speculate how Bakhtin would have responded to Lotman in his post-binary phases, where Lotman investigates such concepts as the biosphere, semiosphere, and the creative potential of the "intersection" [*peresechenie*] and "explosion" [*vzryv*] (for that final phase, see Yu. M. Lotman, *Kul'tura i vzryv* [Moscow: Gnosis/Progress, 1992]).

[22] A comprehensive study of Bakhtin and Lotman in their respective intellectual evolu-tions is yet to be attempted. For an excellent discussion of this one aspect—the juxtaposi-tion of Bakhtin's "dialogue" and Lotman's "codes" as they service literary biography—see David M. Bethea, "Iurii Lotman in the 1980s: The Code and Its Relation to Literary Biography," in Arnold McMillin, ed., *Reconstructing the Canon: Russian Writing in the 1980s* (London: Harwood, forthcoming). See also the preface to the Polish-language edi-tion of Lotman's biography of Pushkin, where Lotman explains how the interaction of codes can increase the individuality and creativity of a poet's personality: Yu. M. Lotman, "'Aleksandr Sergeevich Pushkin. Biografiia pisatelia.' Predislovie k pol'skomu izdaniiu," in M. L. Gasparov et al., eds., *Lotmanovskii sbornik* no. 1 (Moscow: ITs-Garant, 1995): 85–88.

needed a global vision and the highly dispersive, individualizing ideas of dialogue, prosaics, and unfinalizability.

The scholars of the Tartu school, one generation younger, were spared the fate of whole careers lived out under Stalin's special brand of *vlast'*. Perhaps for that reason they seemed less haunted by the question of power. Indeed, their first academic contributions were in the "organically" authoritative realms of myth, religion, and folklore, as well as in theories of social ideology and law. Unsentimentally, as scientists, many of them were interested in the sort of individuation that occurs through *submission* to larger imperatives and social structures, not only—as was the case with many of their parents' generation—in personality formation brought about solely through resisting, outwitting, or (more kindly) rearranging authoritative utterances into "internally persuasive words." The Tartu scholars were curious about the interaction of impersonal mechanisms with personal opinion. But Bakhtin, almost sixty when Stalin died, had a relationship to power that was more visceral, superstitiously evasive, and metaphorical than analytical. Rather than study it, he turned away. Till the end of his life, he remained an enthusiast of Friedrich Schelling (a passion of his youth), whose ideas on "objectivity as intersubjectivity" and on nature as a developing, living organism inclined him toward philosophical idealism and Romanticism. His interest in science appears to have been largely biological; in narrative, he focused not on static or spatial features but on everything that was developing through time. Bakhtin's patience with political commands and with the purely mechanical in the universe was extremely short. And he sensed mechanisms at work in signs and codes.

As Communism moved into its final decade, then, it seemed that Bakhtin had been won for the "lyricists"—a motley band of traditionalists, anti-Jakobsonians, antisemioticians, religious revivalists, and Russian nationalists. What had not yet been attempted was an impartial study of Bakhtin's life and texts relatively free of the reclamation wars. That task seemed to be under way with much more vigor abroad. So when borders began to open, Russian researchers hastened to compare notes with their foreign colleagues and to assess the extant properties of their best-selling author. It became clear that a great deal of groundwork remained to be done.

THE 1990s: THE RUSSIAN BAKHTIN INDUSTRY TAKES STOCK

Most necessary to scholars was a decent database and an inventory of primary research materials: memoirs, archives, biographies, bibliographies. The first category, memoirs, was rich and varied—but somewhat profligate. It reflected the tensions of rival discipleships and of Bakhtin's own apparent determination (even in his darkest moods) to be a sanguine, positive-minded mentor to the junior colleagues who had rescued his work from the dead; it had also been compromised over the years by the magnetic force of the Bakhtin cult. Indeed, one of the more attractive weaknesses of cultured Russians of the older generation—as many of us sensed at the centennial—is a tendency to construct "creator cults" around literary and cultural figures, heroic men and women who then become, in effect, secular saints with exemplary biographies that contain canonized truths. The survival and resurrection of Mikhail Bakhtin fits that pattern well. What stress lines had emerged to divide the faithful by the summer of the Jubilee?

First and somewhat awkwardly, the 1995 conference was thinly attended by that group of caretakers who had known Bakhtin personally and over the longest period. The founding disciples—Kozhinov, Bocharov, Gachev, Melikhova—chose not to participate. "Bakhtinology," it appeared, was getting on their nerves. Some made it clear that they did not need the industry because they had known the man: "To *you* he is Bakhtin; to me, Mikhail Mikhailovich." Valuing themselves as "*khraniteli*," preservers of the legacy, they had come to believe that the young, feeding any which way off these theories now that they had become fashionable and free of risk, were simply opportunists or dissipaters. Kozhinov, in particular, felt keenly that today's readers made little effort to understand Bakhtin in his own context.[23] Perhaps this is understandable; the orphaned era of their own youth had offered few role models for literary scholars, and their personal attachment to this dignified pre-Bolshevik intellectual, to whom they had rendered such hazardous and indis-

---

[23] Kozhinov prefaces almost all his new releases from the Bakhtin archive during the 1990s with injured commentary. See, for example, his introductory remarks to the publication, in 1993, of the uncensored version of R. M. Mirkina's student notes taken at Bakhtin's lectures on Russian literature (in Vitebsk and Leningrad) during the 1920s: "There is a widespread notion that M. M. Bakhtin's interests were entirely turned toward the past, as if he did not want contact with the 'trivial hustle and bustle' of the present day," Kozhinov writes. "But I can attest that even in his advanced years Mikhail Mikhailovich (at least until the onset of his fatal ailments) took a lively interest in everything that was happening in Russia and in the world as a whole . . . Yes, now we can make public the [full] text of the notes of these lectures, but it is not difficult to predict that much contained in them will be received by certain circles of readers with bewilderment and even with acute dissatisfaction [his cool or negative assessments of Ehrenburg, Tynianov, and Zoshchenko]. . . . Again I can bear witness to the fact that Mikhail Mikhailovich, even at the end of his life, did not change his attitude toward those and similar phenomena of literature in the twenties. And I myself, almost completely sharing M. M. Bakhtin's opinions, remain deeply convinced that in the not-too-distant future these assessments will become generally accepted, even canonical, in Russian literary thought." V. V. Kozhinov, "Predislovie" to "Iz neopublikovannykh rabot M. M. Bakhtina," *DKKh, no. 1(2) (93):* 90–91, esp. 90.

pensable service, was great. But the generational conflict was further darkened by professional rivalries, Russian patriotism, and anti-Semitism. The Old Guard, our immediate source for most memoir material, had long been breaking up from within. Old Saransk hands resented the higher visibility and status of Muscovites; the latter group disputed among themselves trivial details that poorly concealed larger struggles for territory. One illustration will suffice.

In 1988 Vadim Kozhinov recalled one of the 1960s pilgrimages to Saransk, including this colorful detail. After fifteen minutes in Bakhtin's presence, a member of their group, Georgii Gachev (the culturologist whose vivid portrait of Bakhtin opened this study) fell on his knees in rapture and implored: "Mikhail Mikhailovich, tell us how to live so that we can become like you!"[24] Gachev himself later expanded on this bout of reverence in an interview he provided for one of the new Bakhtin journals:[25] "Bakhtin himself . . . became for us something like a living church," Gachev remarked. "From him and from [his wife] Elena Aleksandrovna there radiated a holiness, a nobility of spirit, a certain martyrdom. . . . We all clustered about him, and each brought some unripened thing of his own to talk out. Bakhtin personally was silent; it was enough for him simply to be an ear and listen, for when you have tuned up such an ear in yourself, you have tuned yourself up to your own optimum." Gachev was not alone among the Old Guard in mythologizing Bakhtin's reticence to initiate discussion and his willingness to remain silent on the subject of his own biography. "He was, I repeat, a person who profoundly did not like outpourings of a personal nature," Kozhinov wrote in 1991. "Only now and then would individual phrases about his origins or his life accidentally burst forth. I did try several times to draw him into conversation, asked him to tell me something about himself, but each time I heard the same answer: it's not yet time, not yet time. . . . Yes, this man had his own aura."[26]

[24] See Vadim Kozhinov, "'Tak eto bylo,'" in *Don*, no. 10 (1988): 156–60. In his collection of portraits of Russian thinkers from Pushkin to Losev entitled *Russkaia Duma* (Moscow: Novosti, 1991), Georgii Gachev begins his sketch of Bakhtin as follows: "3.04.88. Bakhtin—this is the City (and not Nature), Peopledness, multi-voicedness (and not silence), dialogue (not a unified Logos), polyphony (multi-soundedness), pluralism and not unity, strong tea (not birch tree juice), and a nocturnal seminar until morning . . . Not God, but your neighbor, that was the accent" (105).

[25] "'Tak, sobstvenno, zaviazalas' uzhe tselaia istoriia' (Georgii Gachev vspominaet i razdumivaet o M. M. Bakhtine)" [In this way, actually, the whole story got started (Georgii Gachev reminisces and reflects on M. M. Bakhtin)], interview with Gachev conducted by Ivan Lapin, in *DKKh, no. 1(2) (93)*: 105–8, esp. 106.

[26] "Kak pishut trudy, ili proiskhozhdenie nesozdannogo avantiurnogo romana (Vadim Kozhinov rasskazyvaet o sud'be i lichnosti M. M. Bakhtina)," interview with Kozhinov conducted by Nikolai Pan'kov, December 1991, in *DKKh, no. 1 (92)*: 109–22. Quoted material occurs on pages 111–12.

As Bakhtin's image became an increasingly valuable commodity, genre scenes such as Gachev at Bakhtin's feet—and others of similar hagiographic cast—became themselves a point of dispute. In 1993 Bocharov upbraided Kozhinov in print: "I don't recall Gachev on his knees in front of Bakhtin. We were either sitting, or perhaps someone was standing. It's unpleasant to admit to oneself that one could forget such a prominent fact. But Gachev doesn't remember it either; I asked him. I'm not casting doubt on Kozhinov's communication. I fully admit that he alone might remember what the two of us do not remember." Tactfully, Bocharov then questioned the whole ethics of eyewitness memoirs and the urge of the memoirist to fill out the story with fantasies.[27]

Meanwhile, the backlash was gathering strength. Outsiders to the Bakhtin industry—newly minted converts to Freud, Derrida, and a hermeneutics of suspicion—began to resist the entire hagiographic enterprise. To some of these moderns, Bakhtin's fame, his seeming benevolence, and his reluctance to join the twentieth century in his literary tastes were being exploited quite simply as face-saving nostalgia. Vadim Linetsky, for example, opens chapter 8 of his 1994 tract *Anti-Bakhtin: The Best Book on Vladimir Nabokov* with the following declaration: "It's good that Bakhtin exists. Now we can hide our creative infantilism behind someone else's broad shoulders, we can refer to him, point our finger, nod our heads: Bakhtin. If Bakhtin weren't there, it would be awful to imagine how nowadays we could look in the face the civilized world that surrounds us. Seventy years of barbarism, cretinism, degeneration. But— we managed to get by. In a Saransk storeroom, on a faraway shelf, they found him, exhumed him, shook off the dust, shoved him forward— look, envy us: Bakhtin."[28]

The picture is further complicated by the role Bakhtin came to fill for subsequent, and culturally quite distinct, Soviet generations. The first memoir accounts to be published were written by members of the Old Guard who were, of course, very young in the early 1960s; by the time of their formal reminiscences, they remembered Bakhtin in the grateful way that impressionable junior scholars revere an older mentor. Intimacy with Bakhtin—a man of reserve and formally correct relations—was difficult to achieve; it was only natural that a certain rivalry as regards services rendered would break out among his aides. Competitive saint's lives were composed. Vladimir Turbin (1927–1993), Bakhtin's personal aide for

---

[27] S. G. Bocharov, "Primechanie k memuaru," in *NLO*, no. 3 (1993): 209–10, esp. 209.

[28] Vadim Linetskii, *"Anti-Bakhtin"—Luchshaia kniga o Vladimire Nabokove* (Sankt Peterburg: Tip. im. Kotliakova, 1994), 58. The final line is a paraphrase from Mayakovsky's hectoring propaganda poem "Verses about a Soviet Passport" (1929), which ends: *"Chitaete, zaviduite: ya—grazhdanin sovetskogo soyuza!"* [Have a look, envy me: I am a citizen of the Soviet Union!].

twelve years in Saransk and Moscow and a respected literary scholar in his own right, was touchily proud of his status as *kamerdiner*, or "valet," to Bakhtin's daily bodily needs; at the time of his own death, Turbin left behind a sacralized memoir entitled "The Famine and Pain of Mikhail Bakhtin."[29] Semyon Konkin, Bakhtin's colleague at Mordovia State Teacher's College from 1936 to 1959 and Turbin's bitter foe, produced his own counterbiography of Bakhtin, in which he roundly abuses Turbin for peddling a misty image of Mikhail Mikhailovich as "not of this world," as a "'secret' peering into our contemporary world from 'over there,'" as a heroic figure left starving and friendless in the poorly provisioned Russian provinces and thus in need of being rescued by big-city Moscow intellectuals.[30]

Such possessive moves on the Bakhtin "icon" became common in the inner circle. But then more neutral reminiscences by Bakhtin's own contemporaries and co-survivors from the Stalinist period began to appear. Especially interesting in this regard is the testimony of Leonid Pinsky (1906–1981)—Renaissance scholar, author of a classic text on Shakespeare, former Gulag inmate—who knew Bakhtin and his wife well in the 1960s and 1970s. In his correspondence with Pinsky, Bakhtin expressed more undisguised pessimism than he ever allowed himself to display with the disciples half his age.[31] It was Pinsky, for example, who mentioned to a fellow literary scholar, Grigory Pomerants, that in 1974 he had asked "one of the most noble of Russian minds [Bakhtin was meant] whether or not good would eventually triumph"; and Bakhtin's answer had been, "'No, of course not.'" (In reporting this exchange, Pomerants remarked

[29] See Vladimir Turbin, "Golod i bol' Mikhaila Bakhtina" in *Literaturnaia gazeta*, 15 June 1993; see also "O Bakhtine," in V. N. Turbin, *Nezadolgo do Vodoleia* (Moscow: Radiks, 1994), 443–70. Turbin stresses the ever present fear of hunger that accompanied the Bakhtins until old age, the painkillers he was continually requested to procure, the exile that saved the couple from starving in the cities; and he called for a "poetics of biography" which could accommodate a "biography of the saint's-life type" that Bakhtin in fact represented—and that "repeated in no small part the biography of the Russian people" (449).

[30] S. S. Konkin and L. S. Konkina, *Mikhail Bakhtin (Stranitsy zhizni i tvorchestva)* (Saransk: Mordovskoe knizhnoe izdatel'stvo, 1993), 17. "In the grocery stores of Saransk in the 1950s–1960s there was no shortage of foodstuffs," the Konkins remark with some irritation. "One wouldn't even have to write about this, if it weren't for the strange reminiscences of certain friends of M. Bakhtin that have appeared in recent years. In particular we have in mind the series of article-reminiscences by V. Turbin" (270–71).

[31] "Iz semeinogo arkhiva L. E. Pinskogo (publikatsiia i predislovie N. A. Pan'kova)," in *DKKh, no. 2(7) (94)*: 55–118. The editor Nikolai Pan'kov points out in his preface that Bakhtin's "monumental optimism" was in fact "the consequence of a strong concentration of will" for the benefit of his young intellectual charges (55); but that to Pinsky, Bakhtin had no problem remarking on his illness, his anxieties, and the "depressed condition of his soul" (from a letter of 21 February 1963), 58.

that thinkers like Bakhtin, who have pondered deeply the nature of time and process, rarely speak of "triumph" or victory; those were the words of the Apocalypse, not of Christ.)[32] Pinsky considered Bakhtin a philosopher of European scope and existential depth. But such an assessment was not to everyone's post-Stalinist taste. Kozhinov, for one, confessed to having discovered native Russian culture through Bakhtin; it had been a breath of revivifying air after the fraudulent internationalism of Communist rhetoric. Throughout the 1960s quarrels broke out between Pinsky (an old-school, Russian-Jewish intellectual) and the much younger Kozhinov, emerging chauvinist, who revered "Mikhail Mikhailovich as one of the greatest incarnations of Russia."[33]

This generation gap between Bakhtinists survived well into the 1990s—to be visited on a new layer of scholars, the first never to have known the master personally. Bocharov politely detached himself from the fray, devoting himself to editing the *Collected Works*. Gachev turned his attention to culturology and the typology of nations. And in a 1992 essay, Kozhinov unceremoniously dismissed Makhlin and other younger scholars who had been bold enough to acknowledge the influence of non-Russian ideas on Bakhtin and the legitimacy of non-Russian Bakhtin scholarship.[34] Insisting that Western consciousness was "monologic in principle" and thus unable to grasp the principles of genuine dialogism, Kozhinov considered foreigners' fascination with Bakhtin to be little more than a fad filling the post-Structuralist void. With their superior financial resources, Western intellectuals had bought up Bakhtin and had begun to publish

[32] As mentioned by Grigory Pomerants in " 'Dvoinye mysli' u Dostoevskogo," in G. Pomerants, *Otkrytost' bezdne: Vstrechi s Dostoevskim* (Moscow: Sovetskii pisatel', 1990), 225–26.

[33] See Kozhinov's remarkably unembarrassed testimony to Nikolai Pan'kov in *DKKh no. 2(7) (94)*: 112–18, esp. 116. Bakhtin's Russianness, according to Kozhinov, was manifest in his recommendation to his disciples that they read Vasily Rozanov (who "opened up Russia in all its depth, fullness, and contradictoriness"); whereas Pinsky and Pomerants are vaguely aligned with (a presumably cosmopolitan) "Soviet patriotism" that did not acknowledge "Rozanov, Bakhtin, even Dostoevsky, and that 'accepted' Pushkin and Tolstoy only in a reduced and lab-prepared form."

[34] Vadim Kozhinov, "Bakhtin i ego chitateli" [Bakhtin and his readers], *Moskva* (July 1992): 143–51; repr. in *DKKh nos. 2–3 (93)*: 120–34. The essay is noteworthy for its aggrieved tone and its gratuitous, ad hominem insults to Michael Holquist (who, Kozhinov claims, reneged on a dedication to him and collapsed in the face of "Western pressure" to modify—that is, to qualify—his original image of Bakhtin as primarily a Russian Orthodox thinker). Kozhinov's reminiscences can also, on occasion, be persuasive, flexible, and nonpartisan—qualities much more in evidence when he grants interviews to American scholars. See, for example, his wide-ranging discussion of authorship, religion, intellectual roots, and relativism in Nicholas Rzhevsky, "Kozhinov on Bakhtin," in *New Literary History* 25, no. 2 (Spring 1994): 429–44.

books on him—while Russia lay impoverished. Kozhinov also claimed that Bakhtin's dialogism had been inspired not by cosmopolitan outsiders and pan-Europeanists such as the eminent German-Jewish neo-Kantian philosopher Hermann Cohen (a thinker whom Bakhtin greatly admired), but rather by the fifteenth-century Transvolga hermit and mystic, Saint Nil Sorsky. In the same spirit he argued that the sources of Bakhtinian carnival should be sought not in Rabelais's corrupt Catholic West but in the purifying laughter of the Byzantine holy fool.

All who remember Bakhtin during his final two decades, however, generally agree on his public personality. By the mid-1990s the canonized image was that of a self-effacing, chain-smoking, bemused old man, not given to polemics, congenial and yet (unless pressed for details in a formal interview) indisposed to talk about himself. He was a man more of Chekhov's temperament than of Dostoevsky's or Tolstoy's. A moving glimpse was left by one academic acquaintance who visited Bakhtin in his final year, 1975:

> In Bakhtin's little apartment, an unhurried discussion was going on among the guests, who were literary scholars (the host, as usual, preferred to listen). And suddenly, quite unexpectedly, apologizing for not having forewarned their host (Bakhtin did not have a telephone), two correspondents from the Polish press walked in and began to interview Mikhail Mikhailovich in a most lively way. Bakhtin smiled miserably, begged their mercy, promised to send written answers in a day or two, but the newspaper men were not to be put off, they quickly set up their microphone apparatus, shoved a mike almost into Bakhtin's mouth and showered him with questions, which he answered slowly, wearily, aloofly, laconically. In the world of newspaper correspondents and the spinning of microphones, Bakhtin looked ancient, outdated, lonely, lost.[35]

The centennial year called forth a flood of further commemorative portraits. Bocharov began to publish long past—but now acutely recalled—conversations with Bakhtin that purported to settle uncertainties about disputed authorship, religious belief, and political convictions.[36] Such reminiscences have enriched and complicated Bakhtin's image, but they are not, of course, neutral.

---

[35] B. F. Egorov, "Slovo o M. M. Bakhtine," in *B sb I 90*, 4–6. A transcript of this Polish interview was published as Mikhail Bakhtin, "O polifonichnosti romanov Dostoevskogo," *Rossiia/Russia* 2: 189–98 (see n. 6, above).

[36] S. G. Bocharov, "Ob odnom razgovore i vokrug nego," *NLO*, no. 2 (1993): 70–89; see also the abridged, somewhat imprecise translation by Stephen Blackwell and Vadim Liapunov as Sergey Bocharov, "Conversations with Bakhtin," *PMLA* 109, no. 5 (October 1994): 1009–24. Most recently, see Sergei Bocharov, "Sobytie bytiia: O Mikhaile Mikhailoviche Bakhtine," *Novyi mir*, no. 11 (1995): 211–21.

Even more enigmatic than the genre of the Bakhtin memoir is the Bakhtin archive. In Russia as elsewhere (but perhaps more intensely in Russia where distrust toward official documents is matched by an enthusiasm for sacralized biography and relics), scholars with access to personal papers have tended to sit on them and trickle out their contents piecemeal to select petitioners. In the case of Bakhtin, inventory and access have been sporadic. For years manuscripts and personal belongings were scattered throughout Moscow and Saransk, in cardboard boxes, in the private apartments of a handful of disciples. The preservation of these papers has been an act of love under archaic conditions. (Computer backup is only now becoming routinely available to Russian textologists, so the crumbling school notepads that Bakhtin covered with his commentary have been deciphered and painstakingly recopied by hand, often onto equally perishable material. To the despair of archivists and present-day transcribers, till the end of his life Bakhtin wrote exclusively with a sharpened lead pencil on soft paper.)[37] Previously unpublished material, none of it too startling, continues to appear in the journals: theater reviews and working notebooks from the Saransk years; references to Bakhtin in family archives (the Kagans and Pinskys); notes taken by colleagues during Bakhtin's lectures in Leningrad in the mid-twenties; the full stenographic transcript of Bakhtin's dissertation defense in 1946; portions of the Rabelais dissertation (focusing on Shakespeare) that had been excised while editing for the book.[38] The modest fund of Bakhtin's own extant personal letters is slowly being published.[39] Brian Poole, a Canadian

[37] Konkin and Konkina, *Mikhail Bakhtin*, 270.

[38] In 1992 *Voprosy filosofii* [Questions of philosophy] printed several dozen pages of Bakhtin's "additions and changes" to the Rabelais project; see M. M. Bakhtin, "Dolponeniia i izmeneniia k 'Rable,'" *Voprosy filosofii*, no. 1 (1992): 134–64. These "Additions" are included, with detailed and highly professional commentary, in *MMB: ss 5 (96)*, 80–129, 473–92. The text, prepared by Leontina Melikhova, deals with the question of official versus unofficial seriousness, carnival echoes, the role of gesture in Shakespeare's dramas (including a Freudian reading of *Hamlet* as a displaced *Oedipus Rex*), the name (lofty/ sacred) versus the nickname (low/profane), and makes insightful, if somewhat disjointed, comments on Goethe, Heine, Dostoevsky, and Dante. The excerpt has been translated by Harold D. Baker and is included in his volume *The Unknown Bakhtin* (Ardis, 2000).

[39] The first documents to be published were the Bakhtin-Matvei Kagan correspondence, including seven letters by Bakhtin from 1921, largely relating to his poor health and possibilities for employment; see "M. M. Bakhtin i M. I. Kagan (Po materialam semeinogo arkhiva)," ed. K. Nevel'skaya [Iudit Kagan], *Pamiat'*, no. 4 (1979, Moscow; 1981, Paris): 249–81. Approximately this same selection was reprinted in *DKKh, no. 1 (92)*: 60–88. Vladimir Turbin made available letters Bakhtin wrote to him in the 1960s, all brief and inconsequential (cf. V. N. Turbin, "'Ni proizvedenii, ni obrazov Dostoevskogo . . . i v pomine net': Pis'mo M. M. Bakhtina ot 19 ianvaria 1963 goda," in *B sb II 91*, 371–73. A modest set of letters to Leonid Pinsky was published in *DKKh, no. 2(7) (94)*: 55–62. For a

scholar working in Marburg, Moscow, and Berlin, spent several years tracking down the full, seven-hundred-page proto-text of Bakhtin's magnum opus on the *Bildungsroman*.[40] (The page proofs for this massive volume perished when a bomb hit the Moscow publishing house where it was in production during World War II—after which Bakhtin, in a story that has become so famous it was repeated, somewhat garbled, in the mid-1990s by the chain-smoking hero of the American film *Smoke*, "smoked away" four-fifths of his back-up copy, that is, used it for cigarette papers during the lean war years.) Bakhtin's sources for his other more ambitious works have also been partially assembled. As we await the full *Collected Works*, however, no comprehensive catalogue or inventory of extant archival holdings exists.

The final category of source material on Russian soil—annotated scholarly editions, bibliographies, and biographies—is in a somewhat happier state. The first bibliography (ninety-five pages) of works by and about Bakhtin in Russian and Western languages was published in Saransk in 1989; in 1995 this list was updated in a comprehensive centenary bibliography of recent work (from 1988 to 1994, more than one thousand entries) covering Russian and the major European languages.[41] By the millenium, if work goes according to plan, the occasional sporadic reprint will have been superseded by the authoritative *M. M. Bakhtin: Sobranie sochinenii* [Collected works] in seven volumes (1996–99), ongoing under Bocharov's editorship, with thoroughly updated commentary and textology.[42] Volume 5, the first to be published, appeared in

good sense of the courteous, resigned tone the elderly Bakhtin sustained with younger colleagues, the most interesting set of letters in print are those between Kozhinov and Bakhtin, 1960–65, mostly on the Dostoevsky and Rabelais books but with comments on Solzhenitsyn, Kozhinov's own scholarship, and so on; see "Iz pisem M. M. Bakhtina," *Moskva* (November–December 1992): 175–82.

[40] Brian Poole, then in the German and Comparative Literature department at the University of Marburg, spent two years (1989–91) in Moscow researching Bakhtin's lost book (only seventy pages of which were published). Among the seven hundred pages of "preparatory material" for the *Bildungsroman* project that Poole examined in Bocharov's Bakhtin archive was a detailed (thirty-page) plan for the book, which contained a close analysis of Goethe as well as an impressively full bibliography of works that Bakhtin consulted.

[41] The pioneering work was G. V. Karpunov, L. S. Konkin, and O. E. Osovskii, *Mikhail Mikhailovich Bakhtin: Bibliograficheskii ukazatel'* (Saransk: Mordovskii gosudarstvennyi universitet, 1989); the centennial update is "Bibliographia Bachtiniana: 1988–1994," in T. G. Yurchenko, ed., *M. M. Bakhtin v zerkale kritiki*, part 4 (Moscow: Labirint, 1995), 114–89. The most recent comprehensive bibliography in English of works by and on Bakhtin—including interviews, lecture notes, translations, dissertations, and special journal issues—has been compiled by Harold D. Baker (University of California, Irvine), 1996.

[42] Published by "Russkie slovari," Moscow. Annotations and textological scholarship on the *Collected Works* are being done by major Bakhtin scholars of the older generation: S. G. Bocharov, L. A. Gogotishvili, L. V. Deriugina, V. V. Kozhinov, N. I. Nikolaev, L. S.

1996; it contains more than twenty texts from the Saransk years (1940s–1960s), the majority of them previously unpublished and unknown.

Several journals devoted exclusively to Bakhtin's legacy, with a reliable distribution network and multinational editorial boards, are now well launched. Of these, the most ambitious have proved to be the *Bakhtinskii sbornik* [Bakhtin anthology], based in Moscow-Saransk and begun in 1990 as an annual publication; the quarterly *Dialog Karnaval Khronotop* (established with Soros funding in 1992 in Vitebsk, now in Belarus', Bakhtin's refuge during the Civil War), which fills four two-hundred-page issues a year with archival material, reviews, interviews, and translations of non-Russian work;[43] and a series specializing in Bakhtin as philosopher, *M. Bakhtin i filosofskaia kul'tura XX veka* (St. Petersburg, 1991). These are the large-scale projects—and by 1997, it should be noted, all three faced severe financial crisis and possible collapse for want of sponsors. But there has been an abundance of more modest provincial publications, proceedings, and conference series that tell their own intriguing story. That story is worth sampling, for the role of the provinces in the Bakhtin reclamation project is part of a larger cultural shift.

Between 1985 and 1995—that transitional decade during which Soviet Communism was destabilized and then dethroned—a great deal was written in the Russian and Western press about "discrediting the center." Although usually deployed politically, the phrase had an academic and cultural aspect to it as well. Under the Soviet system, higher education and publishing had been highly centralized: books appeared with an unambiguous "M." [Moscow] or "L." [Leningrad] to mark the place of publication, and the prestigious universities of those cities were greatly coveted. At the expense of the countryside, urban populations were guaranteed the best provisioning, both of commodities and culture. But once the command economy collapsed, the center lost its priority funding and the ability to enforce its fearful mandates. The *provinces* (a term that in Russian has implied not only "provincial" but also primitive, scarcely civilized, without the benefit of material or intellectual progress) began to

---

Melikhova, and I. L. Popova. According to the editor's note prefacing volume 5, material in future volumes will be distributed as follows: vol. 1, philosophical aesthetics of the 1920s; vol. 2, *Problems of Dostoevsky's Creative Art* (1929), and an appendix—"Lecture Notes of Bakhtin's Course on Russian Literature," by R. M. Mirkina; vol. 3, theory of the novel (1930s); vol. 4, the book on Rabelais and material relating to it (1940–70); vol. 5, works of the 1940s to the beginning of the 1960s; vol. 6, *Problems of Dostoevsky's Poetics* (1963) and works of the 1960s to the 1970s; and vol. 7, works of "Bakhtin's circle."

[43] For a review of *Dialogue. Carnival. Chronotope* in English, see Anna Matzov, "Dialog Karnaval Khronotop," in Scott Lee and Clive Thomson, eds., *Le Bulletin Bakhtine/The Bakhtin Newsletter*, no. 5 (1996) (Special Issue: "Bakhtin Around the World"): 211–23.

hold on to their goods and come into their own. It was as if Bakhtin's famous model of the centralizing "centripetal" forces in a given culture undermined by its dispersing "centrifugal" forces had finally come home to erode his own domestic monolith.

For Bakhtin, we must not forget, was most definitely a creature of the outlying regions, a man at home on society's margins. Born in Oryol, raised in Odessa, jobless in the late 1910s to the early 1920s on the western fringes of the USSR (now Belarus'), unemployed in Leningrad, exiled in mid-life to distant Kazakhstan, his first (and only) secure job was at a modest teacher's college in Saransk, two hundred miles southeast of Moscow. As Bakhtin's academic home for almost twenty-five years, this institute—upgraded in 1957 to Mordovia State University, with an active publishing house of its own—inaugurated an annual lecture series in honor of Bakhtin in 1989; in that year, an all-Russian Bakhtin Society was founded there as well.[44] From the start of the boom, enthusiasm ran high in provincial centers with a "Bakhtin connection." I glimpsed this new balance of power in the early phases of the postcommunist transition in Moscow, May 1991, during a discussion with Leontina Melikhova, Bakhtin's student and personal aide during his final years and currently one of the archivists for the *Collected Works*. She was staunchly on the side of the urban saviors of Bakhtin. "How is morale among the Russian *Bakhtinisty*?" I asked. "In Moscow right now, it's bad," she replied. "Everyone is fearful, we're running out of food, out of paper, out of jobs." "And in Saransk?" I asked. "There, everyone is very optimistic," Melikhova remarked with a good-humored shrug. "After all, there was never any sausage in Saransk."

In our slow reconstitution of Bakhtin's "Russian face" we should attend first of all to the provinces. Although other Bakhtinian locales have not been silent (Odessa, Makhachkala in Dagestan), the most valuable of the "provincial"—non-Moscow/Petersburg—contributions to Russian Bakhtin studies have come from Vitebsk in Belarus', site of Bakhtin's intellectual apprenticeship, and Saransk, the "academic" hometown of his mature years. Festschrifts, anthologies, conference papers, archival publications, and fresh dissertations are clustered in those two places. By 1996, at both locations, Bakhtin Centers were projected or operative, with varying degrees of official sanction and funding. And after a decade

---

[44] The first Bakhtin lecture series was announced in a press bulletin, "Pervye saranskie bakhtinskie chteniia," 16–19 oktiabria 1989 (Saransk: Mordovskii gosudarstvennyi universitet), 16 pp. A "Bakhtin Society" was founded in Saransk and incorporated in 1991 with by-laws, a governing presidium, and local branches throughout the country; see the seven-page pamphlet "Ustav Obshchestva M. M. Bakhtina" [Statutes of the Bakhtin Society] (Moscow: Moskovskii gosudarstvennyi universitet, 1991). Plans were announced in 1996 for an International Bakhtin Society centered in Minsk.

of dependence on the pioneering Clark-Holquist biography (which has long circulated in unofficial translation), in 1993 Russian readers were treated to the first full-length domestic biography of Bakhtin, written by his colleagues at the university, the father-and-daughter team Semyon and Larisa Konkin. Published by Mordovia State Book Press and entitled, Soviet-style, *Mikhail Bakhtin: Pages from His Life and Creative Work*, it is a workmanlike, reverent, fiercely pro-provinces monograph that makes little effort to conceal its contempt for the big-city Bakhtin industry.[45] Unsurprisingly, reviews have been mixed. The shift in emphasis, content, and reception of these Saransk publications over the last twenty years can serve as an index to the "re-imaging" of Bakhtin from local pedagogue to international guru and spiritual guide.

In the first Saransk anthologies (mid-1970s to mid-1980s), Bakhtin was invoked conventionally as an academic philosopher and historian of literature. The earliest collection (1973), a routine festschrift, covered a wide and uncoordinated number of topics.[46] A decade later, another modest set of essays appeared, prefaced by the obligatory editorial noting Gorbachev's appreciation of the Russian intelligentsia and the Party's support for socialist art.[47] In this 1985 volume, which appeared on the very cusp of perestroika and of Bakhtin's runaway international fame, the Bakhtinian legacy to world culture already seemed to have an uneasy, potentially destabilizing open-endedness about it. Nervously the editors remark that "the name of Bakhtin is often uttered in vain, used in instances and for purposes far from literary and not at all scholarly" (4).

[45] Konkin and Konkina, *Mikhail Bakhtin*, 397 pp. (see n. 30 above). The biography incorporates many new documents, especially on Bakhtin's arrest and on his teaching years in Saransk (along with much undistinguished paraphrase of Bakhtin's ideas). Among the biography's most unforgiving critics has been Vadim Kozhinov, who reacted strongly to what he alleges are "*konkinskaia lozh*'" [Konkinian lies], that is, self-serving anecdotes to slander the Moscow Bakhtin group and to benefit the Saransk professoriat. Kozhinov especially resented the Konkins' purported removal from the 1973 festschrift of an essay by Vladimir Fyodorov, a gifted young Bakhtin scholar from the city of Gorky, when the young man was harassed by the KGB for possession of samizdat materials. "Konkin immediately *threw the essay out of the collection*," Kozhinov remarks with disgust. "And for including Fyodorov's article in the book, the worst that could have happened to Konkin in the 1970s would have been some rebuke from a petty party committee." Kozhinov challenged Konkin publicly for this, and, Kozhinov notes placidly, "understandably, Konkin began to hate me." See Vadim Kozhinov, "Ob odnom 'obstoiatel'stve' zhizni M. M. Bakhtina," in *DKKh, no. 1 (95)*: 151–60, esp. 155, 156.

[46] The festschrift included essays on the carnivalesque image, ancient Russian laughter, Russian translations of Shakespeare's *Richard III*, Edgar Allen Poe's stories, and the poetics of *Candide*. This first commemorative volume celebrated Bakhtin's seventy-fifth birthday and fiftieth anniversary of the onset of his scholarly career (Konkin, *Prob p&ist lit 73*).

[47] Konkin, *Prob n nasl MMB 85*. This volume marked Bakhtin's ninetieth birthday and the tenth anniversary of his death.

By 1989 national pride and then Communism itself had begun to disintegrate. Endorsement by the Party or by the general secretary had become irrelevant, and retrofitting Bakhtin to past culture was clearly no longer sufficient; the needs of the present were too compelling. Russian intellectuals confronted a political and spiritual void. A second generation of Bakhtin scholars, trained philologists and philosophers rather than personal aides and intimates, had matured in Saransk (Oleg Osovsky, Vladimir Laptun, Nikolai Vasiliev) and in Vitebsk (Nikolai Pan'kov); accordingly, Bakhtin was provided with a new genealogy. For some time the Soviet press had been nourishing a renewed public interest in prerevolutionary Russian ethical thinkers. Especially popular were the turn-of-the-century idealists, humanists, and religious disciples of Vladimir Soloviev, as well as the émigré philosophers Nicholas Berdyaev and Semyon Frank—philosophers who in their youth had tasted, then rejected, Marxism. In a flurry of publications Bakhtin began to be assimilated, at first gingerly and then more boldly, to this neo-humanist, non-Marxist group.

One native son wrote, "1989 in Saransk can with full justice be called the Year of Bakhtin."[48] The first Bakhtin bibliography was followed by a booklet, *Mikhail Mikhailovich Bakhtin in Saransk: A Sketch of His Life and Activity*,[49] which provided fresh details about Bakhtin's university career and pointedly linked him with the new revolution (or rather the undoing of the Revolution) then at its peak. The authors resolutely emphasized Bakhtin's resistance to Stalinism. Far from being the passive and accommodating jester some accounts made of him, Bakhtin is shown to have suffered major difficulties during the purge year of 1937. During that hazardous period, and again in the early 1950s before Stalin's death, the so-called bourgeois objectivism of his teaching almost cost Bakhtin his job (8–9). As noted earlier, recently published materials make it clear that this reputation was not a later fabricated martyrology. Testimony from several generations of students during these marathon teaching years in Saransk reveals Bakhtin to have been an unruly, stubbornly independent pedagogue, impatient with political controls on literature and dangerously devoted to teaching the primary literary text.

Yet another Saransk publication from 1989, *The Aesthetics of M. M. Bakhtin and the Present Day*,[50] provided even more inspiration for courageous, right-minded living. The hour of the placid festschrift was over. This little booklet—a compilation of sixty proposals by scholars throughout the Soviet Union—was intended as guidelines for an annual Bakhtin

---

[48] With these words A. F. Eremeev opens his "Predislovie" to *MMB: ENS 92*, 3.

[49] Karpunov, Boriskin, and Estifeeva, *MMB v S 89*. Two of the three authors knew Bakhtin intimately (one lived in the same apartment complex), and all three have published widely on Bakhtin in scholarly forums and local papers.

[50] Eremeev et al., *Est MMB i sov 89*.

lecture series to be held each October in Saransk, and it attached the master's voice to increasingly anxious questions. In fact the single most popular focus had become Bakhtin's early writing on moral philosophy and the hope it held out for a practical ethics of everyday life and thought.

By 1992, the second winter of Russia's discontent, this ethical message became more insistent—and Bakhtin's ribald, carefree, non-cost-accounting carnival side had all but disappeared from view. Since Bakhtin's early writings on ethics have existed in English for a relatively short time (*Art and Answerability* [1990]; *Toward a Philosophy of the Act* [1993]) and since they began to be widely used in the West only in the mid-1990s, it might be helpful to illustrate this shift toward moral philosophy with some specifics from the Russian press. We say "press"—but the written record here is perilously transitory. The publications in question, dating from Russia's early post-censorship years, range from snappy paperbacks to scratchy bound typescripts in tiny print runs, barely legible and only one cut in quality above the old illicit *samizdat*. The profusion of these flimsy, perishable booklets—many in the genre of "conference volume" and soon superseded by sturdier, computer-processed, better subsidized publishing ventures—allow us to glimpse the postcommunist Russian Bakhtin industry in the making.

Take, for example, the conference volume that emerged from the second Saransk lecture series held at Mordovia State at the end of January 1991, entitled *Bakhtin and the Methodology of Contemporary Knowledge in the Humanities*.[51] As before, Bakhtin is credited as a good reader of literary texts and a respected scholar of Dostoevsky, Rabelais, and the eighteenth-century novel. But far more important, he is now seen as the source for a model of the world that is purposefully opposed to "scientific socialism" and its schematic visions. Over half the sixty-five entries in this booklet concern the dynamics of building an individual personality (in art and in life) that is sensitive to, but not enslaved by, its social environment. Meditative in tone, only marginally about literature, the recurring topics are confession, the crisis of the moral deed, art as a form of dialogue, and the relationship between knowledge and communion. Several of the essays expand on Bakhtin's distinction between *explanation* and *understanding*, one of the enduring divides in his thought.[52]

---

[51] Sukharev et al., *MMB i met 91*. The entries are divided into three sections: (1) "Bakhtin's creative work and general methodological problems of knowledge in the humanities"; (2) "Bakhtin and problems of moral philosophy"; and (3) "Investigating multiple ways of assimilating Bakhtin's aesthetic legacy."

[52] In *MMB i met 91*, see G. I. Ruzavin (Moscow), "Problema interpretatsii i ponimaniia tektstov v trudakh M. M. Bakhtina," 16–18, esp. 18; and V. V. Kashin (Orenburg), "M. M. Bakhtin ob urovniakh ponimaniia," 20–22.

This binary pair is not, of course, original with Bakhtin. *Das Verstehen*, "the sense of a thing in its meaningful context," is a god-term in the philosophy of Wilhelm Dilthey, founding theorist of the modern humanities and a thinker to whom Bakhtin was cautiously indebted.[53] But Bakhtin considered Dilthey too "monologic" (unfortunately the charge is not elaborated), perhaps because the German philosopher, for all his rich, empirical, fragmented exposition, was ultimately devoted to dividing the world into formal disciplines. Bakhtin everywhere prefers the homelier, more habitual scenario. Explanation is monologic. It is based on the assumption that I "come to know something first" and then explain what I have learned to others afterward. As a mental process, then, explanation is abstract and in principle independent of its addressee; it need acknowledge only one active subject, the person who grasps a concept and then proceeds to explicate it to someone else. But to grasp the meaning of a thing internally, for itself and for one's own self, is not, Bakhtin insists, to understand it. Genuine understanding is always dialogic: I come to understand something only, and for the first time, while I am attempting to explain it to you. In the process you must respond, resist, develop it in your own way, fail to get it—in short, *become yourself*, just as I become myself, through the exchange. Neither party should seek "essences" (there are none), nor perfect reconstructions of a past context, nor full consensus. And at no point does either side know anything for sure.

As a model for the way words work in novels—and as therapy for intimidated or silenced personalities—Bakhtin's understanding of understanding is enormously attractive. Reminiscent of John Dewey's enlightened pedagogy, the notion has little shock value on North American soil; after all, debates in the open and a renegotiation of opinion are the singular pride of a liberal democracy's self-image. But in post-Soviet society it had the ring of the radically new. Officially, political consensus had been by decree. Even unofficially, if measured against intuitivist or Orthodox Christian notions of "communality," Bakhtin's ideal of ever abiding uncertainty and outsideness seemed strange and daringly short on faith. For many Russians of that old regime, both dissident and establishment, Bakhtin's countermodel was overwhelming. As one contributor to the Saransk volume put it gratefully, Bakhtin arranges the world so that the very act of understanding becomes "an affirmation of one's own self and

---

[53] Three references to Dilthey occur in the late writings, all laconic: a remark to the effect that the assumption by Dilthey and Rickert that the natural and human sciences are separated by an "insurmountable barrier" had itself been surmounted ("From Notes Made in 1970–71," *SpG*, 145); and then two brief mentions in "A Methodology for the Humanities": the sentence fragment "Dilthey and the problem of understanding" (*SpG*, 161), and, more enigmatically, "Dilthey's monologism has not been completely surmounted" (*SpG*, 162).

. . . a right to one's own point of view."[54] With the addition of a spiritualized vocabulary, some refinement in philosophical terminology, and a growing interest in placing Bakhtin among other European thinkers, that ethical focus has remained in force to the present day.[55]

Thus did these early Russian conference volumes open up sides of Bakhtin that have been less in evidence for an Anglo-American audience—perhaps because for us they are less strikingly new. Our own current fascination with group identity (paradoxically nourished, in the work of some scholars, by Bakhtinian notions of dialogic community and collectivist carnival) tends to obscure the self-reliant, individualizing side of Bakhtin. Precisely that privatizing aspect of our American heritage, toward which ex-communist societies turned with such hopeful relief when their tyrannical economies first fell, has been under attack for some time by theorists who would deconstruct the "bourgeois Enlightenment subject." But if due process, litigation, private property, and the language of contracts come easily to us, thoroughly familiar in all their positive and nasty aspects, more difficult for our tradition, perhaps, has been to justify an absolute value judgment passed on the content and outcome of a dialogic process. Here a dialogue between former East and current West over Bakhtin's understanding of dialogue has much to offer both sides. The following example is illustrative.

What, we might ask, can dialogic process reasonably be expected to do? Chapter 3 is devoted wholly to this question as it relates to literary texts—but we might prefigure the issue here in light of the ethical aspects of the Bakhtin "industry" just reviewed. Bakhtin has appealed to hardcore relativists in part because the polyvalent and polymorphous inclusivity of his ideas, along with his insistence on the validity of every concretely positioned point of view, suggests that in a dialogic universe there *is no truth*. All talk, it is said, offers some valid thing. American social critics writing on the new pragmatism today, however, have become acutely aware that "allowing discussion to proceed" and "giving all parties their say"—as virtuous as these processes are—is no substitute for rooting out lies or for resolving a conflict morally. Russian theorists internalized this lesson with exceptional quickness. Sensitized to the potential

---

[54] M. V. Loginova (Saransk) in *MMB i met 91*: "Dialektika ponimaniia i vyrazitel'nosti v sisteme kul'tury," 24.

[55] The final collection of conference papers surveyed for this study—the Third International Bakhtin Readings in Saransk, which took place within a week of Bakhtin's hundredth birthday in October 1995 and was published in two volumes under the title *M. M. Bakhtin and Thinking in the Humanities on the Threshold of the Twenty-first Century*—followed the pattern of earlier proceedings, with more than 150 entries distributed equally across the fields of ethics, culturology, moral philosophy, and socially informed aesthetics (*MMB i gum mysh I and II*).

for abuse when truth is made endlessly negotiable, they tend to prefer the more old-fashioned stance that there is a truth, yes, and dialogism vis-à-vis that truth means no more than what is meant in democratic countries by minority rights, namely, *that you and I have equal rights to seek it.*[56] The reasons for this convergence are curious. On Russian soil, for a host of historical reasons, habits that encourage independence of thought and civic autonomy ("liberal values") were championed, at the turn of the last century, by philosophical idealism. The "hands-on" radical activists, most of them devoted materialists, were utopians and ambitious social experimenters who brought on the bloodletting of revolution; it was the sober, no-nonsense metaphysical idealists so influential on Bakhtin's circle—religious philosophers and neo-Kantians—who insisted on individual "oughtness" [*Sollen, dolzhenstvovanie*], on pragmatic, step-by-step personal growth in a compromised (but ultimately responsive) world, and on the concrete "non-alibi for existence" as a way out of moral confusion. The eminent philosopher Sergei Bulgakov addressed this issue in 1902, in a passage from his essay in *Problems of Idealism* that closely recalls Bakhtin two decades later:

> The moral law, notwithstanding the absolute nature of its dictates, is realized only through concrete goals, in concrete life. This sets a new task for moral life—to fill the empty form of absolute "oughtness" with concrete relative content, to find a bridge from the absolute to the relative. . . . As with everything relative, reason travels a precarious path here: ideas of good and evil are disputable, mistakes are possible, only the very concept of good and evil that unites all people is beyond dispute. A human being, to the extent that he has succeeded in achieving an understanding of reality . . . selects from the boundless sea of evil precisely that which can and should be eradicated at this very moment by his own particular efforts; he selects that upon which it is appropriate for him to concentrate his struggle at this given moment.[57]

Is Bulgakov's ethical position here that of a Jamesian pragmatist or an idealist? Bakhtin would locate it outside those categories altogether and insist that it is simply the position of an "understanding person," a person committed to answer for the reality of an immediate context. That context is expected to *talk back.* Such a scenario, so against the grain of

[56] See, for example, the discussion surrounding this issue in Bakhtin, *PDP*, 285: "What monologism is, in the highest sense. A denial of the equal rights of consciousness vis-à-vis truth (understood abstractly and systemically)."

[57] S. Bulgakov, "Osnovnye problemy teorii progressa" [Basic problems of the theory of progress], in I. P. Novgorodtsev, ed., *Problemy Idealizma* (Moscow: Moskovskoe psikhologicheskoe obshchestvo, 1902), 1–47, esp. 39. I draw on (and somewhat adjust) the excellent translation being prepared by Randall Poole for the first scholarly translation into English of this important anthology, forthcoming from Yale University Press.

Promethean or utopian thinking, is now being eased out of Bakhtin's early ethical writings by Russian scholars invigorated through contact with pre-Soviet thought on the nature of moral obligation. It is a healthy corrective to Bakhtin's more loosening effects on moral theory in the West.

Russian Bakhtinists are thus at a philosophical watershed. The extant primary texts are largely in print. Russians are more weary of the cult than we. They, too, desire to peel away ideological accretions and discourage facile, lazy applications of Bakhtin's key terms.[58] For not all things that interact or lie side by side are dialogic; not every inversion or comic act of defiance is carnival, and just because Bakhtin believed in the restorative effects of laughter and in the freedom implicit in open-ended texts does not mean he was a relativist or that we should laugh away his paradoxical formulations and take his words to mean anything (or nothing) at all. Impatience with imprecision and inflation is felt both by advocates who wish to "cleanse" Bakhtin (thus restoring his usefulness and authority) as well as by detractors who would like to diminish his influence.

The problem was well expressed in a 1993 essay by A. M. Ranchin, "The Bakhtin Temptation."[59] We turn Bakhtin's ideas into banalities when we confuse their message with their mode of argument, Ranchin insists. Bakhtin might advocate "play" and unfinalizability in narrative, but the analyses he offers are not apologetic, jesting, or illogical. Bakhtin was no prophet, no "carrier of a secret," no creative writer, and—although he could employ Aesopian language when necessary, like any serious intellectual working under Soviet conditions—he was neither tentative nor particularly accommodating toward his critics. He owned his own word (albeit not a final one), and this critical word, as far as the record reveals, suffered little self-doubt.

By 1995 such criticism had gained momentum, the predictable undertow moving against what many considered to be a profligate Bakhtin tidal wave. It soon acquired terminological sophistication and even a journalistic home: the Moscow-based *Novoe literaturnoe obozrenie* [New literary review], or *NLO*, in which Ranchin's essay appeared. *NLO*, founded in 1992, had become the vanguard post-Soviet "thick journal" for high-quality, serious integration of Western theory with Russian primary texts and philological traditions. On the terrain of literary politics, it

---

[58] As early as 1989 there was concern about the dilution of Bakhtin's categories. "In our country," the editor of the first volume of Saransk lectures ruefully notes, "for all the mass use of Bakhtin's name in practically every printed text and manuscript . . . we more often encounter mere play with the terms 'chronotope,' 'outsideness,' 'insideness,' than we do serious methodological application of them." See A. F. Eremeev (Sverdlovsk), "Rezervy izucheniia estetiki Bakhtina," in *MMB i sov 89*, 5.

[59] A. M. Ranchin, "Iskushenie Bakhtinym," in *NLO*, no. 3 (1993): 320–25.

tended toward a pro-Structuralist, Tartu school line; for several years it had been running articles unsympathetic to Bakhtin and relentless in their search for flaws or contradictions in his method. Late in 1995 several pieces appeared in the spirit of a necrologue to the centennial.

Yuri Murashov's essay "The Revolt of the Voice against Writing: On Bakhtin's Dialogism" might serve as exemplary.[60] Irritated by Bakhtin's bias against Structuralism, Murashov conducts his own postmortem on Bakhtin's late essay "Toward a Methodology for the Humanities." His special target is that essay's oft-cited distinction between the double-voiced "depth" of the humanities and the impersonal, single-voiced "precision" of the harder sciences (in effect, the "understanding" versus "explanation" distinction noted above). Why, Murashov wonders, has the term *precision* [*tochnost'*] become one of abuse? By opposing the act of "getting to know another personality" (presumed to be complex, deep, unresolved, unproblematically good) to the supposedly more primitive act of "getting to know a thing" (simple, quantifiable, limited, dead), Bakhtin implies that Structuralist scholars, to the extent that they trust the "thing-like" traces of artistic intention, are in some mortifying way hostile to the interests of the creating author or the living text. Bakhtin does not bother to "penetrate into the 'undefined' or 'infinite' depths of the structuralist text" (26), Murashov notes, nor is he curious to see those things of beauty—however mute or fixed—that might be revealed by such analysis.

But there are more serious deficiencies in Bakhtinian method, we learn. With some malice, Murashov proceeds to probe them. Bakhtin indicts the "collective of literary professionals" for pursuing "personal, merely practical interests," and "to this egoistic voice of the literary professional or Structuralist, Bakhtin opposes his own voice" (27). Bakhtin would have us believe this voice is magnanimous and open-minded. Unlike the structuralizers' voice, it is "uninterested in any conclusions that might be drawn from its own theory." It is outside time, space, and history, floating somewhere in that vague but highly privileged "great time." Murashov then asks why Bakhtin "so cleverly conceals his own personal egoism as a theorist and a literary scholar, his own pretenses to truth in his own final word, his own individual monologism?" (28).

In response to that rhetorical question, Murashov deploys a move familiar to us from deconstructionist critique. The real culprit and foe for Bakhtin, he claims, is writing itself, the status of print as a "thing." Bakhtin links "monologism with writing and dialogism with the oral or voiced form of language, with its bodied-ness" (29); his pro-voice prejudices

[60] Yurii Murashov, "Vosstanie golosa protiv pis'ma," in *NLO*, no. 16 (1995): 24–31. Further page references are given in text.

incline him to bear a grudge against all inscribed traces. To be sure, Murashov's indictment squares poorly with the reality of Bakhtin the singer of novels, who celebrates the ability of precisely the written word to resurrect whole worlds across distant and alien millennia. But passions can run high and indiscriminate on the pages of *NLO*. In the tradition of the Russian "thick journal," it sustains itself through controversy—and the Bakhtin cult has become one of its recurring irritants.

The same 1995 issue carried a review article by A. T. Ivanov entitled "Bakhtin, Bakhtinistika, Bakhtinologiia," ostensibly covering a number of centennial productions—journals, anthologies, and monographs.[61] Although scarcely touching on the seven items under review, Ivanov does dwell on a distinction that sums up well the tensions sensed among readers of Bakhtin. It is expressed in a struggle of suffixes. Competition has arisen, he notes, between "Bakhtinistics" and "Bakhtinology." The former (favored by the Tartu school) has modest, reclamatory, philological aims. It asks such questions as these: How can a literary text be better understood using Bakhtin's categories? Can these categories be refined and tightened? How might a scholar utilize Bakhtin to facilitate access to the languages of a past age? Ivanov regrets that this service function has lost currency in an era of inflated critical personae. (Apparently it was Yuri Lotman himself who, at a Tartu conference in 1969, remarked prophetically and without enthusiasm that "soon we shall become witness to the birth of a new science: Bakhtinology.")[62] With the advent of -ology, Bakhtin began to be abstracted, "de-philologized," metaphysicized, canonized as a mystical "Russian thinker"; the question became not how to read texts with precision but rather "how salvation is possible with the help of Bakhtin" (334). "The Bakhtin of Bakhtinology was not a philologist or literary scholar and not even a philosopher," Ivanov remarks, "but a wise man, a teacher, an ethical mentor who evaluated all of culture from a position of higher knowledge."

According to Ivanov, practicing Bakhtinologists are essentially cultists who engage in a series of highly suspect intellectual moves. First they identify Bakhtin's ideas with his biographical life. Then they assume that every event in that life (which becomes a "text") must therefore be significant. Next follows a "spiritual askesis": to enter the significant world of Bakhtin's life—to "receive the right to enter"—ordinary readers must "do something with themselves," "consciously reject their own past experience," alter their "thinking body." Then comes the most dangerous

---

[61] A. T. Ivanov, "Bakhtin, Bakhtinistika, Bakhtinologiia," in *NLO*, no. 16 (1995): 333–37, esp. 334–35.

[62] As reported by Konstantin Usupov in his prefatory note from the editor, "Ot redaktsionnoi kollegii," in *MMB i fil kul XX, 1 (91)*, 5–6.

step of all: the Bakhtin of Bakhtinology "can only be understood in his own personal language" (335). Since that language is not to be found in impersonal—and thus accessible, verifiable, falsifiable—textual mechanisms but only in some purported "dialogue" set up by the Bakhtinologist, inevitably more attention is paid to the self-expressive fantasies of the critic than to Bakhtin's own writings (not to mention any primary literary texts). Bakhtinologues, it turns out, are always in crisis, chronically anxious (as their guru had never been) over what cannot be (or has not yet been) expressed. Yet paradoxically, time and room can always be made for expressing one more of their own speculations or doubts. Such critical production in the postcommunist era, Ivanov concludes with some exasperation, is not a revival of literary scholarship and not the cutting edge of anything. It is a "neoconservative revolution in the humanities" plain and simple (336). Unsympathetic as it is, this centennial retrospective of the "Bakhtinological turn" on the pages of *Novoe literaturnoe obozrenie* gives an outsider's perspective—and perhaps not wholly inaccurate—on the complexity of Russian attitudes toward Bakhtin that have been traced in this chapter. There will be occasion later in this study to amplify further its unkinder sides.[63]

[63] In the heated context of these *NLO* diatribes, one can appreciate the sane comments of Lydia Ginzburg, who offered an enlightened compromise in the debates over *tochnost'* [precision] in the humanities. Touching on Bakhtin in a 1978 interview—she was appreciative of his mental energy but wary of his methods—Ginzburg remarked: "I think that the humanities has its own type of precision. Precision of a specific sort. And it will avenge itself if it is forgotten. This precision has various levels. At the base of everything lies factual and documented precision, the accuracy of the apparatus. . . . and alongside this, as it were, material precision, there is the logic of explication, the precision with which the devices of synthesis and analysis are applied. And finally there is the inner precision by which a given concept is constructed, and its accurate expression in the word" ("Razgovor o literaturovedenii" [1978], in Lidiia Ginzburg, *O starom i novom* [Leningrad: Sovetskii pisatel', 1982]: 43–58, esp. 48). Ginzburg, Tynianov's most gifted student and perhaps the best representative of Soviet "Structuralism with a human face" after Yuri Lotman, had this to say further on Bakhtin: "And what is truth in literary scholarship? Take a phenomenon such as Bakhtin. Let's say, his idea of polyphony in Dostoevsky . . . by no means do all agree that an ultimate authorial word is absent in Dostoevsky. I also do not share many of Bakhtin's ideas (not to mention their automatic application in works by many of his imitators). Bakhtin is remarkable not because he said things that were irreproachably true but for quite another reason. For his huge spiritual energy, his strength of thought, a tirelessly working mind that along the way gave rise to such fertile concepts" (49). See also V. Baevskii's diary entry from November 1986, where Ginzburg's opinion of Bakhtin is given a somewhat different slant: "The formal method was very broad," Ginzburg is reported to have said. "And like every broad phenomenon, it incorporated into itself even those with whom it quarreled. Such was the case with Bakhtin. His notion that in Dostoevsky the idea becomes the flesh of the text, an element of artistic form, coincides with the ideas of the formal school. Then he became fashionable, everywhere people saw carnival and polyphony. He himself was partly guilty for this. First he pointed to polyphony in Dostoevsky, and that was

To grant Bakhtin the courtesy of a final responsive word in the Bakhtinology debates (and one that luminously illustrates his own category of
"understanding"), we might draw on a reminiscence by the director of
the Moscow Dostoevsky Museum, Galina Ponomareva. In a 1994 interview she recalled numerous discussions with the aging Bakhtin on the
subject of Yuri Lotman. "When I said that Lotman's Structuralism
seemed to me unproductive . . . M. M. agreed—and at the same time
disagreed. He agreed that such self-sufficiency was dangerous, but on the
other hand he immediately corrected himself: 'But of course, Lotman
himself fully understands that!' "[64]

Do the competing images of Bakhtin in his homeland submit to a single
generalized portrait? Can this portrait be put to work? The task in Russia,
it appears, is less and less a matter of making Bakhtin immediately applicable to crisis conditions. Bakhtin's own indifference to the noisy political
panaceas crowding in on him during most of his mature life has always
been part of his huge appeal. As suggested above, Russians read Bakhtin
as a culturologist rather than a politically acute multiculturalist. And
when real-life problems begin (that is, when Western multiculturalists
become most irritable and activist), Russian culturologists, Bakhtin included, tend to take a benignly Formalist turn, becoming specifiers, spec-
ulators, and theorists rather than engaged social critics. They are professional academic humanists in the most bookish sense of that word.

As such, present-day culturology represents a departure from mainstream Russian radical thought and its mystique of revolution. The elitist
Bakhtin pointedly resisted that mystique. His notions of progress, as well
as the goals he posited for interpersonal dialogue, were unambitious. As
Vitaly Makhlin has observed of these early dialogic models, the most innovative debates of the 1920s occurred not within "theories claiming to
be revolutionary" but among people of a "new traditionalist consciousness, . . . a new radical conservatism": conservative "because it involved a
dialogue with humanist and Christian tradition and not their dialectical
'removal' "—and thus a dissenting voice within the extremist tradition of
the Russian intelligentsia.[65] And Makhlin adds: "[Bakhtin's] was a conservatism more radical than any sort of superficial revolutionism." In this
sense, the reviewer Ivanov from *Novoe literaturnoe obozrenie* was quite

---

very interesting. Then he extended the idea to the novel in general, and it no longer
worked. It all fell apart" (V. Baevskii, "Dve stranitsy iz dnevnika," in Isupov, ed., *Bakhtinologiia 95*, 11.

[64] G. B. Ponomareva, "Vyskazannoe i nevyskazannoe . . . (Vospominaniia o M. M. Bakhtine) [interview from November 1994], *DKKh, no. 3 (95)*: 59–77, esp. 73. Further page
references in text.

[65] V. L. Makhlin, *MB: FP 90*, 20.

correct in his impatient remark that Bakhtinian method constitutes a "neoconservative revolution in the humanities." Indeed, many Russian intellectuals today would consider such an old-fashioned return to options that were alive and debated in the 1920s a great good fortune for Russia's future.

Chapter 2 will move back to that very decade and survey the reception of Bakhtin's work during his own career in print (1929 to 1975)—a journey to a land and culture that seems increasingly sealed in a glass jar. We might pose one final question as preparation for this retrospective glance. How did Bakhtin react to the Revolution that defined the life of so many in his generation? In his discussions with Viktor Duvakin, fifty years after the event, Bakhtin insisted that he was dismayed by the fall of the monarchy and irreconcilably opposed to the Bolsheviks from their very first days in power. But what of the testimony of Bakhtin's actual texts in their own time? Was there an implicit politics to his philosophy as he worked it out from the 1920s through the 1970s?

The question of revolution focuses much of what is most confusing in Bakhtin. There is in his life and writings a manifest absence of rage, of despair, of radical stops and clean starts. He almost never took offense—and that alone separates him from much of today's ideological criticism. He had the highest respect for Western literary traditions, both canonical and noncanonical, and the deepest reverence for authors and "subjects," of whose death he had not heard and would not have acknowledged. Although as a very young man he had planned to write a treatise on the ethics of politics, in his extant work almost no attention is devoted to practical political action as a beneficial organizing force in society. The closest he comes to political radicalism is probably his idea of carnival. But the politics of Bakhtinian carnival—that irreverent, unfinalizable material utopia fantasized during years of famine and terror by a deeply nonutopian thinker—is (to say the least) highly peculiar. Its participants could never be disciplined or marshaled into any centripetal event such as "class struggle," coherent rebellion, or effective legislation on behalf of social change.

As a provisional answer to this complex question of Bakhtin's politics, I suggest that he be called an "antirevolutionary." Not "counter-," just "anti-": a person who viewed the dynamics of the world within quite other parameters. He rejected from the start the binary logic at the base of the most successful revolutionary thinking of his time, that is, the Marxist-Leninist model. That model, we must now make an effort to remember, was dialectical and linear to a rigidly "efficient" degree. It taught its converts that in order to make sense out of change, one must analyze it into a system. Whatever does *not* fit that system is relegated to the realm of "spontaneity" or anarchy—to be cast out, brought under control, or annihilated. What does fit the system is made abstract, general, arranged dialectically, and called (again to use the Leninist category) "consciousness." Only this consciously systematic component was deemed real and worthy of work; for its sake, the future mattered more than the present and sacrifice was valued over individual survival.

Bakhtin—a consummate and not too badly compromised survivor—understood consciousness in an entirely different way. To such binary paradigms he would have responded that the world is simply not set up as a battleground between system and chaos. No life even remotely familiar to us from our everyday experience offers those two options in any clean or useful way. And thus Bakhtin rejected both poles: the first, a "Hegelian" (and later a semiotic or a Freudian) extreme that assumes "everything means something and is going somewhere"; the second, a relativist (and later poststructuralist) view that assumes "nothing can mean anything and thus we cannot go anywhere." As an alternative to that grim fantastical choice, Bakhtin believed that the world, as we are thrust into it, is a world of *potential* form. But the realization of form is never instantaneous, it is not an "uncovering" of some preexistent thing. Patches of form arise as the result of intelligence, work, and moral choice; to survive, they require a nurturing environment. It would seem that discrediting the absurd dichotomy between "system or nothing," which eliminates duration and devalues individual effort, was the single major task of Bakhtin's long life.

Ex-Soviet intellectuals, who are undoing their Revolution and at the same time reconfiguring Bakhtin, read this challenge to "system-or-nothing" thinking as a protest against the political thought that had defined their age. For what a system-or-nothing grid eliminates first of all is freedom; as the next step, it eliminates the experience of real time. At stake here is not so much political freedom—fate has not been generous to Russia in that realm, and Russians have managed to produce phenomenally free thoughts under the most imprisoned circumstances. The freedom is spiritual: the sense that the human psyche is, by definition, free to shape its own development; that in this project it has access to unexpected potential; that it is conscious; and that, as Bakhtin put it, this "consciousness is much more terrifying than any unconscious complexes"[66] because, unlike the unconscious, it is obliged to choose and to answer for its own responses. When, during the centennial, it was remarked that "Bakhtin was a free man," the word was used in this sense.

What might such freedom mean in the realm of literary interpretation and the word? Here, too, Bakhtin is profoundly "antirevolutionary." Authors and critics, he insists, are bound together by aesthetic love. Theirs

[66] Bakhtin, *PDP*, 288.

is an endlessly parenting function (the real lesson to be learned from all those hopeful, fertile carnival bodies), and the ground for this activity must be constantly monitored. For whatever the role of truth and faith in Bakhtin's thought—and on those central matters, the verdict is still out—there can be no question that Bakhtin would be quite helpless without *trust*. That trust begins between an author and a reader. Casual toward his own written legacy, reverent toward the literary work he had chosen to study, Bakhtin would most certainly side with that dean of Anglo-American literary critics, Frank Kermode, in his struggle against a hermeneutics of suspicion. "The success of interpretive argument as a means of conferring or endorsing value," Kermode writes, "is not to be measured by the survival of the comment but by the survival of its object. Of course, an interpretation or evaluation may live on in the tradition on which later comment is formed, either by acceptance or reaction; but its primary purpose is to provide the medium in which its object survives."[67]

Bakhtin expressed a similar ideal in an archival fragment first published in 1994 but jotted down in the early 1960s, on the virtues of *soglasie* [agreement; literally, *so-glasie* (co-voicing)]. We might consider it Bakhtin's normative statement for the "aesthetic love" of criticism. Like dialectics, dialogue requires firm boundaries; but unlike dialectics, it requires neither opposition nor even transitory resolution. In Bakhtin's words: "Co-voicing [agreement] as the most important dialogic category. . . . Agreement is never a mechanical or logical identity, and it is not an *echo*; behind it there is always a distance transcended, a drawing close (but not a fusing). Its 'co-soundings' are infinitely distant and barely detectable. In agreement there is always an element of the unexpected, of the gift, of the miracle, because dialogic *co*-voicing, by its very nature, is *free*—that is, it is not predetermined, not inevitable."[68]

How a philosopher-critic of this temperament fared in the polarized climate of Soviet Russia is the subject matter of the following chapter.

[67] Frank Kermode, "Disentangling Knowledge from Opinion," in his *Forms of Attention* (Chicago: The University of Chicago Press, 1985), 67.

[68] Bakhtin, M. M., <K pererabotke knigi o Dostoevskom. II>, ed. Vadim Kozhinov, in *DKKh, no. 1 (94)*: 70–82, esp. 70. This essay, which represented Bakhtin's initial and much more ambitious plan for revising the Dostoevsky book, was superceded by the more modest set of guidelines (and even those, unfortunately, were not fully incorporated into the second edition) translated as Appendix 2 in *PDP*, 283–302. This passage is amplified and annotated in *MMB: ss 5 (96)*, "Dostoevskii. 1961," 364, 668–78.

CHAPTER 2

Retrospective: Domestic Reception during Bakhtin's Life

IF ONE FOLLOWS only written traces and official reviews, Bakhtin's scholarly profile in his own country exhibits a strange curve. He broke into print in 1919 with a tiny six-paragraph essay, "Art and Responsibility," in a provincial journal. Nothing further appeared under his own name until 1929, when the publication of *Problems of Dostoevsky's Creative Art* coincided with its author's arrest and exile. Although Bakhtin wrote copiously throughout the 1930s and during the war years, defending a doctoral dissertation in Moscow in 1946, he formally reentered the world of published scholarship only in 1963, with the revised edition of his book on Dostoevsky. From that year on, waves of increasingly early material filled in the lacunae. The dissertation on Rabelais was reworked as a book in 1965; a collection of essays with the indeterminate subtitle "From Various Years" (largely 1924 to 1941, but with some interpolations as late as 1973) appeared in 1975, the year of Bakhtin's death. Only between 1979 and 1986 did manuscript materials crucial to any informed study of Bakhtin's mature work at last see the light of day: philosophical writings from the early 1920s, packaged together with his (also unfinished) very last essays. For those interested in the genesis of Bakhtin's ideas, primary material was published backward. Fame unfolded around texts for which Bakhtin's early readers—as well as his early translators—were frequently unprepared and caught without basic vocabulary.

This publication history has also shaped Bakhtin's professional image. Although the young Bakhtin began his intellectual career working in the areas of ethical philosophy and psychology (on which he lectured and wrote extensively, but published nothing), because the book on Dostoevsky remained his only published work for more than thirty years, and because his dissertation—a minor academic scandal—had focused on François Rabelais, Bakhtin's reading public knew him exclusively as literary scholar and critic. As we now know, Bakhtin preferred the more comprehensive status of *myslitel'*, "thinker." In Russian parlance, that word designates an intellectual with eclectic interdisciplinary interests and a philosophizing bent. Bakhtin, as shall become clear, was a thinker who not so much utilized his thought to illuminate literature as he utilized literature, quite selectively, to illustrate the course of his thought.[1]

Along such a reception curve, with its bulges and fallow stretches, official feedback tended to cluster around two poles. At one end was the 1920s, specifically 1929; at the other, the 1960s–1970s. These were the opening and closing decades of Bakhtin's intellectual biography. In a realm as sensitive to politically correct readings as the Soviet literary profession was obliged to be, "reception clusters" like these can take on ominous internal coherence. Since Bakhtin's present fame is such an established fact, it might come as a surprise that the reviews of his work, taken as a whole, were unenthusiastic. Part of the coolness, to be sure, was owing to academic turf wars and to Soviet political constraints—as well as to the conservative, soberly "philological" traditions of Russian literary scholarship. But Bakhtin also attracted serious, independent readers who raised cogent objections to his major operating assumptions. The present chapter discusses several of the more durable knots of controversy, concentrating on those reviews that set a pattern for later readings (as well as misreadings) of major concepts in Bakhtin's world.[2] It is

[1] In a memoir—notoriously unreliable—from the mid-1980s, Bakhtin is reported to have drawn a distinction in his final years between philosophy ("a special realm of human knowledge, like mathematics") and two other modes of thought often confused with it: wisdom [*mudrost'*] generated by wise men, and rumination [*razmyshlenie*] practiced by thinkers. Socrates was a wise man; Berdyaev, Shestov, and Sartre were thinkers; the greatest (perhaps the only) philosopher of the twentieth century, according to Bakhtin, was Martin Buber. See Maiia Kaganskaia, "Shutovskoi khorovod," in *Sintaksis*, no. 12 (Paris, 1984): 139–90, esp. 141.

[2] When the "official reception of Bakhtin" began is not easy to resolve. The so-called disputed texts that appeared under the names of Bakhtin's associates, Voloshinov and Medvedev, between 1926 and 1929 did attract considerable critical attention, but on this issue Gary Saul Morson and I endorse a non-conflationist position (see our *Creation of a Prosaics*, ch. 3, 101–19), preferring to treat these works as the property of their signatories and respecting Bakhtin's formal unwillingness to reclaim them. More recently, in 1993 and 1994, respectively, Sergey Bocharov ("Primechanie k memuaru," 71–79) and Vadim Kozhinov (Rzhevsky, "Kozhinov on Bakhtin," 433, 438–39) have restated the counter-case, that Bakhtin dictated these texts to their signatories. With rare exceptions (Nikolai Vasiliev and Medvedev's heirs in Petersburg), Russian Bakhtinists agree with this latter view. The disputed texts are now being reissued in Russian in a new paperback series edited by V. L. Makhlin entitled *Bakhtin under a Mask* [*Bakhtin pod maskoi*] (Moscow: Labirint, 1993); vol. 1 in the series is Voloshinov's *Freudianism*, vol. 2 is Medvedev's *Formal Method*; vol. 5, no. 1 (1996) contains shorter articles published under the names V. N. Voloshinov, P. N. Medvedev, and I. I. Kanaev. Makhlin calls this strange "gifting" of a book a "phenomenal culturological experiment," a "paradoxical interaction of author and hero" not in the literary realm but—a much rarer thing—in literary scholarship. Bakhtin's motives, according to Bocharov, ranged from intellectual generosity, despair at the fate of his own essays in the marketplace after 1924, and the fact that "they were my friends, they needed books, and I

perhaps appropriate that the first three decades of Bakhtin's scholarly reputation were linked closely with Fyodor Dostoevsky, a writer whose own twentieth-century rehabilitation was as precarious and controversial as that of his most accomplished critic.

DOSTOEVSKY, I (1929)

We begin, then, with 1929 and the critical reaction to *Problems of Dostoevsky's Creative Art*.[3] (This first edition, which does not exist in English, differs from the expanded 1963 version in many details but especially in its tiny chapter 4—which, in the second edition, was expanded into a lengthy discussion of genre theory, menippean satire, and carnivalization.)[4] The Dostoevsky book was published *after* Bakhtin's arrest. Its best-known review, rumored to have played a crucial role in commuting Bakhtin's death-camp sentence in the Far North to a much more benign exile in Kazakhstan, was written by Anatoly Lunacharsky, prominent Bolshevik and later Commissar of Enlightenment. The fame of this review, and the fact that it was on balance sympathetic to Bakhtin, has obscured two realities. First, Lunacharsky, in many ways an astute and informed critic, was indeed sympathetic to Bakhtin but by and large for the wrong reasons—out of political caution or because he simply misread the text. Second, of the remaining half-dozen professional responses between 1929 and 1930 that are worth taking seriously, most were unambiguously hostile to Bakhtin's interpretation of Dostoevsky. To get a feel for this premiere critical climate, we shall consider briefly the commissar's pioneering review and then two much less charitable discussions.

Lunacharsky's review of Bakhtin, "On Dostoevsky's 'Multi-voicedness,'" appeared in the October 1929 issue of *Novy Mir*.[5] It opens on

---

still intended to write my own" [from a discussion of 21 November 1974]. Even Bocharov, however, argues that the names of the purported authors are an essential part of the books as dictated. For these and related reasons, the present chapter will not include discussion of the reception of the Voloshinov/Medvedev texts.

[3] M. M. Bakhtin, *Problemy tvorchestva Dostoevskogo* (Leningrad: Priboi, 1929). For synopses of the reception history of both editions, see O. E. Osovskii, *Chelovek. Slovo. Roman.* (Saransk: RIK "Trio," 1993), ch. 4; and the six-volume history of twentieth-century Dostoevsky criticism by Yu. G. Kudriatsev, completed in 1979, excerpts reprinted as "Bakhtin i ego kritiki (Otryvki iz shestitomnogo issledovaniia 'Vokrug Dostoevskogo (k kharakteristike vremeni)'," in *DKKh, no. 1 (94)*: 111–39.

[4] For a brief discussion of the differences between the two editions, see Morson and Emerson, *Creation of a Prosaics*, 84–86.

[5] The review is frequently anthologized. Cited here from A. V. Lunacharskii, "O 'mnogogolosnosti' Dostoevskogo (po povodu knigi M. M. Bakhtina *Problemy tvorchestva*

Bakhtin's strengths. He is applauded for his discovery of the "extraordinary autonomy and full-weightedness of each 'voice'" in Dostoevsky's novels and for perceiving behind those fictional voices richly developed "convictions" or "points of view on the world." Lunacharsky then tempers this suspiciously idealist position by emphasizing Bakhtin's insistence—in contrast to discredited Formalist doctrine—that Dostoevsky was preoccupied with real-life ideological dispute, not only with questions of literary craft. Much space is devoted to the connection between Dostoevsky's world and the ugly social reality of early capitalism (a point stressed far out of proportion to Bakhtin's transitory and cosmetic mention of it). Then Lunacharsky turns to the flaws. Bakhtin, he argues, is narrow in his definition of polyphony, too eager to give pride of place to Dostoevsky as an absolute innovator. A committed Marxist, Lunacharsky prefers to see great creative principles arise out of concrete socio-economic conditions—and ideally, out of conditions that can be shown to recur in other European cultures, each maturing in its own time but according to universal criteria. Contrary to Bakhtin, therefore, who argues that Dostoevsky as novelist breaks conceptually new ground, Lunacharsky insists that a vigorous, early-capitalist-era polyphony governs the distribution of voices in Balzac's novels and, at an appropriately earlier stage for England, in Shakespearean drama as well. Shakespeare, in particular, is singled out as one of the most stylistically diverse and deliberately "impersonal" of authors, "maximally untendentious and thus extremely polyphonic."

Lunacharsky is also vexed by Bakhtin's overall image of Dostoevsky as social moralist and thinker. He considers this image altogether too open-ended, indifferent to resolution, and stripped of that "colossal striving toward god" and cosmic harmony that all readers intuitively sense in the great writer. But here the commissar adroitly rescues Bakhtin through what might be called the "Lenin defense." (In several appreciative prewar essays, Lenin had defended Leo Tolstoy—aristocrat, landowner, pacifist, moral idealist—as a genius who, although flawed ideologically, was nevertheless acceptable to the radical Marxist pantheon because his inner tensions reflected, as if in a mirror, the contradictions that culminated in the Bolshevik Revolution.) Dostoevsky, too, had held some unfortunate personal beliefs: monarchism, faith in Orthodox Christianity, aggressive and imperialistic chauvinism, disgust at the nihilism of Russia's nascent revolutionary intelligentsia. But such a personality has exemplary educa-

---

Dostoevskogo)," in A. A. Belkin, ed., *F. M. Dostoevskii v russkoi kritike: sbornik statei* (Moscow: GosIzdatKhudLit, 1956), 403–29. A mediocre English translation has been published under the title "Dostoyevsky's 'Plurality of Voices,'" in A. Lebedev, comp., *Anatoly Lunacharsky: On Literature and Art* (Moscow: Progress, 1973), 79–106.

tional value for socialist Russia, Lunacharsky argues, because Dostoevsky, like the "crippled titan" Tolstoy, reflected in his divided soul the contradictions typical for his epoch. And although he was, of course, technically able at any time to wave his "conductor's baton" and restore order, Dostoevsky as novelist chose not to integrate his fictional worlds into one triumphant whole. Such a whole was unavailable to Dostoevsky because the man "was not master of his own home." Lunacharsky concludes that the novelist's fragmented consciousness and compassion for the downtrodden continued to suggest "principles of materialistic socialism" as an alternative to the avowed, politically reactionary convictions that are a matter of record. However energetically the great writer spat on, humiliated, and exiled this socialistic alternative to his private Underground, it would return again and again to haunt him in polyphonic confrontations.

What can be said of this reading of Bakhtin's monograph? First and most obvious, Lunacharsky does not take the book on its own "Formalist" terms. As Bakhtin put the matter in his foreword: "The present book is limited to theoretical problems of Dostoevsky's creative art . . . We have had to exclude all historical problems. . . . [Our topic is solely Dostoevsky's] revolutionary innovation in the realm of the novel as an artistic form" (3–4). Lunacharsky undermines this attempt on the part of Bakhtin to keep his treatment of Dostoevsky prudently distanced from history, religion, and politics. To him it was simply not acceptable, within the Russian critical tradition and his own ideological system, to ignore a writer's moral judgment on life or to evaluate literary achievement independent of socioeconomic determinants. Evoking the hideous social effects of the Orthodox Church and Russia's embryonic robber-baron capitalism, Lunacharsky concludes on the confident statement that "Dostoevsky has not yet died among us or in the West because capitalism has not yet died."[6]

Even where he does acknowledge the importance of form, Lunacharsky discerns it but dimly. Most damaging of all—for it sets tenacious precedent—he misreads polyphony. Lunacharsky defines polyphonism variously as an absence of authorial tendentiousness, as "extreme objectivity," as the "absolute autonomy of characters," and thus as the "lack of a whole." Polyphony, he writes, "is an orchestra not only without a con-

[6] When Bakhtin revised his book in the early 1960s he included a review of Lunacharsky's review, gently chiding the commissar for these misgeneralizations (*PDP*, 63, 32–36). Drama—even the great Shakespeare's—can contain only "embryonic polyphony," Bakhtin argues, for although drama can be multileveled, it cannot contain multiple worlds. And to Lunacharsky's suggestion that polyphony is the result of a historical epoch (early capitalism) or of individual biology/biography, Bakhtin remarks: "Great human discoveries are made possible by external conditions, but they do not die along with the epochs that gave them birth."

ductor but also without a composer whose score some conductor might conceivably perform." Lunacharsky indeed gets polyphony wrong; but in justice to him, this key concept (which Bakhtin, as late as the 1960s, confessed had been widely misunderstood) is only now being untangled. The intense, subtle degree of authorial self-control and risk required to make polyphony work can really be grasped only with the help of those early self-other scenarios that Bakhtin elaborated in his initial period as a philosopher, in manuscripts that lay unpublished until the 1970s and 1980s. Overall, Lunacharsky's account of Bakhtin's book did the fledgling scholar an enormous service. Modestly enthusiastic, politically correct, perhaps even cunningly naive, it was instrumental in saving Bakhtin's life. In spirit, it has little in common with the intellectually more rigorous and infinitely less generous hatchet work of his fellow reviewers in the Party, two of whom we will now consider.[7]

The first of these reviews, by I. Grossman-Roshchin, appeared in 1929 in *Na literaturnom postu* [On literary guard], a short-lived (1926–32) but influential journal of leftist criticism and theory associated with the Union of Proletarian Writers.[8] As did Lunacharsky, Grossman-Roshchin seizes on those rare pages in Bakhtin that mention capitalism and hint at class struggle. But unlike the well-disposed commissar, this second reviewer exposes Bakhtin's strategy immediately. Thus, one can argue, he gets more of Bakhtin right. Suspicious of opportunistic Marxist window dressing, Grossman-Roshchin is quick to grasp the "unscientific" and eclectic nature of Bakhtin's literary sociology. Bakhtin's description of the literary artwork—the product of multiply refracted social evaluations—is castigated as "a strange, slippery, ambivalent formulation." Indeed, this sociology has no firm grounding in social class nor are its contradictions organized into stages or struggles. "There's not a whiff here of the Marxist principle of objective cognition," the reviewer notes darkly.

Grossman-Roshchin's most serious reservation (and perhaps clearest insight) comes with Bakhtin's theory of Dostoevskian character. If, he argues, Dostoevsky does in fact strive to draw all external reality into the hero's self-consciousness—if he does empower his heroes to speak their own "fully weighted" personal truths on their own individual behalf—then "outside forces" in his novels cannot be said to exist autonomously or to condition human consciousness in any reliable way. This possibility unnerves the reviewer. "After all," he argues from a materialist perspec-

---

[7] Brief discussions of these early unfriendly reviews can be found in Konkin and Konkina, *Mikhail Bakhtin*, 166–70; and Osovskii, *Chelovek. Slovo. Roman.*, 55–60.

[8] I. Grossman-Roshchin, "O 'sotsiologizme' M. N. [*sic*] Bakhtina, avtora 'Problemy tvorchestva Dostoevskogo'" [On the "sociologism" of M. N. [*sic*] Bakhtin, author of *Problems of Dostoevsky's Poetics*], in the section "Dni nashei zhizni: o poznavaemosti khudozhestva proshlogo," *Na literaturnom postu* 4, no. 18 (1929): 5–10.

tive, "the sociohistorical process sometimes does go on 'behind the back' of heroes, even heroes of Dostoevsky's type!" It is not given to human beings to be conscious of all things at all times. Thus, while praising Dostoevsky's goals, Bakhtin allots too much respect to an individual's initiating and synthesizing powers in a world that Marxist ideology defines as highly determined, a world more likely to induce in its inhabitants "false consciousness" than self-consciousness. (As we shall see in chapter 3, this angle of objection to Bakhtin's Dostoevsky will later become a staple of Marxist-bred critics, even passionately dissident ones like Yuri Kariakin.) On balance, Grossman-Roshchin would classify Bakhtin with such nineteenth-century populist critics as Pyotr Lavrov and Nikolai Mikhailovsky: unscientific, sentimental, subjective, who did not analyze Dostoevsky's technique as much as pander to readers' tastes by psychologizing the characters and lamenting his "cruel talent." Bakhtin's error, to be sure, is not emotional voyeurism of this sort but its opposite extreme: he assumes that consciousness is always attainable and everywhere its own positive reward.

Equally offensive to Grossman-Roshchin is Bakhtin's celebration of the "adventure plot." Here, the reviewer assures us, Bakhtin "finally shows his hand." This plot type, which Bakhtin (in the first edition of his monograph) makes so fundamental to Dostoevsky, can provide no more than a skeleton on which to hang melodrama and freewheeling dialogue, expose human relations beyond time, space, and social class, and multiply crisis situations in which characters—to their own and others' surprise—can be born anew. As such, adventure plots are irresponsible and profoundly non-Marxist constructs, hardly socialized or historicized at all. But, Grossman-Roshchin notes peevishly: "Try to reproach Bakhtin for ignoring the social-class aspect of things! Bakhtin will answer: I beg to differ, on page such-and-such, did I not talk about capitalism, did I not say that the structure of the novel is defined by social existence? And then?— Then he can calmly proceed to declare that the hero is not predetermined and not delimited by social environment. And the wolves of Marxism are satiated and the lambs of idealism are whole." Russian idealists always avoid open battle, Grossman-Roshchin concludes. But in Bakhtin, "Yes, idealistic roots are deep."

Several anonymous reviews in fellow journals repeated these charges, although with even less nuance and patience. "What social groups are the 'carriers' [of value] in Dostoevsky's works? Where is the class leitmotif? We find out nothing about such things in Bakhtin."[9] These complaints are summed up in our final signed review from this early period: Mikhail

---

[9] From an unsigned review in *Oktiabr'*, no. 11 (1929); see Kudriatsev, "Bakhtin i ego kritiki," 118.

Starenkov's "Multi-voiced Idealism," which appeared in an issue of *Literatura i marksizm* in 1930.[10] Not only is Bakhtin faulted therein for a methodology that reveals nothing new ("Marxists have already resolved the problem of the relationship of art to reality"); his whole mechanism for linking author to hero to world is shown to be corrupt. By insisting that Dostoevsky designated the self-consciousness of heroes as his artistic dominant—and the dominant concern of his novels as well—Bakhtin effectively "drives out reality, leaving only consciousness." Citing Feuerbach and Georgy Plekhanov (the time was still to come when one would have to quote Lenin and Stalin on these matters), Starenkov gives the lie to the ancient idealist theme that "the world is [but] a representation of the world" through an analysis of Makar Devushkin, hero of Dostoevsky's short maiden novel *Poor Folk*. Devushkin's lonely lot as a petty clerk is painfully real, Starenkov insists, regardless of what one thinks about it. Bakhtin's views to the contrary, "consciousness remains part of reality and not the other way around."

Bakhtin is no more successful, in Starenkov's opinion, with that most radical of Dostoevskian narratives, *Notes from Underground*. The attempt to depict a hero entirely "from within" is by definition doomed—and not only for the commonsensical reason that consciousness must be registered as an inside reaction to an outside stimulus, of which here there is none. In addition, such a project is too formalistic, too dominated by questions of pure function (the "how" stripped of "who" and "why"). Badly simplifying Bakhtin's text but nevertheless on to a kernel of truth, Starenkov suspects that Bakhtin's passion for "self-consciousness as the dominant" is an attempt to insulate his method against causality, genesis, ideological systems, and external reality—the stuff of life, in other words, and the stuff of a genuinely progressive literary science as well. (This criticism, too, will be revisited in chapter 3 in greater and harsher detail.) Bakhtin's enthusiasm for the "adventure plot" is again decried as a cover-up for pursuing an ahistorical Dostoevsky. Concentrating as he does on the workings of language and on ideas voided of specific content, Bakhtin, in Starenkov's view, advances an understanding of the word that is "just as autotelic as that proclaimed by the Futurists and Formalists." And yet Bakhtin resists organizing these words or ideas into any hierarchical, impersonal system (above all, the author's), for then these words would become "no one's" and thus, in his terms, invalid. By 1930, Starenkov reminds us, even the most stubborn and doctrinaire Formalists had abandoned such "historyless," "contentless" paradoxes.

---

[10] M. Starenkov, "Mnogogolosyi idealizm (o knige M. M. Bakhtina 'Problemy tvorchestva Dostoevskogo')," in *Literatura i marksizm*, no. 3 (1930): 92–105.

In sum, the "immanentist" Bakhtin, in his analysis of Dostoevsky, resurrects what was least persuasive about both Formalism and Idealism. He then compounds that sin by drawing no distinction between a philosophical and an artistic resolution to the many impoverishing ideas (monologism in all its guises) that confront our era. Starenkov considers all talk on Bakhtin's part about the "social character" of ideas to be a deliberate mystification, a show of "idealistic pluralism" that conceals mere "ideological mimicry." Or, as he puts it in his conclusion: "Our scholar has entered a concert hall, heard a multi-voiced sound, and failed to discern a unity in that sound. To visit concert halls is a pleasant and innocent activity—but one that falls outside the tasks of contemporary Marxist literary scholarship, for whom the time of the carefree Mozarts has passed; its future belongs to the Salieris."

As critics of Bakhtin's Dostoevsky, Grossman-Roshchin and Starenkov—the Salieris of their epoch—do not impress us today. Nor do they impress Russian literary historians from later, less fettered decades.[11] But in two areas, surely, these early critics saw more clearly than those theorists in Europe and America who continue to mine Bakhtin's thought for its radical materialism and "Marxism." First, these hostile, politically correct Bolshevik reviewers from the 1920s immediately discarded the possibility of any serious Marxian orientation in Bakhtin's book—as did, of course, Bakhtin himself. Second, Starenkov is right on the mark in his observation that Bakhtin, although displaying a certain susceptibility to Formalist methodology, at the same time fails to distinguish between a philosophical and an aesthetic solution to some highly complex ideas. Not only does Bakhtin "fail to distinguish"; he outrightly insists that techniques of art, to be aesthetically legitimate, must be capable of extending and refining philosophical problems that cannot be resolved—that cannot even be conceptualized—in any other way. Thus does this philosopher-critic's notion of polyphony, and later his idea of the novel as a genre, become "philosophy by other means." Starenkov certainly did not intend his observation as a compliment. But it was shrewd all the

---

[11] Kudriatsev is extremely impatient when discussing this period and these critics ("Bakhtin i ego kritiki," 127–29): "The task of these activists is not to explain, not to prove, but to pass sentence. So Starenkov says that Bakhtin's approach 'has nothing to do with a Marxist explication of the idea . . .' So it doesn't. So what. You go live with your Marxism, and we'll live without it. So any Bakhtin in any free society would have answered. But you couldn't answer like that in our country. . . . Starenkov properly understood Bakhtin and did not try to hide his understanding. He grasped the essence of the book, which was directed against the monologism of thought that had rooted itself in society. How perceptive of him. . . . Such an assessment was logical. The entire path of the new society and new literary scholarship led up to it. Everything that is authentically artistic is pluralistic. Only what is official is monologic. The latter tries to uproot the former."

same; for he scarcely could have had access to those hundreds of un-published pages of early writings on ethics and aesthetics in which Bakhtin worked out this wonderful idea.

Responses to *Problems of Dostoevsky's Creative Art* written by Russians but published outside Soviet Russia constitute a separate, although lesser category.[12] The émigré press was cautious but on balance positive. Overall it saw in Bakhtin a welcome alternative both to the "narrow Formalistic approach" and to the "so-called 'Marxist method,'" the two wings of radical critical thought that had come to dominate their former home-land.[13] In a 1934 survey of Soviet Dostoevsky scholarship undertaken for a German literary journal published in Leipzig, the well-known Dostoevsky scholar Vasily Komarovich—Bakhtin's contemporary in Lenin-grad, fellow arrestee and political exile—provided what is perhaps the exemplary "intrinsic" (as opposed to crudely ideological) critique of the book from this early period.[14] His reservations were to surface in the 1960s and again in the 1990s. Polyphony, Komarovich asserts, advertises itself as an alternative way of viewing the structure of the great novels. But in fact polyphony illustrates only local dynamics, not structure at all, and even those insights draw largely on the shorter works. Such dynamics of consciousness are not unique to Dostoevsky in any event, being adap-tations of the familiar European genres of the confession and epistolary

[12] See O. Osovskii's commentary in "Kniga M. M. Bakhtina o Dostoevskom v otsenkakh literaturovedeniia russkogo zarubezh'ya," in *B sb II 91*, 379–85.

[13] Quotes in the text are from the most positive review from the diaspora, by R. Pletnev, writing from Prague. But Pletnev has his reservations. "Reading the book for the first time, it is difficult to avoid the impression that the author has his hands on the key that opens all doors leading to the secret inner chambers of artistic creativity. But in fact far from every-thing fits under the formula of multi-voicedness." Pletnev mentions such works as *Notes from the House of the Dead, The Gambler, The Village of Stepanchikovo*, and the single-voiced monolithic word of Makar Dolgoruky, the elders Tikhon and Zosima, Prince Mysh-kin, and (surprisingly) "that typical, monolithically single-voiced figure," Razumikhin. In the great novels, Pletnev asserts, monologic segments clearly echo, intersect, and interact with dialogic ones; "Bakhtin," he concludes, "is better at parts than at wholes." For Pletnev's review, see "Kritiky a referaty," *Slavia: Časopis pro slovanskou filologii* [annual] 9 (Prague, 1930–31), 837–40. The book was also noted appreciatively by the Dostoevsky scholar P. M. Bitsilli in a 1930 Paris review of a Dostoevsky anthology published in Prague and edited by the psychoanalytic critic A. L. Bem; Bem himself wrote a review for *Slavishche Rundschau*, no. 1 (Berlin, 1930), in which he admires Bakhtin for providing a "finished system" but regrets his reluctance to see an authorial "third" at work in the novels guaran-teeing unity, and his exaggeration of the "inner sociality" of the word. For translations into Russian of Bem's and Komarovich's reviews, with excellent commentary by Vitaly Makhlin in defense of Bakhtin, see *MMB v zerk 95*, 67–92.

[14] V. Komarovič, "Neue Probleme der Dostojewskij-Forschung 1925–1930, part 2, in *Zeitschrift für slavische Philologie*, Bd 2, ½ (Leipzig, 1934), 227–34. For a translation into Russian of the relevant portions on Bakhtin, again superbly annotated by Vitaly Makhlin, see *MMB v zerk 95*, 74–92.

novel. Furthermore, the "idea" cannot be said to be the hero in Dostoevsky's works. Human fates are the hero—and both catastrophe and resolution are of the utmost moment. Thus Bakhtin's insistence that the major heroes in Dostoevsky are *heard* rather than seen misreads a great deal, and most particularly the natures of Prince Myshkin and Stavrogin, two characters marked more by the image than by the word. "Bakhtin provides no firm grounding for the form of the 'polyphonic' novel," Komarovich concludes (83). The relative virtues of a visual versus an auditory reading of a cultural act—an issue, as was noted in the introduction, still being discussed in the centennial year—were raised early in the debates over Bakhtin's work.

At home and abroad, then, Bakhtin's book on Dostoevsky was considered eccentric. Its contrary originality and stubborn methodology, so against the grain of its time, put it (in the view of most reviewers) beyond the pale of the profession. Sergei Bocharov is probably correct when he writes, "At the time, it was read through by very few; time passed it by"; what academic reviews of it there were tended to be "inattentive and careless"; in short, the book did not "become an event."[15]

Several constants might be noted in this first period of reception. First, the finer points (indeed, even the blunt contours) of polyphony as a psychology of self-other relations or as a radical new strategy for writing fiction are wholly ignored. Second, critics understood Bakhtin's innovative concept of the "idea as hero" and his belief in the open potential of dialogic words neither as modes of freedom for the protagonist nor as creative flexibility for the author. These concepts were seen as philosophical heresy, pure and simple, or as the critic's willful usurpation of the primary author's rights—a transgression as counterintuitive as the notion that characters can be autonomous of their author. (Which is to say: regardless of his self-protective attempts to hide behind literature, all the same Bakhtin was being read as a philosopher.) And finally, Bakhtin is faulted for his unclassifiable method. He was neither fully a Formalist—a known and identified foe—nor entirely a literary critic in the mold of Russian nineteenth-century Dostoevsky criticism. That tradition, whether it praised its heroes or buried them, shared a common ground with progressive Marxist scholarship, being tendentious itself and prone to define "tendencies" in others.

A certain irony obtains, then, in this retrospective look at the reviews that first introduced Bakhtin to his reading public. As we have seen, among postcommunist Russian intellectuals in the 1990s the regnant image of Bakhtin is that of a pluralist unthreatened by multiplicity but

---

[15] Sergei Bocharov, "Ob odnom razgovore i vokrug nego" [About and around a certain conversation], in *NLO*, no. 2 (1993): 70–89, esp. 85.

aware that "many paths lead to the church"[16]—that is, a pluralist for whom the vertical axis of "transcendent value" is as essential as the horizontalizing moves of interpersonal dialogue. In 1929 Bolshevik critics such as Grossman-Roshchin and Starenkov saw this idealist vertical axis clearly; they understood that "with his reservations and hedgings Bakhtin was being cunning, covering his traces, keeping the bloodhounds off his track."[17] And they condemned these maneuvers as reactionary. Western academic theory thus becomes the last bastion of an even partially Marxist and materialist Bakhtin. This dual trajectory is one of the repeating paradoxes of the present study.

DOSTOEVSKY, II (1963)

Bakhtin revised his Dostoevsky book for a second edition in the early 1960s. By that time, the self-righteous and militant rhetoric that had permeated domestic reviews of the 1929 edition—a first book by a vulnerable, untried, virtually unknown scholar—had retreated nationwide, and in any event could no longer be applied in so crude a form. Bakhtin's name had been mentioned by Roman Jakobson during the eminent linguist's first trip back to his homeland in May 1956; one year later Viktor Shklovsky, the aging Formalist critic, was bold enough to refer in print to the Dostoevsky book. Soviet graduate students in literature sat up and took notice. Bakhtin's name was known in Moscow, where his dissertation on Rabelais, defended in 1946, had attracted considerable attention and even some notoriety; he had become the respected head of an academic department at a solid provincial university. Russian literary criticism, having survived terrors undreamed of by Marxist critics in the twenties, was now blander and more cautious. Independence of mind was no longer an absolute risk.

And, according to some Dostoevsky scholars seasoned enough to remember the advent of both editions, Bakhtin's 1963 revision had also grown more cautious, more politically correct. Its tone was more conciliatory; its historical base was inflated with Russian folklore, and it gestured respectfully toward acknowledged authorities.[18] All the same, mov-

---

[16] For a brief and characteristic summary of the confusions and possible mediating ground between dialogic and monologic procedures, see A. F. Eremeev, "Skol'ko zhe dorog vedet k khramy? (O 'spore' mezhdu tak nazyvaemymi dialogistami i monologistami)," *MMB i gum mysh II 95*, 47–51.

[17] Kudriatsev, "Bakhtin i ego kritiki," 121. "One could not call Grossman-Roshchin stupid," Kudriatsev remarks. "He understands everything perfectly. . . . Only he evaluates everything differently from Bakhtin."

[18] Thus does Yury Kudriatsev, in his 1979 survey of Dostoevsky scholarship during the

ing the resuscitated book into print was a risky, time-consuming, and delicate task. Vadim Kozhinov recalls the three years he spent collecting prominent signatures, daring to make the list public (to the chagrin of the apprehensive signatories) when editors proved cowardly. It was diffi-cult for a young academic to elicit any show of support on behalf of an unrehabilitated author, even from the decent-minded senior profes-sionals; by then establishment figures were wholly unaccustomed to inte-grating private convictions with public actions and did not like being called on it.[19] The book's appearance, therefore, was felt by many to be an enormous spiritual victory. But the polemic that developed over the second edition was disappointingly familiar. To sample the post-Stalinist atmosphere into which Bakhtin was "reborn" for the Russian public, it is sufficient to consider one representative cluster of reviews and counter-reviews that appeared in *Literaturnaia gazeta* during the summer of 1964.

The opening salvo was an essay by Aleksandr Dymshits entitled "Monologues and Dialogues."[20] "Again the book has been read through," he begins. "I read it for the first time thirty-five years ago." Although the original 1929 *Problems of Dostoevsky's Creative Art* indis-putably had become a classic, Dymshits nevertheless registers his "serious and principled disagreement" with Bakhtin over aesthetics and meth-odology. Bakhtin's Dostoevsky "never comes to final conclusions"; his major heroes all find themselves in "uninterrupted dialogues"; as a novel-ist he is "all unfinalizability, undecidability, unclosedness . . . and this said about Dostoevsky, among the most tendentious of writers!" What is more, the entire metaphysical opposition of dialogic to monologic is false. Not only does such a binary simplification distort the rich European

---

Soviet period, evaluate the revised edition—insisting, in mainstream didactic Soviet style, on reading Bakhtin as the conscience of his time and thus as an "Aesopian" social critic. Kudriatsev frequently concurs with Bakhtin's hostile critics as regards Dostoevsky but sup-ports Bakhtin's general thesis where it can be interpreted as a courageous, camouflaged anti-Stalinist polemic. The 1963 edition, he writes, "had become more scholarly sounding, intelligent in its own way but less substantial. Bakhtin was a broken man, as was Dolinin, and he now preferred the laurels of a 'theoretician' to the laurels of a 'warrior.' 'Ethics' was traded in for 'scholarliness' . . . Bakhtin 'scienced up' his book, having weakened its moral charge . . . As a general work of literary scholarship, this work doubtless has value. Ethically it is also valuable. . . . But if the monologization of life, and especially of thinking, had increased extraordinarily and in effect reached its outer limit during the quarter-century after the first edition appeared, then Bakhtin's book in its second, expanded edition was weakened in its protest to the extent that its problem-center had been eroded" (Kudriatsev, "Bakhtin i ego kritiki," 129, 132).

[19] "'Ya prosto blagodariu svoiu sud'bu . . .' (Vadim Kozhinov vspominaet o tom, kak udalos' pereizdat' 'Problemy tvorchestva Dostoevskogo')," *DKKh, no. 1 (94)*: 104–10.

[20] Aleksandr Dymshits, "Monologi i dialogi," in *Literaturnaia gazeta*, 11 July 1964.

tradition of Enlightenment, Romantic, and utopian novel writing, but it consigns to monologicity the Russian novel before Dostoevsky: beloved masterpieces by Pushkin, Gogol, Goncharov, Turgenev, Tolstoy. As a concept, polyphony is incompatible with the theory of social types put forth by Belinsky in the 1840s and long canonized in Russian criticism. In fact, Bakhtin severs Dostoevsky from the Russian realistic tradition and from Realism in general. At fault here is the critic's overconcentration on consciousness; in general, an amateurish passion for psychology in a literary scholar is unseemly and "subjective."

Dymshits associates the above errors (or "myths") with another, more comprehensive error: Bakhtin's fondness for Russian Formalism. Invoking the ominous phrase "Formalist *perezhitki*" (ideologically incorrect "carryovers" or survivals from an earlier era), he insists that Bakhtin "turns the process of artistic creation on its head." Critics deluded in this way need only posit a new device—in this case, a new mode of artistic visualization—and wondrously, the primary author is granted access to new sides of reality; form alone becomes a legitimate source of new content. But it is not only Bakhtin's explanation of Dostoevsky's creative method that irritates Dymshits and strikes him as formalistic. The huge new chapter 4, devoted to questions of genre and menippean satire, suffers from the same flaw. Dymshits complains that Bakhtin's unsubstantiated faith in the "self-development" of genres throughout history generates all sorts of "formalistic miracles." Dostoevsky is excavated for menippean themes, name piles upon name and source upon source, and "the real-life image of Dostoevsky begins to disappear; it becomes a sort of a mosaic, in no way resembling the man himself. . . . Enough! In all this, the erudition of M. Bakhtin is indisputable"—but the harmful effects of Formalism take their toll. In Bakhtin's Dostoevsky, nothing essential is learned from observing "living life." Everything becomes the influence of "genre." Finally, Dymshits suggests that Bakhtin's summons to his readers to "break out of monologic habits" and assimilate Dostoevsky's formal discoveries without passing judgment on the content of his ideas is contrary to approved method in literary investigation. For "as Engels brilliantly demonstrated, there is no art without a tendency." In fact—and on this the review ends—creativity itself starts with a "tendency," that is, with a given writer's societally conditioned direction and purpose [*obshchestvennaia opredelennost'*].

The Dymshits essay terrified Bakhtin's wife. As it happened, both elderly couples, the reviewer and reviewee with their spouses, were vacationing at Maleevka in 1965. Elena Aleksandrovna, wholly devoted to her husband's well-being and alarmed that a negative review might compromise their precarious old age, was on edge all summer for fear they might encounter the "terrible Dymshits" in the cafeteria.[21] But Bakhtin—phlegmatic, prepared for anything, surprised at nothing—was not without support of his own. The Dymshits review evoked a flurry in the academic community that lasted well into 1967. During that first summer, two letters appeared in the literary press directed against Dymshits (although not wholly in defense of Bakhtin), and then the beleaguered reviewer rose to a rebuttal of his secondary critics. Scarcely a decade out of the Stalinist night, this tentative polemic among reviewers, although not yet evidence of real critical pluralism, was all the same a harbinger of more open debates to come.

"Let's Get to the Bottom of Things" appeared in *Literaturnaia gazeta* three weeks after the Dymshits review.[22] Its coauthors Vasilievskaya and Myasnikov note testily that Dymshits claims to be reviewing a classic text but then imparts to the curious reader almost nothing positive about the book. Whereas Lunacharsky in 1929 had found the courage to review Bakhtin's volume sympathetically "in the very heat of the struggle against Formalism" (and on the brink of incalculably more dire struggles), now, during a much safer time, Bakhtin is cited out of context and made to sound retrograde and unpatriotic. The authors challenge the review point by point. Most substantively, they insist that polyphony *is* tendentious (thereby initiating a series of heroic attempts by Russian scholars to grasp one of Bakhtin's most original and resistant concepts)—if by "having a tendency" one means sensing an active authorial purpose at work. Although, to be sure, polyphony is tendentious in a special way.

What is this way? Bakhtin's approach to literature, these reviewers claim, is not so much Formalist as it is *functionalist*. The position of an author in polyphony is dynamic, procedural, dialogic; it "coalesces only in the process of shifting about autonomous and contradictory images." "To the Formalist, form is dead," they write cautiously. "For Bakhtin, form is socially signifying. . . . it is itself a category of content." Dymshits errs, therefore, when he suggests that Bakhtin is unwilling to analyze the idea-content of things. A polyphonic point of view on the world is valuable precisely because it assumes that sort of multiple burden so eagerly, because it enables so many different ideas and ideologies to be authored side by side within a single text. Thus polyphony is deeply humanistic; and thus, contrary to Lunacharsky, Dostoevsky's discovery of polyphony will outlive capitalism. "For," our two critics conclude, "the human be-

---

[21] See E. M. Lysenko [wife of the Renaissance scholar Leonid Pinsky] in interview with Nikolai Pan'kov, "Dva monologa ob odnom dialoge," *DKKh no. 2(7) (94)*: 111.

[22] I. Vasilevskaia and A. Miasnikov, "Razberemsia po sushchestvu," in *Literaturnaia gazeta*, 6 August 1964.

ing will eternally remain the subject and aim of art, which carries forward the best traditions from the deepest past into a legacy of the harmonious and free personality in communist society."

Sentences of the above sort do not go down well today, but in the mid-1960s they still had meaning—and it still mattered who was pulled into their vacuous orbit. Clearly a shift in Bakhtin's ideological support base (not a trivial concern in highly politicized Soviet culture) had come to pass. Let us review the distance traveled. The "proletarian" reviewers of 1929–30 had unmasked Bakhtin as an idealist philosopher, an anti-Marxist infected with pernicious Formalist habits. To Dymshits in 1964, Bakhtin was (much less dangerously) a routine, discredited Formalist. To the coauthors of this counter-review, Bakhtin had become a Marxist-Leninist humanist. That Bakhtin might require no label or politically correct defense was not, of course, a public option during those years. Literature and literary criticism were still too indispensable to Russian identity; official control over both was taken for granted.

One week later, more support for Bakhtin arrived in the form of a second response to the offending Dymshits review. A collective letter to the editorial board of *Literaturnaia gazeta*, signed by five prominent scholars (including Viktor Shklovsky), again took the sorely tried Dymshits to task for "irritating contradictions and unpersuasive conclusions."[23] Why did Dymshits resent the exclusion of classic Russian novelists from the polyphonic canon but neglect to mention Bakhtin's inclusion of many of them in that canon (for example, the approved Chernyshevsky)? And rather than fault Bakhtin for flawed scholarly judgment or lack of patriotism, readers should be grateful to him for detaching Dostoevsky from his most egregious interpreters, from all those tendentious readings that link the great Russian novelist to "reactionary ideology." Such sorry associations are still widespread at home and abroad, reinforced by the Dostoevsky criticism of Silver Age critics such as Merezhkovsky, Shestov, Rozanov—"books," the authors insist, "very popular in the West to this day."

As emotional and conceptually thin as this collective letter is, it did add one vigorous, politically beneficial component to Bakhtin's rehabilitation. To grasp its impact at the time, we must recall the logic of Socialist Realism as it was preached during the Stalinist years. Socialist-realist standards for literary scholarship, in full force a mere decade earlier, were designed to be exceptionalist, distinctive, separate from the bourgeois West and thus protective of Russia's "special path." This exceptionalism, which removed Russia altogether from potentially embarrassing competition with the West, was one powerful source of the doctrine's appeal. To

---

[23] V. Asmus, V. Ermilov, V. Pertsov, M. Khrapchenko, and Viktor Shklovsky, "V redaktsiiu 'Literaturnoi gazety,'" in ibid., 13 August 1964.

literary professionals during the 1960s thaw, however, it was clear that such an aesthetic had brought not only difference but disaster. These now legendary *shestidesiatniki*, the "generation of the [nineteen-] sixties," anxiously sought ways to restore their great (if ideologically suspect) classical writers to freer fields of inquiry, while at the same time respecting the party mandate to retain Russia's distinctiveness, even her incommensurateness, vis-à-vis the West. In this struggle, secondary critics were often moved about as pawns to protect primary authors. Thus Russian Decadent and Symbolist critics of the turn of the century—tagged with the ill-boding phrase "popular in the West"—became, in a deft Aesopian move that all who mattered would understand, disposable fodder in a campaign to reclaim a more complete and integral Dostoevsky. In the worst instance, of course, such a sacrificial move against one's fellow scholars and critics was ungrateful opportunism. In the best instance, however, it was a genuine devotional gesture before literary genius that Russian scholars, ardent servitors of their nation's culture under even the most desperate political conditions, would often willingly proffer.

The same issue of *Literaturnaia gazeta* contained a response from Dymshits entitled "Extravagant Praise or Criticism?"[24] He repeated his earlier reservations about Bakhtin: that dialogism is too vague and "unclosed" a principle to attach to Dostoevsky, admittedly a man of many "social-moral ideas" but who nevertheless strove to propagate the "strong and healthy" ones; that menippean satire in Dostoevsky is greatly overstated by Bakhtin; and that the traditions of Russian Realism are too facilely consigned to the monologic line. He observed, in addition, that Lunacharsky's review, for all its cult status and vital role in establishing the "sturdy reputation of Bakhtin's book as above reproach," was itself "far from uncontested." Dymshits's unsentimental interrogation of so canonized a cultural figure as Lunacharsky did not yet constitute pluralism in the realm of criticism. But it was an encouraging sign.

A postscript to the entire exchange—and an attempt to rehabilitate somewhat the much-harassed Dymshits—was provided by the literary critic Boris Bursov a year later in the journal *October*.[25] "The problems connected with M. Bakhtin's book have a more general and methodological significance," Bursov writes, "so debate should definitely continue." The anti-Dymshits counter-critics had let loose many statements "backed up by no analysis at all"; "no small number of doubtful conclusions" had been arrived at in an "extremely astute and clever but one-

---

[24] Al. Dymshits, "Voskhvalenie ili kritika?" in ibid., 13 August 1964.

[25] B. Bursov, "Vozvrashchenie k polemike" [A return to the polemic], in *Oktiabr'* 2 (February 1965): 198–203. Bursov reprints this essay in his book *Realizm vsegda i segodnia* (Leningrad: Lenizdat, 1967), 249–58, after a lengthy and peevish chapter on "Dostoevsky and Modernism."

sided way." Neither side in the debate has yet clarified the connection between polyphony and dialogue. Bakhtin was not, of course, above reproach. In a new variant on a familiar theme, Bursov faults him for attending exclusively to the rosy side of dialogicity and for assuming that the act of fashioning an inner consciousness is, on the whole, a benign and hopeful process. For if Dostoevsky's heroes do indeed live by their worldviews alone, then the price they pay for this privilege is high. Always probing the extremes with thought experiments and abstract, asocial extensions of an idea, these heroes live a life where the balance between words and deeds is often upset—as it rarely is, say, in a realist writer like Tolstoy, for whom the developing consciousness of his characters is always tightly bonded to productive real-life activity.

Bursov then returns to the sensitive issue of "Bakhtin, Dostoevsky, and the West." Without a doubt, he writes, Bakhtin "objectively provides some nourishment" to bourgeois literary scholarship. In the West, Dostoevsky has long been celebrated not only for his art but also for his "alleged prophecies"—his mysticism, metaphysics, anti-rationalism. And perhaps Bakhtin, even though he neglects Dostoevsky's moral themes, unwittingly does feed this prophecy-fantasy when he hails Dostoevsky as the writer who "gave us the most perfect model of the contemporary world." And is Bakhtin's model of consciousness—made up wholly of struggle, both inside words as well as outside of them—really what the world needs? Bursov recalls the famous remark Leo Tolstoy made to his friend and publisher Nikolai Strakhov about Dostoevsky soon after the latter's death, that the world could not afford to place on a pedestal a man who was "all struggle." Endless dialogism is just such endless struggle. To Bursov, there seemed no way to reconcile polyphony with the minimal requirements for that singular achievement and pride of Soviet literature: the self-confident positive hero.

Bursov's retrospective is interesting for us in one final aspect. The present study opened on the many things Bakhtin is *not*, on the schools into which he does not fit. So far in this chapter we have seen Bakhtin labeled—albeit imperfectly—an idealist philosopher, a renegade Formalist, a problematic Marxist-Leninist humanist. Bursov assesses him otherwise: as a flawed historian. "The root of the shortcomings in Bakhtin's book, in my opinion, is not so much its proximity to Formalism as its summary sense of history," Bursov concludes. For although Bakhtin professes to value particularity and flow, he is prone to "absolutizing the poetics of the novel." In the process the particularities of history are often swept away. Bakhtin employs historical evidence "not entirely concretely," whereas truth, Bursov insists, is always concrete. To illustrate his point, he brings forward Bakhtin's by now familiar—and, in the Soviet context, eternally safe—remark that Dostoevsky's polyphonic novel had been nurtured by the tensions of capitalist development in Russia. But by the mid-1960s literary critics could be somewhat more flexible in their mandatory genuflection before the mystique of Marxist stages. Bursov invokes the remark as a *negative* instance of Bakhtin's blurred sense of historical process. "All of that [Bakhtin's references to links between polyphony and capitalism] is too general to serve as an actual explanation of the uniqueness of the Russian novel," Bursov writes. To understand Russian Realism one need only look carefully at the complexities of Russian history—for it provides sufficient impulses toward polyphony before the onset of capitalism. We have thus come full circle. Bursov's overall reading of Bakhtin's monograph is uninspired. But his review rendered an important service: Bakhtin's original cosmetic reference to a Marxist piety had become again a dispensable cliché, with no political residue pro or contra for the conscientious literary historian.

Thus did Bakhtin reenter Soviet intellectual life. It was by no means a reverent reception, but it was serious, at times substantive, and not devoid of drama. With the republication of the Dostoevsky book, the path was cleared for Bakhtin's other works. For in Russia's ideologically weary society of the 1960s, where censorship was as much a matter of inertia as of positive control over content, the setting of an official precedent (in this case, breaking *back* into print) was, for a former political exile not yet rehabilitated, the crucial first step. Bakhtin's coterie of disciples pushed forward. The same year that Bursov's essay on the Dostoevsky book appeared (1965), a second volume by Bakhtin was published: the reworked dissertation on Rabelais. The critical reception of this new book, now the work of an officially approved Soviet author, would take place on a more scholarly and less defensive plane.

But there were fresh complications. Dostoevsky, for all his ideological unruliness, was nevertheless Russian and canonical; Rabelais was Western and indecent. Carnival laughter on the public square might be indeed "revolutionary" and "of the masses"—points stressed repeatedly by Bakhtin during his thesis defense—but it was also a good deal more dangerous and potentially anarchic than the dialogic word in the novel, a genre designed for solitary individual consumption. If the Dostoevsky book had passed into academic limbo almost as soon as it appeared, then Bakhtin's second book, in contrast, had a trickling twenty-five-year history, controversial at every step. Bakhtin submitted his "Rabelais in the History of Realism" as a dissertation (although he never liked to refer to his book as such) to the Gorky Institute of World Literature in 1940, on the brink of the war; he defended it in 1946, on the breaking edge of a new wave of High Stalinist xenophobia. Notwithstanding a divided vote slightly in his favor, he was eventually certified—in 1951, after a five-year delay—with the lesser academic degree of *kandidat* rather than that of *doktor nauk*. Before the dissertation could be approved and filed in public libraries, Bakhtin was required to cleanse and rephrase those portions of the text that made his work, in the opinion of the Higher Accrediting Commission, "crudely physiological," bawdy, and "ideologically depraved."[26] (The published book was based on this cleansed version of the dissertation.) The full stenographic transcription of Bakhtin's 1946 defense was published only in 1993.[27]

This transcript of the Ph.D. defense provides a fascinating glimpse into the dynamics of Stalin-era academic life. In a procedure that was far from routine for those years, independently minded colleagues within the institute took a bold stand in defense of their wayward candidate. Sound reservations were raised; absurd criticisms were hooted down. The stubborn, outspoken, ill and exhausted Bakhtin, astonished at the tenacity of his supporters, turned communist rhetoric to his own advantage and made a heroic showing against party-minded objections to his work. Of political naiveté there was none. As we know from Bakhtin's personal correspondence with Leonid Pinsky, as late as 1960 Bakhtin considered his work on Rabelais and the history of laughter still unpublishable.[28] By the mid-1960s, however, conditions had changed. Although some of the

---

[26] The phrase here is "ideologicheski porochnoi" (guilty of an ideological sin). See the memoir by Bakhtin's enthusiastic supporter E. M. Evnina, who, as a junior scholar during these years, was required to "remove from the manuscript of her own book on Rabelais all citations and references to Mikhail Mikhailovich's dissertation." The Higher Accrediting Commission (VAK) criticized Bakhtin's work as "Freudian," "pseudoscientific," "formalistic," and disrespectful to the genius of Gogol; Bakhtin was required to make a number of changes in the text before his degree was conferred. See "Iz vospominanii E. M. Evninoi," appendix 3, *DKKh, nos. 2–3 (93)*: 114–17, esp. 117.

[27] See "Stenogramma zasedaniia uchenogo soveta instituta mirovoi literatury im. A. M. Gor'kogo: zashchita dissertatsii tov. Bakhtinym na temu 'Rable v istorii realizma' 15 noiabria 1946 g.," annotated by N. A. Pan'kov, *DKKh, nos. 2–3 (93)*: 55–119. In addition, the issue includes a lengthy background essay by Pan'kov (29–54) as well as four appendixes: the text of Bakhtin's formal dissertation prospectus, or "tesizy"; a conversation with the literary scholar Valery Kirpotin; a memoir on the fate of Bakhtin's dissertation after the defense by a fellow Rabelais scholar, E. M. Evnina, who was banned from citing it; and a brief statement (1944) in favor of Bakhtin's monograph by Boris Tomashevsky. In fairness to academic procedure, however, it should be noted that the *kandidat* degree was hardly cruel and unusual punishment; it was the normal title awarded after a successful defense. The Stalinist academic system—in most particulars modeled after Germany circa 1910— had two levels of Ph.D., and very few scholars made it through to the second stage, even experienced and favored servants of the regime. I thank my colleague Thomas Pavel for this and other helpful comments on this chapter.

[28] See Bakhtin's letter to Pinsky of 26 November 1960: "As regards my work on Rabelais, I am not counting on any possibility of its publication. What is more, it was finished twenty years ago and a great deal no longer satisfies me" ("Pis'ma M. M. Bakhtina k L. E. Pinskomu," ed. N. A. Pan'kov, in *DKKh, no. 2 (94)*: 57).

objections elicited by the Rabelais book are familiar from reviewers' responses to *Dostoevsky's Poetics*, their overall tone and scholarly orientation augured well for Bakhtin's return to a world of Russian literary criticism that was worth taking seriously.

RABELAIS AND FOLK CULTURE

For so long, and with such naive enthusiasm, have Bakhtin's ideas of carnival and the grotesque been extolled by postmodernist readers in the West that it takes some effort to relocate those ideas in the conservative Soviet literary climate of the mid-1960s—a straitlaced, starchy, infinitely more cautious landscape. The publication of *The Creative Art of François Rabelais and Folk Culture of the Middle Ages and the Renaissance* in Moscow during 1965 was a major cultural event.[29] Many senior academics still remembered the stormy dissertation defense two decades earlier and considered the appearance of a book based on that material to be a victory of independent scholarship over the cowed (and cowardly) Stalinist-bred bureaucracy. Accidents of timing also helped: in the early 1960s, N. M. Liubimov's celebrated new Russian translation of *Gargantua and Pantagruel* appeared, which focused attention on Rabelais and, in the academic world, on the paucity of recent Russian scholarship about the great French master. Two pillars of the Russian literary establishment, Viktor Vinogradov and Konstantin Fedin, petitioned a state publishing house to move Bakhtin's study into print as soon as possible. Pinsky wrote a passionately supportive reader's report for the press.[30]

Russian critical response to Bakhtin's *Rabelais* was abundant during its first decade and a half in print. Of this rich harvest, we will consider only four representative reviews. Underlying each is an approach to Bakhtin, to literary criticism generally, and to Russia's own recent past that remained vigorous throughout the de-Stalinization process. The first, a complex and discriminating appreciation of Bakhtin's book by the Kharkov-based cultural historian Leonid Batkin, appeared as a review article in *Voprosy filosofii* at the end of 1967. The second is a passing reference to *Rabelais* by one of Bakhtin's contemporaries and fellow arrestees, the venerable philosopher Aleksei Losev (1893–1988), at the end of his very long, late book *Aesthetics of the Renaissance* (1978); it is the highly emotional testimony of a classicist who was as appalled and disgusted by Bakhtin's vision of carnival as Leonid Batkin had been open-minded and

---

[29] M. Bakhtin, *Tvorchestvo Fransua Rable i narodnaia kul'tura Srednevekov'ia i Renessansa* (Moscow: Khudozhestvennaia literatura, 1965).

[30] For a short history of these two pre-publication years, see Konkin and Konkina, *Mikhail Bakhtin*, 299–301.

intrigued. The third review, which in the old Soviet context was the most comfortable, appears as the final chapter in Vladimir Boriskin's little volume *Atheism and Creative Art* (1986)—a routine contribution by a Saransk academic on the brink of glasnost to the curious, and now entirely defunct, discipline of "scientific atheism." The last entry is by a scholar of Bakhtin's generation who also survived to bridge pre- and post-Stalinist culture: Viktor Shklovsky's essay "François Rabelais and Bakhtin's Book," included in his late (1970) anthology *The Bow-String: On the Dissimilarity of Similar Things.*

None of these responses is unambiguously positive. All acknowledge methodological dangers and moral defects in Bakhtinian carnival—and in Bakhtin's reading of Rabelais—that will be raised in Western criticism only timorously, decades later. And most interesting, all the major arguments pro and contra the dynamics of carnival, the grotesque body and cultures of laughter that we meet in these reviews of the 1960s and 1970s were first broached during Bakhtin's dissertation defense twenty years earlier—in which context Bakhtin himself had a chance (indeed, an obligation) to respond and defend his hypotheses. As a septuagenarian in the 1960s, Bakhtin rarely bothered to rebut criticism (or court praise) when his works finally began to appear in print. He considered himself either above, or to the side of, such dialogue. Thus his required response, at age fifty, to his *opponenty* (the formal examiners at his defense) is one of the few sustained self-reflections we have by Bakhtin on his own work. To be sure, this initial stage in the reception of Bakhtin's Rabelais project is "pre-publication"; but it was official, public, and rapidly became part of academic lore. We will therefore open our review of "carnival criticism" with the 1946 Ph.D. defense. What were the major objections raised to *Rabelais in the History of Realism* at that time, and how did Bakhtin justify himself in light of them?

In many respects, Bakhtin's thesis was ingeniously appropriate for its time and place. Many clichés of communism are realized in it: carnival, after all, could easily be linked with the "common people," the collective body, and a buoyant indifference to individual death. Carnival had the additional advantage of being pro-materialist, anti-Church, disruptive of fixed order, and vaguely "revolutionary" both on its own terms and vis-à-vis more humanistic, Western readings of Rabelais. Although prim, oppressive Stalinist culture had long since ceased to live by those destabilizing Bolshevik slogans, as verbal tags they could still embarrass and deflect. When, for example, Comrade Teriaeva, an examiner of few scholarly qualifications but with rigid Stalinist convictions and a good nose for heterodoxy,[31] accused Bakhtin of not reflecting in his dissertation (sub-

---

[31] For a brief and exasperated professional biography of Mariia Prokofievna Teriaeva, see

mitted in 1940) the spirit of Zhdanov's 1946 proclamation on party-mindedness in literature, and when she condemned his work for resembling more "private research" full of "superfluous references to Saturnalia and phallic cults" than an objective study of class antagonisms, Bakhtin responded in his final statement—with what must have been profound weariness—that his study dealt with one of the world's most revolutionary writers, that he saw no reason to write "what had already been written and spoken," that Comrade Teriaeva apparently wanted him simply to repeat "what she had already studied," and that "I, as a scholar, can be a revolutionary as well . . . I solved the problem [of Rabelais] in a revolutionary way."[32]

There were also responsible objections raised at the defense, however, by those who appreciated fully the value and originality of Bakhtin's work. Where is the spiritually serious side of humanism? Why is the great realist François Rabelais cast backward into the Middle Ages and not forward, progressively, into the Renaissance? On what basis can the dissertator claim that medieval carnival or carnival laughter is so carefree and eternally "cheerful"? Why such simplistic binary thinking, which presumes that grotesque realism is solely the property of the masses—when in fact all strata of society (even those Bakhtin excoriates as "official") can be shown to have indulged delightedly in it? And for that matter, why do the common people in Bakhtin's account only laugh and cavort, when in history they clearly broke their backs with work, suffered, and thirsted to believe? The entire hypothesis of "reduced carnivalization" in subsequent literary epochs struck some examiners as an artificial construct. Can one really leap unproblematically from Rabelaisian folkloric fantasy to Gogol's ambivalent humor or to Dostoevsky's tragic vision?

In his final statement, Bakhtin addressed these reservations, although in no sense apologetically. His kindly, aristocratic demeanor—tolerant of others because he was indifferent to their opinions—glimmers beneath the transcript. "I am an obsessed innovator," he admitted. "Obsessed innovators are very rarely understood." He was deeply gratified, therefore, by the support he had received and grateful for a chance to respond to objections. Yes, in his thesis (far too short for the task he had in mind) perhaps he had exaggerated and simplified cultural traditions as well as

---

N. A. Pan'kov, " 'Ot khoda etogo dela zavisit vse dal'neishee . . .' (Zashchita dissertatsii M. M. Bakhtina kak real'noe sobytie, vysokaia drama i nauchnaia komediia)," in *DKKh, nos. 2–3 (93)*: 29–54, esp. 47–48. For more on these troubles, see Nikolai Pan'kov, "The Creative History of Bakhtin's *Rabelais*," in *Face to Face: Bakhtin in Russia and the West*, eds. Carol Adlam, Rachel Falconer, Vitalii Makhlin, and Alastair Renfrew (Sheffield: Sheffield Academic Press, 1997): 196–202.

[32] Bakhtin's summary statement [zakliuchitel'noe slovo], "Stenogramma zasedaniia . . . ," 98–99. Further page references given in text.

historical conditions. "I did not present Rabelais in the atmosphere of the French Renaissance. This is true. I did not do so, because in that area so much has already been done, and I would have addressed you here as a mere compiler. And why is that necessary, when those materials are available to everyone? . . . To repeat [what is known] is to beat down an open door" (94). In any future monograph, he assured his examiners, he would balance the record with attention to Rabelais the humanist. But as he had testified in his opening statement, the gothic and the grotesque had fared so poorly in literary scholarship—always partial to forms of "prepared and completed existence"—that in his study he had resolved to "catch existence in the process of becoming" (56) and consider the epoch solely from that "unofficial," as yet uncoalesced point of view. As regards laughter, Bakhtin hastened to assure his audience: "I do not in the least mean to imply that medieval laughter is cheerful, carefree, and joyous laughter" (97). In carnival, laughter and death are intertwined; death and pain are everywhere to be found and are grimly real, only death never has the final word. "Laughter is a weapon, like fists and sticks." But unlike those latter two weapons, which can be wielded effectively in anger and in dread, laughter must be absolutely fearless; and for precisely this reason it is progressive, pointed forward toward the Renaissance. "Laughter liberates us from fear, and this work of laughter . . . is an indispensable prerequisite for Renaissance consciousness. In order to look at the world soberly, I must cease to be afraid. In this, laughter played a most serious role" (98). No, Rabelaisian realism is not degraded, dirty, or an insult to consciousness; it is, on the contrary, a forerunner of all objective critical consciousness. Of course the common people do not only laugh; they have many lives. "But this is the life that interested me, it is deeply progressive and revolutionary. . . . Excuse me if I have not satisfied you with my answers, I am so exhausted, and it shows" (100).

Despite these assurances at the defense, Bakhtin did not alter the text of his dissertation in the "more balanced," humanistic direction indicated before seeking a publisher. In fact, his first attempt to publish was in 1940, soon after he submitted the text to the Gorky Institute. In 1944 he tried a second time to publish the text, also unsuccessfully, although there survives from that period a long set of notes, published for the first time in 1992 under the title "Additions and Revisions to *Rabelais*," indicating the scope of Bakhtin's ambitions for the larger project.[33] Projected chapters were to deal with official (that is, bad) versus unofficial (good) seriousness; with carnival as a universal theory of "limbic" images; with carnivalized aspects of *Hamlet*, *King Lear*, *Macbeth* and presumably

---

[33] M. M. Bakhtin, "Dopolneniia i izmeneniia k 'Rable'" [dated 18/VI/44], prepared for publication by L. S. Melikhova; first published in *Voprosy filosofii*, no. 1 (1992): 134–64, definitively annotated in *MMB: ss 5 (96)*, 80–129, 423–92.

other Shakespearean drama; and there is some loose speculation on the relation of carnival to nicknames and gesture. Regretfully, little of this plan was realized. The sanitized late-1940s version required by the dissertation committee became the "canonical" text (Bakhtin's 1940 Ur-*Rabelais* is still in the archives).[34] And over twenty-five years, these various quasi-public presentations and resubmissions—each with its own reader reports, local audience, and mythology—entered institutional memory. Apocryphal and carnivalized stories began to circulate, such as the (unconfirmed) account by one eyewitness at the doctoral defense that "at the culminating moment, Bakhtin shouted at his opponents: 'Obscurantists! Obscurantists!'—and furiously banged his crutches on the floor."[35] In a word, by the time the typescript finally saw the light of day, it had accumulated a whole shadow history. This shadow added texture and depth to the reviews in print.

Leonid Batkin's review, "Panurge's Laughter and the Philosophy of Culture," was among the most probing of the academic responses to Bakhtin's *Rabelais*.[36] Its title provides the clue. An exemplary depoliticized discussion of two texts (Bakhtin's and Rabelais's), each containing potentially explosive political material, it resembles the early reviews of the Dostoevsky book in this one feature only: it does not approach Bakhtin's study of Rabelais as traditional "philological" scholarship. Batkin appreciates the work first of all as culturology, as speculation on the psychology of fear, and as a meditation on the metaphysics of laughter. It is on this ground, he believes, that Bakhtin is at his most suggestive and should ultimately be judged.

The review opens on the text's sociocultural merits. Bakhtin was among the first modern critics to understand that Rabelaisian "indecencies" were not at all indecent for the sixteenth century. Thus Rabelais should not be read as we moderns tend to read him, as a complicated "protest" against ascetic pruderies (such prudery did not exist)—but more simply as a pleasurable, humorous, instructive book. A large part of its humor lay in a Renaissance worldview that could still grasp directly a spontaneous, contradictory carnal image as a unified whole, without logical or linear explanations. Bakhtin forces us back into this imagic thinking, so integral a part of his author's world. He also focuses our attention on ambivalence itself, not to be confused with mere doubt (which is often paralyzing) or with "double meanings," too easy to factor out and

[34] Pan'kov, "'Ot khoda etogo dela . . . ,'" in *DKKh, nos. 2–3 (93)*: 40.

[35] The eyewitness was B. I. Purishev; the anecdote was related to Pan'kov by Iu. M. Kagan, Matvei Kagan's daughter. See Pan'kov, "'Ot khoda etogo dela . . . ,'" 42.

[36] L. M. Batkin, "Smekh Panurga i filosofiia kul'tury," *Voprosy filosofii*, no. 12 (1967): 114–23.

pin down. Batkin finds a virtue—faintly Marxist—in Bakhtin's daring to construct an image of the ordinary "man of the masses" from a distant period; by and large, he writes, "we judge the culture of people through people of culture," and Bakhtin had the courage to construct an image from the bottom up.

Such were the virtues of the book. Its "inspirational style and fearlessness" were indisputable. As literary history and as a close reading of the primary text, however, Batkin finds the study seriously flawed. His objections echo those of Bakhtin's examiners in 1946. First, the category of "official culture" is impossibly broad, imprecise, unrelievedly authoritarian and monologic. The Catholic Church in France of that period was in fact diversified and divided; Bakhtin paints it, anachronistically, as the Inquisition. Everything official is rendered wholly negative and oppressive: "It is only the common people on the public square who laugh. Beyond the puppet-stalls, Gothic gloom spreads out thickly." Bakhtin declines to acknowledge that the common people could also be the source of gloomy and repressive thoughts—fanaticism, cruelty, eschatological fantasies—or that clerics, knights and merchants, the privileged and commercial classes, also took part boisterously in carnival. In a related point, Batkin notes that Rabelais's humanism fares poorly in Bakhtin's book. From the Abbey of Thélème to a host of other misprisions, Bakhtin simply does not see humanism as a value—it is only a "one-sided seriousness"—and this means he does not see Rabelais.

In fact, the image of the author falls away entirely. If the Dostoevsky book was perhaps too concerned with authorial device, then here, "The Rabelais in Rabelais is forgotten"; literary technique, structure, and creative intelligence are of too little account. Bakhtin makes it look as if the elemental force of laughter emerges and "moves along by itself." This is a serious matter, the reviewer argues, for in fact Rabelaisian laughter comes down to us in an ancient and familiar literary genre, "the laughter that happens at table during a humanists' feast," the erudite, idle, witty, and often wicked talk of educated skeptics. This table talk is ambivalent, Batkin concedes, but not in an especially folksy way: "Laughing and serious tonalities constantly interact and exchange places, estranging one another."

Batkin is further bothered by one "strange and embarrassing aftertaste": the fact that the grotesque is everywhere so privileged over the classical in this study that it becomes a new and oppressive canon. In this regard, Bakhtin appears to resist the passage of time. The more modern, the worse. "Outside of the grotesque there is no salvation," the reviewer notes—and thus everything after Rabelais is seen as an erosion and a falling away. The error here, which Bakhtin avoids in other areas of his study, is to measure the nineteenth (or any other) century by seventeenth-century standards. For there is no reason why the two historical periods should translate into one another at all; each has its own parameters and truths, and between them "misunderstanding is *normal*." Batkin hints here at what is indeed a peculiarly Bakhtinian conundrum, also coloring reviews of *Dostoevsky's Poetics*: on the one hand, a passion for the speculative sweep of history, for genres rooted in an undocumentable, distant past, for vague and amalgamated tales of genesis; on the other, insistence on difference, differentiation, and the possibility of something being absolutely, creatively new.

Batkin's final reservation is one that will ring constantly in post-Soviet criticism of Bakhtin—and most loudly, as we shall see in chapter 4, among philosophers of religion intrigued by links between carnival and Christianity. In Rabelais's work, "not only is there the one-sidedness of seriousness; there is also the *one-sidedness of laughter*, of which M. Bakhtin does not write . . . If Don Quixote is helpless without his rogueish servant, then Sancho Panza, too, is worth very little when not jolting along on a donkey behind his master." The larger point is dialectical. In Bakhtin's notion of carnival, laughter is "negation pregnant with affirmation." But in any given ambivalent laugh, affirmation is relative—whereas negation, it appears, is absolute: in this is its power and fearlessness. Such fearlessness comes at a cost. Ambivalent laughter cannot be the main axis of any cultural development, Batkin argues (somewhat in the spirit of Nicolas Berdyaev), because out of a purely negative principle one cannot *create*; at best, negation can only liberate. Following Bakhtin's logic, the end result of *Rabelais and Folk Culture* would have to be a "Renaissance that was at its zenith when it did not take itself seriously." And although this might be a strong reading of that period, it is scarcely a correct one. Thus Bakhtin's book is best appreciated for its provocative impulse, for the "idea that moves through its historical material"—an idea that is inevitably more accurate in its broad contours than in any of its narrower derivative formulations or close readings.

Overall, then, Batkin considers Bakhtin's *Rabelais* a culturological rather than a philological monograph, stimulating in its metaphysical concepts but disappointing in its exaggeration and reductiveness. At several points, he remarks, "proofs are replaced by declamation about the people's wisdom"; when this happens, "there are no people, only the once-and-for-ever People, i.e., the *Volkgeist*, an abstraction." The rigor and cleverness of humanist thought is either sacrificed outright or turned over to an unheeding crowd. Batkin hints at what will become familiar criticism by the 1990s: that many of Bakhtin's most powerful, apparently universalizing ideas are in fact more closely tied to the specific realities of Stalinism than it might at first seem—that is, they rely for their persuasiveness on reflexes bred in the reader by the constant reality of oppression and terror. Under such conditions, a moment of "liberation from fear" is by itself, and by definition, creative.

Our second response to carnival, not by an intellectual historian but by a philosopher turned aesthetician and classicist, is less evenhanded. Aleksei Losev was known in the 1920s for his non-Marxist work in logic, myth, music theory, and phenomenology. His biography to some extent parallels Bakhtin's: arrested in 1930, sentenced to hard labor on the White Sea Canal, Losev scraped by on uncertain employment in the provinces after his release and, like Bakhtin, was crippled in midlife by a debilitating illness (in Losev's case, progressive blindness). Losev was resurrected in print only in 1953.[37] His second career produced massive, if highly subjective, volumes on the aesthetic thought of the Ancient and Renaissance worlds. *The Aesthetics of the Renaissance* (1978), completed when Losev was a very old man, ends with a chapter on "The Decay of Renaissance Aesthetics," of which eight, almost wholly hostile pages are devoted to François Rabelais.[38] "Rabelais was the greatest French humanist," Losev writes, "but he was also excessively submerged in the chaotic variety of human life . . . a man who drew too frank a picture of life, unembarrassed by its naturalistic details" (586). Raised in the Church and high culture of his age, Rabelais, according to Losev, gives us an inversion, destruction, and *parody* of Renaissance humanism, not its heroic realization. The Abbey of Thélème—that anti-monastery where one neither prays nor works, which posits no guiding order at all, which has no visible means of support, and yet where all is elegant, leisurely, and blooming—is, in Losev's opinion, Rabelais's sober picture of "the utter helplessness and impotence of a comfortable illusion" (the assumption, apparently, that "the state will pay"). Likewise, the "titanism" that inspires those much admired hero-giants Gargantua and Pantagruel conceals the fact that they are simply "bohemians," "rabble," nothing more than coarse, grasping, cowardly, violent nihilists with no "truly durable perseverance to their natures" (588). Such heroes parody the ideal of Renaissance humanism, which was driven by ideas, not appetites. Furthermore, Losev contends, "corporeality" in Rabelais is far removed from the grace and proportionality of the Renaissance body; Rabelaisian bodies are "idea-less, empty, devoid of any content or artistry" (589).

Losev then comments on two well-known recent Soviet books on

[37] For a useful brief introduction to Aleksei Losev (with incidental parallels drawn to the life of Bakhtin), see Scanlan's prefatory essay to part 5, "Finding Philosophy under Soviet Rule," in James P. Scanlan, *Russian Thought under Communism: The Recovery of a Philosophical Heritage* (Armonk, N.Y.: M. E. Sharpe, 1994), 187–94.

[38] A. F. Losev, *Estetika Vozrozhdeniia* (Moscow: Mysl', 1978), 586–93. Further page references given in text.

Rabelaisian laughter, one by Bakhtin and the other by Leonid Pinsky. He faults Pinsky for his reluctance to see, in Rabelais's contradictory and deceptive treatment of the comic, a genuine satanism at work (this question of satanic laughter in carnival will be taken up again in chapter 4). But it is Bakhtin's book that receives the full force of Losev's skepticism and scholarly wrath. He specifically cites Bakhtin to illustrate Rabelais's "vile and repellent aesthetics"—but, he adds, "without linking ourselves in the least to the theoretical or literary constructs of that researcher, which often strike us as highly contestable and at times fantastically exaggerated" (589). Losev sees neither joyful material surplus nor release from terror as motivating Bakhtin's delight in the "material-bodily lower stratum." In Bakhtin's themes he detects only an infantile fascination with excrement, intoxication, and monstrous misshapen growth, all followed by the hope that a folklore miracle would make it right. "The realism of Rabelais is the aesthetic apotheosis of all vileness and obscenity," Losev concludes. "Whoever wishes to consider such realism progressive, go right ahead" (591). Here, indeed, is an eccentricity to match Bakhtin's own. Losev's attack on Bakhtin's *Rabelais*—viewing it not only as one more apologia for a smutty book but as a misreading of an entire epoch—is itself, of course, a critique that Bakhtin predicted and had attempted to deflect. Dignified and darkened, Losev's argument will enter the 1990s debates about carnival, its receptivity to the mythography of Stalinism, and the questionable potential of laughter to nourish genuine spirituality.

Vladimir Boriskin's monograph *Atheism and Creative Art* (Saransk, 1986), incorporates a review of his colleague Bakhtin's monograph on Rabelais as its final chapter.[39] Under the title "The Cheerful Universe (Problems of Atheism in Bakhtin's Book)," the essay is a routine product of a respectable Soviet academic discipline. It presumes as self-evident the truisms of scientific atheism: that a divine Creator would be in competition, not cooperation, with human creativity; that God is jealous and grim whereas "the people" are spontaneously labor-loving, cheerful, self-reliant, and strive toward spiritual autonomy; and that faith in a materialistic universe is a surer route to the realization of humanistic ideals than any mystic or metaphysical alternative. Although Boriskin acknowledges that religion can, on occasion, contribute to culture, as a professional in his field he must hold that "creativity, by its very nature, is incompatible with dogmatism and passivity, traits especially characteristic of religious consciousness" (5–6). Such obstinate parameters almost disqualify Boriskin as a serious reviewer of Bakhtin's monograph. But it is of

---

[39] V. M. Boriskin, ch. 4, "Veselaia vselennaia," in *Ateizm i tvorchestvo* (Saransk: Mordovskoe knizhnoe izdatel'stvo, 1986), 93–108. Further page references given in text.

some interest to the present study, I believe, that Bakhtinian carnival, with its abundance of schematic binaries—"official"/"unofficial," "the authorities"/"the people," "one-sided seriousness"/"cheerful relativity"—alongside its often unstoppable slide toward mindlessness, can be fit with such ease into these standard party-minded norms. It helps to explain the exceptional survival record of the carnival idea, which has proved to be, in widely differing political environments, among Bakhtin's most cunning, malleable, and robust concepts.

As Boriskin reads the work of his Saransk colleague, *The Creative Art of François Rabelais* is thoroughly Soviet in content and spirit. Aleksei Losev was wrong to despise Rabelaisian aesthetics, Boriskin writes; further, Losev's impetuous "opinion" concerning Bakhtin's so-called fantastically exaggerated reading of Rabelais in terms of the lower bodily stratum is simple evidence that opinion is no match for a "clearly expressed concept" (96–97). Whereas Losev, with his ill-tempered "opinion," can merely discredit in a negative spirit, Bakhtin's concept permits him to look on life's processes cheerfully and optimistically. His monograph is thus precious to the antireligious cause, because it documents Rabelais's success at achieving an *artistic* (not merely a rational or intellectual) representation of atheism and its humanistic fruit.

Boriskin cannot, of course, claim the same "concept" for Rabelais himself, a man raised in the Church and, as a fictional artist, deeply committed to pursuing a dialogue—however daring in its comic irreverence—between secular and sacred forms. ("True," Boriskin admits, "Rabelais's [actual] relationship to religion has so far been assessed very cautiously" [99]). But the formal claims of art or Church occupy Boriskin very little, in Bakhtin's monograph as well as in Rabelais's original. "M. M. Bakhtin's concept makes it possible to draw some conclusions about the *uninterruptability of atheistic traditions* in human culture," he writes (95), with the facility of a mind well trained at linking official slogans into dull bland chains. "At the base of this concept lies the teaching of historical materialism on the deciding role of the popular masses in history. The common people are always the creator of history, even during the gloomiest epochs, since they are the main productive force of society, its main builder of material and spiritual values. The laboring activity of the people is always to some degree a creative act. . . . The people laugh not only because they need a break from labor, a rest, a relaxation; they laugh from a spontaneous sense of their own real strength" (95).

Working within his formulas, Boriskin nevertheless takes some care not to distort outrightly. "Bakhtin does not identify Rabelais's worldview with atheism," he admits; "first, because that worldview is directed not only against religion but against the entire value system of feudal society," and second, because it is not negating but "life-affirming, striving toward the future." Atheism is "only one side of Rabelais's naively materialistic and spontaneously dialectical worldview" (97–98). Boriskin alludes vaguely near the end of his review to a "contemporary understanding of atheism" that is more flexible and spiritually uplifting than the "insufficient, limited nature of purely rationalistic atheism" (98). The advantage of this more up-to-date definition, apparently, is that it requires no firm stand on the question of God. All that is needed is a popular base, a belief in communal labor, reverence toward physical matter, and optimism in the face of death. On these grounds, Boriskin concludes, both "Rabelais's novel and M. M. Bakhtin's book are permeated practically on every page with the ideas of atheism" (99).

There are two reasons, I suggest, for keeping Boriskin and his rote Marxist science in mind. Both will resurface when we consider the fate of Bakhtin's carnivalesque in the post-Soviet period. First, like Batkin before him, Boriskin grasps clearly that Bakhtin cannot be read as a literary critic or as a historian of carnival in the narrow sense of the word. Apply those standards (as, say, Viktor Shklovsky does in our next entry) and imprecisions and contradictions will abound (97). For the moment of carnival that Bakhtin celebrates is not so much a social phenomenon or a fixed date on the church calendar as it is an attitude, a holiday attitude—and by "holiday" [*prazdnik*] is meant any peak point or threshold that is (in Boriskin's words) valued for the aspect "of change and renewal in it, its striving toward the future" (105). Carnival is not an institution, nor can it be judged by any of its (often nasty) material traces. It is simply a name given to that moment of enablement—inevitably transitory—during which the self feels itself to be an agent in the world, that moment when a human being no longer feels helpless, nor prays, nor begs. As Bakhtin writes in his *Rabelais*, this enabling moment is the "victory of laughter": "not only a victory over the mystic terror of God, but also a victory over the awe inspired by the forces of nature, and most of all over the oppression and guilt related to all that is consecrated and forbidden . . . This truth was ephemeral; it was followed by the fears and oppressions of everyday life, but from these brief moments another unofficial truth emerged . . . Laughter is essentially not an external but an interior form of truth.[40]

Carnival, therefore, does not and cannot hope to change the world; it can only change our inner relationship to that world. (Near the end of his life, Bakhtin himself would jot down a similar sentiment as regards consciousness expressed through the word: words free my "I" from the necessity to act upon the world by transforming that I into a witness or

---

[40] Mikhail Bakhtin, *Rabelais and His World*, trans. Hélène Iswolsky (Bloomington: Indiana University Press, 1984), 90–91, 94.

a judge.)[41] Unlike the vigilant Bolshevik critics who condemned Bakhtin's Dostoevsky book for its philosophical idealism in 1929, Boriskin does no more than gesture lamely at this profoundly anti-Marxist conclusion.

The second reason for attending to state-sponsored atheism is more generic. Boriskin's facile assimilation of Bakhtin's "concept" is good evidence that the carnivalesque, like the rogues and fools of the entr'acte, is an adaptable, pliable, immortal creature. The virtues that Boriskin claimed for "contemporary atheism" within his appreciative but pedestrian critique were precisely the ones that had saved Bakhtin during his embattled dissertation defense. And they are the same virtues being claimed, in the postcommunist era, by thinkers sympathetic to a Christian outlook and eager to affix Bakhtin to it. That carnival, one of the great liminal moments in human culture, can literally justify and generate *anything* has fueled the search for some deeper principle to which it might be attached.

One final response remains to be considered. Viktor Shklovsky's "François Rabelais and Bakhtin's Book," surely the best-known review to be written by one of Bakhtin's own contemporaries, is cast in that pathbreaking Formalist's trademark aphoristic style.[42] Shklovsky on Bakhtin is a curiously illuminating dialogue. Focusing on the categories of menippean satire and carnivalization as Bakhtin employs them in both his Rabelais and Dostoevsky books, Shklovsky finds fault with a great deal. This in itself is instructive. As a very young man in the 1910s and 1920s, Shklovsky had launched his own precocious career with sweeping manifesto-like statements of the sort he now finds unprofessional in Bakhtin. What are his major complaints?

First, Shklovsky regrets that Bakhtin fails to document the target of Rabelais's parody, namely, the Bible and Holy Writ. For Rabelais maltreats these texts in a masterfully crude and cavalier way, deliberately reducing their authority to that of pagan Greek or Roman myth. Bakhtin's research on Rabelaisian devices is "interesting and significant," Shklovsky admits, but he is bothered that in Bakhtin's account no one seems partic-

---

[41] "The reflection of the self in the empirical other through whom one must pass in order to reach *I-for-myself* . . . The absolute freedom of this I. But this freedom cannot change existence, so to speak, materially (nor can it want to)—it can change only the *sense* of existence (to recognize it, to justify it, and so forth); this is the freedom of the witness and the judge. It is expressed in the *word*. Authenticity and truth inhere not in existence itself, but only in existence that is acknowledged and uttered" ("From Notes Made in 1970–71," in *SpG*, 137–38).

[42] Viktor Shklovskii, "Fransua Rable i kniga M. Bakhtina," in *Tetiva: O neskhodstve skhodnogo* (Moscow: Sovetskii pisatel', 1970), 257–96. Further page references given in text.

ularly insulted or threatened by any of it. "Rabelais's carnival was pointed and offensively parodic . . . it parodies the church, the courts, war, the illusory right of some people to oppress others." Bakhtin, however, presents these matters as benevolent folklore carnival—reversible, timeless, utopian; "he does not point out precisely against whom the parody is directed" (264). Shklovsky's dissatisfaction here is understandable; with his lifelong enthusiasm for parody as the prime mover of political as well as literary consciousness, he could hardly be expected to endorse Bakhtin's philosophically quite dissimilar understanding of carnival laughter. For Bakhtin, true laughter was always ambivalent and two-way, a vehicle of freedom for all sides and thus unencumbered by practical politics, a settling of scores, or the residue of real historical events. Shklovsky's other reservations are more substantive.

The familiar observation that Bakhtin loses sight of Renaissance humanism is again repeated. But true to his Formalist inclinations, Shklovsky emphasizes the strictly literary dimension of this oversight. A key mediator for Rabelais was Aristophanes and ancient Greek comedy (almost unremarked by Bakhtin). And overall, Shklovsky notes, Bakhtin's treatment is so partial to the lower body and its palpable mute functions that it fails to transmit a sense of the "literariness" of the audience, that "the participants in a given carnival spectacle were extraordinarily educated men who presumed that their readers would be ironists and erudites" (259). Such bias against high culture creates a host of problems. Among them, Shklovsky intimates, is the whole "carnivalization" thesis, a problem in the Rabelais study as well as in the inserted chapter on menippean satire in the Dostoevsky book. By what logic can one call the post-Rabelaisian carnival impulse degraded or "reduced"? Dostoevsky, after all, was a reader, a writer, a novelist. But for Bakhtin, who tends to equate all contradictoriness and parodic complexity in novels with the menippean spirit—so much so, in fact, that "the concept of 'menippea' encompasses almost all of literature" (293)—the Russian novelist "is, as it were, explained by carnival" (268). For Shklovsky, such an equation is an offense against literature. Bakhtin should have made the genres of epic and tragedy more central to Rabelais's and Dostoevsky's art; he also should have acknowledged that participation in a carnival spectacle is entirely alien to the private experience of reading a book. Since reading requires such very different skills than life on the public square, no novelist of genius would wish to transpose its effects directly—nor would he consider any reduced ability to do so a special handicap.

The indiscriminate maw that "menippean satire" becomes in Bakhtin's vision of the world prompts Shklovsky to his final criticism. In both the Dostoevsky and Rabelais books, real history (and real literary evolution) is too often dissolved in myth. Taken abstractly, carnival indeed does repeat; but in human experience, "utopia and satire are historical" (270). Not every conflict is a carnival one. Bakhtin's books, however, are marked by a "generalizing of conflicts, [a tendency to understand their dynamics] outside a pattern of conscious shifts in literary forms. . . . Bakhtin fuses repetitions into immobility" (271). He thus unwittingly repeats the mistake of Freudian psychoanalysis—in which an obsessive attention to "the most ancient and conservative instincts" renders "absolutely incomprehensible the historical development of art" (287). Curiously, in his review of Bakhtin on Rabelais, Shklovsky's surviving Formalist sensitivities are both incited and at the same time laid bare. In the 1920s, we recall, Bakhtin and members of his circle wrote and lectured copiously against the impersonal schema, ahistoricism, and mechanistic devices so dear to early Formalist critics. Shklovsky was their most polemical mouthpiece. Now, half a century later, Shklovsky—who had long since mellowed into a traditional, less aggressive, and less imaginative literary historian—sees in Bakhtin, and is inclined to censure, the excesses of his own youth.

Despite this cautious initial reception, Bakhtin's general hypotheses on folk laughter and the carnival grotesque quickly entered mainstream Soviet scholarly discourse. By the early 1980s standard historical surveys—such as Aron Gurevich's *Problems of Medieval Popular Culture*—already referred to Bakhtin as an innovator and a classic.[43] Bakhtin was "a name linked with a decisive revolution in the study of the popular culture of the Middle Ages," a scholar who understood, as his predecessors had not, that a palpable sense of the period had to be built from the bottom up, however unpracticed scholars might be in handling such "unsublimated" material. Bakhtin is still faulted for his one-sided treatment of official culture, which is denied any complex dynamics of its own; he is still called to task for ignoring the fact that carnival inversions must always reinforce—and thus respect—that which they mock; and Gurevich notes that Bakhtin's emphasis on urbanized ("public-square") carnival fails to account for the vast, more shapeless peasant component. But Bakhtin is not Curtius, Gurevich reminds us. He is not an annotator of details but an innovator, a stimulus, a prompt. "After Bakhtin's works appeared, it became difficult to study medieval culture from the old positions—even if we admit, as we must, that Bakhtin sooner fixed our attention on the problem of popular culture in the Middle Ages than solved it" (273).

---

[43] A. Ia. Gurevich, *Problemy srednevekovoi narodnoi kul'tury* (Moscow: Iskusstvo, 1981), esp. 272–73. In a forum marking the fiftieth anniversary of the dissertation defense, Gurevich called carnival a "scholarly myth." *DKKh, no. 4 (96):* 5–45, esp. 14.

Bakhtin himself expressed little interest in the critical turmoil around his two major works of literary scholarship, in print at last. In the occasional personal letter to a friend he would remark on his growing weariness, or on the difficulty of arguing his ideas with the force they deserved; but, as with the scandal over the *kandidat* degree, he habitually shrugged off dissent and dissuaded those who wished to lobby on his behalf. According to Kozhinov, Bakhtin was capable of such equanimity because he did not consider himself a literary scholar at all but a philosopher—and, as Bakhtin himself had quipped, "a philosopher must be no one, because as soon as he becomes someone, he begins to adjust his philosophy to his professional obligation [*dolzhnost'*]."[44] Bakhtin did not live to see the bulk of his intact philosophical writings transcribed, cleared for publication, and entered into public debate. He barely survived to the page-proof stage of his most wide-ranging and influential essays, the fruit of the exile years: his work on the history and theory of the novel.

THE 1975 ANTHOLOGY: ESSAYS ON THE NOVEL

The five-hundred-page *Voprosy literatury i estetiki. Issledovaniia raznykh let* [Problems of literature and aesthetics: Studies from various years] was published posthumously in Moscow in 1975. This omnibus anthology, covering a half-century of literary activity, gathered together several shorter projects and fragments, two important lectures, and two book-length texts: the ramblingly theoretical "Slovo v romane" [Discourse in the novel; or better, "How words work in novels"] and an apparently incomplete history of time-space relations ("chronotopes") in prose genres.[45] As with the earlier two books, the content of this volume was not wholly unfamiliar to the Russian academic community. The longer works, completed in Kustanai and Saransk by the end of the 1930s, had been distributed to friends in manuscript. In the fall of 1940, Bakhtin delivered a paper at the Gorky Institute in Moscow on the prehistory of the novelistic word; in May 1941 he read a paper on "The Novel as a Literary Genre," which appeared in the 1975 anthology under the title

[44] As related by Kozhinov to N. A. Pan'kov, in "'Ot khoda etogo dela . . . ,'" in *DKKh*, nos. 2–3 (93): 29.

[45] M. Bakhtin, *Voprosy literatury i estetiki. Issledovaniia raznykh let* (Moscow: Khudozhestvennaia literatura, 1975). The anthology includes all the programmatic essays translated in *The Dialogic Imagination: Four Essays by M. M. Bakhtin* (Austin: University of Texas Press, 1981), plus others. One important entry included in the 1975 Russian volume (on pages 6–71) but omitted, because of its chronological distance from the other essays, from the English edition is Bakhtin's 1924 essay polemicizing with the Formalists ("The Problem of Content, Material, and Form in Verbal Art"). It appeared in English only in 1990, as an appendix in the Liapunov edition of *Art and Answerability*.

"Epic and Novel." But the fact that these earlier, more theoretical works had their official debut in print only *after* Bakhtin had been resurrected through two controversial "single-name" monographs (first on Dostoevsky's polyphony, then on Rabelais's carnival) tended to mute their reception. Compared to cultures of laughter or words with a loophole, terms such as *chronotope, dialogized heteroglossia, hybrid construction, voice zone, multi-languagedness,* and *materialist aesthetics* sounded dry and abstract. (Unfortunately most of these concepts were subsequently caught up in the cult and moved quickly in critical discourse from unexamined neologism into cliché.) Reviews of the 1975 volume are distinguished by their somewhat sluggish attention to what, over time, would prove to be highly original and productive interpretative categories. Only later would it be suggested that Bakhtin had wrought these terms out of German nineteenth-century aesthetics reinterpreted in the light of the theory of relativity.

The lack of depth or focus in these early reviews was not the fault of shortsighted or unappreciative critics. Quite the opposite; since Bakhtin died the very year the book appeared, and since the new volume contained essays composed over a fifty-year period, reviews were cast in a mixed intonation, obituary and eulogy competing with scholarly assessment. Bakhtin was indeed celebrated. But it was celebration with a leeway and an exempting edge, a sense that this was the work of a highly gifted but eccentric outsider, whose recent passing made serious criticism unseemly and comprehensive overviews still premature. What is more, much in the new volume simply did not fit within the existing conventional frameworks for thinking about novels.

Russian literary professionals had long discussed the novel as a genre biographically, philosophically, thematically, historically. But a rigorous "theory of the novel" had not been put forward with any success. In the opinion of the Formalists who worked on prose, the novel was simply an "accretion," little more than a short narrative grown long by the inserted devices of retardation, digression, and techniques of estrangement. When Bakhtin turned his attention to the novel early in that decade, he found the prior research at his disposal scattered and unsatisfying.[46] He fully

---

[46] One attempt in the second half of the 1920s must have been known to Bakhtin: Boris Griftsov, *Teoriia romana* (Moscow: Gosudarstvennaia Akademiia khudozhestvennykh nauk, 1927). Celebrating the novel as "the sole verbal artwork of modern times," a "half-art" that can absorb any other form "with no theoretical prejudices" (10), Griftsov admits that such tolerance has made the genre inaccessible to theorists. As will Bakhtin, Griftsov finds fault with most of his predecessors. The novel did indeed emerge from rhetoric (such was Gustav Shpet's thesis), but only when rhetoric had ceased to serve ethical goals and had already decayed into casuistry. Its evolution is difficult to demonstrate since one cannot distinguish between imitation and convergence. And, although Formalist studies were then the fashion,

appreciated the reasons. The novel's protean nature, its ability to incorporate self-parody without ceasing to be itself, and its openness to the "feel" of the present (that is, its ability to invite into its own present tense any number of readers from later times and make them feel at home, with something to say and contribute) made the very question of an adequate theory of the novel awkward for a literary tradition.

Equally difficult for the anthology's initial audience was that Bakhtin's treatment of the novel, to be properly grasped, had to be prefaced by an entire philosophy of language. Problems of individual style were revealed to be problems—or potentials—inherent in the way words work, both in novels and in general. As Bakhtin argues in "Discourse in the Novel," even when a novelist strives to achieve a unified and authoritative voice, without distance, refraction, or reservations, the very fact that these words are deployed in this genre means that they are not undisputed, that they must be overtly justified and motivated. And from this imperative comes what the Saransk scholar Oleg Osovsky has called the "anthropocentrism" of Bakhtin's theory of the novel. Novels, like people, are living organisms; they "listen," "speak," and adjust to their environment. If healthy, both novels and people strive toward the same thing: constant differentiation and a chance to defend their individual positions in a world that knows neither absolute authority nor fixed plots. Both evolve toward an ever higher, more articulate consciousness.[47]

Finally, it could be argued that these essays, while possessing the usual soporific and anesthetizing virtues of straight theory, are no less subversive in the realm of literary studies than Dostoevsky had been, stripped by Bakhtin of his plots, or Bakhtin's Rabelais, reduced to joyful obscenities

---

Griftsov argues that novels are not well served by them since little attention is paid to the boundaries *between* prose genres (prose genres were assumed simply to "grow in" to one another). Not surprisingly, Griftsov's "several methodological conclusions" are almost all negative warnings (140–48): do not tie the evolution of the novel to literary schools; do not attempt an exhaustive typology, for there are never enough categories and no list of distinctive features will ever be sufficient. As regards immanent principles, he comes up with only one: "The novel lives by controversy: by quarreling, by struggle, by a contradictoriness of interests, by contrasts between what is desired and what actually exists" (147). Bakhtin will pick up where Griftsov ends. In a Formalist spirit, he will specify a "dominant for the novel," the primary feature defining its "literariness": this very motif of contradiction and struggle. But he will distance this struggle from any crude identification with real-life battlefields or social class. He will relocate it within the novel's own professional medium: the contradictory, multi-voiced utterance. And language, thus understood, becomes a carrier not of plot, economic pressures, or formal literary devices, but of consciousness itself, intended to benefit first and foremost the densely populated, *created* world of the novel and not the creators and consumers of that world (authors, readers, analysts).

[47] See O. E. Osovskii, *Chelovek. Slovo. Roman.*, ch. 4, "Teoriia romana Bakhtina i nekotorye problemy izucheniia romannogo zhanra," 83–84.

and indecencies on the carnival square. The first reviewers of the 1975 anthology might have been hesitant and disoriented for this reason, too. Bakhtin's earlier books had offered rebelliously unconventional readings of great (and unconventional) rebel-novelists; this new volume of essays took on placid, canonized authorities who had long permeated Soviet culture and provided its basic terms of reference. Among those challenged was Hegel, with his doctrine that the novel was a degradation, a prosaicization, and a falling off of poetry and epic; Bakhtin was being quite heretical, therefore, when he argued that human personality in the novel is *more* triumphant and heroic (although differently so) than in the loftier genres. Closer to home, Bakhtin also took on his shadow rival in Moscow, the dean of Marxist critics Georgy Lukacs. Several decades earlier Lukacs had preached (in Hegel's spirit) that the epic was the product of an integrated world and the novel the genre of "transcendental homelessness," fragmented, inward-looking, pessimistic. Seeking contacts in the capital after his term of exile was over, Bakhtin made a bid to displace this august predecessor in the realm of novelistic theory by reversing the ethical charge on Lukacs's categories. (For Bakhtin, of course, the novel was *happily* fragmented; only multiplicity and open-ended surplus could guarantee a vigorous and socially informed whole that was flexible, outward-looking and optimistic.) But the largest authority Bakhtin challenged, one could argue, was the ancient founder and canonizer of all poetic forms. As Vladimir Turbin recalls:

> Bakhtin spoke and wrote very often about the rare opportunity that had fallen to the lot of our generations: to witness how the novel is created, a genre for which he predicted a fertile future. And this prognosis would have to be understood not "according to Aristotle," but . . . according to Bakhtin. . . . From the novel's point of view, the epic is monotonous, bombastic in an unlifelike way; from the epic's point of view, the novelistic world is unorganized, devoid of order. . . . [Bakhtin's] achievement, most probably, is not that he had the courage—in addition to all the other calamities he was called upon to endure—to contradict the methodology of a Dymshits. Dymshits is not at issue here; the issue here is Aristotle.[48]

The task Bakhtin assumed, then, was to think about literary genre in a way that would specifically benefit the novel—that is, define genre in terms of character rather than plot, and in a *non-normative* way. Turbin remembers how Bakhtin, "in the foggy twilights of Saransk," would repeat "as something simple and long since resolved" that "we think not in

---

[48] V. N. Turbin, "Karnaval: Religiia, politika, teosofiia," in *B sb I 90*, 6–29, esp. 18. Of all Bakhtin's students, Turbin has made most central to his own work the idea that the world is arranged and perceived entirely through genres.

words, but in genres."[49] The implications of this statement are far-ranging. Words are separate building blocks, versatile and polysemantic, marked by the intonation of the individual who utters them. A genre is an orientation or "field," whose parameters are more or less fixed by an interpretive community that pulls words into its orbit and dictates how, in that context, they are to mean. By linking genre with inner mentation, Turbin suggests an analogy. Just as each "I" instinctively relates to its own thinking processes—and to its own individuality—as to a dynamic process that potentially can produce something unclassifiably new (that is, something "novel") and yet still recognizably "its own," so each "I" should approach a given genre as if it were still alive, as if it were an energy rather than a form. Identity is achieved not by the end product, by the "material" or the repeatable rules that can be extracted from the form, but by *how* material is processed (how I create) and what I do with your response to me. With this "responsive" rather than referential definition of genre in place—a definition maximally distant from Aristotelian poetics and its hierarchy of plots, formal features, and effects—suddenly all the drawbacks of the novel become its singular advantage. Each of the essays in the 1975 volume contributes to this character-centered, process-oriented, nonnormative task. It is hardly surprising that Bakhtin's early reviewers could not make immediate sense of it. To sample the range of critical reactions to the anthology, we will consider three items: the most famous eulogy-obituary to be written on the occasion of this book (and of Bakhtin's death); one counter-eulogy in response to it; and then a mainstream 1970s version of the professional review.

"The Personality and Talent of a Scholar," by the eminent classicist and philosopher Sergei Averintsev, appeared in 1976.[50] It struck a reverent, exceptionalist tone that hitherto had been rarely heard outside Bakhtin's own circle. As a specialist in ancient literature and biography, Averintsev inevitably has a problem (as have many professionally trained classicists in Russia and abroad) with some of Bakhtin's more sweeping formulations. He is bothered, for example, by the huge role Bakhtin assigns to carnivalization in Roman culture—a culture that in Averintsev's opinion is "relatively naive" in comparison with the "polyvalent irony, clever taunting, extremely subtle modulations and transitions between laughter and seriousness" characteristic of the ancient Greeks (61). (A centennial memoir by one of Bakhtin's former students, an undergraduate at Mordovia State Teacher's College in the late 1940s, reverses the

---

[49] "Vmesto vvedeniia," in V. N. Turbin, *Nezadolgo do Vodoleia (sbornik statei)* (Moscow: Radiks, 1994), 31.

[50] S. Averintsev, "Lichnost' i talant uchenogo," in *Literaturnoe obozrenie*, no. 10 (October 1976): 58–61. Further page references given in text.

impression Averintsev received from the published essays: the memoirist recalls that Mikhail Mikhailovich devoted "more than half the semester to Homer and only three or four lectures to Roman literature," which he considered "derivative and less important.")[51] Averintsev has no intention of pursuing these small matters of balance or focus. In the terms of chapter 1, he prefers to remember Bakhtin more as a lyricist than a physicist, and he measures him largely by "lyrical" criteria. Bakhtin, Averintsev writes, "is a wisdom lover [*liubomudr*] among the specialists" (59). Scholarship is wary of this status, for precisely the reasons Turbin gives: it is easier to think responsibly and professionally about normative features than about potentials. Bakhtin resists that greatest of all hazards in the humanities: stripping down reality into "planes" or "projections" that are then allowed to define our professional lives. Each scholar chooses a manageable and methodologically sound strip (or "projection") of reality with which to work. It then requires, Averintsev confides,

> a huge spiritual effort to empathize with the ontological priority of reality over that projection. The net of coordinates, laid down solely in order to see the thing properly, takes on flesh, looms up harshly and precisely before the mind's eye, impressing the imagination with its intellectual rigor, and meanwhile the thing itself is forced to back off, retreat to the background, as if ashamed of its own imprecision, incorrectness, inappropriately enigmatic aspects. And then, one after the other, more or less professional works appear, marked by a scholastic correctness, at times even intellectual energy, and there is everything in them except the feeling that the historical event being examined actually took place in the world of human beings . . . [Before us and our students there is always] the threat of losing the object, the threat of a dehumanized humanities, humanities without a human being—which is a rather wretched joke.

In place of those dry inventions of the conventional academy, Averintsev writes, Bakhtin offers "philosophical anthropology," the "ability to see the literary word as a human word" (60). Bakhtin's dominant was freedom but understood in a peculiar sense: the freedom of any thing to exit from its own prior identity. Far from presuming a fragmented, alien-

---

[51] Bakhtin "constructed his course on ancient literature in a very original way, different from Tronskii's textbook that we were using," the memoirist recalled. "The midpoint of the semester approached, but Mikhail Mikhailovich was still reading Homer; it was already almost the end of the year and we were still hearing about Greek literature. In the entire course, only three or four lectures were devoted to Roman literature. Mikhail Mikhailovich emphasized that Roman literature was secondary, and he was concentrating his attention on the most important—and about the rest, we could find out for ourselves from the textbooks." See Yu. D. Ryskin (b. 1924, by profession a literary scholar and bibliographer), "Moi vospominaniia o M. M. Bakhtine," in *MMB v zerk 95*, 111–13, esp. 111–12.

ated, or incoherent universe, this exiting act positively requires the spa-
tiousness of a whole; it cannot be confined to a predetermined "strip" or
projection. And since such an exit will always increase individual responsibility rather than diminish it, freedom of this sort has nothing in common with license or anarchy. It cannot, however, be contained in the
accepted institutionalized ways. Thus must Bakhtin resist the formal
method, one-way satire, and Aristotelian frameworks—all of which are
demonstrably most at home with categories of *imposed* identity: literary
devices rather than consciousness, ridicule rather than reciprocal laughter,
plot rather than character. As organizing principles, those modes of
thought are helpless before entities that can redefine themselves from
within.

But Averintsev, himself a meticulous philologist, must sooner or later
confront the nature of Bakhtin's approach to the scholar's task. His angle
here resembles Gurevich's view of Bakhtinian carnival: it is not an answer
for all time, and not every reader's preferred Rabelais, but as a stimulus it
is unparalleled. "Bakhtin's thought sought broad heuristic perspectives,"
Averintsev concludes, "but not 'scientific or scholarly results' in the usual
sense" (61):

> What was said by him was said not so that the reader trustingly accept his
> theses as "the final word of scholarship" or—vice versa—set about disputing
> and refuting them, but so that the very structure of the reader's mind, in the
> process of reading, somehow become different. Agree or don't agree, that's
> not at issue here: there are books after which it is simply impossible to work
> in the old ways (even though one cannot extract from them any ready for-
> mula for working in a new way). There is no need to take Bakhtin at his
> every word, no reason to understand him too literally; his own weakest mo-
> ments come when he is too inclined to take himself literally . . . The fact is,
> in Bakhtin's scholarly-philosophical prose the word is also, in its own way,
> not equal to itself. What, then, can one "borrow" from Bakhtin? One should
> and must learn his freedom. Let each of us learn from it to the extent of our
> powers.

Averintsev's review—part eulogy, part apologia, part exhortation—was
followed in the same issue by a rejoinder, bluntly entitled "The Real
Content of the Search," from the veteran establishment Dostoevsky
scholar Georgii Fridlender.[52] An editorial note at the end of the cluster
assures the reader that neither entry pretends to "an exhaustive assessment of the anthology [under review], and even less of Bakhtin's entire
output as a scholar"; it then adds, somewhat defensively, that Frid-

---

[52] G. Fridlender, "Real'noe soderzhanie poiska," *Literaturnoe obozrenie*, no. 10 (October
1976): 61–64.

lender's "methodologically more disciplined article" serves "as a supplement and corrective" to some of Averintsev's more "agitated" commentary (64). Such is indeed the case. Fridlender objects to the condescension and intellectual disrespect implicit in eulogies of the sort Averintsev provides. Bakhtin, after all, had considered himself a scholar "in the usual sense"—and would have wanted to be judged on the "*istinnost'*" [truthfulness] of his ideas, not only on their ability to provoke and destabilize. (Again, in the familiar terms of this study, Bakhtin's constructs might not be of sufficient rigor to please the "physicists," but they were certainly not offered as poetry.) "Does not Averintsev, in his review, speak more about Bakhtin himself than about the content of the book?" Fridlender asks (61). To do so is a mistake, for although Bakhtin's ideas have become faddish, excerpted, and applied out of context, the memory of the deceased is not served by blurring them further.

Fridlender then indicates what he believes to be the salient scholarly contributions of this new volume of essays. Disappointingly, they turn out to be—if not wholly politically correct—then at least well within the approved parameters of Brezhnev-era literary activity. The ever cautious Fridlender first welcomes Bakhtin's criticism of the Formalist school and its hedonistic, materialist aesthetics. He then marshals evidence to show that Bakhtin passed through a "serious Marxist school" (his proof: that Bakhtin, in his work on Dostoevsky, approached the novel both as a structure and as a humanized system—as if Marxism had a monopoly on those qualities); eventually Bakhtin arrived at a sociologically informed poetics that rejected both Symbolism and Idealism. His treatment of the "alien word" is both more flexible than the Formalist device and more subtle than the class-bound, crude "pseudo-sociologism" of (the officially purged and discredited) Pereverzev. Fridlender regrets that the anthology did not include Bakhtin's prefaces to two volumes of the *Collected Works of Tolstoy* (curious but mediocre commissioned pieces, written in a Marxist vein, on the dramas and the late novel *Resurrection*, which Bakhtin himself later disavowed), and predictably he finds the short piece included there on Rabelais and Gogol (often criticized because it was so counter to the canonized Soviet view) not persuasive. Overall, Fridlender considers the book of essays "highly significant for the struggle against Formalism and against the anti-historicism of bourgeois literary studies" (64).

A non-Russian reader of Fridlender's review would scarcely guess that the omnibus anthology *Problems of Literature and Aesthetics* contained any of the essays made famous in its later, somewhat abridged English-language version, which appeared under the far catchier title *The Dialogic Imagination*. None of the pathbreaking theses are summarized; no important terms are explicated. If Averintsev was wholly taken up with apologetic eulogy for Bakhtin's "outsideness" to philology as usually practiced, then Fridlender is at pains to integrate Bakhtin as quickly as possible into the Soviet literary establishment, to re-create him as an insider to its tradition—with its litany of government-issue friends and enemies. A year after this exchange, a lengthier review by Dmitri Zatonsky in *Voprosy literatury* (1977) finally surveyed Bakhtin's accomplishment on its own terms.[53]

Zatonsky neither apologizes for his subject nor polishes up his image. But he does intimate that the outsider/insider distinction, so dependent on the vagaries of politically driven Soviet norms for professionalism, is not a particularly fruitful one. More important by far, Zatonsky suggests, is to grasp Bakhtin's own integrity and coherence as a thinker, both over time and in his own time—which, with this new anthology of essays early and late, has at last become possible. Taken together with the previously published studies of Dostoevsky and Rabelais, the new volume suggests the creative trajectory of Bakhtin's life.

For Zatonsky, most remarkable about the anthology is its "undatedness" and intellectual "wholeness." Most of the essays are forty years old, he notes; very little was changed in preparation for publication. Yet we do not sense these texts as "old" or outdated; they are innerly consistent to an astonishing degree, supplementing one another and coalescing into a recognizable voice. Bakhtin's two monographs, by now more than a decade old, had been read by their initial reviewers as interpretations of those two novelists. Naturally, complaints had abounded that there was more complexity and nuance to Dostoevsky and Rabelais than could be registered through the features Bakhtin often obsessively highlighted. As Zatonsky remarks, there is a "certain one-sidedness" in Bakhtin, "connected each time with the bull's-eye aim he takes at the object he is investigating, his almost deaf and blind concentratedness on it"; he is not afraid to repeat a point, "varying it only slightly, shifting his major propositions just a tiny bit to one side or the other, as if hammering them in place with nails" (258). Such a methodology has its advantages. "The tenseness, intensity, dynamism of the search guarantees a forced entry into the heart of the phenomenon"—even though one must constantly introduce correctives and point out arbitrary assumptions in the method, since "its creator did not bother to do this" (258–59).

The theoretical essays at last make it clear that Bakhtin was not primarily an explicator of individual literary worlds. He was a genre theorist who made use of individual writers to explicate a larger thought. And that thought, Zatonsky suggests, is itself powerfully centripetal and sys-

[53] D. Zatonskii, "Ob estetike, poetike, literature," *Voprosy literatury*, no. 4 (1977): 254–64. Further page references given in text.

tematic. Now that we have a clear exposition of Bakhtin's guiding ideas, we can see that the "books on Dostoevsky and Rabelais, of course, developed and affirmed the same Bakhtinian ideas" (256). We had assumed that those volumes were about *The Brothers Karamazov* or *Gargantua and Pantagruel.* "But that's not what they were for Bakhtin. For him, Dostoevsky and Rabelais were in the first instance not creative individualities but models, intersections of the rule-bound regularities and laws of genre. To be sure, this had been no absolute secret earlier. But a book like *Problems of Literature and Aesthetics* turns the hunch into a certainty" (257). Much in the anthology is fragmented, unfinished, poorly worked out; not everyone is up to handling it [*ne kazhdomu po plechu*]. "But it is Bakhtin at his most typical."

Zatonsky then summarizes the genre laws Bakhtin claims to have uncovered, emphasizing the most programmatic of the essays, "Epic and Novel." Impressed with the three lapidary genre criteria for the novel that Bakhtin lays out (its special use of time, space, and utterance), he praises the "originality of thought and the abundance of new, unexpected foreshortenings" that permit Bakhtin to view frequently described objects in a unique way. But several aspects of Bakhtin's thesis and exposition trouble Zatonsky. The chronotope essay is cripplingly open-ended. Bakhtin's repeated insistence that novels can be explained totally by the workings of the dialogic word is simply Formalist stubbornness, his own prosy equivalent of their partiality to mechanistic or linguistic solutions. And in the realm of historical poetics, Bakhtin's curious tendency to "operate on a scale of centuries, not to say millenia"—and then to give more credence to factors buried deep within ancient traditions than to the immediate historical period during which a novel was written—can only raise suspicions (263).

"In some things Bakhtin erred, in places he was incorrect," Zatonsky concludes, "but he was a discoverer." On such slender identifying credentials, this reviewer—unlike the previous two—finds an appropriate place for Bakhtin in the Russian tradition, locating him both inside and alongside it. Bakhtin belongs with the unclassifiable polymaths Veselovsky, Zhirmunsky, Likhachev, all three boundary-crossers in literature who were drawn to philosophy. Zatonsky is a wholly conciliatory critic. In the end, he too prefers to generalize on the overall value of innovation in the humanities rather than examine, if only in a few select details, the benefits and costs of Bakhtin's framework for literary scholarship. And thus, although the fad for Bakhtin spread wildly in the 1980s, the immediate reception of these Russian essays could not match the later, rapid, almost unconsidered bestsellerdom of *The Dialogic Imagination* in English-speaking countries.

Why this was so is a matter of our respective academies. In Russia

Bakhtin had a history: he was a dissident, a non-cooperator, an outsider who had been largely ignored by the Soviet literary establishment (on balance a somber, unspeculative body) since the early days of the regime. In the West Bakhtin was a name. By the 1970s the triumph of Structuralism—and, truth be told, a more modest and increasingly eccentric factual base among students of literary history—had created a receptivity to the large scheme, the grandiose binary, the provocative, easily paraphrasable statement from an intellectual guru. Such indeed were the strengths and intonations of Bakhtin's middle-period essays, as well as of his *Rabelais*. Bakhtin is accessible. He is so suggestive and in places so imprecise that he gives tertiary critics—you and me—a great deal to do in our own voice, filling in, refashioning, talking back. As we shall see repeatedly in part 2 of this study, it is just this open invitation to the impetuous, underprepared reader that the anti-Bakhtinians most resent. In the opinion of the scholar who has become their unacknowledged dean, the eminent poetician and polymath Mikhail Gasparov, what Bakhtin most loved was to "expropriate others' words." Gasparov made this remark in a tiny but trenchant essay from 1979, which launched the counter-cult. Expropriation is a double-edged move, Gasparov argued: while it could further one's freedom and widen one's options, it could fatally compromise the scholar's task. Above all, Bakhtin believed in "an active attitude toward the inheritance. Things are valuable not in themselves, but for the use to which they have been put and, more important, to which they can be put. . . . The literary work is not made from words, but from reactions to words. But whose reactions? . . . Bakhtin is the mutiny of the self-asserting reader against the pieties imposed on him."[54] Gasparov's anxieties are those of the professional guild. The Russian academy, Germanic in its philological traditions, its best representatives superbly trained, and staffed largely by cautious, obedient ideologues, has resisted endorsing excessively "readerly" rights. Even when it was willing to overlook Bakhtin's manifest indifference to political sloganeering, it insisted on a proper deference to documentation, scholarly precedent, and textual detail.

Here Bakhtin is indeed vulnerable. In his own way he was didactic, even pedantic. His generosity in gifting his ideas to others was legendary. But he did not attend particularly to the ownership of ideas, nor did he worry that his own strong critic's voice, intruding into a text, might interrupt or unbalance it. Immensely well read himself, he was not always

---

[54] M. L. Gasparov, "M. M. Bakhtin in Russian Culture of the Twentieth Century" [originally appeared in Lotman, Vyach. Ivanov et al., eds., *Vtorichnye modeliruiushchie sistemy* (Tartu, 1979), translated and with notes by Ann Shukman, *Studies in Twentieth Century Literature* 9, no. 1 (Fall 1984): 169–76]. It should be noted that Shukman's commentary, inexplicably, interprets this manifestly anti-Bakhtin document as a "passionate defence of the libertarian Bakhtin" and a "rescue operation."

wholly precise. His implied reader is that supremely knowledgeable, interested interlocutor, neither above nor below the critic but his potential equal, who feels no need to test a new proposition by the old rules nor any pressure to take it on faith—a reader who is secure enough simply to entertain a new idea and respond to it. As we noted at the beginning of this study, Bakhtin's 1924 essay on "The Problem of Content, Material, and Form," published for the first time in *Voprosy literatury i estetiki*, opens on a remarkably self-confident note for an apprentice scholar: "We have freed our study from the superfluous ballast of citations and references," Bakhtin announces; "for they lack any direct methodological significance in studies of a nonhistorical nature, while in a compressed work of a systematic nature they are entirely superfluous. For the qualified reader, they are unnecessary, and for the unqualified, useless."[55]

This aristocratic tone runs like a shimmering thread through the whole of Bakhtin's career. Recall again, for example, Bakhtin's comment to Duvakin on his friend Maria Yudina, who "could not be fit into the framework of any profession" for she was "absolutely not official . . . like me, by the way." Or recall Bakhtin's own fastidious reluctance ever to refer to his study on Rabelais as a dissertation and his assumption, during his defense, that disagreement with his thesis was because he had failed to present his case or because "innovators are rarely understood"—not because he might be wrong. Bakhtin did not judge others harshly, this is true. But by the same token he apparently felt little obligation to submit himself to the judgment of others, especially corporate or "official" others—nor did he feel he had much to gain or lose by their approbation. Such "Old World" stubbornness was much remarked on during the Saransk teaching years, where (if we are to believe the eyewitnesses) Bakhtin's indifference to party guidelines, his irritation at rote pedagogy, and his contemptuous dismissal of required literary topics in the classroom stupefied and thrilled his students.[56] It is only natural that the official literary profession moved slowly in rehabilitating this wayward son.

Let the last word on the reception of this anthology belong, then, to Bakhtin himself—appropriately, perhaps, in his role as appreciative critic of another scholar's work. By the early 1960s Bakhtin's own pathbreaking essays on the novel had lain twenty years without hope of publication; there would be another fifteen years to wait. Neither the Dostoevsky

---

[55] "The Problem of Content, Material, and Form in Verbal Art," in Bakhtin, *A&A*, 257.

[56] For material—not necessarily objective—on Bakhtin's teaching practice, both at the high school and then at the college level, from personal Saransk archives, see Konkin and Konkina, *Mikhail Bakhtin*, chs. 6, 7. For Bakhtin as literature teacher in a Kimry high school, 1941–44 (where he shocked the students by refusing to read Mayakovsky, even though that official poet was in the obligatory "program"), see 229–30; for memoirs by students at Mordovia State Teacher's College and later University, see 259–60, 264–66.

nor the Rabelais study had yet been resurrected. Fully anticipating trouble for his unconventional approach, Bakhtin (who disliked letters and rarely revealed himself in them) provided a summary of his own long-maturing ideas about the novel in an unexpected place: a personal letter to Vadim Kozhinov, dated April 1961, in response to having read the latter's just completed manuscript, "The Rise of the Novel."[57] This "unofficial" or casual review, from the still unpublished master to his soon-to-be-published disciple on nothing other than the passion of the master's life, is a poignant one.

Bakhtin is fulsome in his praise of his junior colleague. He declares Kozhinov's book (which duly appeared in 1963) to be almost epic—not novelistic—in its wholeness, "fashioned from one piece," without any "dead spots" or "material irrelevant to the thought or unnecessary for the thought," a "rare combination of strict scholarly thinking and a genuine understanding of art and artistic taste." But Bakhtin had several minor reservations, most of them related to the role of the "serious-comic genres" and to the actual historical starting place of novelistic consciousness. Kozhinov had elected to begin his survey in the second half of the sixteenth century; Bakhtin would move much further back. He recommends this backward shift because it is not so much the novel itself—almost unidentifiable as a formal category—as it is a "feeling" for the novel's use of language that a scholar must trace. And when language is the object, Bakhtin writes, such a feeling [*oshchushchenie*, the palpable texture of a thing] takes not mere generations but whole geological units of time to coalesce and become coherent. "At the base of novelistic language," Bakhtin writes in his letter (177–78):

there lies an absolutely new *feeling for the word* as artistic material, a new *position* for this word in relation to the depicted object, to the author himself, and to the reader. A novel depicts not only the human being and his life, but the *fundamentally speaking* human being and a *multi-languaged*, speaking life. The word here is not only the *means* of depiction but at the same time the *object* of depiction. . . . Such fundamental changes in the artistic function of the word, or so it seems to me, were prepared for throughout almost the entire Middle Ages, under conditions that favored an intense and complex play among the forces of language, in the most varied genres—artistic, quasi-artistic, not artistic at all—all of which prepared the language of the novel. Both of my comments, as I already said, do not touch the essence of your remarkable book. . . . And now you must, with full confidence in the seriousness, significance, and necessity of your book, set about

[57] "Iz pisem M. M. Bakhtina" [Bakhtin's letters to V. V. Kozhinov, 1960–1965], ed. V. V. Fyodorov, in *Moskva* (November–December 1992): 175–82, esp. 177–78.

insuring its publication in its primordial [i.e., uncensored and unedited] form.

The Rise of the Novel was published as planned. But Kozhinov was so persuaded by Bakhtin's generous-spirited "correctives" to his monograph that he later rejected all requests by his own publisher to reissue it. To-gether with Sergei Bocharov, Kozhinov continued his dogged, and often seemingly hopeless, efforts on behalf of Bakhtin's long-forgotten work—efforts which, in 1963, were on the brink of their first success. By 1975, the year of his death, Bakhtin himself had become a major player among the "intense and complex forces of language" of his own increasingly multi-languaged age.

POSTHUMOUS: THE FIRST MANUSCRIPTS AND FINAL ESSAYS

The posthumous appearance, in 1979 and 1986, of Bakhtin's earliest philosophical writings and latest ruminations on the humanities[58] takes us beyond the framework of the present chapter—back, in fact, to the pre-ceding chapter that covers the boom to the Jubilee. But several aspects of the final publishing phase are worth brief attention in light of this recep-tion history. Let us recall the patterns. From the early Bolshevik screeds to the Brezhnev-era reviews, Soviet critics overall were less sympathetic and more suspicious of Bakhtin's "creative dismissal" of previous can-onized scholarship than were Western critics in response to any of the Bakhtin best-sellers. Soviet reviewers were also quicker to see Bakhtin as a thinker who used literature to illustrate his philosophical principles—viewed by them variously as criminal, curious, enlightening, and liberat-ing—rather than as a literary professional who drew on philosophy to illuminate a literary author or text. And lastly, the Russian reviews (even the most positive) were highly sensitive to the harmful effects of a cult,

---

[58] There were two major publications in Russian, which in English translation were dis-tributed into three volumes (all published by University of Texas Press). The first anthology is M. M. Bakhtin, *Estetika slovesnogo tvorchestva* (Moscow: Iskusstvo, 1979), containing "Art and Answerability," "Author and Hero in Aesthetic Activity," "The Novel of Educa-tion and Its Significance in the History of Realism" [the surviving fragment], "The Problem of Speech Genres," "The Problem of the Text in Linguistics, Philology, and other Human Sciences," "Toward a Methodology of the Human Sciences," jottings from 1970–71, and the 1970 open letter to *Novy Mir*. The latter half of the contents of this volume (1940s–1970s) was translated by Vern W. McGee in *Speech Genres and Other Late Essays* (1986); the material from the 1920s was translated by Vadim Liapunov in *Art and Answerability: Early Philosophical Essays by M. M. Bakhtin* (1990). A second Russian installment of prior philosophical writings was published in 1986 as M. M. Bakhtin, "K filosofii postupka," in *Filosofiia i sotsiologiia nauki i tekhniki: Ezhegodnik 1984–85* (Moscow: Nauka, 1986), 80–160. This text was translated and expertly annotated as a separate volume by Vadim Lia-punov entitled *Toward a Philosophy of the Act* (1993).

where faddish citation or superficial application would replace a responsible examination of Bakhtin's terms and method. Indeed, within literary studies and outside it, Soviet experience offered sobering lessons on that score. By the 1980s, with the appearance of Bakhtin's dense and difficult early writings on post-Kantian ethics, the necessary theoretical ground had been laid. Russian sociologists, aestheticians, cultural anthropologists, and moral philosophers began to read Bakhtin with increasing seriousness. As Vitaly Makhlin correctly summed up this final phase: "Bakhtin's *Aesthetics of Verbal Creativity* [the 1979 volume, where the bulk of the early work was first published], in the form in which it has come down to the reader, [came to be seen as] the 'source and secret' of his entire system."[59]

To close this chapter we shall sample only one review, by Vladimir Novikov, that appeared in the literary magazine *Novy Mir* in 1981.[60] Ten years earlier, Bakhtin had been asked by the editorial board of this same controversial, open-minded journal to comment on the future of literary studies. Now, posthumously, his earliest and latest writings (along with some student notes taken during Bakhtin's lectures on literature in the 1920s) were themselves being surveyed as foundational for a theory of the humanities.

Novikov's review, entitled "The Word and Glory" [in Russian, *Slovo i slava*] begins where Bakhtin himself began, with the problem of the word as a phenomenon of culture. Are words a "medium of information"? A "means for selecting and juxtaposing values"? Phatic material we utter back to assure others of our presence? The word is all those things; when the tools and timing are favorable, words serve to stitch an individual voice into a culture. But as regards fame, Novikov notes that it did not serve Bakhtin during his own lifetime. Rather, Bakhtin's fame served his readers. The works on Dostoevsky and Rabelais, forgotten or shamefully delayed, reappeared precisely when Soviet readers were ready for them, the 1960s: Stalinism was disintegrating, censorship was loosening its moronic grip, and literary scholarship was deeply needful of liberated thinking. "Bakhtin's fame helped to break down barriers that had separated literary scholarship from literature on the one hand, and from the reader on the other" (257).

Then a trivializing counter-trend developed, which Novikov laments. "Insane citation-itis" and the extraction of truisms became the rule: the irresponsible reader was born. "Bakhtin's name traveled far beyond the bounds of professional literary circles. . . . A name that ought to have resounded as the decisive antithesis of all frivolity and vulgarity was en-

---

[59] V. Makhlin, "Bakhtin i problemy 'novoi nauki,'" in *Voprosy literatury*, no. 8 (1987): 213–21, esp. 213.

[60] Vl. Novikov, "Slovo i slava," *Novyi mir*, no. 4 (April 1981): 256–60.

tered as a consumer item into every 'gentleman's toilette': a leather jacket, a ticket to the Taganka Theater, a few citations from Bakhtin . . . The time has come to consider our spiritual ecology." Oddly, considering that Bakhtin had become so famous, very little had been written on him beyond the scholarly preface or book review. Here is a man whose entire life had been devoted to investigating consciousness and the creating personality—and yet his own personal style and approach to the word remained curiously unexplored.

The most valuable contribution of Bakhtin's just published manuscripts will come in precisely this realm, Novikov suggests. Although the essays—unprepared for print and thus untouched by the censor's pencil or editorial prejudice—are cast in a formidable "scientific-philosophical style," overflowing with "cumbersome syntactical constructions and ramifying, abstractly logical computations," the overall effect of Bakhtin's critical prose is to create an "emotional, richly multivalent *image of creativity*" (258). By concentrating thus on the process of creation, "Bakhtin provides his own solution to the riddle and secret of inspiration: the artist creates a new *other* consciousness and attempts to grasp it fully, while not dissolving in it."

Novikov does not deny that this model has shortcomings. "Bakhtin taught us to believe in the artist we were studying, to perceive every literary work as a unique unrepeatable event—in general, to relate to a creation of art as if it were a human being. But this human being lived in a highly specific Bakhtinian world" (259). Despite Bakhtin's much-vaunted openness and tolerance, then, "the radiant lucidity of his aesthetic glance is harnessed to the highly individual structure of his own scholarly world. For Bakhtin, there were no gradations or degrees of evaluation. Artistic systems that were innerly alien to him ended up, as it were, in an outsiderly position vis-à-vis his own system. They simply cannot be described adequately by Bakhtin's devices. Such, for example, happened with Leo Tolstoy. . . . If we are better to understand and appreciate [Bakhtin's] world, we must clarify what is not worth our while seeking in it." Novikov closes on the observation that scholars from various fields—cultural history, anthropology, Dostoevsky studies—had already begun to quarrel with Bakhtin and that this is a good thing, much better than thoughtless fame or citation-itis. It would guarantee the return of responsible readers.

The subsequent fifteen years of that polemic, which has constructed whole subsidiary disciplines out of Bakhtin's strong ideas and probed unforgivingly into the weak, provides the subject matter for part 2 of this study. "An aesthetic idea is alive only as long as one can argue with it," Novikov remarks at the end of his review. At the time, no one could have predicted for that truism its actual tempestuous future.

Part II

LITERATURE FADES, PHILOSOPHY MOVES TO THE FORE (REWORKING THREE PROBLEMATIC AREAS)

DESPITE the political conformity and Aesopian language mandated by Communist conditions, the reception of Bakhtin by Soviet critics was diverse, learned, and thoughtful. Has the collapse of state censorship made the reclamation of Bakhtin easier or has it served to distance his thought even further from the tension-filled relations that gave rise to it? The question is complex. Certain Soviet-era constraints—the necessity to lie, the benumbing quota of obligatory references to party-approved authorities, omnipresent toadyism and intimidation, getting killed for what one wrote—were wholly bad. Other aspects were humiliating in many instances but could also be reassuring, when they contributed to a sense of intellectual continuity or spiritual community (for many, these bonds became all the more sustaining as the random repressions and deprivations of everyday life increased). The Russian critic's sense of membership in a well-subsidized literary profession devoted to conservative textology on a stable literary canon was for many intellectuals their genuine "homeland," and they enjoyed a general social consensus about the elevated status of literature and the word. As state subsidies for the humanities disappeared in the 1990s and the lowest cultural common denominators swarmed in from the West, certain Soviet-era attitudes toward scholarship appeared to many, in retrospect, to have been partial blessings.

Bakhtin's adult life passed entirely in the Soviet period, and he wrote constantly throughout its very worst years. By temperament, conviction, vagaries of health, and accidents of geography, he remained unofficial and on the "outside." But a recurring theme of the present study is that Bakhtin was to a certain extent an outsider by choice and would prefer to be remembered as a survivor rather than a victim. Although periods of bitterness and despair surely occurred, by all indications he was unwilling to view himself as compromised beyond recognition or driven into a realm where personal responsibility no longer applied. Protective coloration was of course essential. As we have seen, Bakhtin understood exactly how to negotiate the routine obeisances to Stalin required of any academic, and especially one in his position of pedagogue to future teachers of the young. But he was gentle with those forced to use words in ways beyond their control. As he wrote at the end of the 1950s in "The Problem of the Text," in a passage that has made some of his readers uneasy, worse always than an untruth is a failure to respond. "Even a word that is known to be false is not absolutely false," Bakhtin wrote. "It always presupposes an instance that will understand and justify it, even if in the form: 'anyone in my position would have lied too.'"[1] For all the risk of such position-based ethics, however, the most present danger in post-Soviet reclamations of Bakhtin is not to be found here.

A more serious temptation is the easy reflex of flipping the sign. The fact that Marxism is now a discredited political and economic doctrine cannot serve as an argument for or against Bakhtin's interest in that intellectual movement. Because the Bolsheviks did not believe in God and because they have now been exposed as liars and crooks is not in itself proof for the existence of God—nor does the fact that Bakhtin intensely disliked the atheism of the Revolution transform him into a mainstream "Christian believer," or his work into a theology in code. Because borders are now more open and ideas and goods flow across them more freely does not mean that Bakhtin was against the constraints, delimitations, or restrictions that a border imposes. Quite the contrary, as we shall suggest: It is Bakhtin's distinctively wise understanding of limits that prevents him from becoming a fully reliable "theoretician" and thus separates him from much Western postmodernist thinking. Although his categories often fall out into comfortable dyads (monologism/dialogism, carnival life/official life), in the details Bakhtin was not a particularly binary thinker. And thus signs—and even more so the flipped sign—have proved inadequate to the overall patterns of his thought.

Part 2 of this study examines the fate of three concepts in Bakhtin's world where controversy has been so active, interesting, and evenly balanced pro and contra that this danger of merely "inverting the sign" is greatly diminished. In their original exposition, these ideas arose in connection with artistic matters: Dostoevsky's polyphony, the dialogism and heteroglossia of the novel, Rabelais's carnival, and the obligatory "outsideness" of all ethical and aesthetic positions. But—as was chronicled in part 1—under the impact of the early manuscripts, the posthumously published late essays, and Bakhtin's own admissions soon before his death, the ground for these "literary" judgments broadened as Bakhtin's image changed and deepened.

---

[1] "The Problem of the Text in Linguistics, Philology, and the Human Sciences: An Experiment in Philosophical Analysis," in *SpG*, 127.

"There exists a widespread notion," wrote two Bakhtin scholars at Moscow State University in 1991, "that Bakhtin was a philosopher only in his very first works of the Vitebsk-Nevel period, when he was planning to compose a philosophy of law, morality, and aesthetic activity . . . [But] Bakhtin remained a philosopher in his philosophical-culturological research as well, even in his literary-historical study of Dostoevsky."[2] This is true, but it is not much of a clarification. What was the relationship between literature and philosophy in Bakhtin's worldview? Galina Ponomareva recalls one discussion where, in response to her jesting remark that literary scholarship was a "secondary superstructure" erected over original creativity, Bakhtin answered "with his inimitable grin and puffing away on his cigarette, 'Yes, yes, yes, for after all, it is a parasitical profession.'"[3] In 1994 one Voronezh Bakhtinist remarked ruefully that although "the philosophers have now definitely seized the initiative from the literary specialists" in explicating Bakhtin's thought and had succeeded in exposing an abundance of "contradictions, miscalculations, and unclear spots in Bakhtin's constructs," nevertheless "the most basic, primary questions associated with his legacy remain without an answer."[4] As literary and cultural critic, Bakhtin was speculative, creative, controversial. As a philosopher, he was simply incomprehensible.

What is more, he had pretensions. Vadim Kozhinov recalls submitting for Bakhtin's approval a brief sketch, written about his mentor for a seventy-fifth birthday festschrift, which summed up Bakhtin's intellectual project in the following way: an "organic fusion of the systematicity, objectivity, and consistency of German philosophical thought with the universal breadth and depth of Russian spiritual creativity."[5] Bakhtin, we are told, agreed completely with this formulation, adding (in Kozhinov's recollection) that he regretted the undisciplined state of Russian philosophy, which so often chose to "squeeze its eyes shut and leap over abysses" rather than "look into them straight with a calm and fearless gaze." According to Kozhinov, ever since his youth Bakhtin had wished "to transform Russian thought into a creative structure just as 'finalized' as German thought." Was this consummate structure ever built, and—if it was—have Bakhtin's explicators been successful at uncovering it?

As literature faded from view or became largely illustrative, the search for Bakhtin's elusive "first principles" began. Only recently have Russian scholars trained in the classical texts of nineteenth-century European phi-

[2] E. V. Volkova and E. A. Bogatyreva, "V bol'shom vremeni kul'tury: M. M. Bakhtin," in *Vestnik Moskovskogo universiteta*, seriia 7: *Filosofiia*, no. 1 (1991): 48–58, esp. 51.

[3] G. B. Ponomareva, "Vyskazannoe i nevyskazannoe . . . ," *DKKh, no. 3 (95)*: 66.

[4] V. A. Svitel'skii (Voronezh), "Idei M. M. Bakhtina i sovremennoe izuchenie russkoi literatury XIX veka," in V. L. Makhlin, ed., *MMB i PGN 94*, 118–23, esp. 119.

[5] Vadim Kozhinov, "Bakhtin i ego chitateli," *Moskva* (July 1992): 143–51, esp. 146.

losophy begun to analyze the actual style and logic of Bakhtin's "philoso-phizing," its tissue of unidentified quotations, voice zones, and hidden polemics.[6] At times the search has turned aggressive—and unkind—in its attempt to reconstitute, "after Bakhtin," the purported lost literary whole of Dostoevsky or Rabelais. To some it has seemed that Bakhtin's aes-thetics, pared back to its roots and initial conditions, departs so pro-foundly from what most of us mean by "art" that we do him a service by ceasing to consider him an aesthetician at all. Such an anti-cult animus is most evident in the opening chapter of part 2, on recent rethinkings of polyphony, dialogism, and the Dostoevsky book—although carnival has come in for its share of blows as well. This criticism would doubtless not have had the benefit of Bakhtin's response, for by all accounts he was constitutionally unable to feel insulted or pricked to irate self-defense. But the vigor of the debate would have delighted the man who provided the pretext.

[6] See, for example, N. K. Bonetskaia, "O stile filosofstvovaniia M. Bakhtina," in *DKKh, no. 1 (96)*: 5–48. Bonetskaia pays special attention to Bakhtin's polemic with Rickert and to the "I"-centeredness of Bakhtin's early philosophy (the necessary priority of *otsenka* [eval-uation] over *tsennost'* [value]).

CHAPTER 3

Polyphony, Dialogism, Dostoevsky

LET US RECALL the basic theses of Bakhtin's book on Dostoevsky. It begins with a familiar Formalist complaint: that literary scholars, dazzled by Dostoevsky's contributions to theology, moral philosophy, psychology, and Russian nationalism, have failed to appreciate his even greater contribution to *literary* art. This oversight Bakhtin intends to correct—with, however, a concept of "literariness" that most Formalist critics would have found highly suspect. Whereas the Russian Formalists preferred to examine hard-edged mechanical or impersonal devices such as defamiliarization, retardation, parody, the "stringing" of events and stepwise construction in an author's literary texts, Bakhtin focuses almost entirely on a single (and decisively soft) "device": human consciousness.

In order to examine degrees of consciousness in the aesthetic realm, Dostoevsky created—or perhaps discovered—polyphony. According to Bakhtin, this idea was so radical that it caused a genuine paradigm shift, a "Copernican revolution," in the history of the novel. In the prior more "Ptolemaic" worldview, an author sits at the center of things like Jehovah, passing out bits of consciousness piecemeal to the characters taking shape under the authorial pen, just enough to each person so that the cast of characters could obediently act out its predetermined roles. But Dostoevsky, Bakhtin intimates, endorsed a more "New Testament" model of authorship, one based on unresolvable paradoxes and parables rather than on certainties handed down as law. The rewards might appear unjust and the ends unclear, but the method increases the chances that both author and hero will genuinely learn from the process of defining each other. Incarnation—which is delimitation—always means increased vulnerability. When polyphonic authors "come down to earth" and address their creations not vertically but horizontally, they are designing their characters to know, potentially, as much as authors know. Such authors frequently craft a hero of whom they say: He has to do that, but I do not know why. How might I encourage him to show me his reasons?

To strengthen this reciprocal relation, Bakhtin claims, Dostoevsky designs as the hero of his novels not a human being destined to carry out a sequence of events—that is, not a carrier of some pre-planned "plot"—but rather an *idea-hero*, an idea that uses the hero as its carrier in order to realize its potential as an idea in the world. The goal then becomes to free up the hero from "plot," in both the sinister and humdrum sense of that word: from all those epiclike story lines that still clung to the novel with their routinized, and thus "imprisoned," outcomes, and also from events in ordinary, necessity-driven, benumbing everyday life. For *events*—as the biographies of both Bakhtin and Dostoevsky attest—rarely make you free (Bakhtin all but suggests that we leave this pleasant illusion to Count Leo Tolstoy, who loved life's delightful round of rituals, could afford to lose himself in it, developed an anguish of guilt about it, and came so powerfully to distrust language). Instead of events, Dostoevsky invites his heroes and his readers to experience the richer, more open-ended discriminations and proliferations of the uttered word, in a context where all parties are designed to talk back. In choosing to structure works in this way, of course, the polyphonic author is still authoring heroes and still "writing in" their stories. But by valuing, above all, an open discussion of unresolvable questions, such an author writes them into a realm of maximal freedom.

Polyphony brings further benefits. Once the grip between hero and plot is loosened, and once a dialogue of ideas (rather than a mass of exotic adventures) becomes the common denominator between author, hero, and reader, more space opens up for the reader. Readers can participate actively—which is to say, non-vicariously, on an equal plane—in the narrative. In a novel of ideas, there is no "escapism"; willingly or no, we are all equal communicants. (Or, as Bakhtin seems to be suggesting, no matter how crippled, constrained, or impoverished our lives may be, we can all always listen in and contribute a response.) In terms of their potential to communicate on shared ground, ideas are simply richer than experiences. Dostoevsky's working notebooks testify to his continual surprise at the turns his novels were required to take in order to accommodate the unexpected growth in ideas that were carried—and verbally tested—by his characters.

According to Bakhtin, the polyphonic hero was Dostoevsky's first great contribution to the art of the novel. His second contribution was to a theory of language. Inside every word, Bakhtin maintained, there is a struggle for meaning, and authors can adopt various attitudes toward this struggle. They can choose to cap or muffle the dialogue, discouraging all outside responses to it, and thus employ the word *monologically*. Or they can emphasize the word's so-called double-voicedness by exaggerating one side (as in stylization); by pitting two or more voices against one another while rooting for one side (as in parody); or, in a special, highly subtle category Bakhtin calls "active double-voiced words," by working the debates inside a word so that the parodied side does not take all that abuse lying down but rather fights back, resists, tries to subvert. Dostoevsky was exceptionally skilled at portraying this final, crafty type of word.

These two innovations—the "fully weighted hero" who signifies alongside his creator and the "dialogic word within a polyphonic design"—make up the theoretical core of the book on Dostoevsky. Bakhtin specifically declined to deal with the *actions* of Dostoevsky's heroes—all those scandals, rumored rapes, suicides, murders, instances of child abuse, as well as the sacramental moments of conversion and transfiguration. He also refused to discuss much of the (often quite unsavory) *content* of Dostoevsky's ideas, full of paradoxical wisdom and extravagant generosity but also no stranger to sadism, Russian chauvinism, reactionary politics, and psychic cruelty. Bakhtin sticks close to formal matters. "Miracle, mystery, and authority"—the three keys that will unlock the world, according to Ivan Karamazov's Grand Inquisitor—get no attention at all in Bakhtin's book on Dostoevsky.

Curiously, we do not know if this elegant formal exegesis is in fact the book that Bakhtin really wanted to write. Near the end of his life he confessed to Sergei Bocharov that in his work on Dostoevsky he had been unable to "speak out directly about the most important questions . . . the philosophical questions that tormented Dostoevsky his whole life, the existence of God. In the book I was forced to prevaricate, to dodge back and forth continually. I had to hold back all the time. The moment a thought got going, I had to break it off."[1] But however Aesopian and self-censored the text might be in its two editions, Bakhtin made his peace with the published versions and reconciled himself to being imperfectly understood. He tended, in the words of one colleague, to look at his own works in print quite philosophically, "the way a soul might look down from on high at its own cast-out body."[2]

At first polyphony was simply an enigma. How can created characters "create" themselves? Is not the polyphonic author abdicating responsibility for the finished whole of a literary work? As a literary strategy, polyphony was casually conflated with dialogism, heteroglossia, voice zones, chronotopic analysis—all those now fashionable catchwords that Bakhtin devised later, in the 1930s, to apply to novels in general, not to the prior (and much more restricted) subset of polyphonic novels. But then there appeared on the scene, in Russia and in the West, critics who had studied carefully and claimed to understand both the dynamics of

---

[1] S. G. Bocharov, "Ob odnom razgovore i vokrug nego," *Novoe literaturnoe obozrenie* 2 (1993): 70–89, esp. 71–72; English version, 1012.

[2] G. Pomerants, "'Dvoinye mysli' u Dostoevskogo" [1975] in *Otkrytost' bezdne: Vstrechi s Dostoevskim* (Moscow: Sovetskii pisatel', 1990), 225–34.

polyphony and the logic of its later offspring, "dialogism," and did not like them at all—not for themselves, not as metaphors for human freedom, and not as insights into the workings of Dostoevsky's novelistic masterpieces. This chapter is devoted to those reservations and to subsequent attempts to counter them.

CAN POLYPHONY EXIST? IF SO, DOES IT APPLY?

The first complaints against Bakhtin's image of Dostoevsky concerned quite simply its appropriateness to its subject. Were polyphony and double-voicedness in fact part of Dostoevsky's design? Did the novelist intend the sort of openness for his plots and autonomy for his heroes that Bakhtin claims? Many suspected not. There seemed to be a strong "authority principle" in Dostoevsky—especially in his final novel, *The Brothers Karamazov*—that pointedly resists the decentering impulse.[3] To mention one critical response: In 1989 Yuri Kariakin, Dostoevsky scholar and political gadfly of Solzhenitsyn's generation, published a six-hundred-page book entitled *Dostoevsky and the Brink of the Twenty-first Century*, in which he took his good friend Mikhail Mikhailovich gently to task.[4] Polyphony is a faulty hypothesis, Kariakin argues, because it concentrates solely on verbal dialogue and its current of ideas, tending to ignore the effect of fully embodied scenes. (Dostoevsky was a great master at imagining the scene; it is in this sense, we might add in support of Kariakin's complaint, that he is a "dramatist," and not in the trivial sense that his novels can be reduced or adapted effectively to the stage.) Words come and go, taking pleasure in their own eloquence or ambiguity. But Kariakin insists that in his major scenes, Dostoevsky always included a silent "finger pointing at the truth." The "double-voiced word" (*dvugolosoe slovo*), which Bakhtin recommends as an interpretive unit for the novel, should thus be replaced by a "triple-voiced word" (*trekhgolosoe slovo*), with the word's third "voice" assigned permanently to Dostoevsky as author and, as it were, stage director. For Bakhtin is wrong, Kariakin contends, when he suggests that self-consciousness is the hero of Dostoevsky's novels. *Self-deception* is the hero—and all that polyphonic ob-

---

[3] For the classic Russian argument, see V. E. Vetlovskaia, *Poetika romana "Brat'ia Karamazovy"* (Leningrad: Nauka, 1977); for a pioneering attempt to use Bakhtin as an aid in interpreting that novel's structures of faith and authority, see Nina Perlina, *Varieties of Poetic Utterance: Quotation in "The Brothers Karamazov"* (Lanham, Md.: University Press of America, 1985).

[4] Yurii Kariakin, *Dostoevskii i kanun XXI veka* (Moscow: Sovetskii pisatel', 1989), 649 pp. The "triple-voiced word" is discussed on pages 26–30; the case against consciousness and for self-deception as the "hero" of Dostoevsky's novels is examined on pages 69–72.

fuscation, those thought experiments and endless proliferation of alternatives, all those compulsive storytellers and chatterers, are designed by their author not to provide the major heroes with invigorating, open-ended options but rather to thicken and darken the texture of the work, to increase the obstacles, and to test the heroes on their conflicted way to the truth.[5]

Kariakin's reservations on the structural plane are one type of complaint against polyphony. Other skeptical readers have applied the acid test to which every strong critic must submit, namely, are the feelings and reactions we experience when reading Bakhtin on Dostoevsky at all compatible with our feelings while reading Dostoevsky himself?[6] At issue here are not merely morally repugnant scenes or themes. In *Problems of Dostoevsky's Poetics*, to repeat, Bakhtin deliberately excluded considerations of "content," limiting himself to the workings of language. He remained consistently Formalist in his reluctance to pass judgment on the ideology and virtue of Dostoevsky's plots. But remarkably, given its focus on the word, Bakhtin's book also does not address any ethical or metaphysical problems in the formal realm of language. Consider, for example, his treatment of *Notes from Underground*. The Underground, where consciousness is everything and where words never stick to deeds, is a deconstructor's paradise by postmodernist criteria. Dostoevsky, as we know, considered it a wholly godless place; he intended its chatter to be read not simply as misguided or futile but as demonic, and he lays bare its dynamics with ice-cold satire.[7] Bakhtin does acknowledge that Underground discourse is dead-ended, a *perpetuum mobile* and vicious circle. But ultimately that grim voided place contains for him some fundamentally positive principle, even if taken in this instance to unfortunate extreme: the principle of "unfinalizability." For the logic of the Underground guarantees all speakers who reside there the right to postpone the final

---

[5] For a more comprehensive discussion of *Dostoevsky and the Brink of the 21st Century* and the reservations it raises about Bakhtin's reading of the novelist, see Caryl Emerson, "The Kariakin Phenomenon," *Common Knowledge* 5, no. 1 (Spring 1996): 161–78, esp. 166–69, 173–75.

[6] For two preliminary surveys, see Caryl Emerson, "Problems of Baxtin's Poetics," in *Slavic and East European Journal* 32, no. 4 (Winter 1988): 503–25; and Emerson, "Word and Image in Dostoevsky's Worlds: Robert Louis Jackson on Readings That Bakhtin Could Not Do," in Elizabeth Cheresh Allen and Gary Saul Morson, eds., *Freedom and Responsibility in Russian Literature: Essays in Honor of Robert Louis Jackson* (Evanston, Ill.: Northwestern University Press and Yale Center for International and Area Studies, 1995): 245–65.

[7] The best account of the ideology of *Notes from Underground* remains that by Joseph Frank, in chapter 21 of his *Dostoevsky: The Stir of Liberation, 1860–65* (Princeton, N.J.: Princeton University Press, 1986), 310–37. In a lengthy footnote (p. 346), Frank notes his reservations about Bakhtin's reading.

verdict—and to deliver a supplementary word on themselves that others do not, and in principle cannot, know.

The Underground viewed not as trap but as "aperture" is only one peculiarity of reading Dostoevsky through a Bakhtinian lens. Other critics have noted that Bakhtin's passion for the horizontally cast dialogic word often comes at the expense of Dostoevsky's more vertical gestures, those leaps into iconic or transfigured time-space that provide the great novels with their crowning moments of personal conversion or collective Apocalypse.[8] Bakhtin has little sense of the sublime. With equal fastidiousness he avoids absolute bliss and absolute horror. He never mentions Dostoevsky's quasi-fictionalized prison memoirs *Notes from the House of the Dead*, for example, nor does he make reference to that gallery of tortured and silenced children that are so crucial a part of Dostoevsky's symbolic universe. Part of the problem, surely, is that those silenced victims cannot, or do not, talk (although they can be talked *about*); left solely with the ugly, silent material aftermath of a violent event—a corpse, a suicide, an atrocity that leaves us speechless—Bakhtin as a reader of Dostoevsky's world seems somewhat at a loss.[9] What is strange here, we should note, is not Bakhtin's unwillingness to be mired down (as so many have been) in Dostoevsky's cruel, crowd-pleasing Gothic plots; such plots, after all, were the conventional and thus almost invisible raw material of the nineteenth-century urban novel. More significant is that Bakhtin has also almost nothing to say about the centrally important, affirmative, "godly" dialogic situations—if they happen to be wordless. Among these crucial scenes are Raskolnikov and Sonya on the banks of the Siberian River in the epilogue of *Crime and Punishment*, Prince Myshkin's meaningless babble as he embraces a stunned Rogozhin over Nastasya Filippovna's corpse at the end of *The Idiot*, and—most famously—Christ kissing the Grand Inquisitor after having listened, in silence, to that brilliant and lengthy diatribe.[10] In Bakhtin's readings, however, only the interaction of one verbal utterance with another verbal utterance can be adequate to the most subtle and multilayered messages. By definition, this interaction opens up new potentials. The possibility that verbal dialogue might actu-

---

[8] See, for example, David M. Bethea, *The Shape of the Apocalypse in Modern Russian Fiction* (Princeton, N.J.: Princeton University Press, 1989), esp. "*The Idiot*: Historicism Arrives at the Station," 103–4; and Malcolm V. Jones, *Dostoyevsky after Bakhtin: Readings in Dostoevsky's Fantastic Realism* (Cambridge: Cambridge University Press, 1990).

[9] On this topic, see Natalia Reed's ongoing work on scapegoating and violence in Dostoevsky (and on Bakhtin's inability to address these issues); in particular, her seventy-page Girardian study, "Dostoevsky's 'The Meek One': the Metamorphosis of a Truism" (unpubl. ms., 1996).

[10] Late in life, however, Bakhtin did make these suggestive jottings in a passage devoted to Dostoevsky: "The unuttered truth in Dostoevsky (Christ's kiss). The problem of silence. Irony as a special kind of substitute for silence." "From Notes Made in 1970–71," *SpG*, 148.

ally drain away value or flatten out a subtlety or be so subject to terror and constraint that it depreciates into outright fraud is not for Bakhtin a theoretically serious issue. On principle, he seems reluctant to project a human being so evil, weak, indifferent, or exhausted that he or she can no longer listen to, or author, a useful word.

Let us now move into even more critical and suspicious corners of the Bakhtin industry. On the occasion of the thirtieth anniversary of *Problems of Dostoevsky's Poetics*, the editorial board of the Belarus' Bakhtin journal *Dialog Karnaval Khronotop* distributed questionnaires to two dozen eminent scholars, soliciting their opinions on the role of the book and its author in the history of Russian thought. Returns began to appear in 1994.[11] Although the proper Jubilee praises were sung, several of the scholars polled were clearly irritated at Bakhtin's single-minded pursuit of polyphony into every cranny and at any cost. Polyphony was judged inadequate to Dostoevsky's complexity not only for the old reason—that the voice of the author must always be firmer and more primary than that of the created heroes—but for newly legitimated religious reasons as well. As one contributor put the issue bluntly, "The authoritativeness of the author's word . . . relies on the authority of Christian truths, whose conscious transmitter and preacher Dostoevsky was" (7–8). (Unlike the uglier ideologies of the modern period, we are assured, religious faith "could not be a monologism.") Georgii Fridlender pursued the Christian line further. He classified the Dostoevsky book alongside works by Vyacheslav Ivanov and Nicolas Berdyaev as a prime text in Russian Orthodox "personalism" (14)—although he added that Bakhtin was perhaps too marked by the binary oppositions of his era, which lent his work a structural elegance but also a certain rigidity. By so stubbornly insisting on polyphony, Fridlender notes, "Bakhtin, paradoxical as it seems, was extremely monologic and didactic" (15). The genre theorist Vladimir Zakharov was even less accommodating. Bakhtin "wanted to think freely in a totalitarian society" and yet was destined to work out his major ideas in resistance to Stalinist oppression. Under those conditions, Bakhtin came up with some brilliant formulations—but whatever he did not wish to think about, no matter how central to literary study (Zakharov has in mind his own area of research, the Dostoevskian narrator), he simply ignored. "Without this resistance [to Stalinism], however, he would scarcely have been so original a philosopher . . . May the Bakhtinians not be offended by what I say," Zakharov concluded, "but in many respects, Bakhtin already belongs to history" (9).

---

[11] Anketa "DKKh", "Na voprosy redaktsii po povodu 30-letiia so vremeni vykhoda vtorogo izdaniia knigi M. M. Bakhtina o F. M. Dostoevskom otvechaiut: Budanova N. F., Zakharov V. N., Ponomareva G. B., Renanskii A. L., Fridlender G. M.," in *DKKh, no. 1 (94)*: 5–15. Page references given in text.

Zakharov's verdict, although addressed to a local forum of specialists, cannot be wholly dismissed. At the Bakhtin Centennial Conference not a single paper, by Russians or non-Russians, was devoted to Bakhtin on Dostoevsky. This did not seem to distress his followers. Many defended Bakhtin's admittedly lopsided reading of the great novelist as simply "illustrative" of something more important—the way Freud, say, used the literary image of Oedipus to illustrate his powerful discoveries about the human psyche; thus, it was felt, Bakhtin had little to gain or lose from the grumbling of literary specialists. Why reopen all that, they said; it is old hat, a purely literary matter; the book is a classic of criticism and part of the canon. After all, Russian academics now in their prime had dutifully memorized *Problems of Dostoevsky's Poetics* as undergraduates during the early years of the Bakhtin cult. Its precepts have long been considered as magisterial, grandfatherly, and uncontroversial as, say, those of Wayne Booth, Wellek and Warren, or Northrop Frye.

But let us push the critique further. For there is a group of critics, in Russia and in the West, who find Bakhtin's whole model of polyphony not only untrue to Dostoevsky's primary intentions as a novelist and a thinker, but also inconsistent and somewhat dishonest on its own terms—for psychological and linguistic reasons as well as for ethical ones. These critics are developing an argument that was made forcefully a decade ago by Aaron Fogel, in a fine book on Joseph Conrad entitled *Coercion to Speak*.[12] Fogel's point is that dialogue, as Bakhtin invokes it, is not the normal human relation at all. Most human speech, he argues, is forced and under constraint; although dialogue, when it does occur, can at times be a blessing and a relief, the task of making it happen between two people is difficult, dangerous, and (here is the scary, non-Bakhtinian part) often made worse when we try, against all odds and against the interests of the participants, to "talk things out." A prime exhibit for this truth are the tortured protagonists in Conrad's novels. However Bakhtin might package the matter, Fogel argues, it is clear that much of the time, for a large number of human problems, dialogue is *not* a "talking cure." To sample why not, here are two recent polemics, one by a Russian and the other by a Russian emigré scholar, both deeply skeptical of Bakhtin.

UNSYMPATHETIC CASE STUDIES AND SUSPICIOUS CLOSE READINGS

In 1994 a postmodernist work of literary criticism was published in St. Petersburg entitled *Anti-Bakhtin, or the Best Book about Vladimir*

---

[12] Aaron Fogel, *Coercion to Speak: Conrad's Poetics of Dialogue* (Cambridge, Mass.: Harvard University Press, 1985).

Nabokov.[13] The book is mediocre and derivative (it figured briefly in chapter 1, as exemplary of the crasser sides of the "Bakhtin backlash") but its author, Vadim Linetsky, does direct attention to one vulnerable area in a dialogic poetics. Linetsky alleges that Bakhtin, in his essay "Discourse in the Novel," "reacts rather skeptically to dialogue in the traditional understanding of the word." By "traditional" Linetsky appears to mean all those situations where people simply talk back and forth in good faith—in order to exchange information, give one another cues, reveal their immediate desires, clarify each other's intentions, in short, try to tell the truth as each party understands it at that moment—and thereby resolve, sooner or later, on a course of real action. Linetsky observes that Bakhtin considers such ordinary, practical verbal exchanges to be rather flat and monologic, dismissing them as conceptually trivial and restricting their role to a "compositional" or merely "plot-related" function in the work. Bakhtin does so, Linetsky suggests, because he does not really value practical real-life distance between one person and another—even though all genuinely embodied dialogic exchange must be based on it. Distance is a prerequisite for the effective working of all addressed words, codes, controls, social hierarchies; in fact, Linetsky insists, real distance is required for any "materialization of power" in real life. Without a good intuitive sense of these parameters, none of us would ever open our mouths. And we might add—as an old-fashioned gloss to Linetsky's faintly postmodernist casting of this problem in terms of power—that distance between one person and another is also what enables independence, privacy, and genuine acts of giving, just as it makes inevitable both human loneliness and longing.

Linetsky's reservation could be expanded. As we shall see in chapter 5, Bakhtin builds both his ethics and his aesthetics around the virtues of "outsideness." But one suspects that Bakhtin would prefer us to be not entirely outside, not all that distant from one another: we should hover around a shared boundary, different but not *that* different, curious about others but not threatened by them, speaking not (of course) the very same language but *enough* the same language so as to insure that others hear us and incline toward us—or, as Bakhtin put it disarmingly near the end of his life, "the more demarcation the better, but benevolent demarcation, without border disputes."[14] This scenario is indeed inspirational: boundaries are to multiply, yet disputes are to wither away. But its dynamics apply to only a tiny fraction of the heroes in Dostoevsky's novels—and not, I wager, to the ones who excite us and strike us as the most deeply human, the ones whose maniacal inner workings we would

---

[13] Vadim Linetskii, *"Anti-Bakhtin"—Luchshaia kniga o Vladimire Nabokove* (Sankt-Peterburg: Tipografiia im. Kotliakova, 1994), 84–85.
[14] "From Notes Made in 1970–71," in *SpG*, 137.

expect a literary critic to elucidate. And further: these trapped and maniacal heroes, more often than not, do not thirst after any fancy double-
voiced dialogism, which can create for them only more doubts and confounding options. From within their own unhappy unstable worlds, they
simply want to believe in something; they want to be understood; and
they want to be loved.

An unsettling critique of Bakhtin's image of Dostoevsky can indeed be
mounted along these lines. One place to ground it would be in Bakhtin's
earliest philosophical writings, where he addresses the difference between
ethical and *aesthetic* domains in a work of art.[15] Although this problem
will occupy us more fully in later chapters, a preview might be useful
here. An event becomes "aesthetic," in Bakhtin's world, if there is an
outside consciousness looking in on the event and, as it were, embracing
it, able to bestow on the scenario a sense of the "whole." Such an external (and thus aesthetic) position is available to spectators watching, to
readers reading, and to an author "shaping." But from within the artwork—that is, from the perspective of the created character who is undergoing the particular pleasure or torment in question—events are of
course experienced as partial, unshaped, cognitively open, ethically irreversible, as matters not of art but of life and death. The hero—or at least
the hero in a realistic novel, always Bakhtin's genre of choice—does not
feel his own life to be a fiction. Let us apply this early distinction to some
scenarios of the Dostoevsky book. It will help us glimpse the mechanism
by which Bakhtin, working with such often desperate texts, arrives at his
dialogic optimism.

Take, for example, death. Bakhtin turned to the topic often in his writings, and usually in a spirit of benevolent gratitude: death is aesthetic
closure, that point where creative memory can begin, the best means for
making a gift of my whole self to another. As one Polish scholar has
summed up this position, Bakhtin devised not a neo- but a "post-human-
istic vision of man": if neo-humanism takes the individual personality as
its reckoning point and thus regrets its passing, Bakhtin, with his insistence that an "I" comes to exist only on the border between itself and
someone else, provides us with a model of death that is neither an insult
to consciousness nor a blessing to it but, as an event, simply irrelevant.
Only that which exists *in itself* can die.[16] Those grimmer aspects of
death—its silence, nonnegotiability, unanswerability, aloneness—that so
terrified other Russian writer-philosophers (say, Leo Tolstoy, to whose

---

[15] See the opening segments of "The Problem of the Author's Relationship to the Hero"
and "The Spatial Form of the Hero," in "Author and Hero in Aesthetic Activity," *A&A*,
4–16, 31–46, 73–75.

[16] Dr. J. Wizinska, "Posthumanistic Vision of Man in the Philosophy of M. Bakhtin," in
Yazyk i tekst: Ontologiia i refleksiia (Sankt Peterburg: Eidos, 1992), 320–22.

anxieties Bakhtin seems singularly immune) seem to have persuaded Bakhtin that the whole procedure, being so wordless and so unavailable to my own ended consciousness (*my* death can exist only for others), is not worth taking seriously.

This elegant resolution of the problem of our mortality—again recalling the Hellenistic philosophers—Bakhtin graciously attributes to his own hero and scholarly subject, Dostoevsky. In his 1961 notes for the revision of *Problems of Dostoevsky's Poetics*, Bakhtin remarks that death hardly signifies at all for the great polyphonic novelist. In support of this claim and in contrast to Tolstoy, he points to the fact that "Dostoevsky never depicts death from within [the dying person]"; death is an event solely for another, as yet living consciousness, and thus it "finalizes nothing" in the larger realm of the spirit. And why, indeed, should we fear extinction if—as Bakhtin put the matter movingly—"personality does not die. Death is a departure. . . . The person has departed, having spoken his word, but the word itself remains in the open-ended dialogue. . . . organic death, that is, the death of the body, did not interest Dostoevsky."[17]

Perhaps it did not. But, one might object, surely the death of the body interests Dostoevsky's *characters*. And death obsesses precisely those characters who reside in the novels Bakhtin skirts most widely: the totally ignored *Notes from the House of the Dead*; the novel *Devils*, with its brutal arbitrary murders and its travestied Nativity scene (mother and son, Shatov's beloved family, die almost as an afterthought in the wake of his murder); *The Idiot*, with its horrifying incoherence over Nastasya Filippovna's dead body in the final scene; and Dostoevsky's harrowing death-side monologue "Krotkaia" [The meek one], which unfolds—which could only unfold—over a corpse. In fact, the only death story Bakhtin reads in any fullness is the tiny throwaway tale "Bobok," a menippean satire about obscene graveyard conversations carried on by the dead who refuse to die or fall silent. Bakhtin's less sympathetic critics see something disturbing in this pattern of omissions. Is the man so committed to unfinalizable dialogue, to the good we can do others if only we remain outside them and talking to them (or posthumously remembered as having once talked to them), that he is indifferent to the ethical world as experienced by Dostoevsky's heroes, to its innerness and breaking points? For surely Dostoevsky, as author, did not intend his absorbed and captivated readers to react with bland hope or benign resignation, relegating all those ultimate life-and-death questions to some ephemeral dialogue in the sky; he was counting on horror. The unfinalizability is only in Bakhtin.

---

[17] "Toward a Reworking of the Dostoevsky Book," in *PDP*, 290, 300.

Death, then, is similar to aesthetic wholeness in that it, too, is the product of a dialogic situation: it requires an outsider, or a *socium*, to bestow it. In Bakhtin's exegesis, this bestowal is simply not felt as murder. In fact, Bakhtin is as curiously untroubled by dying as he is by the possibility that outsideness will turn alien or hostile—although the best students of Dostoevsky routinely have found these two anxieties central. Gary Saul Morson, for one, has argued cogently that for Dostoevsky, an astute student of the fundamentally *social* vices, the state of being "external to" and in social relation puts one at great moral risk.[18] As the novels demonstrate, we are indeed indispensable to one another—but for reasons that give no cause for rejoicing. Sociality is scandal space, the site of voyeurism. ("In Dostoevsky's novels," Morson writes, "suffering, shame, torture and death usually take place before a crowd of spectators who indulge in the quintessential social act of gaping. In Dostoevsky, the first sign of our essential sociality is that we are all voyeurs. . . . Nobody had a deeper sense of the social as an arena of gratuitous cruelty.") Reacting to this truth, several American scholars are now supplementing Bakhtin's "aesthetic" interpretations of Dostoevsky with darker ethical correctives that work with more than just words. Among the most useful of the philosophers invoked is the late Emmanuel Levinas and his philosophy of human obligation arising from eye-to-eye contact with a living, suffering—even if wholly silent—face.[19]

These final considerations bring us to the most sustained criticism yet raised against Bakhtin's reading of Dostoevsky and against polyphony in general: that by the literary scholar Natalia Reed.[20] Reed approaches polyphony from a Girardian perspective, insisting on its mimetic origins. She contends that the polyphonic model—and by extension dialogism as well—is rooted in Bakhtin's desire to improve on the monologic creative

[18] Gary Saul Morson, "Misanthropology," *New Literary History* 27, no. 1 (Winter 1996): 57–72, esp. 62, 71.

[19] See Leslie Johnson, "The Face of the Other in *Idiot*," *Slavic Review* 50, no. 4 (Winter 1991): 867–78; and Val Vinokurov's trenchant critique and expansion from a Levinasian perspective in his "The End of Consciousness and the Ends of Consciousness: Re-reading *Idiot* and *Demons* after Emmanuel Levinas" (unpubl. ms., 1996). Vinokurov writes of Myshkin: "The Prince is simply profligate toward the face, and thus unable to live with the politics, the agony and violence of choosing between faces that justice demands when I and the other are not alone in the world. His departure is Christ's failure on earth. One should not be too ready to fill in the blank of Dostoevsky's doubts by insisting so wholeheartedly on Myshkin's potential. The world does not fail Myshkin. The world *cannot fail.* Only the individual can fail against the resistance of the world. He can also, unlike Myshkin, succeed."

[20] Natasha Alexandrovna Reed, "Reading Lermontov's *Geroj našego vremeni*: Problems of Poetics and Reception," Ph.D. dissertation, Harvard University, September 1994, esp. ch. 3: "Baxtin's Theory of the Polyphonic Consciousness: The Dialogue of Self without Other," 304–73.

act and as such does not welcome real others at all. It might welcome them for a moment, as a temporary stimulus or trigger, but it rarely has the patience to orient outwardly toward another person's words and acts *over time*. In fact, Reed argues, if you consider the stories that Dostoevsky really tells (that is, if you reject Bakhtin's hypothesis that the novelist did not care much about stories and plots but cared only about putting a mass of "embodied ideas" into circulation), you will realize that double-voiced words, as Bakhtin claims to find them in Dostoevsky, are not put to work in a sustained "multi-perspectival" way at all. "Outsideness" is not much of a value, either for the major novelistic heroes or for Bakhtin the critic. The dialogues that matter to Bakhtin are all already internalized, detached in a trice from their original speakers, whose further words and emerging needs in their ongoing lives become irrelevant to the inflated, autonomous, curiously timeless consciousness of the central character. And this consciousness proceeds to generate plots that are ghastly.

Let us expand on Reed via Bakhtin's analysis of Raskolnikov's famous internal dialogue in the opening chapters of *Crime and Punishment* (*PDP*, 73–74). This is the moment in the novel when Raskolnikov, having read his mother's letter with the details of his sister Dunya's fate, Svidrigailov's attempted seduction, and the impending marriage to Luzhin, links these events with the drunkard Marmeladov's lachrymose story in the pub and resolves to repudiate a world that has been thus arranged. Bakhtin calls this dialogized inner monologue a *microdialogue*, one that "re-creates" the autonomous voices of the participants; as Bakhtin writes, at this point "dialogue has penetrated inside every word, provoking in it a battle and the interruption of one voice by another" (75). Such microdialogues are said to have a markedly good effect on readers, who find themselves stimulated and open to new, multiple points of view. "Every true reader of Dostoevsky," Bakhtin concludes, "can sense [a] peculiar *active broadening* of his or her consciousness, not [so much] in the assimilation of new objects . . . [as in] the sense of a special dialogic mode of communication with the autonomous consciousnesses of others, something never before experienced, an active dialogic penetration into the unfinalizable depths of man" (*PDP*, 68).

But is this in fact what occurs? To a certain extent, of course, Raskolnikov reading his mother's letter and angrily debating its sentiments and intonations with himself is a model for mental activity in general: we take events in, set one voice against another, prod ourselves to respond, and in this way eventually manage to focus our own thoughts. But this process should at no point be confused with communication. (Dostoevsky himself makes this fact clear about his hero six paragraphs into *Crime and Punishment*: Raskolnikov lapsed into oblivion on the street, "no longer noticing what was around him and not wishing to notice. He only muttered something to himself from time to time, out of that habit of monologues he had just confessed to himself.") As readers we might indeed want to talk with Raskolnikov—he is an interesting fellow. But is there any indication that he might wish to talk with us—or with anyone, for that matter—in the simple "traditional" sense of dialogue, which at least admits the possibility of hearing something new outside one's own system? Quite the contrary: the novel as published still bears traces of its early draft in first-person confessional narration, and Raskolnikov's self-obsessed consciousness continues to serve as the dominant fulcrum for its ideas and events.

How does that consciousness actually work? Raskolnikov hears a random story from a drunk in a tavern or he receives a letter from his mother whom he has not seen for years, and suddenly he is off. Everyone in the world becomes "a Sonya," "a Svidrigailov," "a Dunya." These voices in Raskolnikov's inner speech come into "a peculiar sort of contact," as Bakhtin puts it, "one that would be impossible among voices in an actual dialogue" (*PDP*, 239). Impossible, yes, because voices in an actual dialogue would not tolerate contact on those terms. And is contact established in this way necessarily a good or honest thing? Does Dostoevsky intend this contact among ideas *within* the hero's consciousness to result in the authentically productive and spiritually broadening microdialogue that Bakhtin claims it must become?

The opposite case could easily be argued. When Bakhtin insists that Dostoevsky's world is fundamentally organized and visualized in categories not of evolution but of *coexistence* and *interaction* (*PDP*, 28), we should be alert to the sinister and inhumane aspects of that scenario. What Bakhtin calls microdialogue might more closely resemble a lunatic inner monologue that has been—for lack of genuine empathy, interest, or lived experience on Raskolnikov's part—simply embellished and exacerbated by other people's utterances. For the most powerful instinct in Raskolnikov (considered as a human being, not just as a repository for ideas) is always to stop talking with "real others" as soon as possible, to detach the words uttered by those others from the experience or the truth that had given rise to them, and to start using those words to rearrange the world according to his own prior and fixed notions of it. It would appear that Dostoevsky was acutely aware of this dynamic. He intended his gifted but appallingly self-absorbed Raskolnikov to be perceived, if anything, as thoroughly monologic because of it. After all, Raskolnikov was created after the Underground Man and is a refinement on his type. Unlike that earlier, overtly grotesque and thus less threatening image, however, Raskolnikov has high intelligence, beauty, boldness, the ability to act. But he shares with his predecessor the inability to listen.

Among those who might agree with this hypothesis is Bakhtin's slightly younger contemporary, Lydia Ginzburg. One of Russia's best readers of Rousseau, Proust, Herzen, and Tolstoy, Ginzburg was drawn to explicate literary worlds that were as hospitable to the Tolstoyan hero as Bakhtin's world was structured to wall that type of hero out. Ginzburg is not sympathetic to Bakhtin's notion that Dostoevsky's characters, being "idea-persons" in pursuit of higher concepts, are thereby less selfish. "Tolstoy discovered the first principles of shared spiritual experience as it relates to the contemporary person, and this person is not even aware that he conceives of himself in Tolstoyan terms, that in fact he has no other choice," she writes in *On Psychological Prose*. "To be sure, this character might find it more *interesting* to conceive of himself in Dostoevskian terms, since doing so would allow him to focus attention on himself."[21]

In her exposé of the "dialogue" that Bakhtin foists on Dostoevsky, Reed would agree. She argues that the consciousnesses of others are *not* autonomous in such "thought experiments" as Raskolnikov's internalized letter scenario (Reed, 370)—and neither there nor in a host of other so-called microdialogues is there anything resembling a reciprocal act of communication. Thus when Bakhtin, explaining the essence of dialogic discourse, states with approval that "to think about others means to *talk with them*" [*PDP*, 68; Reed, 315], Reed objects strenuously. To communicate with others is *not*, she insists, merely to think of them, merely to carry on a mental conversation with them at one's own leisure and convenience.

In short, Natalia Reed sees polyphony as a rapid, profound, and profoundly selfish *internalization of relationships*—a removal of human relations from the realm of responsible outer actions (or *inter*actions), involving unpredictable unmanageable others, into the safer realm of inner words and domesticated verbal images of the other. We may expand Reed's comments into yet another realm. At several points Bakhtin claims that polyphony in a novel serves to "put the unfinalizable idea on trial." And in ethical life, an *un*finalized thing cannot be tested or put on trial. Trials follow completed deeds; they have verdicts, sentences, punishments. People are acquitted, locked up, shot. In benign contrast to the real courtroom trial, ideas in inner dialogue always have loopholes and a chance to be re-uttered. Again, it is instructive to note which texts in the Dostoevsky canon Bakhtin reads at length and with his most characteris-

---

[21] Lydia Ginzburg, *On Psychological Prose*, trans. and ed. Judson Rosengrant (Princeton, N.J.: Princeton University Press, 1991), 243 (translation somewhat adjusted). It seems plausible that this somewhat arch retort is Ginzburg's response to Bakhtin's remark, in *Problems of Dostoevsky's Poetics*, that "all of Dostoevsky's major characters, as people of an idea, are absolutely unselfish, insofar as the idea has really taken control of the deepest core of their personality" (*PDP*, 87).

tic brilliance: *Notes from Underground, Crime and Punishment,* "The Meek One," "Bobok," "The Double," Ivan Karamazov and his Devil—plots or scenes where one event, one moment of crime or mental breakdown, is followed by a huge amount of talking to oneself. Bakhtin does not have much to say about narratives that are devoid of a single crisis or crime and its obsessive internalization (meandering novels like *The Idiot*) or a dark masterpiece like *The Devils,* where corpses explain nothing and dialogues remain largely on the outside, used by deluded men and women to deceive others or to declaim false truths—used for anything, one could argue, except to enrich the self with interesting and wholesome options.

Bakhtin, it is true, intends the comparison between Dostoevsky's novel and polyphony as "a graphic analogy, a simple metaphor," nothing more (*PDP,* 22). But the term *polyphony*—which he often employs alongside another musical metaphor, *counterpoint*—is surely meant to evoke, at a minimum, the image (or sonority) of a multiply harmonized texture, a fabric of discrete interwoven strands receptive and inviting to others. As we have seen, skeptics would sooner call it a soliloquy of the isolated, narcissistic self. Furthermore, it is a soliloquy that, by its very dynamics and the doors it shuts behind itself, beckons the speaker toward violence. (A self thus conditioned must battle its way out in blindness or in anger.) The revisionists also insist that Dostoevsky, who was not at all naive about the difficulties of honest dialogue, would concur. What Dostoevsky was parodying, Bakhtin took for authentic coin. The novelist understood full well (in fact he devotes one small scene in his novel *The Adolescent* to just this uncomfortable social truism) that a real other, a genuine interlocutor (of the sort you rarely meet in the literary passages Bakhtin selects for analysis) is always free to walk in on me at inconvenient times, walk out on me at will, speak inpenetrable nonsense, ignore me altogether, abuse me in ways I am not prepared for, even kill me off. In contrast to such recognizably real-life dialogic scenes, the Bakhtinian microdialogue can be philosophically satisfying, open-ended, full of the anguish and articulation that is so electrifying to Bakhtin and stimulating to the reader because it begins and ends on the thinker's terms. It never leaves the terrain of a single person's head. And because it does not, because it is not forced to tack back and forth in "traditional" dialogic exchanges for its nourishment, it can have horrendous consequences—such as murder—in other people's real worlds. Dostoevsky was a profound student of such solipsism. He identified it with the pathology of the Underground. And it is worth noting that Dostoevsky prefers to bring his salvageable heroes—Raskolnikov or Dmitry Karamazov—to public trial as a prelude to their ultimate resurrection rather than leave them muttering to themselves, even as he condemned court procedures and despaired of the law.

Thus the anti-Bakhtinians distrust how Bakhtin interprets Dostoevsky's understanding of language. Reed even intimates at several points in her study that like most desk-ridden, reclusive intellectuals, Bakhtin—at least in his high polyphonic phase—unconsciously creates as the ideal interlocutor someone who responds to others' needs only when all that is left of them is their *words:* no deeds, no bodies, no one-way actions and irreconcilable conflicts, no stubborn deadlock that can be broken only by coercion. (According to Bakhtin, the genuine heroes of a polyphonic novel are consciousness and ideas; thus the events that trigger the necessary talk can be of the most melodramatic and banal kind.) Bakhtin insists that plot per se did not matter to Dostoevsky. But in fact any stripping away of plot events would be quite a sinister move, Reed argues, when considered from the human perspective *inside* the text. In her opinion, Bakhtin gets rid of Dostoevsky's plots not in order to "free the hero"— that is, to free up an epiclike character from his epithet, an Achilles from his heel, to take a closed biography and endow it with new potentials— but in order to free up the *author*, who can then transfer his own monologic torment to the hero, and at the hero's expense. If Bakhtin had bothered to submit even one of the novels to sustained structural analysis, or if he had chosen to attend at all to the emotional world of Dostoevsky's obsessively driven and unhappy cast of narrators, he would have seen that this polyphonic "freeing up" is simply a fiction of his own devising. Bakhtin, these critics believe, overestimates the power of language to rescue us. For him, an utterance will sooner work to multiply meaning and enrich mental options than to misrepresent, mislead, or misperceive reality. Thus Reed would sympathize (although for very different reasons) with those early Bolshevik reviewers of *Problems of Dostoevsky's Art* who insisted that Bakhtin's polyphony, designed to absorb every significant thing into consciousness, is at base idealist, asocial, and fundamentally immoral. For the refusal to finalize any judgment is an escape from the consequences of authentic residence in the world.

According to the revisionists, then, such polyphonic manipulation of ethical choice—rendering it reversible and always "inner"—cannot be the major mechanism at work in Dostoevsky's novels. It cannot, because Dostoevsky is himself a discriminating moralist who arranges matters in his fiction so that major heroes are run not by ideas, as Bakhtin claims, but by *doubt*. These heroes do not wish to be polyphonically "free" of commitment. Rather, the opposite is true: they want desperately to believe, and they cannot. They examine options in order to be rid of them, to move forward into the deed, not merely to elaborate more options.

About passionate desire and passionate doubt—both fueled by the pursuit of real, elusive people who change over time—Bakhtin, in the opinion of these critics, hasn't a clue.

Is this critique just? Again, it depends—quite literally—on one's point of view. For what Vadim Linetsky, Yuri Kariakin, Lydia Ginzburg, and others who take Bakhtin seriously but with a severely critical eye have done in their analyses of polyphony is to consider a given experience or event in Dostoevsky's texts not "externally"—as a reader, a philosopher, a scholarly critic—but from the simple, trapped perspective of the created hero, whose free-standing interests Bakhtin claims to champion (and whom Natalia Reed considers a victim of Bakhtin's "surrogate plot," the great dialogue between author and hero). The method has merit, I might add, because ordinary, untutored readers of novels (the audience for whom Dostoevsky actually wrote) identify in this way instinctively; it is one of the great pleasures of the genre. Put yourself in the hero's place. The first thing you will insist on is that consciousness alone does not make a biography. My plot, after all, is my life. I do not want to be liberated from it. And least of all do I wish to be liberated by an author who values only my verbal residue and my trail of ideas, not my decisions, unspeakable losses, and irreversible events. Dialogic communication, if it aspires to an ethical position, must mean more than simply "Leave me alone to think about what you just said."

Dostoevsky, these critics insist, was fully aware of the solipsism in any "dialogue of ideas" that only pretends to fulfill a communicative function. For dialogue is measured by many criteria—precision of expression, proper timing, impact on the listener, subsequent modification of behavior—and makes use of various instruments, of which words are only one. (In 1996 one practicing psychotherapist in the New Russia concluded an essay on Bakhtin and family counseling with a section whose title was surely inspired by Christ's response to the Grand Inquisitor: "Silence as the Heights of Dialogue.")[22] No reader would dispute that novelistic worlds are reached *through* words. But once we are inside that world, the real power of the genre is in the interpersonal space, the scene called forth, the entire complex that we (along with the characters) see and feel, not only what we hear, speak, and think. Therefore, these critics do not agree with Bakhtin when he states, in a passage written just before revis-

---

[22] T. A. Florenskaia, "Slovo i molchanie v dialoge," in *DKKh, no. 1 (96)*: 49–62, esp. "Molchanie kak vershina dialoga," 60–62. Remarking on the unexpected ability of therapists to sense quickly the sort of language that will penetrate the most recalcitrant subject and have an effect, she then notes that dialogue requires not verbal language per se but only an act in which one's "dominant orientation is toward the interlocutor"; only under conditions of "the most intimate spiritual closeness" is silence between two people, "understanding without words," possible.

ing the Dostoevsky book, that "language and the word are almost every-thing in human life."[23] They sympathize, rather, with Alexei Kirillov, the monomaniacal, wierdly inarticulate nihilist in Dostoevsky's *The Devils* and one of that novel's few attractive, kindly, and honest figures, when he says to his would-be murderer in the final conversation before his suicide: "All my life, I did not want it to be *only words*. This is why I lived, because I kept on not wanting it. And now, too, every day, I want it *not to be words*."[24]

Curiously, some centennial rethinkings of the Dostoevsky book by phi-losophers have endorsed this critique of logos-centric dialogism—but in an effort to redeem, rather than to undermine, Bakhtin's interpretation of Dostoevsky. In a 1995 paper the Moscow philosopher Natalia Bonetskaia defended Bakhtin's second edition, and particularly its massive insert on menippean satire, as a belated discovery on Bakhtin's part that the 1929 study was indeed inadequate to the darker sides of his subject.[25] The rosy, sentimental-Romantic view of reciprocal dialogue that governs the 1929 original version was simply too partial a picture to be allowed to stand, she argues; Bakhtin eventually wanted to "get at more than merely the poetics" (30) and felt obliged to address the real pathos and perverse intonation of Dostoevsky's world. And what, Bonetskaia asked, could be more hysterical, chaotic, hellish, anti-dialogic than the spirit of carnival? If dialogue is "personality, reason, freedom, the realm of meanings, the light of consciousness and perhaps of Logos," then carnival is the existen-tial void, "the appearance of Dionysian chaos, a darkening of reason, and the triumph of the elemental unconscious, the night of human nature" (28). As shall become clear in the following chapter, such a reading—although ingeniously motivating the move from the first to second edi-tion of the Dostoevsky book—requires a demonic view of carnival that Bakhtin's own demonstrably passionate attachment to the concept poorly accommodates. In another attempt to tie Bakhtin's shifting image of Dostoevsky to some rational pattern, the prominent sociologist Yuri Davydov reminds us that Bakhtin matured exceptionally early as a thinker: by his early twenties he had already absorbed (and criticized) Kant, Windelband, Simmel, Rickert, Scheler—and then began to seek out a creative intelligence broad enough to test this wisdom. Bakhtin "constructs his own sort of philosophical cyclotron and finds the atom

---

[23] "The Problem of the Text in Linguistics, Philology, and the Human Sciences: An Ex-periment in Philosophical Analysis" (1959–61) in *SpG*, 118.

[24] Fyodor Dostoevsky, *Demons*, trans. Richard Pevear and Larissa Volokhonsky (New York: Knopf, 1995), part 3, ch. 6 ("A Toilsome Night"), 615.

[25] N. K. Bonetskaia, "K sopostavleniiu dvukh redaktsii knigi M. Bakhtina o Dos-toevskom," *Bakhtinskie chteniia*, vyp. I (Materialy Mezhdunarodnoi nauchnoi konferentsii), (Vitebsk, 3–6 July 1995). Vitebsk, Belarus': 1996.

which it splits. That atom is the literary art of Dostoevsky." Husserlian phenomenology, not Raskolnikov's selfish internalizations or gratuitous unkindness, is the criterion by which the success of Bakhtin's thought must be measured.[26]

Can a balance on dialogue be achieved between Bakhtin's admirers and his detractors? By judging Bakhtin's account of Dostoevsky negligent in this matter of responsible relationships with real others in real time, the anti-Bakhtinians raise substantial questions about the ethical center of his entire enterprise. Does dialogism affirm self and other or does it efface both sides? Scholars at work on Bakhtin's Silver Age context have hinted at links between his thought and Solovievian and Symbolist experiments of the Russian Decadent period—which were, after all, not that distant from the young Bakhtin in Petrograd. Leading poets of the prewar period were experimenting with nonconsummated marriage, homoerotic utopias, metaphysical equivalents of the nuclear family, and extravagant projects for transcending death. Under the influence of Platonic philosophy, they advertised a wide variety of self-absorbed, autonomous, sterile structures for intimate love.[27] Can it be said that Bakhtin's self-other paradigms belong to that company?

Let us turn to Bakhtin's own self-evaluation. In the early 1960s he summed up Dostoevsky's major innovations in the art of the novel with the following three postulates.[28] First, Dostoevsky is credited with structuring a "new image of a human being that is not finalized by anything (not even death)"—to which Bakhtin adds, with his customary inspirational stoicism, that such a human image is unfinalizable because "its meaning cannot be resolved or abolished by reality (to kill does not mean to refute)." Second, Bakhtin claims that Dostoevsky devised a way to represent, through words, the "self-developing idea, inseparable from personality." And third, Bakhtin honors Dostoevsky as the writer who discovered dialogue "as a special form of interaction among autonomous and equally signifying consciousnesses." We might inquire how much of this three-part assessment is still intact.

The first and third "discoveries" have come under sustained attack. The most articulate opponents of Bakhtin today argue that Dostoevsky did indeed believe that "to kill was to refute"—and to neglect the importance of all the killing that goes on in his novels is simply to misread the

---

[26] See the discussion of Davydov's paper at the October 1995 Bakhtin centennial readings at the Moscow Dostoevsky Museum, in N. A. Pan'kov, "Bakhtin na fone Dostoevskogo," *DKKh, no. 2 (96)*, 134–37, esp. 137.

[27] For an excellent discussion, see Olga Matich, "The Symbolist Meaning of Love: Theory and Practice," in Irina Paperno and Joan Delaney Grossman, eds., *Creating Life: The Aesthetic Utopia of Russian Modernism* (Stanford: Stanford University Press, 1994), 24–50.

[28] "Toward a Reworking of the Dostoevsky Book [1961]," in *PDP*, 184.

novels. They have also argued that interaction within those novelistic worlds does not take place among "autonomous and equally signifying" voices: it takes place between mortal bodies, and the interaction there is either deadly political and manifestly unequal, as when Raskolnikov assaults an old woman with an axe and Pyotr Verkhovensky stalks Kirillov with a gun, or—if we are dealing with polyphonic dialogue rather than with murder—the interaction, more often than not, is narcissistic, isolating, and indifferent to the real world (to death in the first instance, but also to any vulnerability or desire coming from, or directed toward, a needful other). Dostoevsky saw this misuse of language and parodied it. He was far more attuned to the healing effects of *non*verbal communication—silence, icons, genuflections, visual images—than he was to the alleged beneficent effect of words. And thus, as regards the second achievement with which Bakhtin credits Dostoevsky—the "self-developing idea" fused to personality and freed from the distractions and humiliating constraints of plot—many readers consider this more a recipe for monologue than for dialogue. I have my idea, you have yours, and we will feed them to each other without listening to each other until each of our ideas has ripened and the novel is over.

This critique has been taken—unjustly but provocatively—to an even more sinister extreme by one group of Russian postmodernists, the Conceptualists. They see something suspicious and evasive in the obsession with "dialogue" and "naming" that marks so many Russian philosophers, in whose ranks they now enroll Bakhtin.[29] In theory, they say, Bakhtin might have believed that "to exist [authentically] means to communicate dialogically," but in practice this "dialogic utopia" ends up as a "neurosis of incessant talk" that pretends to provide options for real people trapped in real places but in fact makes it altogether too easy and attractive for us to separate words from any ordinary real-life referents. Conceptualists claim there is a venerable Russian tradition of putting words in circulation for their own sake—and its genealogy reads like an honor roll of Russian literature. The starting point is Nikolai Gogol, whose genius created unprecedentedly palpable reality out of waxy masses of words and sounds that lacked any referent; the brooding talkers and dreamers of Dostoevsky and his devoted servant Bakhtin are two intermediary steps; and the proud inheritor, they insist, is Stalinist Russia. For as the Conceptualists' chronicler Mikhail Epstein has noted, the autonomy of the

---

[29] Speaking of Dostoevsky, the conceptualist artist Ilya Kabakov has remarked that the incessant chatter that fills the novels does not "test an idea" at all; those endless debates succeed only in drawing in and implicating the reader to such an extent that "the thread is lost," the chains of debates grow to "monstrous length," and all parties forget what is at stake (Il'ia Kabakov, *Zhizn' mukh / Das Leben der Fliegen* [Kölnischer Kunstverein, n.d.], 128).

uttered word in Russia did not further the interests of civil liberty or freedom. Instead, it has lent a sort of voodoo authenticity to fantasy constructs, including those fantasies that could inflict a great deal of public harm: "It was the hidden assumption of the Soviet system, after all, to give the status of absolute reality to its own ideological pronouncements."[30]

The psychoanalytic critic Aleksandr Etkind provides a concrete example. "Let us imagine Soviet interrogators, contemporaries of Vygotsky and Bakhtin," he writes in *Sodom and Psyche*, his 1996 collection of essays on the intellectual life of Russia's Silver Age. "What they needed was the fact of an accused person's confession, because the other extra-verbal reality did not exist. Whether or not the accused was lying, slandering himself, doing it under threat or in order to bring an intolerable torture to an end—all that was unimportant, because something other than words was required in their account: feelings, acts, situations. . . . In the Soviet person, there is nothing that is not expressed in words. Except for words, nothing exists."[31] Thus do the Conceptualist critics and their ideological allies wish to de-Stalinize Russia by fighting against the proliferation of ecstatic, indestructible, floating words and ideas, the sort of words that during the Communist period almost boasted their independence from the world as it really was. Such words, precisely because of their immortal status, are exempt from judgment and can be irresponsible, promiscuous, lie-bearing. Therefore the Conceptualists build up and smash images, analyze museums and bomb sites, compile lengthy treatises documenting the life of the housefly. Far more ethical than to work with the ever renegotiable poetic word, they argue, is to acknowledge a perishable world full of mortal, destructible, fully ordinary and thus precious events and things.

We have now come full circle. The polyphonic Bakhtin, freedom fighter and champion of the individual voice, has become solipsistic

---

[30] Epstein has thus argued the Conceptualist case contra Bakhtin, drawing on one of their prominent practitioners, Ilya Kabakov: "For Bakhtin, the dialogic relationship is the only genuine mode of human existence: addressing the other through language. For Kabakov, this obsession with dialogue bears witness to the lack of any relationship between words and a corresponding reality . . . Kabakov sees this inclination for verbosity as a symptom of Russia's fear of emptiness and the implicit realization of its ubiquity. . . . For Bakhtin, to exist authentically means to communicate dialogically, which allows us to interpret Bakhtin himself as a utopian thinker seeking an ultimate transcendence of human loneliness, alienation, and objectification. Kabakov advances a postmodern perspective on this dialogical utopia, revealing the illusory character of a paradise of communication" (Mikhail Epstein, "The Philosophical Implications of Russian Conceptualism," paper delivered at the American Association for the Advancement of Slavic Studies, Washington, D.C., October 1995).

[31] Aleksandr Etkind, *Sodom i Psikheia: Ocherki intellektual'noi istorii Serebrianogo veka* (Moscow: ITs-Garant, 1996), 296.

Bakhtin, Stalinist fellow traveler. This is truly a monstrous trajectory. To soften its effects and do justice to the man, we now attempt, as we bring to a close this first problematic reassessment of the legacy, a defense of Bakhtin—who remains, after all has been rethought and resaid, one of the most powerful thinkers of our century.

"THE TORMENTS OF DIALOGUE": IN DEFENSE OF BAKHTIN

In a 1994 issue of *Filosofskie nauki*, to honor the upcoming centennial, the literary scholar and philosopher P. S. Gurevich published a lengthy (and rather negative) review of leading American Dostoevsky scholarship under the title *Muki dialoga*—the torments of dialogue.[32] He considers much Western work that draws on Bakhtin rather primitive, in part because it "ignores the polyphonic nature of polyphony itself" and too often endorses some monologic slice of an idea that is then allowed to regiment and dictate the whole. The polyphonic principle should not be viewed as simply one more method for analyzing artistic practices, Gurevich concludes. "Dialogue, polyphonism are passwords to a new cultural paradigm—which, with difficulty and through all the sluggishness, monologism, and torments of communication, is cutting itself a path" (31). This sense of dialogue's great difficulty, the enormous pressure and precision required to carry it out honestly, is a useful preface to any rehabilitation of Bakhtin's central concept. For the Conceptualists are wrong about Bakhtin and words. Although Bakhtin was certainly pro-language— he was, after all, a philosopher of language, that was the subject of his research—he did not share any of the transfigurational attitudes toward the word endorsed by Symbolists, avant-garde Futurists, and later by the state-sponsored Socialist Realists. He did not believe that one could subdue nature through words; he was no proponent of the theosophist doctrine that "naming could control the unknown" or that knowledge of the sign permits one to manipulate reality. The sentiments underlying Andrei Bely's essay "The Magic of Words," with its invocation of a *zvukovaia taina* or a "secret to the very sound of things," were wholly foreign to Bakhtin. Accordingly, he steered clear of the theurgist, incantational, mystagogical, and occult theories of language so in vogue during his

---

[32] P. S. Gurevich, "K 100-letiiu so dnia rozhdeniia M. M. Bakhtina: Muki dialoga," in *Filosofskie nauki*, nos. 4–6 (1994): 15–31. The scholars discussed are R. L. Cox (*Between Earth and Heaven: Shakespeare, Dostoevsky, and the Meaning of Christian Tragedy*; Robert Belknap, *The Structure of "The Brothers Karamazov"*; Gary Saul Morson, *The Boundaries of Genre: Dostoevsky's "Diary of a Writer" and the Traditions of Literary Utopia*; Joseph Frank, *Dostoevsky: The Years of Ordeal, 1850–1859*; and Robert Louis Jackson, *The Art of Dostoevsky: Deliriums and Nocturnes*. Further page references given in text.

youth. And of course he had scant sympathy for the Symbolist and Futurist concept of time as millenarian, where empirical speech matters less than hieratic speech prophecy. In sum, for a Russian literary critic, Bakhtin was remarkably phlegmatic about the ability of literary consciousness to transform the world. His *logos*-centrism, such as it was, differed profoundly from that of his contemporaries. He was ambitious for the word in another way.

Let us suspend our reservations about Bakhtin's reading of Dostoevsky, then, and consider an attempt to examine this "new cultural paradigm" at its root, in one scholar's reconstruction of Bakhtin's original context. Some of the harsher objections to its later applications in literature might be mitigated or appear in more sympathetic light. In an essay published in the 1991 volume *M. M. Bakhtin and Philosophical Culture of the Twentieth Century*, Boris Egorov relates dialogism to the revolution in scientific thought preceding and following the Great War.[33] During that decade, he reminds us, the positivism, linearity, and "singularity" of nineteenth-century thinking across a wide number of fields (philosophy, political economy, biology, and the natural sciences) gave way to new "pluralist" and multi-perspectival models, inspired by Einsteinian thought (15). The more strictly scientific fields made this transition with remarkable speed—and, Egorov notes, Bakhtin was determined that literary consciousness not fall behind. The young, intellectually precocious Bakhtin was passionate about a global coordination of paradigm shifts; a humanist, he poorly concealed his competition with the exact sciences. (This being so, Egorov finds rather odd the "hostile coldness" on Bakhtin's part toward the Russian Formalists, themselves self-proclaimed scientists and specifiers, and, in turn, that group's "total indifference to the appearance of Bakhtin's book on Dostoevsky" [16]. The indifference could easily be explained, however, by the fact that the Formalists—such as remained of them by 1929—were in no position to take a stand for anyone, least of all a fellow scholar already under arrest.)

Bakhtin's determination to connect the principles underlying modern physics with the principles animating human culture reflected the maximalist, unifying aspirations of Russian thought in general, to which Bakhtin was in no sense immune. (Here Egorov would sympathize with Gachev's suggestion that Bakhtin was more under the influence of Soviet-style transfiguration fantasies than it at first appears.) Such ambitions are always alluring and always dangerous, Egorov remarks. For natural science is obliged to reckon neither with memory nor faith—and in any event cannot afford to legitimate itself through such factors—whereas human

---

[33] B. F. Egorov, "Dialogizm M. M. Bakhtina na fone nauchnoi mysli 1920-kh godov," in *MMB i fil kul XX, 1 (91)*, 7–16. Further page references given in text.

culture (and especially culture as understood in the religious circles that Bakhtin frequented throughout the 1920s) cannot afford to ignore them. Such postulates as "universal relativity, dialogic ambivalence, the insta- bility or transitoriness of all sensations and concepts," if moved mechan- ically from science into the humanities, could result in a destruction of "the very bases of human culture: the durability of traditions, ethical commandments and prohibitions, and other so-called eternal categories" (15). Principles of relativity and ambivalence function differently among human beings than among particles of the universe. During a scientific revolution of such magnitude, only religious faith, with its a priori ideals and monologic dogma, "could offer a substantial counterweight to all the varieties of subjectivism and relativism" that would otherwise spin out of control. Bakhtin, a believer, presumed this counterweight to be in place. Religious consciousness would provide the proper discipline for dialogic relations occurring under the newly "relativized" conditions. But as So- viet history unfolded, cultural professionals in Bolshevik Russia (begin- ning with the atheistic Formalists) were increasingly incapable of preserv- ing, and soon even of perceiving, this anchor of Bakhtin's thought.

How might Egorov's reminder help us to modify the severe judgment that Natalia Reed and others have passed on Bakhtin's polyphonic image of Dostoevsky? Perhaps Reed is unjust when she detects only solipsism (and thus, presumably, a personality's craven desire to escape into silence or to safety) in Bakhtin's readings of those Dostoevskian heroes who appear to internalize dialogues instantly and dispense with real others. Such a reflex is no passage to safety and certainly no route to be con- sciously preferred. For "persons of the idea," the inner self is never an escape. It is a trap. Real others, if the afflicted hero can find them and hold on to them, are the escape. After all, Raskolnikov—plagued with "universal relativity," "dialogic ambivalence," the "transitoriness of con- cepts," all the latest legal, scientific, and atheistic ideas—manages to rid himself rather easily of his immediate interlocutors (the pawnbroker, his best and most loyal friend Razumikhin, his devoted mother and sister); those are the people who could have offered him his only relief by tying him to the miracle of real interactive life. Having thrown them over, he is at last free to experience the most excruciating torments of dialogue— precisely when left alone with himself. (Only Sonya, note, will not be put off by his cruelty, and at times Raskolnikov hates her for it. His own family loves him in much too normal a way to endure such treatment; his mother goes mad, and up until the very end his sister is in anguish, seek- ing "reasons.") Without a doubt, the lonely microdialogue that plagues Raskolnikov is not answerable or responsible. It does not give real others the chance to intervene, talk back, offer help, pass condemnatory or mer- ciful judgment, finalize an image. But the point to emphasize, it would seem, is that obsessively inner dialogue—although a very bad habit—is not a coward's way out. The exclusive innerness of dialogue does not alleviate a life situation, enrich a consciousness, or make one more creative. It is a disaster. Raskolnikov knows this.

And surely to demonstrate just how disastrous this reflex is, be it voluntary or not, is part of Dostoevsky's larger purpose. So Linetsky is wrong, I believe, when he suggests that Bakhtin does not appreciate ordinary dialogue, dialogue "in the traditional sense of the term." There is every indication that Bakhtin follows Dostoevsky closely in his reverence for such crystalline moments, which are awarded to innocent children, to beloved elders, and to the state of prayer. (Just such a dialogic moment descends on Raskolnikov when, after Marmeladov's death, he asks Sonya's stepsister Polina to love him and pray for "thy servant Rodion.") But if the hero of a novel functions not as a character acting out an uncomplicated plot function but as an *idea-person* [*ideia-chelovek*, a "person born of the idea"[34]]—that is, if a person is run by living concepts rather than by biology, a detective plot, or grace—then such ordinary, declamatory, preciously wonderful dialogues are extremely difficult to conduct. Such is the natural logic, or pressure, of polyphonic design. Sonya Marmeladova, almost wholly silent and rarely in control of her words, stands on the threshold between inner and outer acts. By contemplating her iconic image, Raskolnikov is driven forcibly over that threshold back into real-life communication (to confession and public trial)— not out of guilt, for he avoids acknowledging his guilt, but out of weariness and loneliness, for that reconciling step is the only relief possible from the cacophony of unfinalized inner dialogue.

This "microdialogue within" is a torment. But it must be said, lest it look like easy salvation is just around the corner, that macrodialogue in the outer world—while more open to change and offering (as Porfiry Petrovich assures Raskolnikov) "more fresh air"—need not, by any means, be truth seeking or consolatory. Read Bakhtin carefully, and you will see that nowhere does he suggest that dialogue between real people necessarily brings truth, beauty, happiness, or honesty. It brings only concretization (and even that is temporary), and the possibility of change, of some forward movement. Under optimal conditions, dialogue provides

---

[34] See *PDP*, ch. 3, "The Idea in Dostoevsky": "It is not the idea in itself that is the 'hero of Dostoevsky's works,' as Engelhardt has claimed, but rather the *person born of that idea*. It again must be emphasized that the hero in Dostoevsky is a person of the idea: this is not a character, not a temperament, not a social or psychological type; such externalized and finalized images of persons cannot of course be combined with the image of a *fully valid* idea. It would be absurd, for example, even to attempt to combine Raskolnikov's idea, which we understand and *feel* (according to Dostoevsky an idea can and must not only be understood, but also "felt") with his finalized character" (85).

options. But there can still be mutual deception, mountains of lies exchanged, pressing desires unanswered or unregistered, gratuitous cruelty administered on terrain to which only the intimate beloved has access. By having a real other respond to me, I am spared one thing only: the worst cumulative effects of my own echo chamber of words.

This being the case, one could argue that Kariakin, too, is only partially correct when he regrets the absence of a "finger pointing toward the truth" in Bakhtin's polyphony. For an ethical trajectory could be seen as inherent from the start in this spiraling alternation between "polyphonic" internalization of dialogue and then escape from its unbearable torments. Moral growth might even be inevitable in novels of the sort Dostoevsky designed, where the chief crime is not murder, not even psychic cruelty, but the drive for excessive autonomy and the human failing that fuels this drive, which is spiritual pride. If I proudly internalize all dialogue so as "not to depend" on another's personality or body or service or idea—I will *never* be alone or at peace again. Inner dialogue will give me no rest: again, not because I feel guilty, repentant, or even interested in another person's point of view (Raskolnikov was none of those things, even at the end) but because only concrete external others, in responding to me, can check the monstrous growth of my own view of things. Only the other can finalize my thoughts long enough for me to get outside them, assess them soberly, and thus stand a chance to tame or modify them. Since no major Dostoevskian personality can survive a state of hyperactive inner dialogue for long, either suicide or some form of religious conversion out of that solitary vortex is unavoidable.

In sum, critics of dialogism and polyphony are correct that Bakhtin underestimates (as Dostoevsky never does) the sheer viciousness of the criminal imagination. True, Bakhtin was thoroughly familiar with bodily pain, not surprised by cruelty, and not offended by death. He can also be faulted, it seems, for a lack of interest in the negative emotions and venial sins that, for many readers, constitute the core attraction of Dostoevsky's plots: lechery, lying, jealousy, greed, violence. To Gasparov's complaint that Bakhtin is too quick to encourage us to "expropriate others' words" and turn them to our own selfish use, Bakhtin would nod sadly in agreement: indeed, there is no reason why this process of appropriation need be virtuous, happy, healthy, or just—but it is universal. Although unimpressed by many of the stimulants natural to novels, about the inescapability of dialogue and the cost that dialogue exacts, Bakhtin is not naive.

What are those costs, the risks and routine torments of dialogue? To answer this question, we should leave the specifics of Dostoevsky's crisis-ridden texts behind, for Bakhtin—as provocative as he is on that novelist—did not find in him an entirely conducive vehicle for his most precious ideas. Dialogue is a risk precisely because it is so ordinary, prosaic, undramatic. We risk dialogue whenever we take on a responsible, but provisional, commitment—which is continually. And here we might expand on one aspect of Egorov's hypothesis that Bakhtin, an admirer of those breakthroughs in physics that revolutionized science during his adolescent years, should be aligned with the physical scientists rather than the metaphysical Symbolists. At issue is the concept of relativity.

It is important not to confuse *relativity* with *relativism* in disputes over the virtues of dialogue, for the two words are not at all the same. Precisely because we live in a universe governed by relativity, relativism, as a working principle for ethics, is so undesirable and dangerous. (It is of some interest that Bakhtin's best friend and closest intellectual mentor, Matvei Kagan, a gifted mathematician and student of neo-Kantian philosophy in Berlin during the First World War, was apparently sought after in Berlin as a secretary by both Paul Natorp and Albert Einstein. The theory of relativity was not perceived as incompatible with the teachings of transcendental idealism.)[35] Sensing the confusion between relativity and relativism still operative after forty years, Bakhtin added this sentence to his revised Dostoevsky book, almost as an afterthought: "We see no special need to point out that the polyphonic approach has nothing in common with relativism (or with dogmatism)" (*PDP*, 69).

Why was it important to Bakhtin that polyphony not be seen as relativistic? Because, we might suggest: If there existed a single unitary standard by which all acts could be judged, it would be easy to chart the moral (or immoral) life. But since there is no such single standard, every individual consciousness must define for itself local constraints; it must pass its own judgment, take a stand even when blinkered, seek out and defend the truth as he or she sees it.[36] Much more inner discipline and

---

[35] In the early 1990s Brian Poole, now at the University of Berlin, worked several years with the Kagan family in Moscow (Matvei Isaevich's widow and daughter Iudit Matveevna), helping to prepare the rich Kagan archive for publication and researching Bakhtin's huge, lost *Bildungsroman* project. Unfortunately, little of Poole's superb, meticulously scholarly work is yet in print in any language, although he is a contributing editor to the *Collected Works of Bakhtin* and under contract to translate into English the Bakhtin-Duvakin interviews. I draw here on his "Rol' M. I. Kagana v stanovlenii filosofii M. M. Bakhtina (ot Germana Kogena k Maksu Sheleru)," *B sb III 97*, 162–81, esp. 176, and later on personal correspondence.

[36] Sergei Bocharov's irritation at the Bakhtin industry and its proliferation of schools and rules is based on just this conviction about his mentor. As he put it in his November 1995 centennial remarks at the Moscow Dostoevsky Museum: "It seems to me that the credo of Bakhtin's own moral philosophy is contained in this proposition: that 'oughtness' is not moral but singular. What does that mean? It means that 'oughtness' is mine, i.e., singular. Another person has another 'oughtness,' i.e., we always act and must act at our own peril and risk, and not according to some general rule—of course checking out an overall general norm or code but each time interpreting it in one's own way." Pan'kov, "Bakhtin na fone Dostoevskogo," *DKKh, no. 2 (96)*, 132.

active articulation is required in an Einsteinian universe than in the more stable, straightforwardly anchored models of the cosmos that preceded it. Once completed, each loop connecting one person to another in a specific time and space takes on nonnegotiable importance—because each of these loops is *in principle* negotiable; in a world where no single God or "god-term" binds events together, it is even more true that from each particularized vantage point "all is *not* permitted" and every side is *not* equally valid. (How unpersuasive is Ivan Karamazov's remark: "If God is dead, then all is permitted." On the contrary, because God might well be dead, for that very reason all is not, and cannot be, permitted. Now I must decide for myself what to forbid and what to permit, and the burden of a discriminating personal decision weighs much more heavily than any penalty for disobedience to a known law.) In "Toward a Philosophy of the Act," Bakhtin sketches such an individualized cosmos in this way: "Rays of light, as it were, fan out from my unique singularity, which, passing through time, confirm the human way of history."[37] We sense in such a passage Bakhtin's trademark preference for stating his truths in a major key. But a confirmation of the human way that relies on nothing more grand or authoritative than my own singular, tiny, local dialogic gestures, which may or may not be registered and elicit a response, requires a great deal of tolerance and patient work.

Bakhtin's notion of architectonics (the "non-alibi in existence") and later the ground rules he lays down for dialogue are predicated on just this reality. Individuation is impossible to avoid. Dialogue (both inner and outer) is extremely difficult, prone to distortion, but probably inescapable. Despite these handicaps, however, individuals must be able to defend each act they commit and each judgment they pass. To make any of it succeed even minimally, the world requires trust—and because Bakhtin appears to presume the existence of that trust, his "cleansing" of Dostoevsky has come under special suspicion. Bakhtin is faulted as evasive, naive, complacent toward evil. The charge is all the easier to sustain because Bakhtin is not an especially astute *visual* witness; he does not dwell on the palpable results of evil deeds and is not one to stumble over a dead body in the middle of the road. Perhaps because his methodology does not seek to "see" deeds—in the way that a Structuralist seeks to plot data on a field, with all the effects pinned into place—but rather concentrates on auditory points of exchange, on the words and intonations accompanying or describing these deeds, he is more inclined to presume negotiability, detect a double-voicedness, grant a second chance. What Bakhtin's ethical system will not tolerate, however, is relativism,

---

[37] "Toward a Philosophy of the Act," 60 (Liapunov translation adjusted). See also the introduction in Gary Saul Morson and Caryl Emerson, *Rethinking Bakhtin: Extensions and Challenges* (Evanston, Ill.: Northwestern University Press, 1989), 24, 9–10.

when that principle is invoked to release us from the obligation to evaluate and commit. Polyphony, I suggest, is Bakhtin's metaphor for the increased burden dialogue must bear in an Age of Relativity.

Let us now sum up the fate of polyphony. Bakhtin was fascinated with scientistic models and—we are told—sought to establish a moral philosophy rigorous enough to rival the Germans. He had come to maturity in an era fascinated by numerical manipulation and classification: series, sets, groups, the emergence of sociology as a profession. Numbers lent themselves to grids and structures. And much like Wittgenstein at a slightly later time, Bakhtin was concerned to preserve the principle of relationalism without endorsing systematic structuralism (and why indeed should relationships, to be valid, organize themselves into a system?). Still, as the most thoughtful Bakhtin scholars now acknowledge, a pure and unalloyed polyphony challenges not just systematic thought but also the very integrity of the personalities it pulls in.[38] Bakhtin himself returned to the ambiguities of the method a half-century after he had coined the concept, in this note: "The peculiarities of polyphony. The lack of finalization of the polyphonic dialogue . . . These dialogues are conducted by unfinalized individual personalities and not by psychological subjects. The somewhat unembodied quality of these personalities (disinterested surplus)."[39] Disinterested, perhaps even "somewhat unembodied," these "unfinalized individual personalities" who engage in polyphonic dialogue constitute a wondrous population: secure, raised on the virtues, free of embarassing dependencies. It is not easy to see ourselves in it. And from

---

[38] Russian philosophers have thoroughly explored the shortcomings of the dialogic model and the danger of taking Bakhtin's ideal of polyphony too literally. As Liudmila Gogotishvili paraphrased the familiar complaint in her 1992 essay on the problem of Bakhtin's "evaluative relativism": "If speech belongs in turn first to me, then to the other, then to us, then to some third, and there is no superior possessor of meaning who might cap this uncoordinated clamor of voices with its own centralizing word, then it follows that the meaning of speech in Bakhtin's scheme of things loses all its objective features. If there is no direct word, that is, no word issuing forth from a stable 'I' or 'we' and confidently addressed to its object, it means that linguistic form cannot have any truth-significance at all. As a matter of principle, such a word cannot contain in itself the truth of the world" (145). In her attempt to answer this objection, Gogotishvili points to the old error of assuming that people are like things, that they can attach themselves to values with no work or risk, and that a truth need be singular or eternal. *Absolute polyphony*, she admits, is impossible (152). Nor is it desirable: the author's center must remain the clearing house. But polyphonic aspirations are not for that reason fraudulent, reductive, or self-serving. Polyphony is a generator. It generates boundaries, which are required to keep individual voices vulnerable and distinct from one another. For "the absence of a unified and singular direct word . . . is what protects the cultured word from barbarism" (172). See L. A. Gogotishvili, "Filosofiia iazyka M. M. Bakhtina i problema tsennostnogo reliativizma," in *MMB kak filosof 92*, 142–74.

[39] "From Notes Made in 1970–71," *SpG*, 151.

our outsiderly perspective, therefore, we must confirm that as a reader of literary and real-life scenes there are certain things Bakhtin cannot do.

First, as a rule, Bakhtin does not do beginnings and ends. He only does middles. Wholly committed to process and to the dynamics of response, Bakhtin concerns himself very little with how something *starts* (a personality, a responsibility) or how it might be brought to an effective, well-shaped end. This neglect of genesis and overall indifference to closure left a profound trace on his thought, imparting to his literary readings their strange, aerated, often fragmentary character. The passion for the ongoing middle of a text also separates him profoundly from his subject Dostoevsky, perhaps the nineteenth century's greatest prose poet of original sin, Revelation, and Apocalypse.[40]

Second, Bakhtin cannot hear a fully self-confident monologue anywhere. As he matured, he became increasingly adamant on this point. In his view, even language deliberately employed "monologically"—in ultimatums, categorical farewells, suicide notes, military commands—in fact wants to be answered; it wants to be taken as only the penultimate word, and the person who utters such bits of monologic speech is always hoping that the person who hears it will care enough (against all odds and linguistic cues) to answer back. Within such heightened fields of expectation, a failure to respond is itself a response, giving rise to its own fully voiced anguish. As long as we are alive, we have no right to pull out on another person who addresses us in need—and no right, apparently, to be left alone. No single moment is *ever* wholly authoritative or closed for Bakhtin. Even dying, it turns out, is no guarantee of an escape from dialogue.

In some jottings on "Dostoevsky's quests" written in his working notebooks near the end of his life, Bakhtin included this enigmatic little sequence: "The word as something personal. Christ as truth. I ask him."[41] Later in the same passage, Bakhtin remarks without elaboration: "The juxtaposition of truth and Christ in Dostoevsky" (150). Reference here is to the letter that Dostoevsky wrote from his Siberian exile to Madame Fonvizina in March 1854, with its famous remark that "if anyone could

---

[40] Without a doubt, beginnings and ends fascinated the novelist. To be fascinated does not mean to understand their causes, however. See, for example, these lines from Dostoevsky's essay "Two Suicides": "We know only the daily flow of the things we see, and this only on the surface; but the ends and the beginnings are things that, for human beings, still lie in the realm of the fantastic" (October 1976 entry in Fyodor Dostoevsky, *A Writer's Diary*, trans. Kenneth Lantz, vol. 1 [Evanston, Ill.: Northwestern University Press, 1993], 651). Although Bakhtin remarked on several occasions that faith in a "miracle" [*chudo*] was both necessary and proper in life, he was far less willing than Dostoevsky to theorize about "fantastical" or mystical material.

[41] "From Notes Made in 1970–71," in *SpG*, 148. Further page references given in text.

prove to me that Christ is outside the truth and if the truth really did exclude Christ, then I should prefer to stay with Christ and not with the truth."[42] How might Bakhtin have expanded on this juxtaposition? He would argue, I think, that Christ had come to seem "more true" to Dostoevsky largely because, by that time in his life, Dostoevsky had put in so much energy trying to understand Him, had received so many varied "answers" within himself, had returned so often to the same beloved set of parables and pondered them so deeply, that it no longer mattered what issues had been resolved or concretely "proven" by the image and example of Christ.[43] For what matters ultimately to human beings and what generates value in our lives rests on two factors: first, where we turn for help, and then, the *time put in*. Thus I should not ask such questions as "Who am I?"—an essentialist paradox that admits of no answer—but rather, "How much time do I have to become something else?" The choice to spend time with another personality and to take its approach to the world seriously is itself the core and substance of truth.

From this we might conclude that Bakhtin appreciated truth and religious faith in his own somewhat secular, thoroughly dialogized way. He was, to be sure, a believer, active in the underground Russian Orthodox Church; in the 1920s he lectured on Kant and religion; his thought was never atheistic. But if we take his corpus of writings as a whole, Bakhtin seems to be saying: What I need to remain spiritually alive, what anyone needs, is not necessarily faith in God. What I need and cannot do without is the faith that someone else has faith in me. This, surely, is what Georgii Gachev had in mind when he opened his irreverent memoir on the master with the following observation: that while Bakhtin, in the "prayer hall" and "cultural church" of his nocturnal seminars, shared some traits with the proselytizing Baptists, there was "not much Russian Orthodox Christianity in his religiosity": "Not God but one's neighbor, that was his accent: 'Where two (dialogue!—G. G.) have gathered in My name, there am I also among you': love your neighbor and you realize God . . . In Bakhtin's understanding of *sobornost'* [spiritual community],

---

[42] *Letters of Fyodor Michailovich Dostoevsky to His Family and Friends*, trans. Ethel Colburn Mayne (New York: Macmillan, n.d.), 71.

[43] In a 1995 memoir Sergei Bocharov recalls that Bakhtin was in the habit of dividing "truth," *pravda*, into two parts: there was the "truth-miracle" (*pravda-chudo*), which was always unexpected and unprepared for, and then there was the debased category of "truth as force" (*pravda-sila*), "totalitarian truth." Bocharov recalls that very much in this Christological spirit Bakhtin had often remarked that "truth and force were incompatible" and that truth therefore could never conquer or triumph. If present at all, it would always be in a subordinated and humbled guise. See Sergei Bocharov, "Sobytie bytiia: O Mikhaile Mikhailoviche Bakhtine," in *Novyi mir*, no. 11 (1995): 211–21, esp. 213, 215.

everyone gazes not upward, toward heaven, nor forward, at the priest or the altar, but at one another, realizing the kenosis of God, on the low horizontal level that is our own."[44]

Such sectarian and communitarian emphases were not uncommon among Russian nineteenth-century novelists and might well have interested Bakhtin himself. But many readers feel uncomfortable—and properly so—when such a diluted notion of the Christian faith is applied to Dostoevsky. As Gachev notes, in Bakhtin's cosmos "there is no Creation as a given, for the world is created each time—in communication, in an encounter, in our efforts to listen to each other . . . In this sense Bakhtin is an anti-Hellene and anti-Platonist" (107). This overwhelming preference on Bakhtin's part for Creation-in-process must temper our reading of his book on Dostoevsky.

The cautionary note sounded above prompts us to a third and final area where Bakhtin cannot be expected to perform. Somewhat like Dostoevsky's Idiot Prince Myshkin—and very unlike Dostoevsky himself—Bakhtin was temperamentally unfit for polemics. He would not condemn or exclude. All memoir accounts of Bakhtin emphasize this aspect of his mature personality: whether because of tolerance, languor, aristocratic disdain, commitment to dialogue, carnival optimism, Christian meekness, or simply fatigue, chronic illness, and pain—there was, as one Jubilee memoirist put it, a sort of "lightness," *legkost'*, to Bakhtin's person that made it absolutely impossible for him to take a firm or final stand on a question, to impose rigid constraints, or to endorse any form of violence.[45] This "lightness" has proved a serious obstacle to politicizing his thought. It shaped his understanding of dialogue in Dostoevsky as well.

Let us close this chapter not on a polemical "response to criticism" in Bakhtin's own voice (such a response was never forthcoming) but on a juxtaposition of worldviews at, as it were, one critical remove. The parties involved—one anti-Bakhtinian and one Bakhtinian—are of equally long and dignified standing. The dispute between them has larger implications for literary study than the eccentric, rather too crisis-ridden tableaus of the Conceptualists might suggest. Speaking for the opposition is Mikhail Gasparov, a leitmotif of the present study, who was already doing battle with the cult in the late 1970s, lamenting Bakhtin's miserable written record of hostility to poetry and challenging the popular comic nihilism

---

[44] See Georgii Gachev, "Bakhtin," in *Russkaia duma: Portrety russkikh myslitelei* (Moscow: Novosti, 1991), 105–18, esp. 105, 106. Further page references given in text.

[45] Sergei Averintsev, "V stikhii 'bol'shogo vremeni,'" *Literaturnaia gazeta*, no. 45 (15 November 1995): 6.

of carnival.[46] As we have seen, one of his recurring targets is the aggressive, self-assertive Bakhtinian reader, whom Gasparov considers an unduly privileged product of a dialogic approach to the world. In a 1994 article reviving the debate entitled "Criticism as an End in Itself," Gasparov, with his trademark bluntness and good humor, reiterated his dismay.[47]

In that essay, Gasparov laments current habits in the academy that encourage too loose and undisciplined a "dialogism" vis-à-vis one's object of study. Across a wide range of disciplines, he remarks, the desire has taken hold to make everything "speak to me, and on my own terms." This reflex leads to other bad habits from the Bakhtinian arsenal: a tendency to place too much value on prosy paraphrase or "internally persuasive discourse" (with its assumption that my own groping words are always worth more than any text I might memorize intact or wish to recite, unaltered, from someone else); the concomitant celebration of a code-free world; and thus the careless application of the word *dialogue* to what should be delicate tasks of scholarly reconstruction. Gasparov associates the solipsistic tendencies of post-Structuralist criticism with the assumption (silently laid at Bakhtin's door) that dialogue between a reader and a text is easy, pleasant, and for the critic to define the terms. Such critics proceed "from the assumption that if I am reading a poem, then it was written for me." But every step of my life, Gasparov writes, persuades me that

> nothing has been created or adapted for me in this world. . . . philology is in the service of communication. This communication is very difficult. I consider unjustifiably optimistic the current metaphor which says that between a reader and a work of art (or between anything at all in the world) a dialogue is taking place. Even when living people converse, we often hear not a dialogue but two chopped-up monologues. As the dialogue proceeds, each side constructs an image of the other that is convenient for it. One could talk with a stone with equal success and imagine the stone's answers to one's questions. Few people talk to stones nowadays—at least publicly—but every energetic person talks with Baudelaire or Racine precisely as with a stone, and receives precisely the answers that he or she wants to hear. . . . When we read the ancient *Conversations in the Kingdom of the Dead*—between Caesar and Sviatoslav, between Horace and Kantemir—we smile. But when we ourselves dream up a conversation with Pushkin or with Horace, we treat it

[46] See M. L. Gasparov, "M. M. Bakhtin in Russian Culture of the Twentieth Century," trans. Ann Shukman, in *Studies in Twentieth-Century Literature* (Fall 1984): 169–76, and its update by Ol'ga Sedakova in "Dialogi o Bakhtine," *Novyi krug*, no. 1 (Kiev, 1992): 113–17.

[47] M. L. Gasparov, "Kritika kak samotsel'," in *NLO*, no. 6 (1993–94): 6–9. A translation exists as "Criticism as a Goal in Itself," *Russian Studies in Literature* (A Sampling of *New Literary Review*) 31, no. 4 (Fall 1995): 36–40.

(alas) seriously. We do not wish to admit to ourselves that the spiritual world of Pushkin is for us just as alien as the world of an ancient Assyrian or [Chekhov's] dog Kashtanka. Questions which are major for us did not exist for him, and vice versa. (8–9)

Gasparov's critique of lazy dialogue in the academy is wide-ranging. But his position has not gone unchallenged. In a memoir that appeared late in 1995, Sergei Bocharov, the most reliable of that devoted group of scholars who served the master in his final decades, reviewed the case for Gasparov's "nonacceptance" of Bakhtin.[48] Responding to the essay "Criticism as an End in Itself," Bocharov remarked that the resistance to Bakhtinian method by Russia's most eminent poetician is based on a misreading. Gasparov despairs that we might ever enter into authentic dialogue with Pushkin or with Horace, Bocharov observes, because "Gasparov's position vis-à-vis a past culture (Horace or Pushkin or a scholarly book on Dostoevsky from the 1920s, it's all the same) is *as if to a foreign language*, which one must study as one does English or Chinese" (212). But Bakhtin was convinced that another's consciousness is not only a language. Once contact is made with it, it opens up in ways that cannot be "learned" by any norm-driven grammar at our disposal. Indeed, the modernist move that reduces the world to linguistic paradigms was quite alien to Bakhtin, for whom language could never be reductive and consciousness could never simply be "read." With all the humility in the world, the "text" of this consciousness cannot be recuperated or straightforwardly served—because it does not exist as such before I approach it. A dialogue of cultures (or even a dialogue between you and me) will not yield up the lucid satisfactions of a poem.

Dialogism uses language, but the "first philosophy" that underlies it is not (in the usual sense of the term) linguistic. It relies on an interactive logic that strains words to the limit—encouraging them to take on intonation, flesh, the contours of an entire worldview. The carnival world, it has been argued, is even more interactive—and the role allotted to words in that world far more problematic. It has an even longer, more distinguished record of fanciful application and creative abuse. We will now sample that debate.

[48] Bocharov, "Sobytie bytiia: O Mikhaile Mikhailoviche Bakhtine" (see n. 43 above). Quotation occurs on page 212.

CHAPTER 4

Carnival: Open-ended Bodies and Anachronistic Histories

"M. BAKHTIN possessed a genuinely philosophical gift for broadening out problems."[1] With this sentence, E. Yu. Savinova opens her 1991 essay entitled "Carnivalization and the Wholeness of Culture"—and as evidence of this breadth, she brings forward the fact that Bakhtin's "research into the writings of Rabelais resulted in the discovery of a completely new layer of culture in the Middle Ages and the Renaissance, which, in turn, altered the entire picture of the development of human culture." Savinova overstates, but in spirit she is correct. Of all Bakhtin's ideas, "the problem of carnival" has proved the broadest, most appealing, most accessible, and most readily translated into cultures and times distant from its original inspiration.

This ready translatability has been both a handicap and a boon. The handicaps are of the same variety that Mikhail Gasparov held against Bakhtinian dialogue: facile analogies, indiscriminately "open" documentation, overgeneralization, a dismissal of history, potential abuse of power by the critic. But the boons brought to the academy by Bakhtin's carnival have also been very real. Three years after the Rabelais book was published, an enthusiastic review article by a Soviet sinologist appeared in the professional journal *Narody Azii i Afriki* [Peoples of Asia and Africa] entitled, simply, "Reading Bakhtin."[2] The body of the article is devoted to the role played in Chinese culture by holidays, festive processions, and folk wisdom in anecdotes about Confucius. Its author credits Bakhtin for providing her with the scholarly precedent. Such irreverent celebratory rituals are underresearched in a field like sinology, she notes, which has been dominated for so long by the study of powerful, serious, duty-laden religions. Reading Bakhtin's book on a French writer opened up rich possibilities for her study of China; in fact, she writes, "The 'popular laughing carnival culture' he discovered makes available a new, fruitful elaboration of the two-cultures problem in every national culture" (106). Like Freud's fantasy of a single family romance that unfolds in each hu-

---

[1] E. Yu. Savinova, "Karnavalizatsiia i tselostnost' kul'tury," in *MMB i fil kul XX, 1 (91)*, 61–66, esp. 61.

[2] L. D. Pozdneeva, "Chitaia M. Bakhtina," in *Narody Azii i Afriki*, no. 2 (1968): 94–106. Further page references given in text.

man psyche without exception, Bakhtin's carnival idea has the thrill of a cultural and biological universal.

As a communication model, carnival dynamics has much to recommend it. The suspension of everyday anxieties during "holiday time" and "carnival space"—the specific locus being the vulnerable, yet superbly shame-free, grotesque body—rids both me and my most proximate neighbor of the excessive self-consciousness that keeps both of us lonely, our words insipid, and our outreaching gestures timid. (Remarkably, Bakhtin—a chain smoker and tea addict—attends almost not at all to the chemical side of carnival, that is, to intoxication, addiction, and drunkenness, although any practical understanding of holiday bawdiness or vulgarity is unthinkable without it.)[3] For the carnival self is not a wholly conscious entity. Its ideal is the open-ended irregular body, which has no need for visions of symmetrical beauty, feats of self-discipline, or acts of genuine intimacy. If the products of the mind (words, verbal dialogue, polyphonic maneuvers) are fastidiously individualizing and take a great deal of work to get right, then an imperfect body, by contrast, is something each of us possesses by definition—indeed, almost by default. However we age, we will, in the natural order of things, have more of such a body, not less. To affirm it, therefore, requires no special effort; in fact, to affirm it is an enormous relief.

It follows that entry into the world and worldview of carnival costs ridiculously little. Even without any special accent on the grotesque, we would all probably agree that much of our basic physiology—what Bakhtin calls the "lower bodily stratum"—is identical, involuntary, nonnegotiable. Its processes and appetites can thus be said to constitute (in a metaphor popular with postmodern critics) a common "language," native to all humans. And yet, as Bakhtin describes it in his *Rabelais*, the common language of bodies is of a certain highly convenient sort.

---

[3] On this issue see Marty Roth, "Carnival, Creativity, and the Sublimation of Drunkenness," in *Mosaic* 30, no. 2 (June 1997): 1–18 (University of Manitoba Press). On the mystique of a good cigarette for Bakhtin, see Galina Ponomareva's remark that the first question Bakhtin asked her during their initial meeting was whether she smoked. Answering in the negative, she relates, "at that moment I discovered how important it was for him—I wouldn't want to say it was a sacred ritual, but still—this communion while smoking, even if at times a wordless communion." Visitors could easily "sniff their way" to the Bakhtins' totally fumigated apartment in Saransk and Moscow. See G. B. Ponomareva, "Vyskazannoe i nevyskazannoe . . . (Vospominaniia o M. M. Bakhtine)," in *DKKh, no. 3 (95)*: 59–77, esp. 61. Consider also the (by now apocryphal) comment Bakhtin made to one of his undergraduate advisees in Saransk, who "always saw him sitting at his desk . . . and uninterruptedly smoking: as soon as one cigarette was finished he immediately lit up another. A cup of strong coffee. 'For some it is harmful to smoke,' [Bakhtin] often said; 'for others it is *necessary* to smoke.'" See Yu. D. Ryskin, "Moi vospominaniia o M. M. Bakhtine," in *MMB v zerk 95*: 111–13, esp. 112.

Whereas verbal languages must be learned, internalized, teased out of the mind—and even then they can be easily "misspoke," at the level of form as well as intent—the body (and even more, the grotesque body) cannot make a misstep or a mistake. It is already out of step; in any case a *faux pas* would not be noticed or remembered. This body is inviting and available to all without discrimination.[4] Its energy and material structures are displayed on the surface and turned toward the outside world in a frank, friendly way. Such communal baseness, the vigor of "le bas corporel," is the foundation of Bakhtin's carnival logic. Fueled by denunciation and aggressive rhetoric but apparently tainted by neither, its laughter is in equal parts defiant and rejuvenating. Since the grotesque body costs nothing to keep up, does not care if it wears out, has neither vanity nor fear of pain, cannot be self-sufficient, and is always "a body in the act of becoming," it is guaranteed triumph over classical form, institutional oppression, and individual death.

The optimism of all this is dazzling. Grounded in Rabelais but not limited to him, Bakhtin's concept of the grotesque body at home within *smekhovaia kul'tura*, a "culture of laughter," has proved irresistible. It is sensed by all as potentially subversive and yet, unlike so many subversions elaborated by intellectuals, it is not elitist (for we are working here—literally—with the lowest common human denominators). No wonder, then, that carnival and its corollary values moved with astonishing speed to inspire Paris 1968, British postcolonial theory, Latin American literature, continental and American feminist thought. On Russian soil, however (as we saw in chapter 2), Bakhtin's carnival idea had a difficult and suspicious reception from the start, indeed, from the very day of the dissertation defense.

This chapter examines some of the recurring paradoxes and continuing fascinations of Bakhtinian carnival as it was discussed in Russia during the early 1990s. By that time, the fundamental problems with the concept had long been acknowledged by detractors and enthusiasts alike. No one doubted that Bakhtin's image of carnival was utopian fantasy. It had long been a matter of record, stressed by cultural historians both East and West, that real-life carnival rituals—although perhaps great drunken fun for the short term—were not necessarily cheerful or carefree. In its func-

---

[4] See Mikhail Bakhtin, *Rabelais and His World*, trans. Hélène Iswolsky (Bloomington: Indiana University Press, 1984), esp. ch. 5, "The Grotesque Image of the Body." One unfortunate mistranslation in this uninspired but serviceable English version is the rendering of *chrevo*, Russian for the "belly/womb" or generalized region of digestive and generative functions, solely as "bowels" (cf. 317). There the grotesque body, forever outgrowing and transgressing itself, allots an essential role to "those parts . . . in which it conceives a new second body: *chrevo i fall* [the belly/womb and phallus]" (not, as Iswolsky has it, "the bowels and the phallus").

tion as society's safety valve, as a scheduled event that worked to domesticate conflict by temporarily sanctioning victimization, medieval carnival
in practice could be more repressive than liberating. Bakhtin's reluctance
to highlight the crucial role of violence during carnival baffled many of
his readers. And then there was the stiff binary nature of Bakhtin's social
history, which presented such a strange image of popular appetites and of
upper-class taste. As one American critic put the matter in a 1987 review,
"Bakhtin and the World of Rabelais Criticism": "It is not surprising that
Bakhtin, writing in a Marxist society, defines popular culture by opposition to official or establishment culture, thus basing his definition on class
distinctions. Even laughter is class specific: the culture of the power establishment is serious; that of the people essentially comic. Deprived of
power, folk culture appropriated laughter and made of it a powerful, liberating, generative force."[5]

Contrary to Bakhtin's vision, the reviewer notes, "the powerful, the
wealthy, the learned were actually bi-cultural and did not consider the
marketplace alien territory; popular culture was universal culture." Since
Bakhtin, however, reads so much of Rabelais's novel through the lens of
preliterate (and arguably Slavic) folklore and thereby de-historicizes the
literary text, French medieval society appears rigidly, artificially stratified.
Bakhtin functions here more as a mythographer than as a literary scholar
or social historian. Many felt that mythography suited Bakhtin's scholarly
intention as well, burdened as it was with such Aesopian tasks. By supplementing his schematicized, quasi-historical picture of Rabelais's
France with a fund of timeless folk images, Bakhtin could preach to his
immediate Soviet audience detachable, thinly disguised psychological
universals that were relevant to any (and most persuasively, to his own)
time.

These reservations about Bakhtin's *Rabelais* were effectively summed
up from a Russian perspective by the late Aleksandr Pankov in his centennial study *The Key and Clue to M. Bakhtin.*[6] According to Pankov, Bakhtin's most repudiated value—traces of which could be found at the negative pole of every Bakhtinian binary—was *ofitsioz*, "officialese culture,"
the world as it looks when approved and controlled from the political
center. Repelled from his earliest years by *ofitsioz* wherever it was found,
Bakhtin "strove to extract from medieval ideology itself the principle of
cultural two-worldness [*dvoemirie*]; he subjected living material to a ty-

---

[5] Mary B. McKinley, "Bakhtin and the World of Rabelais Criticism," in *Degree Second* 2
(1987): 83–88, esp. 85. McKinley is reviewing Richard M. Berrong's ambivalent, but on
balance adversarial, *Rabelais and Bakhtin: Popular Culture in "Gargantua and Pantagruel"* (Lincoln: University of Nebraska Press, 1986).

[6] Aleksandr Pankov, *Razgadka M. Bakhtina* (Moscow: Informatik, 1995), 157–73. Further page references given in text.

pological cleansing . . . and at times the material clearly resisted" (168). Bakhtin's "body of the people" lost all historical or literary reality, becoming directly mythological and populist (but in the nineteenth-century Russian, rather than medieval French, sense of that word). The folk, *narod*, were invested with a Romantic, "metaphysical vital value"; although presented as wholly spontaneous, self-absorbed, and un-self-reflecting, this folk also functioned for Bakhtin as a progressive mechanism that could move history (171). With such a romanticized "people" in place, official culture could then be reinterpreted negatively as an "artificial construction, genetically 'alien,'" an imposition and a burden; Bakhtin's social history could unfold in a quasi-fictional realm that "at times began to recall the Wall between 'city' and 'nature' in Zamyatin's [dystopian] novel *We*" (171–72).

Pankov's reading echoes much recent American criticism of Bakhtinian carnival. Other Russian responses to *smekhovaia kul'tura*, however, have been particular to Bakhtin's own homeland. Inspired perhaps by the universalism of Bakhtin's claims—and by the obvious infusion of Russian folklore into his analysis of this foreign culture and foreign literary text—some Russian cultural historians began to explore the "transposability" of Rabelais-style grotesquerie into specifically Russian history. In 1976 the great medievalist Dmitri Likhachev, in collaboration with A. M. Panchenko, published a controversial volume entitled *The "World of Laughter" of Early Russia*. The two authors drew suggestive parallels between the Bakhtinian-Rabelaisian phenomenon of carnival laughter and Russian medieval theatricals, literary parody, Ivan the Terrible's terror-guard *oprichnina*, and holy foolishness. Yuri Lotman and Boris Uspensky, on the alert during this maiden season of the Bakhtin cult for just such speculative academic folly, responded with a lengthy, thoughtful rebuttal in *Voprosy literatury* a year later.[7]

The Tartu school scholars asserted that the Likhachev-Panchenko team had read Russian medieval behavior out of context. Although an intriguing thesis within Western European cultures, Bakhtin's principle of ambivalent, tolerant, two-way laughter "lies outside the severe religious and ethical constraints imposed on the behavior of a [Russian] person of that time." Russian life was governed by a different, more rigid binary, the opposition of sanctity and Satanism (153–54). A medieval Russian subject could seek success in life either through prayer or through black magic. But in neither route was a belly laugh or guffaw an ambivalent

---

[7] Yu. Lotman and B. Uspenskii, "Novye aspekty izucheniia kul'tury Drevnei Rusi," *Voprosy literatury*, no. 3 (March 1977): 148–66. A flawed translation by N.F.C. Owen can be found in Ju. M. Lotman and B. A. Uspenskij, *The Semiotics of Russian Culture*, ed. Ann Shukman (Ann Arbor: Michigan Slavic Contributions No. 11, 1984), 36–52. Further page references given in the text are to the Russian edition.

gesture: robust laughter was always unambiguously blasphemy, a tool of Satan. Medieval theatricals, likewise, were not participatory, quasi-"carnivalized" events carried on without footlights or spectators; they were didactic, judgmental, quite often tyrannizing. Holy fools, too, were much more complex than carnival jesters. Their outrageous behavior was meant to humiliate, in imitation of Christ, either the spectator or the fool; but such behavior was not meant—as Bakhtin's carnival laughter manifestly was—to liberate or to empower. In short, Lotman and Uspensky argue that in medieval Russian culture, laughter and the inversion of sanctioned values (even when institutionalized by codes or rituals) were understood by those who partook of them not as emancipated behavior but as *anti*-behavior. Freedom did not figure into the picture at all.

In a lengthy footnote to their rebuttal, Lotman and Uspensky sound a warning. "We are witnessing more and more often the tendency not to develop Bakhtin's ideas or devise sensible arguments out of them, but to extend them mechanically into areas where their very application should be a subject of special concern," they caution. "Taking on the functions of a scholarly ornament, Bakhtin's thought, complex and controversial, has been oversimplified and made too comfortable" (153). The Tartu scholars were seasoned skeptics. Even for a committed and disciplined Bakhtinian critic, however, the idea of carnival presents a dilemma. It both fits, and radically does not fit, the other god-term in Bakhtin's cosmos, which is dialogue. To be sure, some blunt parallels are easy to draw: verbal dialogue works with the *dvugolosoe slovo*, or double-voiced word, and carnival interaction takes place between *dvutelye obrazy*, or double-bodied images; both value exchange over stasis or essence. But beyond that point, so much in the two worlds appears mutually contradictory. Dialogue individuates, carnival absorbs and effaces; the speaking person is mortal, the grotesque body immortal; the perfect home for maximally dialogic language is the privately consumed novel, whereas Bakhtin's version of the public square—for all its excellence as the site of carnival—is a place of monosyllabic obscenities and hawkers' cries, more suited to a Dionysian book burning than to sedate book reading. (Is the carnival body even literate?) But let us assume, as evidence suggests, that Bakhtin was not wedded to the historical truths of carnival practice. The concept of carnival was precious to him more as a spiritual attitude, as a "loophole" for the psyche, and as a concrete manifestation of hope in a world that otherwise knew little of it. Grotesque bodies, precisely because they are imperfect, require supplementation and reach out to others in a climate of trust; thus they are analogous to needy dialogic words. Have Russian students of Bakhtin successfully sustained this analogy?

Several attempts have been made to do so, usually at a high level of abstraction, with mixed results. In one typical discussion, A. P. Bondarev links dialogue and carnival through Bakhtin's mega-image of the *chrevo* or "belly/womb," that vague overlapping realm in the lower torso that digests, excretes, and reproduces. Carnival events "are fraught or pregnant [*chrevaty*] . . . The culture of laughter is built on oppositions, on the *unity* of analogies and contradictory juxtapositions."[8] Bondarev suggests that this unity is equivalent—albeit in "a logic of images" [*obraznaia logika*]—to the dialogic multiplicity inherent in words. Since the "unexpected mosaiclike combinations" of the grotesque image resemble the irregularities of ongoing conversation, Bondarev is prompted to conclude that "carnival and dialogue, Bakhtin's ontology and logic, form a correlative pair." Just as carnival continually disrupts organized space, so dialogue "seethes with 'provocative' questions, deprives its participants of spiritual comfort and intellectual well-being, reduces everything to naught, ridicules, devalues, annihilates everything that has been laid away or stored up, undoes all the usual protective arguments that have worked so smoothly up to this time" (60).

In Bondarev's reading, what these two concepts share are the (very broad) virtues of destabilization and anti-entropy. For the analogy to work, carnival must be equated with creative potential in general—not merely with sanctioned ritual inversion—and dialogue must be reduced to constant reevaluation and erosion of certainty, ignoring its role in the positive accumulation of a complex identity. Only, it would seem, by interpreting carnival as maximally pluralistic and dialogue as maximally nihilistic can Bondarev bind these two god-terms together. Such analogies are of questionable usefulness.

A far more persuasive argument for linking carnival and dialogue in Bakhtin's thought has been made by the American scholar Alexandar Mihailovic.[9] He pursues the matter along another axis altogether, through the incarnational, eucharistic, and Christological metaphors common to both. In his view, Bakhtin intended his monograph on Rabelais to be read by his fellow Russians not only as viable scholarship but also as a literary and spiritually informed work in its own right, laced with Aesopian references both to Johannine biblical doctrine and to Stalinist reality. (Mihailovic provides an important service to non-Russian readers by pointing out where the standard English translation of *Rabelais and His World* blunts the imagery, reiterated puns, phonetic play, and

---

[8] A. P. Bondarev (Moscow), "Karnaval/Dialog: Ontologiia i logika M. M. Bakhtina," in V. L. Makhlin, ed., *M. M. Bakhtin i perspektivy gumanitarnykh nauk* (Vitebsk: Izdatel' N. A. Pan'kov, 1994), 55–62, esp. 58. Further page references given in text.

[9] Alexandar Mihailovic, *Corporeal Words: Mikhail Bakhtin's Theology of Discourse* (Evanston, Ill.: Northwestern University Press, 1997), esp. ch. 5, "Carnival and Embodiment in *Rabelais and His World*," and ch. 6, "The Word Made and Unmade: Rabelais, Bakhtin, and Stalin." Further page references given in text.

hyperbole of Bakhtin's Russian text. In the original, the effect of this rhetoric is less embarrassing and more incantational.) The carnival imagery of *Rabelais* is related to the almost coterminous essay "The Word [Discourse] in the Novel" as matter is related to spirit. It is that word "made flesh."

In Mihailovic's view, Bakhtin intended us to take this incarnational metaphor absolutely literally. The analysis of a burlesque anecdote from the German Renaissance scholar Schneegans, developed by Bakhtin in his chapter on "The Grotesque Image of the Body" (*Rabelais*, 304–10), strikes him as key: the grotesque body of a stutterer, butted in the stomach by the Harlequin's head, gives birth to the word. Utterances are born out of a body made grotesque in the labor of generating them—and the comic intervention of an impatient second party is indispensable midwife to the event. The word, then, originates as something material, theatrical, inevitably assisted by others, "ejected" beyond its boundaries, all of which mimics in a strange way the position of the Third in a trinity: "the offspring of the body during the comic or carnivalesque moment" (151–52). Mihailovic interprets Bakhtin's extended attention to this scene as indication of his enthusiasm for comic debasements of incarnation and as Aesopian commentary on the Chalcedonian ideal of consubstantiality. Additional "carnal" analogies are uncovered in Bakhtin's text as well: the material benefits of sexual over asexual reproduction, the parallel physiological reliefs of laughter and of birthing, and the absolute need of every uttered word for an embodied answering word. "Bakhtin's literary universe," Mihailovic writes, "is completely intolerant of parthenogenesis" (179).

Against this general background, we might distribute Russian responses to Bakhtinian-Rabelaisian "cultures of laughter" into three groups. There are those scholars who would redeem carnival and integrate it into Bakhtin's thought, often—as Mihailovic has done—in an overtly Christian context. At the other pole are those who are opposed to Bakhtinian carnival and appalled by it, as Aleksei Losev was in his *Aesthetics of the Renaissance*. These critics wish to expose it, together with its cast of grotesque criminal bodies, as destructive both of humanism and (in the post-Soviet context) of Russia's nascent liberalism—upon which, they feel, rest all fragile hopes for a rule-of-law state. The anti-carnival group, in turn, contains several factions, not always easy to distinguish. One wing maintains that Bakhtin himself, in his Rabelais book, was being satirical and Aesopian. It takes for granted that Bakhtin was suspicious of carnival ecstasy and fully alert to the ghastly parallels between a collective body sustaining itself on individual deaths and the coterminous rhetoric of Stalinist Terror. (As we shall see below, Mikhail Ryklin, while prudently ambivalent about Bakhtin's own intent, reads the lessons of carnival along these lines. And Mihailovic, in this spirit, points out convincing analogues between the Show Trials of the late 1930s and Bakhtin's ostensible celebration of "praise/blame" [*khvala/bran'*] on the public square [*ploshchad', ploshchadka*]—the latter term doubling for the executioner's block [199–203].)

Archival material recently unearthed lends some credence to this darker position. Deeply pessimistic jottings Bakhtin made during the war years (1943–46), transcribed from crumbling notebooks and published only in 1992, suggest that he was quite willing to submit the wholesale corruption of images and words surrounding him to the rigors of theory.[10] In these wartime notes, for the first time we glimpse a Bakhtin for whom "image-bestowing" and "form-shaping" instincts are not benign. When he invokes the problem of the image [*obraz*] in these notes, he clearly has in mind not the blessed icon or the sunlit, inflated folkloric masses of carnival time-space but rather the vast, flat, evil, hectoring poster art of the Stalin era. In this negative space, words and images express destructiveness in different ways. The evil peculiar to images is inert, a deadening "thing-ness," a "today-ness" that is deceptively "always ready to pass itself off . . . as a servant of the future" (154). If imposed from above (as these public images were), at a distance, secondhand and without love, an image always bears traces of its origin in violence. In contrast, the desecration peculiar to language is energetic: the lie. "The lie is today's most ever present form of evil," Bakhtin writes. "The word does not know whom it serves. It emerges from the dark and does not know its own roots. Its serious link with terror and violence. The authentically kind, unselfish, and loving person has not yet spoken, he has realized himself in the spheres of everyday life, he has not attached himself to the official word, infected with violence and the lie; he is not becoming a writer" (155, 154).

Thus have random archival finds and unexpected primary sources fed a second, less bucolic portrait of Bakhtin. It now competes with the sunny, cheery relativity of the Rabelais book, completed during those very years, overcasting it with parody and double meaning. But scholars less charitable to Bakhtin would dismiss this dark wartime testimony as transitory and incidental. These critics hold that Bakhtin was overall so enamored of his utopian carnival idea, so in need of its spiritual balm and convinced of its salvific qualities, so (perhaps) even conditioned by the lies that fueled the rhetoric of his era that he was taken in by the deceptions of carnival and remained blind to its potential for abuse.

---

[10] M. M. Bakhtin, "Iz chernovykh tetradei," ed. Vadim Kozhinov, texts transcribed by V. I. Slovetskii, in *Literaturnaia ucheba*, bks. 5/6 (September, October, November, December 1992): 153–66. Further page references given in text.

Exemplary of this group is the émigré culturologist Boris Groys. In his 1989 essay "Between Stalin and Dionysius," Groys insists that we look soberly at the political implications of Bakhtin's theories, preferably in the spirit of his own inquiry into the totalizing fantasies of the 1920s Russian avant-garde.[11] We will detect the same enthusiasms, the same danger signals. "Liberalism and democracy in their usual understanding," Groys writes, "evoke acute antipathy in Bakhtin." And he continues:

> They are synonymous for him with automatization, self-enclosed individuality, rupture from the unified cosmic life and, consequently, reasons for the emergence of seriousness, moralizing, and the collapse of humor and carnival . . . One should not even speak of democracy here: no one is given the democratic right to shirk carnival, to not take part, to remain on the sidelines. On the contrary, precisely those who try to do so are the first to be subject to well-deserved "cheerful vilifications and beatings." According to Bakhtin, this nightmare is transformed into carnival thanks to the laughter that accompanies it. . . . This laughter is born of the faith that the folk is something materially larger than a gathering of individuals and that the world is something more than all the things in it, which is to say, this laughter is born of a faith in totalitarianism.[12]

Thus do some students of carnival make common cause with those postmodernist anti-dialogians who, as we have seen, hold Bakhtinian *logos*-centrism in criminal regard. Bakhtin, in their opinion, should be considered part of the problem of Stalinism, not part of its unmasking.

A final group of scholars prefers to investigate carnival and its mechanisms more neutrally. For them, as for the Tartu school semioticians in the ideal instance, the role of scholarship is not to "apply" an idea but to analyze it, to inquire where it might be helpful in organizing other data gathered independently of it, and—especially important when one is dealing with gurus and cults—to fix limits to it, to determine at what point it falsifies material or fails to fit. In their opinion, Bakhtin's thought is misused when read as theological or political commentary. Whatever a

---

[11] Groys is best known for his thesis that Soviet totalitarian art (Socialist Realism in its most rigid phase) is a natural extension—not an aberration—of principles that governed the Russian avant-garde, most especially its disgust for the natural world as we are cast into it and a passion for cosmic re-creation regardless of human cost. See Boris Groys, *Gesamtkunstwerk Stalin: Die gespaltene Kultur in der Sowjetunion* (Munich, 1988), trans. Charles Rougle as *The Total Art of Stalinism: Avant-garde, Aesthetic Dictatorship, and Beyond* (Princeton, N.J.: Princeton University Press, 1992). Groys is a controversial player in the Bakhtin industry, coming in on the dark side of the ledger; he is opposed with some heat by scholars more compassionate toward Bakhtin's intellectual position, such as Vitaly Makhlin.

[12] Boris Groys, "Mezhdu Stalinym i Dionisom," in *Sintaksis 25* (Paris, 1989): 92–97, esp. 95. See also B. Groys, "Totalitarizm Karnavala," *B sb III (97)*: 76–80.

concept might have meant for its founder, subsequent scholars should treat it objectively, as an explanatory or historiosophical principle. In the case of carnival, the concept can be shown to interact over time with other Bakhtinian principles, most instructively the dialogic or polyphonic. Only such patterns are a scholar's proper concern. To get some feel for this most famous (and most curious) of Bakhtin's legacies, these three categories of response to carnival will now be sampled.

PRO: CARNIVAL AS INCARNATION, EUCHARIST, SACRAL MYTH

We begin with the varied group of redeemers and integraters. These critics welcome carnival laughter and its grotesquerie as positive virtues, considering them of one piece with Bakhtin's other teachings and valuable to philosophy independent of any local Russian subtexts. They are inclined to interpret Bakhtin's lifelong enthusiasm for carnival and its special brand of body dialogue as more or less "single-voiced"—that is, as a direct expression of an affirmative value system that nevertheless required a degree of camouflage during the Soviet years. In their opinion, the appeal of carnival for Bakhtin was less social than spiritual. Although none has given the topic Mihailovic's detailed and dispassionate treatment, most associate this spirituality with the Russian Orthodox faith.

The connection between Bakhtin and Christian (and Judeo-Christian) thought is touched on throughout this study, but nowhere discussed in detail. It might be helpful, therefore, to provide some background here, in the context of carnival, noting the scope of Russian research in this realm. Systematic investigations into Bakhtin's relation to twentieth-century religious philosophers in Western Europe (largely German: Franz Rosenzweig, Martin Buber, Ferdinand Ebner), undertaken by Vitaly Makhlin and others, are at last beginning to appear.[13] Parallels—albeit at a high level of abstraction—have been drawn between Bakhtin and such Orthodox religious philosophers as Pavel Florensky and Nikolai Lossky.[14] Russian scholars of a neo-nationalist bent have been quick to point out that Bakhtin condemned not Christianity in general but only the institutionalized Catholic Church of Rabelais's time; in opposition to that Roman fallacy, with its worldly power and cult of violence, the Eastern

---

[13] See, for an initial research plan, the graduate seminar lectures published as V. L. Makhlin, *Ya i drugoi (Istoki filosofii 'dialoga' XX veka)* (Sankt-Peterburg: Russkii khristianskii gumanitarnyi institut, 1995).

[14] See, for example, V. V. Babich, "Losskii i Bakhtin: Opyt sravneniia," in *DKKh, no. 4 (94)*: 34–57; for a brief general overview of compatibilities, see Donatella Ferrari-Bravo, "More on Bakhtin and Florensky," in *Critical Studies* 2, no. ½ (1990) [Special Issue on "Mikhail Bakhtin and the Epistemology of Discourse," ed. Clive Thomson]: 111–21.

Orthodox liturgy can incorporate without strain all the tangible, participatory, self-humbling aspects of carnival behavior. As we see from the following passage by the eminent contemporary Greek theologian Christos Yannaras, Bakhtin's "carnival complex" of values—the embodied word, the grotesque body, the legitimacy and redeemability of matter, interpersonal contact as definitive of life—all find ample expression within such a worldview:

> The eucharistic liturgy has its own aesthetics, stemming from the same ontology of the Church's truth and ethos. This has nothing to do with the conventional aesthetics of harmonious proportions, with the categories of beauty and ugliness or symmetry and asymmetry, nor with arbitrary individual devices meant to be impressive or imposing. The aim of Orthodox church art is not to delight the senses or the mind, but to reveal to both the truth and the inner principle or "word" of things: the personal dimension of matter, its capacity to manifest the personal operation of God the Word, to give flesh to Him who is without flesh and to contain Him who cannot be contained. . . . In the Orthodox eucharist, nothing is theory, autonomous doctrine, or abstract reference: all is action, tangible experience, and total, bodily participation.[15]

In a pathbreaking 1991 essay entitled "Carnival and Incarnation: Bakhtin and Orthodox Theology," the Canadian scholar Charles Lock noted additional compatibilities.[16] Unlike the Western Church (which demoted and exiled the flesh as sinful) and unlike Western philosophy from Descartes on (which preached a separation of body and mind), Eastern Orthodox theology never endorsed those Neoplatonist divisions and dichotomies. The Incarnation had rendered such distinctions invalid. Lock suggests that Bakhtin, in his work on Rabelais, pursued an Orthodox reverence for matter under the convenient rubric of approved Marxist-Leninist materialism. For this task, the great French novelist (also no prim Neoplatonist as regards the body) was the perfect academic subject: for in "incarnational Christology," Lock reminds us, "there can be no privileging within matter; even the excremental can be sacramental" (73). Thus the incarnated world, expressed with maximal compactness in the lower bodily stratum, cannot be equated with degradation or dissipation. It is the harbinger of an ideal. Such a body is heroic in times of deprivation and is always granted a Resurrection.

Since deprivation—famine and pain—was Bakhtin's experience over

---

[15] Christos Yannaras, *The Freedom of Morality*, translated from the Greek by Elizabeth Briere (New York: St. Vladimir's Seminary Press, 1984), 95–96.

[16] Charles Lock, "Carnival and Incarnation: Bakhtin and Orthodox Theology," *Journal of Literature and Theology* 5, no. 1 (March 1991): 68–82. Further page references given in text.

long stretches of his life, the bread and wine exchanged during Holy Communion took on an elevated, albeit everyday, meaning. As Lock writes: "For Bakhtin, food is always festal. . . . For the Neoplatonist, hunger is a humiliating reminder of the body's lack of self-sufficiency; for the Orthodox, it is an affirmation of the body's connection, through orifices and apertures, with the cosmos" (74). Then Lock makes a summarizing point, which marks off his own Christianized reading of Bakhtinian carnival from some of the later, more suspicious criticisms on Russian soil:

> It should hardly need to be said that in his celebration of the body Bakhtin does not advocate a return to the bestial, is not nostalgic for the unself-consciousness of animals—a nostalgia or temptation not unknown to Tolstoy, Rousseau and others. The carnival is not a given of nature, nor can it be achieved by will: it must be officially sanctioned—produced and tolerated by what is *not* carnival—and temporally circumscribed. Bakhtin's lament is that these conditions no longer obtain, and especially and most regrettably could not obtain in the Soviet Union. There the dictatorship of the proletariat meant that folk culture was imposed and decreed from above as the *only* culture. If folk culture is hegemonic there can be no carnival, no rebellion from *below*, no celebration of the lower bodily stratum, because there is no axis to provide degrees of comparison. (75)

Lock's hypothesis is plausible—and a great deal more palatable, I suggest, than Boris Groys's ironclad linkage of carnival vision with totalitarian practice. Bakhtin was indeed apprehensive about democratizing and secularizing processes that could erode a feel for boundaries or enfeeble the sort of transfigurations possible only during carnival moments within a faith community. Evidence for this anxiety in his texts is muted because Bakhtin, as a rule, is not an anxious writer. Beyond the occasional working notebook, we have no detailed autobiographical record of his life or thoughts during the most stressful Stalinist decades, when the carnival idea was ripening (Bakhtin's oral memoirs break off in the late 1920s). But Vladimir Turbin has testified at length to his mentor's uneasiness on this matter of carnival's passing.

"Bakhtin often remarked that 'we were entering a non-carnival era,'" Turbin wrote in one of his several emotional memoirs on those years.[17] "Life had made Bakhtin witness to a planned, comprehensively thought-out destruction of carnival. . . . this anti-carnival took place on the ruins of churches, for without a church, carnival is impossible: a person during carnival is a person who is again undergoing rebirth. He leaves the building of the church, and, having departed, finds himself on the threshold,

---

[17] "O Bakhtine," in V. N. Turbin, *Nezadolgo do Vodoleia* (Moscow: Radiks, 1994), 443–70, esp. 459, 461.

as it were on the border between two worlds: the higher world, symbolized by the cathedral he has left behind but cannot fail to remember, and the lower, material world. . . . Carnival is an interpretation of the material world from the point of view of the spiritual, nonmaterial world." Such a threshold position was psychologically indispensable for Bakhtin, Turbin argues elsewhere, because Bakhtin's long life was governed by two constants to which a carnival worldview was the only reliable antidote: pain and hunger.[18] Turbin senses a nostalgia in Bakhtin's formulations about carnival, even when embedded in the most scholarly contexts. Only carnival, it appears, held out hope of resurrection to hopelessly flattened matter and thus could arrest the desacralization of the world.

Such speculation on the connection between Bakhtin's ideas and Christian faith is now routine in Russia. (So much so, in fact, that the theme "Bakhtin and the Divine" has no risk left to it at all; in the mid-1990s, a counterwave against the excessive theologizing of his thought was already being felt.)[19] But the topic could not be investigated openly—much less dismissed openly—until the end of state-sponsored atheism. At that time it became the fashion to mine once dissident, now redeemed Russian thinkers for Christian subtexts. In assimilating Bakhtin, Russian theology proved itself marvelously elastic. Carnival emerges as a sort of "church in reverse," an Orthodox site for metamorphosis and miracle in opposition to the Latin heresy of hierarchies, military orders, and corrupt officialdom. Such a reading had the advantage of answering both to Bakhtin's aversion to *ofitsioz* and to his anxiety about our entry into a "non-carnival era"—a dystopian nightmare where the state becomes all there is. In part because the Orthodox Church has been associated with ultra-nationalist politics, however, carnival understood as Communion has been slow to receive in Russia the impartial treatment given it by Western scholars. What is more, a certain nervousness about carnival in practice—its potential for anarchy and victimization—has tended to encourage a demonization of carnival rather than a celebration of its possibly sacral roots. Many Russians would concur with Natalia Reed's wary remark in response to Turbin's (obviously exultant) recollection of Bakhtin's insistence that the Gospels were carnival, too: "Indeed they are. Up to and including the mob-lynching of Christ."

"Christianized" interpretations are not, however, the sole conduit for

---

[18] V. N. Turbin, "Karnaval: Religiia, politika, teosofiia," in *B sb I 90*, 6–29, esp. 10–13.

[19] As one speaker put it at the Third Saransk International Bakhtin Readings in October 1995, "Some people say that the 'primary author,' the 'highest instantiation' for Bakhtin, is God. It is hard to agree with that statement. Significantly, even when talking of Dostoevsky and his understanding of faith, Bakhtin gives a purely culturological definition of that faith." See L. A. Zaks (Ekaterinburg), "'U mira est' smysl' (Dukhovnoe mirozdanie M. Bakhtina)," in *MMB i gum mysh II (95)*, 54–57, esp. 56.

sympathetic Russian readings of carnival. There is also a less inflammatory tradition of inquiries into pre-Christian, pagan "holiday time" as the ritualistic core of every carnival worldview. In such an approach, the sacralization of matter need not result in any "theologizing" of reality—that is, reality need not be transformed into an illustration of divine intent or process. Scholars of this persuasion argue that Bakhtin, as a student of folklore, was after larger game. He desired to integrate laughter into a more archaic worldview, one markedly pre-Platonic, where the very distinction between Creator and created, noumenon and phenomenon, was dissolved—or perhaps not yet drawn. Russian scholarship is strong in such theorists. Among Bakhtin's contemporaries writing in the 1930s and 1940s, for example, was Vladimir Propp, the great Soviet folklorist and Formalist, who demonstrated in several controversial studies that ritual laughter frequently accompanied death and magically transformed it into new birth.[20] The founding text for reading Bakhtin in this tradition appeared in 1968—a review essay on the Rabelais book by Grigory Pomerants, published as a companion piece to the sinologist's "Reading Bakhtin" in the journal *Peoples of Asia and Africa*. Entitled " 'The Carnival' and 'the Serious,' " Pomerants's essay adopts an intellectually satisfying strategy that later proved very effective in other confused areas of Bakhtin's legacy.[21]

Pomerants welcomes the fact that Bakhtin's book on Rabelais—like his earlier volume on Dostoevsky—was a best-seller and a cultural event. But he admits that close scrutiny by specialists has revealed both books to be insufficient to the complexity of their subject and, to some extent, internally inconsistent. In Bakhtin's defense, Pomerants argues that the Rabe-

[20] Propp notes, for example, that laughter, a uniquely human reflex, was routinely proscribed in the Kingdom of the Dead (living interlopers could be identified by their laughter). In a discussion of the other death-defying qualities of the laughter reflex, Propp devotes some attention to the classic example of "so-called sardonic laughter," researched by his German colleagues: "Among the very ancient people of Sardinia, who were called Sardi or Sardoni, it was customary to kill old people," Propp notes. "While killing their old people, the Sardi laughed loudly. This is the origin of notorious sardonic laughter, now meaning cruel, malicious laughter. In light of our findings things begin to look different. Laughter accompanies the passage from death to life; it creates life and accompanies birth. Consequently, laughter accompanying killing transforms death into a new birth, nullifies murder as such, and is an act of piety that transforms death into a new birth." (One can see why a scholar of Groys's cast of mind, sensitive to totalitarianism's drive to legitimate itself through the archaic folk, might be made uneasy by such naturalization of the links between laughter and murder.) See Vladimir Propp, "Ritual Laughter in Folklore (Apropos of the Tale of the Princess Who Would Not Laugh [Nesmejana]," in Propp, *Theory and History of Folklore*, trans. Ariadna Y. Martin, Richard P. Martin, et al., ed. Anatoly Liberman (Minneapolis: University of Minnesota Press, 1984), ch. 9 (124–46), esp. 134.

[21] G. S. Pomerants, " 'Karnaval'noe' i 'ser'eznoe,' " in *Narody Azii i Afriki*, no. 2 (1968): 107–16. Further page references given in text.

lais book is not necessarily, and certainly not solely, about Rabelais; it is stronger than its own argumentation and point of departure. A "carnival sense of time is a much later rethinking of holiday rituals that arose considerably earlier, in the atmosphere of another culture more primitive, more integral, more emotional" (107). Although the structure, organization, and titling of Bakhtin's monograph urge us to misread in this way, carnival should not be measured by its Renaissance manifestation first and only afterward, in order to obtain the necessary "proofs," traced back in time to its possible sources. If read in that retrograde way, carnival will inevitably be understood in a sixteenth-century European manner—as a suspension of duties, a "rest from work," an interval and interruption between fixed ticks of the clock. But such a picture, Pomerants intimates, is already a degeneration.

For genuine holiday time cannot be part of the everyday world and is not an intellectual construct. Archaic holidays knew rhythms and pulsations, but not a "concept of time" in the sense Bakhtin implies. Thus holiday consciousness cannot be understood as merely hydraulic, as a moment of release or a loosening of strictures laid down by oppressive institutions. It is a psychological, biological, perhaps even a spiritual necessity, intuitively grasped by organic societies and sanctioned not sociopolitically but by "another sphere of existence" altogether, the "world of ideals" (107). "The essence of the holiday is liberation from the practical [delovoi] orientation of the mind, liberation from the dismemberment of the world into north and south, big and small, past and future; it is an experience of the world as a unity, as an 'eternal present'" (108). Europeans, tethered to time even as they seek to construct for themselves an exit out of it, have lost this fullness of holiday consciousness.

Interestingly, this "holiday" moment, sensed by Pomerants in the 1960s as crucial to the carnival idea of the 1930s and 1940s, might have much earlier origins in Bakhtin's thought. According to the Kagan family archivist Brian Poole, among the more durable legacies of the Marburg school in the 1910s (of which Bakhtin, through his close friend Matvei Kagan, had become an avid student) was Paul Natorp's notion of "breath," "the breathing of the cosmos," "rest" [otdykh], a "break from labor" [peredyshka]—all words that in Russian are related to dukh, spirit. For Natorp, art and life met on the boundary between labor and rest, between (metaphorically) inhaling and exhaling. Kagan himself, in a 1924 essay on the meaning of art, describes just such a creative peredyshka in terms that closely parallel Bakhtin's meditations, much later in the Rabelais book, on the "breathing space" of carnival.[22]

And so, Pomerants suggests, to explore the truth of Bakhtin's carnival

---

[22] Brian Poole, "Nazad k Kaganu," *DKKh, no. 1 (95)*: 38–48, esp. 42–44.

idea we must begin not with the Renaissance French writer Rabelais but with a more archaic, "cosmically breathing" source. For this purpose he recommends African cultures—which, until exposed to the doctrine of "development" and "European efficiency" [*delovitost'*] in the twentieth century, did not suffer from a time fetish (116). Holiday consciousness was highly developed in these cultures as a variety of the sublime: "vertical" in orientation, worshipful, and serious. We should not take Bakhtin's strictures against "one-sided seriousness" too quickly to heart, Pomerants counsels us. They are clearly a later overlay, a response to institutions and political constraints that Bakhtin himself found oppressive, for "reverence is just as human and natural as are laughter and dissipated behavior" (109). To understand the roots of carnival, such binary oppositions as "laughter/seriousness" or "atheism/religion" are reductive and misleading. A more valid opposition is between *prazdnik* and *budni*, the myth-opoetic creative holiday versus the efficiency-driven weekday (110).

If a balance is not achieved between these two modes, Pomerants concludes, the results for individuals and cultures can be dire. Either "a new, unhealthy dialogue inevitably arises, between the efficient, rational consciousness and an 'underground' irrational unconscious," or, on a national scale, the result can be fascism. "For if a European of the nineteenth century could point with reproach to Africa's isolated, not very numerous instances of cannibalism, then the traditional African of the twentieth century could point with some reproach to Europe's Hitler" (116).

Such ruminations over the distortions and repressions of the carnival impulse, formulated on the boundaries between anthropology, myth, and national guilt, will become common in the post-Soviet period. To be sure, domestic self-criticism of Stalin will replace the obligatory Soviet-era reference to Hitler; some critics will link the "immortal, laughing body of carnival"—co-opted by the state, stripped of any authentic or spontaneous sense of "holiday time," and associated with the Grinning Lie—to the worst abuses of their own prior regime. To these 1990s readings we shall turn presently. In Pomerants's conventionally Soviet-style discussion of holiday consciousness from the manacled year 1968, it suffices to note that Bakhtin is presumed to embrace pre- and non-Christian folklore straightforwardly, not as an Aesopian cloak for banned religious symbols. Bakhtinistics in this descriptive, ethnographic vein has continued to the present day, a counterpart to the positive influence of Bakhtin on folklore and folklife studies in the West.[23]

---

[23] In one centennial essay, for example, "holiday culture" is examined as an essential, healthy ritual, validated both biologically (human biorhythms that dictate periodic rest for the body) and cosmically. Authentically popular—not state-sponsored—holidays always cel-

Even when dealing with morally neutral categories like "liminality" and "cyclicity," however, Russian ethnographers acknowledge a tension between carnival consciousness and religious (or moral) culture. With a Freudian anxiety that contrasts sharply with Bakhtin's own less burdened conscience on these matters, these scholars are prone to apologize for this tension. The Saransk Bakhtinist Oleg Breikin, paraphrasing a famous line from Pushkin's dramatic narrative "Mozart and Salieri," states bluntly that "civilization and carnival are incompatible things"; "carnival must die for the social life of the tribe to triumph."[24] If in primordial mythological consciousness good and evil were fused, then under conditions of our modern "utilitarian consciousness"—which attempts (Breikin would say, unsuccessfully) to duplicate that earlier and irretrievable state—"carnival very quickly degenerates into naked hedonism or, worse, into a Satanic witches' sabbath that leads to the degradation of personality" (72–73).

CONTRA: DEMONIZATION, STALINIZATION

We now leave the realm of the Church and pagan reenactments of Creation for the far other shore: carnival as negative and degenerative energy, as a "Satanic witches' sabbath." The association is not new. We sampled one such response in chapter 2 (Losev's disgust at Rabelaisian aesthetics and at Bakhtin's celebration of it); also, passing reference was made in the present chapter to another skeptical critique, Lotman's and Uspensky's rebuttal of a scholarly monograph that had identified a "laughing culture" in Russia's own medieval past. This anti-carnival side of the debate has been fueled by two scholars whose contribution to Bakhtinistics, in different ways, strives to tighten and discipline the legacy. The first is the prominent philosopher of religion Sergei Averintsev, whose sympathetic attitude toward Bakhtin's "humanism for nonspecialists" we have already encountered. He appears in this chapter as an au-

---

ebrate the reenactment of the primordial moment of Creation out of Chaos, during which "everyday, profane space-time becomes sacralized." See L. S. Dmitrieva, "Teoreticheskie problemy prazdnichnoi kul'tury v rabotakh M. Bakhtina," in *Bakhtinologiia*: 27–31, esp. 29. See also T. Yu. Krylova, "Problema sootnosheniia karnival'nogo i khristianskogo mirovozzreniia," *MMB i gum mysh I (95)*, 169–70, where "pre-logical myth" is seen to link the two worlds.

[24] O. B. Breikin, "Karnaval kak element mifologicheskogo soznaniia," in *MMB i PGN 94*, 72–74, esp. 73. In a related (unpublished) paper entitled "The Problem of the Correlation of Carnival Consciousness and Religious Culture," Breikin opens with the question: "Is it possible to find a point of intersection between Christian morality and the carnivalistic type of thought?"—and concludes that it is not.

thority on Russian attitudes toward laughter within the context of medieval Christian culture. The second, Konstantin Isupov, is an intellectual historian from St. Petersburg and editor of its major Bakhtin festschrifts. Isupov updates the Losev-Bakhtin polemic over carnival by returning to Bakhtin of the 1920s and placing his thought in Old—not New—Testament subtexts. His speculations on the underside of carnival are more unnerving than those discussed earlier by Boris Groys or Alexander Etkind, manifestly secular philosophers with extensive experience both in the West and with Western texts. Isupov's work, as we shall see here and in chapter 5, is permeated by a certain dread and mystery; he, too, reads Bakhtin as a "Russian thinker," but not at all as our sacralizers are wont to do.

Having passed the midpoint of the present study, however, we might pause on these two scholar-critics and take stock. Averintsev and Isupov are exemplary "Russian critics of critics." Both have been profoundly influenced by Bakhtin, and both are made anxious by this influence—although not in the Bloomian sense. (Russian cultural tradition tends to be agglutinative and embracing, more likely to idolize forerunners than to annihilate them. Although competition does of course take place among peers over the meaning of the legacy, personal rivalry with one's own mentor or object of study plays no fundamental role in the story of Bakhtin's reclamation.) Nevertheless, Averintsev and Isupov are each troubled by the degree and quality of critical energy that Bakhtin has released into the field of ideas—in this case, through that most accessible concept, "carnival laughter"—and made uneasy precisely by the effect on the field *as a field*, that is, on the sorts of questions that will subsequently be asked, or overlooked, within it. Their treatment of Bakhtin reflects this anxiety.

Among the carnival revisionists, Averintsev is a curious case. Sensing a profound moral principle in Bakhtin's teachings and yet confronted with carnival's indisputable profligacy as an ethical framework, Averintsev sets out, in the two essays discussed here, to test that apparent contradiction. The results are uncertain; he is distracted from a critique of the ideas by the image and appeal of Bakhtin's life. Although Averintsev has not left any detailed memoirs, scattered references in the work of others to his relations with Bakhtin suggest a personal affinity that goes deeper than scholarly debt and respect. Apparently Bakhtin confessed to Averintsev at one point, sorrowfully, "I was not better than my time."[25] The dignity and pathos of that remark, made by a scholar-survivor of Bakhtin's gener-

---

[25] "Ya byl ne luchshe svoego vremeni." Natalia Bonetskaia relates this comment, which Averintsev had passed on to her. See N. K. Bonetskaia, "Zhizn' i filosofskaia ideia Mikhaila Bakhtina," *Voprosy filosofii*, no. 10 (1996): 94–112, esp. 95.

ation, moved Averintsev profoundly; the "detour into the human" that one senses in Averintsev's essays is surely linked to the Christological appeal Bakhtin had for an academic of his keen spiritual orientation.

In his 1988 essay "Bakhtin, Laughter, Christian Culture," Averintsev addresses the ancient question of whether Christ laughed.[26] Would an answer in the negative cast doubt on the existence of a "culture of laughter" within Christian societies? Ingeniously, Averintsev approaches the problem through physiology. *Smekh* [laughter], he points out, is not a steady state like smiling, cheerfulness, or humor. It is a burst, "a profoundly dynamic event—at one and the same time a movement of the mind and a movement of nerves and muscles: a rupture and an impetuous explosion . . . not an enduring condition but a transition, whose entire charm and meaning lies in its momentariness" (8). Timing, tempo, and impermanence is all. A prolonged act of laughter, Averintsev observes, is immediately felt as intolerable, unnatural, even grotesque, as something exhausting for the body and senseless for the spirit. What, then, are the ethical and philosophical implications of this *mgnovennost'*—the mandatory "instantaneousness"—of laughter?

Citing Bergson, Averintsev addresses this issue by considering, first, how a transition differs in value from a duration. Laughter is always experienced as movement "from a certain unfreedom to a certain freedom," which is to say that laughter is "not freedom, but liberation." As such, there is an inevitable mechanical and involuntary aspect to it, the initiating gesture of a person who is not yet free; if there is any reason to believe that Christ did not laugh, it was because He was, at all times and as a steady state, completely free. "At a point of absolute freedom, laughter is impossible for it is superfluous" (9). If liberation is the end point of laughter, however, we must ask further: freedom from what? For Bakhtin, laughter enables not rebellion against the material givens of the world but freedom from "social masks, imposed on a frightened person by 'official culture'"; its target was not so much another person as it was "physical difficulty" and "human weakness" in general. The relevant image here is that of the Christian martyrs, laughing at their executioners to keep up their courage: laughter is "a solemn vow directed [internally] toward the powerlessness that a person is forbidding himself to feel" (10).

The laughter Bakhtin sees in Rabelais, then, is not the literary construct of an individual mind but a "universal philosophical and anthropological paradigm," the "laughter of a hero over the coward in his own self." Such self-ridicule [*samoosmeianie*] presumes a bifurcation of the self within the laughing person. With its biblical parallel in the man who

---

[26] S. S. Averintsev, "Bakhtin, smekh, khristianskaia kul'tura" [1988 in *Rossiia/Russia*, no. 6], repr. in *MMB kak filosof 92*, 7–19. Further page references given in text.

"believes, and entreats God to help him in his unbelief," it is an ancient means by which "the conscious and the unconscious unceasingly provoke each other and exchange roles" (11). Averintsev admits that Bakhtin's vague, abstractly ecstatic treatment of Rabelaisian laughter can easily appear utopian and naive. But for Bakhtin, again, laughter does not describe a state of being (and much less a state of reality); it is a line of defense, a state of mind, or rather the threshold between two states of mind. Contrary to the reading Isupov provides below, such laughter is not necessarily of the devil. It is wholly prior to distinctions of good versus evil, functioning more as a primordial element that detaches us temporarily from the world as we were thrust into it, thus restoring us to strength.

Although laughter is not demonic or evil in its essence, it can—and will—be utilized to *serve* evil. Averintsev closes his essay with a discourse on the terror of laughter. Bakhtin's categorical statement that "violence never hides behind laughter"[27] strikes him as utterly odd, since "the whole of history literally shrieks against that statement"; after all, the mocking of Christ on the cross was itself "a return to the very sources of a popular culture of laughter" (13). Blood is at the base of every carnivalization. And if Rabelais's heroes do not go out of their way to shed that blood, this is not because popular laughter is peace-loving or benevolent but because "Rabelais was a humanist, with the mentality of a humanist" (14). Examples to contradict Bakhtin's benevolent understanding of laughter abound closer to home. In Russian history, Ivan the Terrible was a great fan of jesters and of vicious, ambivalent rituals of humiliation; likewise, "the Stalinist regime simply could not have functioned without its own sort of 'carnival.'" Averintsev intimates that such regimes find their ideal raw material in bodies that are needful, disorganized, and grotesque (despite, we might add, today's fashion for considering the efficient, glossy, autonomous body the "fascist" one): "Totalitarianism has always known the value of the unfinished, the unclosed, the malleable," Averintsev notes, and it is expert at exploiting these qualities for its own purposes. The subjects of authoritarian regimes "must be unfinished and adolescent, in a state of becoming, in order for them to be educated, reeducated, 're-forged'" (16).

All the same, Averintsev insists that Bakhtin's carnival idea is internally consistent, pure in both spirit and intent. Problems arise only when this idea is historicized and attached too literally to a single author—Rabe-

---

[27] The reference is probably to this passage in Bakhtin's notebooks from 1970 to 1971: "Irony (and laughter) as means for transcending a situation, rising above it. Only dogmatic and authoritarian cultures are one-sidedly serious. Violence does not know laughter" (*SpG*, 134).

lais—or to a single book. Then the charge can indeed be brought that Bakhtin "absolutized laughter" and mistakenly applied to the late Middle Ages the term *official culture* (in fact suitable only for "mature absolutism") (17). But such simplifications are a reflection of Bakhtin's years of exile and silence; isolated, unpublished, Bakhtin nourished himself on philosophical universals. And whereas "concepts can be disputed, the experience of the soul cannot."

In a second, briefer essay, "Bakhtin and the Russian Attitude Toward Laughter," Averintsev is less the philosopher and more the cultural historian.[28] He opens with an observation about language: in folk sayings and proverbs, laughter [*smekh*] is constantly rhymed with sin [*grekh*]. This semantic connection, he argues, is part of a larger network of linkages and taboos. In Russian, for example, it is quite impossible to say, "The saint told a joke"—that is, the sentence can be uttered, but like an oxymoron it produces no living image; it falls apart because jokes, like laughter, are the realm of the devil. Averintsev then speculates on possible reasons for this cultural fact. Western Catholicism made an effort to "tame laughter, domesticate it, integrate it into its own system" (342). This integration was achieved with the help of the calendar; there were specific, delimited days or zones where "the forbidden" became "the possible." But in Russian culture, such a line was never clearly drawn. Laughter remained an unregulated and dangerous primordial element—and *smekhotvorstvo*, breaking into laughter or causing others to laugh, remained a sin at all times. Even the *iurodivyi*, or holy fool, did not act foolishly for laughter's sake. A lighthearted or boisterous response to holy foolishness was sinful; it would not do to "laugh when we should sigh, weep, and tremble" (342). However, the popular association of *smekh* with *grekh* does not mean that Russians are grim or disinclined to laugh. "Rather the contrary," Averintsev observes—and not entirely happily. Because of its demonic connotations, laughter was perceived as license, as a reaction to the world that could not be monitored within any agreed-on limits. Thus it lacked internal calibration and moral discrimination; even a little bit of it was wholly bad. "There was always a huge amount of laughing going on in Russia, but to laugh there was always more or less forbidden . . . This is a very Russian problem, the conflict between comic genius and Orthodox conscience; it literally drove Gogol into his grave" (343).

The solution that Bakhtin devised to this problem was also, in Averintsev's opinion, very Russian. The monograph on Rabelais, as is proper for

---

[28] S. S. Averintsev, "Bakhtin i russkoe otnosheniie k smekhu," in *Ot mifa k literature. Sbornik v chest' Eleazara Moiseevicha Meletinskogo* (Moscow: Rossiiskii universitet, 1993), 341–45. Further page references given in text.

an academic work on a foreign author, relies largely on non-Russian primary material and documents. But everywhere Russian folkloric motifs, nature worship, and pre-Christian sensibilities penetrate and condition the whole. Most significant, Bakhtin slotted "Rabelaisian" laughter into Russian categories of time, more open-ended and unmonitored than their French counterparts. (Throughout his study, Averintsev avers, Bakhtin "insufficiently appreciated" the "calendar limits" and "conventionality" of Western laughter.) Bakhtin's image of carnival laughter in Renaissance France is not conditioned by the moderate, civilizing social norms of the Western Church but instead possesses the Russian attributes of a force all-powerful, out of bounds and out of control. Thus we arrive at the peculiar "purity" of the illusory utopia that rises out of Bakhtin's book on Rabelais. A Russian would appreciate, far more acutely than a native of Rabelais's own homeland, the "nowhere-ness" of this utopia, which in the Russian context is not only a desired future ideal but a miraculous illusion, a "union of what cannot be unified." Such a "utopia of Laughter with a capital L"—laughter with no demonic overtones—could only be imagined within a *Western* society sensed as entirely "other" to Russia. But powerfully for its Russian audience, the raw material of this laughing utopia is permeated by an energy and illicitness of East Slavic origin.

Thus Averintsev intimates that Bakhtin's book on Rabelais is marked by a curiously compact "outsideness" and "otherwise-ness" [*inakovost'*]. Its mix of alien and domestic perspectives, making it "other" to Russian experience and "other" to medieval France as well, has contributed to its astonishing popularity and transposability and also to its vulnerability as literary history. In closing, Averintsev quotes Leonid Pinsky on Bakhtin's passion for juxtaposing and intersecting cultures. "The idea of personality, supposedly a Western idea, is demonstrated by Bakhtin through the work of the Russian writer Dostoevsky [Pinsky noted]. And the idea of communality, supposedly a Russian idea, through the work of the Western writer Rabelais" (344).

Konstantin Isupov, trained as an intellectual historian rather than a classicist or philosopher of culture, is nowhere near as generous to Bakhtin. He is repelled by those who would assimilate Bakhtin to the more obscurantist recesses of "Russian national-religious thought" (such as Kozhinov) and suspicious of "spiritual" parallels that smooth over logical contradictions and attempt to soften their practical consequences. Seeking to uncover the now distant questions that Bakhtin's ideas were designed to answer, Isupov has labored to reconstruct the intellectual environment that surrounded Bakhtin in the 1920s. His reconstruction supplies the religious dimension that Egorov, in his elaboration of Bakhtin and the scientific revolution, had taken for granted.

Centrally important to Bakhtin at the time was a community of socio-religious thinkers, among whom Isupov singles out Aleksandr Meier (1875–1939). Arrested in 1928 alongside Bakhtin in the "Resurrection Affair" and awarded a ten-year sentence in the death camp at Solovki, Meier belonged to that gifted group of philosophers in Petersburg who, having tasted Marxism in their youth, sought in their maturity to promote a peculiarly Russian fusion of socialist collectivism with early Christianity.[29] Isupov concentrates on Meier's—and Bakhtin's—enduring enthusiasm for salvific models of self-other relations. These models originated with the Symbolist generation, were made famous in the classroom by Bakhtin's professor of philosophy at Petrograd University, Aleksandr Vvedensky, as "the problem of another person's 'I'" [*problema chuzhogo ya*], and were widely discussed in the 1910s and 1920s in both secular and spiritual circles. Their unifying motif was the interrelated Christian and apocalyptic theme of Eros, Heart, and Sacrifice.[30] In Meier's version of this triad, what shapes and saves us is the other—the other's voice, presence, worldview—to whom anything of our own must constantly, and gratefully, be sacrificed.

Here Isupov sees a problem, the same one that troubled critics of dialogue and polyphony in the previous chapter. What, ultimately, can be meant by "ours" and "others,'" when two parties continually defer to each other in authority and content? Where can we look for a point of origin and locus of responsibility? Self and other hold each other hostage. If the other can at any time be raided to feed an arbitrary succession of "I's," then the integrity of the other will always be insecure or swallowed up, in cruel symmetry and endless regression. (The identity of each "I," as other to another, is of course no more secure.) "Bakhtin highly valued the Christian mythologeme of the sacrificial victim [*zhertva*] as the ideal norm," Isupov writes. "But in fact it is the other who turns out to be sacrificed in his model, an other in whom any approaching 'I' finds its own authentic contours and the unity of its personality. The actual fate of the 'other' in the finale of this procedure does not interest Bakhtin" (65).

As Isupov draws out its implications, Bakhtin's self-other paradigm appears quite hopeless. Eschewing all sentimentality, he classifies it as one of "those nostalgic monsters that emerged from the autumn twilight of the Russian religious renaissance."[31] In an intimate chamber-room con-

---

[29] On Meier, Bakhtin, and the "Voskresenie" group, see N. P. Antsiferov, "Tri glavy iz vospominanii," in *Pamiat': Istoricheskii sbornik*, no. 4 (Paris 1981; Moscow 1979): 55–152. See also K. G. Isupov, "Ot estetiki zhizni k estetike istorii (traditsii russkoi filosofii u M. M. Bakhtina)," in *MMB kak filosof 92*, 68–82.

[30] See K. G. Isupov, "Mikhail Bakhtin i Aleksandr Meier," in *MMB i fil kul XX, 2 (91)*, 60–121, esp. 61–66. Further page references given consecutively in text.

[31] Isupov, "Mikhail Bakhtin i Aleksandr Meier," 65.

text, Isupov admits, the scenario might still work to everyone's benefit. In a climate of trust, among close friends, gestures of mutual "sacrifice" and local adjustment are attenuated, concrete, kept in check by shared experience and habits of reciprocity. The danger comes when "Bakhtin's act of humility before a sacrificial victim" is transformed, under pressure of Stalinist maximalism, into abstract rhetoric and an idealization of carnival relations. For in carnival we do not know who the other is—indeed, this is part of carnival's appeal—and thus everything really *is* sacrificed: "The personal voice drowns in carnival laughter . . . The carnival crowd, organized into a laughing judgment on both past and future: this is not an alternative to wretched existence and wretched social conditions but simply a yearning for the mythology of an eternal return. . . . Bakhtin's concept of carnival, for all its indisputable attractiveness and fascination, is essentially tragic, for the human being is forgotten in it" (66).

Isupov's criticism of carnival can now be attached to the polemic introduced in chapter 2 between Bakhtin's book on Rabelais and Aleksei Losev's profoundly negative reading of that novelist—and of Bakhtin's book—in the final pages of his *Aesthetics of the Renaissance*. In an essay entitled "The Bakhtinian Crisis of Humanism," Isupov reviews that controversy.[32] This minor quarrel between two philosophers is of more than literary interest, he insists. In fact, it provides a retrospective glance at the entire tradition of Russian thinking about "humanism, mangodhood, the satanic relativizing of all sacral values . . . [and] the experience of the rise and fall of the human being as the central value in God's world" (127). Since Bakhtin's book on Rabelais is so often reprimanded for its neglect of Renaissance humanism, Isupov's strategy here is of some interest. He places Losev's anti-Rabelaisian zeal in the context of Russian models of humanism (he sees three: Promethean competition with God, creative cooperation with God, and a tragic tension between the demands of the human and the divine). And he insists that Bakhtin gave us solely the carnival underbelly of Rabelais's text and world, "leaving out the familiar high-cultured side of the picture," not because that high-culture aspect was already well researched and known to all (as the defendant had claimed during his dissertation defense) but because the wholesale elimination of genuine, value-bearing humanism was essential for Bakhtin's carnival to work at all.

How did the trajectory of Bakhtin's thought lead to an apotheosis in carnival? In the 1920s, Isupov reminds us, Bakhtin and Meier, enamored of a "liturgical-sacrificial ethics of service," strove for a "community of 'others'" in which "worldwide orphanhood" would be successfully tran-

---

[32] K. G. Isupov, "Bakhtinskii krizis gumanizma (materialy k probleme)," *B sb II 91*, 127–55. Further page references given in text.

scended "by an aesthetics of salvation and consummation" (132). Bakhtin's humanism, therefore, had a strong religious coloration from the start. In such a quest Bakhtin did not perceive individual consciousness and identity to be at risk, because the personalist and intuitivist traditions of Eastern Orthodoxy taught that within a Christian community, the full priorities of each individual "I" would be preserved (133). With the discovery of the dialogic nature of language—a crucial step—this abstract and somewhat impractical scenario was stabilized and brought into the immediate grasp of every human being. "Liturgical-sacrificial ethics" could be justified from both an individual and a societal perspective by the process of remembering [*pamiatovanie*]. Since human memory is stored nowhere as accurately and efficiently as in language, through working with words we can come to know what we must answer for, what is "our own" [*svoi*].

What happens, however, under carnival conditions? Time and memory cease to function as components of personality. There is an abrupt loss of personal language, of any sense of "one's own," and a regression to pre-Edenic innocence, helplessness, and incompleteness. As Isupov charts the prehistory of Bakhtin's carnival vision, the path of the "Bakhtinian Adam" moves from an initial competence to finalize another's "I," through a (largely utopian) positing of the personality's autonomous value within a chorus, to the book on Rabelais, where "in general, the 'I' simply falls out of the field of Bakhtin's vision, it ceases to be a problem, and instead dissolves itself in a poetics of socialized agreement. Not only does Bakhtin, in his analysis of Rabelais's prose, part company with the problem of the author. Important is the fact that for Bakhtin, all principled distinction between [a singular] 'I' and the 'I' of a chorus has now disappeared" (134).

Isupov insists that this shift to carnival is more radical than the shift to polyphony accomplished earlier in the Dostoevsky book—where the concept of "one's own" [*svoi*] is boldly extended from author's voice to hero's voice but still coheres as a concept. With carnival, the concept of *svoi* collapses altogether. And when this occurs, the emphasis on blame and responsibility that marks the early writings (the "non-alibi in existence") is transformed "into the laughing alibi of the crowd, which is always right simply because it is the crowd and because it is laughing." Its cultural memory is no longer temporal-historical but has become blindly spatial, eternally returning to the same place. And "humanism, having gazed on the far side of personality, found there a demonic facelessness and the relativized judgment of the mob" (135).

Isupov concludes by asking why Bakhtin might have departed so utterly from his earlier Christian anthropology (139). His answer all but suggests that Bakhtin himself came under the spell of an unclean spirit.

The new choral "I" no longer needed justice or personality: "It is imma-nently vindicated, beyond the realm of sin." Bakhtin effectively returns the conscious "I," a fallen and thus an articulate Adam, to a prelapsarian state where it neither knows nor cares about Good and Evil; mutely, it reenters a "carnivalized Eden." But such an Eden could just as easily be understood as Hell. After all, the only resident within the Garden with any real knowledge is the Serpent. Its laughter is neither humanizing nor humanistic but, ringing out boldly and facelessly on the Edenic equiva-lent of the public square, simply satanic. (At this point we are reminded of Averintsev's dictum that in Russian traditional culture, laughter—however beneficently employed and whatever its happy results—is, by definition, of the devil.) In the absence of any individualizing principle, Isupov concludes, this "demonic humanism" must be judged Rabelais's proper legacy. Thus the body warmth, fertility, and indiscriminate cele-bration so much a part of Bakhtin's family-holiday approach to Rabelais's text are wholly deceptive.

The proper fruits of carnival, Isupov suggests in closing, are not to be found in Rabelais. They are the voided spaces of Baudelaire's *Les fleurs du mal*. That most unsentimental of poets adopted none of the conven-tional decadent poses—"singer of sin, of erotic suicide, the intolerable voyeur"—but attempted the most difficult thing of all for an artist: "to enter into the very heart of Evil" (141).[33]

Thus do Sergei Averintsev and Konstantin Isupov raise old-fashioned tex-tological and ethical questions about Bakhtin's interpretation of Rabelais. Both have tasted of Stalinism and both worked long years—as did Bakh-tin himself—within Soviet academic structures. Although neither is blind to the postcommunist crisis and its anarchic-carnivalesque potential, their critiques do not sound "modern" at all (not to mention "post-"); al-though free to do so, they do not exploit post-Soviet literary strategies or terminology in their discussion. Nor do they "biographize" the intellec-tual passions of their subject (so easy to do, as Vladimir Turbin has shown) by connecting Bakhtin's loss of a leg with his glorification of the grotesque body or his constant hunger with his praise of the carnival feast. Respecting the integrity of the scholar's voice and the privacy of his life, both scholars do homage to the fact that Bakhtin—whatever his

---

[33] Interesting in this regard is Baudelaire's own theory of laughter, which may or may not have been familiar to Bakhtin: "Laughter is satanic; it is thus profoundly human. It is the consequence in man of the idea of his own superiority. And since laughter is essentially human, essentially contradictory: that is to say that it is at once a token of an infinite grandeur and an infinite misery . . . It is from the perpetual collision of these two infinites that laughter is struck." See Charles Baudelaire, *The Painter of Modern Life and Other Essays*, trans. Jonathan Mayne (London: Phaidon, 1964), ch. 6: "On the Essence of Laugh-ter," 153–54.

personal travail—*lived by ideas*; thus they conceive their task, as fellow scholars, to be an inquiry into the logic and appropriateness of those ideas on their own terms. Our final "anti-carnival" response, by the post-modernist cultural critic Mikhail Ryklin, is quite another phenomenon.

Ryklin's career and prospects represent an authentic paradigm shift, not only for Bakhtin studies but for the larger Russian academic establishment. As an update to chapter 1 of this study, which surveyed the reclamation of literary scholarship in the post-Stalinist period, we might pause briefly on the general shape of that career. Born in 1948 and awarded the Ph.D. in 1978, Ryklin is of a generation whose academic—and, we might add, life—experience at no point overlap Bakhtin's. He came to maturity as a member of the dissenting intelligentsia, one of several gifted and restless students to gather around the remarkable phenomenologist, philosopher of culture, and Proust scholar, Merab Mamardashvili. Then, during glasnost, in a move that almost has the ring of carnival about it, Ryklin found himself sponsored by Gorbachev's revisionist state apparatus. Influenced by French models, a scholarly section had been set up within the Institute of Philosophy of the Soviet Academy of Sciences under the title "Laboratory of Post-Classical Studies." It enjoyed the support of those reformers in government circles who were anxious lest Russian state-subsidized scholarship in the humanities, once opened up to the West, reveal itself as pinched, naive, crippled by the accumulated silliness of six decades of Marxist-Leninist ideology, and desperately out of date. Ryklin was among those recruited to staff the laboratory.

These young researchers were granted access to what had once been the Soviet Index: the canonical texts and reigning authorities of the contemporary European and American literary-critical scene. Commanding French, English, and German, Ryklin translated into Russian major works by Lévi-Strauss, Barthes, Foucault, Gadamer, Adorno, the Marquis de Sade. He answered for the entries on Blanchot, Bataille, and Tel Quel in the *Dictionary of Contemporary Philosophy* published in Moscow in 1990. But Ryklin was more than a conduit through which luminaries of continental thought could reach the newly liberated and vulnerable East. He emerged as an energetic organizer and commentator, integrating the latest literary categories into the (by then) rapidly pluralizing Soviet scene. In 1989 he helped to bring Jacques Derrida to Moscow (which resulted in a book of commentary and interviews, *Jacques Derrida in Moscow: Deconstruction, Travels*);[34] for the next three years, Ryklin himself was a visiting fellow at French and American universities. In 1992 his essays on

---

[34] M. K. Ryklin, ed., *Zhak Derrida v Moskve: dekonstruktsiia, puteshestviia* (Moscow: RIK "Kul'tura," 1993), publication financed by the French Ministry of Foreign Affairs and the American firm "East-West Tours and Travel Consulting."

"speech vision," Roland Barthes, French theory, and post-Soviet deconstruction were collected into an anthology, *Terrorologiki* ("Terrorolo-
gics"), published alongside the Derrida book in the Tartu-Moscow series
Philosophy at the Margins.[35]

The pace and depth of this change in Russian critical vocabularies defy
comparison with our earlier "stages." Within ten years Ryklin's generation "at the crossroads" accomplished a task that would have struck
Bakhtin as novelistic to the core: the incorporation of alien literary vocabularies and worldviews into long-ossified, time-sanctioned official genres
of speech. An element of willful subversion was not wanting in all this.
But that, of course, was also in the spirit of Bakhtin—who, recast into
the vague, mind-boggling syntax of postmodernist discourse, became a
key player in Ryklin's deconstruction of the Soviet regime.

Ryklin's major contribution to the Russian debate over carnival comes
in an essay, "Tela terrora" [Bodies of terror], which appeared in the pi-
oneer issue of *Bakhtinskii sbornik* (Moscow, 1990) and subsequently in
English in *New Literary History* (1993).[36] Abstract, theoretical, in parts
quite unreadable, the argument is pursued in such a way that the concrete body and documented life of Bakhtin the man are effectively absent. But in keeping with the norms of much postmodernist criticism,
intimate psychological terms are applied, as it were, to Bakhtin's "virtual
body." In the text of *Rabelais and His World*, Ryklin uncovers both a
"self-therapeutic" aspect and the unconscious reflexes of "trauma."
Bakhtin is said to have discovered in Rabelais a "convenient site" for the
traumatized intellectual's response and resistance to Stalinism (to be sure,
a trauma conditioned by "the unconscious of someone superlatively intelligent" [55]). With the help of a carnival worldview, this trauma could
be enacted and partially exorcized—which explains, perhaps, Bakhtin's
abiding passion for the idea. "The Rabelais book," Ryklin asserts, "is
indirectly dedicated to the terror and dictated by it" (63): "*Rabelais and
His World* is one of the key texts that help us understand the radically
changed situation of a member of the new society's intelligentsia, who
has lost his status as a courier for the whole of society and received in
exchange the fate of a hostage. . . . [By attending to the multicolored
kaleidoscope of the "lower bodily stratum" and folk speech patterns,] the
traditionally trained intellectual could maintain for himself the appearance of cultural continuity and could also distance himself from the more

---

[35] Mikhail Ryklin, *Terrorologiki* (Tartu-Moscow: Eidos, 1992), in the series *Ad Mar-
ginalem/"Filosofiia po kraiam."*

[36] M. K. Ryklin, "Tela terrora (tezisy k logike nasiliia)," in *B sb I 90*, 60–76. Translated
into English by Molly Williams Wesling and Donald Wesling as "Bodies of Terror: Theses
toward a Logic of Violence," *New Literary History* 24, no. 1 (Winter 1993): 51–74. Page
references are to the English text, adjusted where necessary for accuracy.

dramatic, tragic aspects of the new culture that made intellectual life impossible" (55).

To argue this thesis, Ryklin offers a dynamic theory of the logics—or, as he prefers, the "ecstatics"—of terror. Terror is marked precisely by the "insignificance of causes in the face of effects . . . [unfortunately,] we have not yet learned to analyze this enormous priority of effects, and from habit we continue to seek the 'right' causes. But terror is a pure logic of effects . . . a theater that transforms itself into an orgy of effects" (56–57). Traditional scholarship, working from the bottom up, cannot possibly grasp this logic or incorporate it intellectually into a canon. Necessary, rather, is some emotional intonation closer to a "violent ecstatics"—precisely the tone (which Mihailovic called "incantational") that Bakhtin strikes in his *Rabelais*.

This "ecstatics," Ryklin claims, has more in common with vision than with speech. Watching something, being watched, creating a sculptured image: here, in categories of vision, we have the most powerful tool of any terror-culture. Terror relies on a paralysis of normal life processes. The world is frozen in a single glance—immediate, available for simulation, iconic, indifferent to dialogic feedback, tolerant of absolute silence and death. Static visions are the perfect receptacle for the lie. To illustrate his thesis, Ryklin selects the murals, mosaics, and statuary of the classic Moscow Metro stations, constructed as "people's palaces" during the Stalinist years. The proletarian and peasant figures that adorn these underground stations—inconspicuously huge, vacant, fertile, rejoicing, and everywhere redundant, "a dense piling up of bodies"—function, in Ryklin's view, as vampires or zombies, storing up death in themselves. Alone or in groups, they radiate not the "catastrophic excesses" that were in fact occurring (collectivization, the terror-famine, violent urbanization) but "the perfect innocence of primary intentions" (58). For "collective corporeality" is always imperial. It feeds indiscriminately; the buxom bodies ripen on their own, all blankly alike and all unfaltering. When an authoritarian empire begins to crumble, however, when demands for individual rights or personalized expression can no longer be effectively resisted, such gross and self-confident embodiment becomes an anachronism. In a decadent transitional age (Ryklin is writing in 1990, on the edge of the end of the Soviet Empire), it loses its inner logic and becomes emaciated, nostalgic, sentimental, wantonly violent.

Ryklin intimates that imperial Moscow Metro art, if considered in sober retrospective, is a requiem for the individual body. Your body, my body, had become incidental, disposable, mute—and in its place, the collective body of the people was granted all the reproductive and rhetorical rights. *It* cannot die, so its component parts were set free to kill the individual you. The anesthetizing monumentality of this art was so primeval and depersonalizing that no one dared look at it. Collective corporeality, after all, is not meant to be perceived by *individuals*, all the individuals are already inside it (with what organs might that gaze be accomplished? What sense organs do you have left?). Dare to look, and you will be struck blind. Ryklin closes his essay on the grotesque literary miniatures of Yuri Mamleev, a Russian writer long in emigration who is so bewitched by collective bodies, communal apartments, coprophilia and necrophilia that his characters literally consume themselves and have no eyes left to see with (they see with their lower body parts). The craftsmanship of Mamleev, who in Ryklin's hands plays something of the carnival fool to Isupov's Baudelaire invoked earlier, "sinks lower than any literary waterline" (73). Mamleevian grotesquerie does indeed recall the Rabelaisian world that so disgusted Losev and Isupov with its incipient "Satanism." What can be said of these various successive readers of carnival grotesque? Bakhtin, by all accounts, was delighted by its products. Isupov was repelled. Ryklin and Mamleev coolly observe.

In his fascination with state power and his shift of emphasis from the ear to the eye, from auditory message to visual stimulus, Ryklin brings Bakhtin as close to the "postmodern condition" as any critic we have yet considered. Yet for all its theoretical detachment, Ryklin's reading is highly partisan. He suggests that Bakhtin (consciously or not) came to align the image of a terrorized, collectivized Soviet folk with the basic components of a "carnivalistic" worldview, conveniently extracted from Rabelais. This parallel unfolds in *Rabelais and His World* in discrete stages. First, Bakhtin "inverts the logic of terror" by removing real-life bodies from his purview and filling his discussion with "the archetypal pure essence of folk-ness" (53). Then, by permeating his readings with joyous, carefree, impulsive acts that entail no consequences, terror is "ousted to the periphery"; "the folk finds itself deprived of [even] the right to transgressive ritual." Finally, Bakhtin's wholly visual, outsiderly approach to corporeality results in the individual body becoming "an ideally replaceable, synthetic body"—a body in which denunciation (an external, lie-bearing form) can take the place of confession (an internal, truth-seeking form) without a tremor. Ideally, speech stops altogether. Or, as Ryklin expresses it in his own weirdly roughened prose, speech "closes in on itself and gives itself over to a sublime self-devouring. The reality of the denunciation and the shuddering of suffering bodies, confessing their fictiveness under torture, is replaced by the coming-into-being of speech body-giants, gazing as if from the sidelines at the torments of their chance individual incarnations" (54). The invisibility of real everyday bodies and the blind—literally blind—faith in utopia that accompany such Rabelaisian hero-giants were essential for the "ecstasy of terror" to work.

We might now inquire: In this exposé of carnival, does Ryklin himself pursue humanizing ends? Whose side, bluntly put, is he on? Such questions are not easy to ask of postmodernists. Their critical stance, which fears naive sentimentalism most of all, is designed to avoid if at all possible any embarrassing localization along an ethically exposed border. (Ryklin hates Stalinism, but his style shares nothing with Solzhenitsyn's no-nonsense Gulag realism.) Ryklin does not remark on the fact that many of Bakhtin's comments about the body, ominous as they are when read in a Stalinist context, also characterize bodies as Bakhtin represents them in more distant eras—the ancient world, the Middle Ages—in his writings from the early 1920s, long before the Great Terror. Most surprising, however, given the modish diction and cutting-edge French theory of his essay, is how very old-fashioned Ryklin turns out to be within the Russian critical tradition.

Ryklin accepts unquestioningly the elevated role of the prophet-critic. Literature—even in its comic mode—serves social and political life, and it must expose and censure the abominations of that life. Literary scholarship (such as Bakhtin's on François Rabelais) is consequently an Aesopian practice, an "oblique-speak" that morally alert outsiders will grasp but the people in power will not understand. Most old-fashioned about Ryklin's critique, however, is its view of Bakhtin as a "thinker" in Russian society. The energy behind Ryklin's image of Bakhtinian carnival as "encoded Stalinist terror" appears to originate not in the oppressed folk and not in the oppressing state but rather in the anxiety of that time-honored, privileged social class—the Russian intelligentsia, to which Ryklin himself belongs—now faced with the specter of being shoved aside. Accustomed to enjoying the centrality of a Tolstoy or a Solzhenitsyn in the life of its people, at home with the idea of sacrifice for the common good, this cultured class, too, is being forced to resituate itself in post-Soviet reality. It suffers not so much from repression (which was its past burden and banner of glory) as from fears of irrelevance, fears that it might lose influence and audience. As we have seen elsewhere in this study, the self-absorbed theorizing and inflated fantasies of the Russian intelligentsia have come under considerable attack in the postcommunist period. In his essay, with its talk of exorcism and the unconscious, Ryklin appears to assign this routine "intelligentsial" anxiety to Bakhtin—although there is every indication that the aristocratic Bakhtin was just as untouched by this aspect of his reception as by any other.

It is of some interest, then, to note Alexandar Mihailovic's thoughtful, but on balance dissenting, review of Ryklin's essay from a religious perspective. We recall Mihailovic's "Christological" reading provided earlier in this chapter: that for Bakhtin, carnival and grotesquerie do not degrade the spirit but instead serve to elevate matter, in imitation of the

Incarnation and Eucharist. Thus Ryklin's reading, which claims (in Mihailovic's paraphrase) that the grotesque body is an "ultimate totem of ideological monotheism," motivated not by trust or love but by an ancestral "fear of the cosmos," one that "demands the periodic lustration and self-abnegation of the many for the sake of one," is judged by Mihailovic to be "highly idiosyncratic" (191). "In [Ryklin's] article," he concludes, "the carnivalesque becomes the expression of something very much like *thanatos.*" Not tethered by Ryklin's imported terminology or secular framework, Mihailovic further points out that while transubstantiation in fact abounds in Ryklin's image of a grim Stalinist carnival, Ryklin moves it in a direction opposite from Bakhtin's intent, that is, toward increasing *in*substantiability and vacuousness.

As centerpiece of his critique, Mihailovic comments on Ryklin's awkwardness, his suspicion, almost his criminalization of individualized "breakaway bodies." He contrasts this traditionally Russian discomfiture in the presence of the isolated or free-standing person with Bakhtin's own much less anxious view, and with the high value Bakhtin everywhere places on individuating chronotopes. Attending closely to Bakhtin's text, Mihailovic concludes that, contra Ryklin, "Bakhtin actually emphasizes the absorption of the cosmos into the individual, rather than the suicidal merging of the latter into the former" (192). But in Ryklin's more sinister interpretation, as Mihailovic reads it, "the individual body only has substance when it cleaves itself unto the corporate guilt of the collective body; therefore informing [denunciation] becomes the communicative equivalent of bodily assimilation whereas individuation is tantamount to separation from the body. . . . The body that is not identical to others and does not consume or merge with them is tortured for its exclusionariness . . . Sentience belongs to the breakaway bodies, not to the ones that inform on and cannibalize one another; the latter are virtually inert, even inanimate" (194).

Mihailovic concedes that Ryklin's dark reading is a needed corrective to the naively ecstatic reception of *Rabelais and His World.* But he notes that Ryklin never takes into account Bakhtin's manifestly positive enthusiasm for the carnival worldview nor does he entertain a collectivity that might respect, rather than violate, the boundaries of personality. (Epstein might well be correct in pointing out spiritual affinities between communism and postmodernism.) The question of Bakhtin's own ethical position—whether he endorses or parodies this material—cannot be resolved, Mihailovic observes, if carnival is envisioned solely as "a demonic Otherworld" (195). On balance, Ryklin and his fellow transmitters must be credited for bringing these "foreign bodies" of cultural criticism to bear on their famous, still somewhat insulated elder compatriot. But in his motivation and method, Ryklin remains more at home than he suspects. An outside perspective still offers the more evenhanded verdict.

NEITHER FOR NOR AGAINST: CARNIVAL AS ANALYTIC DEVICE

Our final category of response to carnival is neither sacred nor demonic nor defensively protective of humanist values. It is—or attempts to be— neutral and disinterested scholarship. These critics admit that the carnival cluster of images and values was precious to Bakhtin, however he might have deployed it; but they also hold that the "carnival grotesque" is a principle, an option, whose dynamics can be investigated independently of its application to Rabelais's novels or to Stalinist politics. The partisan history of carnival reception has tended to discourage needed research into the metaphysics of carnival-holiday thinking—and even to obscure the contours of the idea itself.

This state of affairs was summed up well by Vitaly Makhlin in 1991, in an essay for the second issue of *Bakhtinskii sbornik* entitled " 'Laughter Invisible to the World': the Carnival Anatomy of the New Middle Ages."[37] At first we were all enchanted by ambivalent laughter, Makhlin notes of Bakhtin's reception in his homeland; now we are all disillusioned with the "cheerful gravedigger." So wide a swing over such a short period has given rise to the desire "to take revenge on Bakhtin, to expose laughter itself as corrupt . . . On the sociopolitical plane, the 'laughing chorus of the people' is understood—at best—as allegory and as a schizoid-analytical substitution of 'bodies of terror,' and at worst as an expression of Russian fascism and Russian Nietzscheanism. On the religious plane, it is taken as an expression and reflection of the 'demonic,' Luciferian principle" (159–60). Such polarized reactions are part of an inevitable backlash, Makhlin remarks. The world of criticism is currently poorly structured to appreciate a position of "outsideness" toward another person that is not solipsistic, parasitic, or formalistic.

According to Makhlin, Bakhtinian laughter can better be grasped as an illustration of a larger principle—one connected, at base, with *how we see*. But unlike Ryklin's postmodernist use of vision, with its arsenal of terms contemporary only to the critic (simulacrum, repression, trauma, "the gaze"), Makhlin draws largely on philosophers familiar to, or contemporary with, Bakhtin himself. In his own time, Makhlin argues, Bakhtin challenged those naive, classical definitions of vision that hold witnessing to be autonomous, authoritative, monologic—definitions that lend legal

---

[37] V. L. Makhlin, " 'Nevidimyi miru smekh.' Karnaval'naia anatomiia novogo sred-nevekov'ia," in *B sb II 91*, 156–211. Further page references given in text.

credence, say, to the status of "eyewitness." For Bakhtin believed that we could often "true up" our vision more honestly by laughter than by seeing. Along with theorists of comedy and anti-utopians before and since, Bakhtin understood laughter as a detaching, humbling, individuating force that helps us to define our properly modest place in the world of other subjects: that of "laughing outsideness" [*smekhovaia vnenakhodimost'*] (194). As such, it is one of the "visible forms and roots of dialogism" (166): I laugh at myself, at my own suffering, at my absurd position in the world, because I cannot know or see the whole picture and someone else is obliged to tell me where I fit. My "I" is a singularity, but one that nevertheless acknowledges itself as only a part; laughter helps us to accomplish that most difficult task, to see ourselves as very minor players in a multitude of other people's plots.[38] Laughing forms are, above all, participatory forms. That is their primary and fully serious function.

Thus we err when we forget that for Bakhtin, the comic was always the "*serious* comic." "Laughing outsideness" is not necessarily a mindless grin or an irresponsible guffaw, nor need it idealize ugliness and formlessness [*bezobrazie*]. In fact, properly applied, "laughter *sobers down* utopian, aestheticized 'seriousness,'" which is always too ecstatic, always threatening to shut up the world with its stiff theories and humorless arrests (195). Further, Bakhtin never intended that his favorite phrase *veselyi smekh*, "cheerful laughter," be taken to mean that all laughter is cheerful; that would be ridiculous, utopian, perhaps even sadistic (200). Bakhtin implies only that the best sorts of laughter are cheerful—because cheerfulness is a prerequisite for openness and an unencumbered mind (201).

Finally, Makhlin readdresses that point which, ever since the dissertation defense, has plagued readers of Bakhtin's Rabelais project. Why was no effort made to account for Renaissance humanism? Even to suggest in what ways it might coexist productively with a culture of laughter? Makhlin's answer draws neither on Stalin nor the Devil but on straight academic and literary history. He conjectures that Bakhtin had concluded, on the basis of his research in the 1930s, that most scholarly authorities on the Renaissance constructed a retroactive and anachronistic image of humanism that was "nothing other than an aestheticized myth, created by the individualistic culture of the nineteenth century," a companion piece to the "Romantic-utopian myth of an 'organic' Middle

---

[38] "I am capable of seeing outside myself, seeing other people and other things, only because I am already seen, acknowledged, and accepted" (168); that is, the sense of wholeness I derive from my own acts of feeling and seeing is also every other person's experience, although a different whole is achieved for every person. Elsewhere, Makhlin commends this act of "finding oneself as an other" for its "ontological modesty and dignity." See V. L. Makhlin, "'Dialogizm' M. M. Bakhtina kak problema gumanitarnoi kul'tury XX veka," in *B sb I 90*, 107–29, esp. 109.

Ages" (203). Such scholarly mythmaking—or "intelligentsial fiction" [*intelligentskaia vydumka*]—was always offensive to Bakhtin, regardless of the worthy values such a myth might carry. The stamp of officialness was too much upon it. And Bakhtin's reaction, in this instance, was to bring the whole weight of carnival to bear against that image. He was not especially concerned with balance. For unlike the academic world of "ready scholarly results" and unlike postmodernist constructs that focus on power (and also, we might add, unlike any construct where justice and memory are indispensable), the "mental energy" of carnival could never become bitter (204). Thus it was impossible to defeat.

Makhlin's route—carnival as a metaphysics of "laughing outsideness"—is one of the more successful neutral approaches to this most controversial concept. We conclude our "nonpartisan" approaches to Bakhtinian carnival with one equally theoretical, but more tied to literary history and to problems in the evolution of genres. For that reason, perhaps, it arose on the boundary between carnival and dialogue, and as an aftermath to Bakhtin's massive insertion of what some have felt to be exaggerated carnival motifs into the revised Dostoevsky book. Can the incompatible theses of polyphony and carnival be effectively combined? Does the new fourth chapter on genre traditions of menippean satire contradict the spirit of Bakhtin's original theses on Dostoevsky?[39]

Some readers, nostalgic for the Soviet order, openly despised the carnivalesque insert in *Problems of Dostoevsky's Poetics*. They used it to lash out at the twin evils of an anarchic Russian present and an irresponsible past (including that morbid scandalmonger Dostoevsky himself, under ban for much of the Soviet period).[40] More sophisticated attempts were soon

---

[39] Saul Morson and I have offered an "opportunistic" hypothesis: In the early 1960s Bakhtin still saw no chance of getting his dissertation on Rabelais into print. He might have thought it prudent to introduce some of those ideas under the guise of a "revision" of an earlier book, even at the expense of internal logic and at the risk of exaggeration (i.e., "Bobok" is a microcosm of all of Dostoevsky's work). See Morson and Emerson, *Mikhail Bakhtin: Creation of a Prosaics*, 456–60. Since that writing, evidence for Bakhtin's lifelong pro-carnival sympathies has persuaded me that opportunism cannot be the whole of it. Bakhtin loved this idea and was eager that scholars whom he respected approve his application of it to the most diverse realms. See, for example, his letter of 23 November 1963 to Leonid Pinsky: "I am now occupied with renovating my 'Rabelais' . . . I would very much like to receive from you even the briefest comments on the fourth chapter of my book on Dostoevsky (if you have had the chance to acquaint yourself with it). This is very important for my work on 'Rabelais.'" *DKKh, no. 2(7) (94)*: 60.

[40] Exemplary here is A. A. Iliushin, whose essay, "Apropos of 'Carnivality' in Dostoevsky," appeared in a 1992 Saransk anthology. The "carnivality" of the 1963 revision is inappropriate and un-Russian, Iliushin remarks, an entirely Western concept. Carnival is supposedly joyous and universal, but Dostoevsky is dreary and grim. Is Dostoevsky therefore tragic? Not really: he is not lofty enough. Dostoevsky is merely sadomasochistic. The whole of Dostoevsky, in fact, is one "Feast during the Plague"—and "now that plague is everywhere

undertaken by scholars determined to "make carnival fit"—without, however, endorsing it in all its Dionysian literalness—into Bakhtin's overall thought and into literary history as a whole. These critics accept the presence of carnival in Bakhtin's vision of Dostoevsky, and even justify it within bounds. But they resist tying carnival to outside, nonliterary causes—as Russian civic critics, from Belinsky to Isupov and Ryklin, have been so fond of doing—and resist as well any facile evocation of inner, psychologized categories such as "trauma." Instead, in the pro-system spirit of late Formalism, these critics believe that any manifestation of art, while neither isolated nor disinterested, can be studied as a relatively autonomous realm of culture. Thus they seek reasons for Bakhtin's shift from polyphony to carnival in the very nature of his categories, in the dynamics inherent to them, and in the alternations and correctives built in to any culture's literary process.

Representative of this group is the prominent Moscow philosopher Liudmila Gogotishvili. Her lengthy essay in *Voprosy filosofii* (1992), with its faintly Formalist title—"Variants and Invariants in Bakhtin"—made a substantial, sobering contribution to the increasingly heated debate between Bakhtin's Christianizers and his demonizers.[41] Her thesis is as follows. The "fulcrum" of Bakhtin's thought has been difficult to find, she writes, because "the inferences to be drawn from his various works (for example, the books on Dostoevsky and Rabelais) are at times not in hidden, but in naked, contradiction" (116). This fact should not dismay us, however, but impel us to seek deeper for the point of their joining. According to Gogotishvili, the "regulative idea" governing Bakhtin as he emerged from his Kantian period was the search for "the particularization of one's own moral reality"—that is, for a point of view on oneself that is singular in the world, that exists authentically and carries absolute value, but that all the same is not "given," that permits itself to be posited and molded as an individual task. Within that task, among the most persistent invariants she identifies in Bakhtin is his *personalistic dualism* (117). By this term she means his commitment to the *non*fusion, or eternal separateness, of self and other. In his early writings on the structure and growth of personality, Bakhtin restates the problem as the juxtaposition between an "I-for-myself" (how my inner potential looks and feels to my

---

and we are not doing much feasting, we understand all of this differently: life has ceased to be feast-like and carnivalesque, this is not the era for it" (86). Faring poorly on the ruins of Communism but still viewing the world through the distorting lens that Soviet pedagogy had turned on the great nineteenth-century Russian classics, Iliushin is disappointed by *both* Bakhtin and Dostoevsky. See A. A. Iliushin, "Po povodu 'karnival'nosti' u Dostoevskogo," in *MMB: PNN 92*, 85–91.

[41] Liudmila Gogotishvili, "Varianty i invarianty M. M. Bakhtina," in *Voprosy filosofii*, no. 1 (1992): 114–34. Further page references given in text.

own consciousness), an "I-for-the-other," and "the-other-for-me" (how others experience my "outerly" completed acts, and I theirs).[42]

According to this paradigm an "unbridgeable chasm" exists between the experience and perspectives of an "I" and an "other." (Such a discontinuity, Bakhtin argued in the 1920s in his lectures on the philosophy of religion, is unshakable and nonnegotiable for the believing Christian.[43] Gogotishvili, too, recommends that we understand Bakhtin's theories of "otherhood" in religious terms.) Despite the current fashion for theories of alienation, this "chasm" is no cause for despair. On the contrary, in a happy paradox, unbridgeability does not disqualify or disable us in our need for others but heightens and refines that need (117). Orthodox doctrine acknowledges no absolute void in the sublunary world. Personality [*lichnost'*], no matter how inarticulate and helpless it might prove vis-à-vis an abstract idea or the laws of nature, can always define itself creatively against another personality. It follows that a healthy self is not one to which other personalities are fused or fixed in permanent relations, but one that retains the ability to negotiate among changing and competing claims. If either the "I" or the "other" comes to dominate a given horizon wholly, monologism results.

Gogotishvili then suggests that Bakhtin's attitude toward literary history, and toward the evolution of aesthetic form within that history, was conditioned by this inviolate distinction between the world of my "I" and the world of others, elaborated very early in his career. As Bakhtin gradually came to model it, literary form evolves in a cyclical pattern, alternating between the polar monologisms of a triumphant "I-for-myself" (where solely my own inner perspectives are real) and a triumphant "I-for-others" (where I am worth only what others see, value, and need in me) (118–21). At each extreme, dialogue collapses into monologue. Each pole has its strengths and its peculiar distortions. The greatest liability of *I-monologism* is its idealism; introspection and abstract ideas become all, everything is arranged along a vertical axis of fixed values, the lonely "I-for-myself" attempts the impossible (which is to do without others), and the inevitable result is the revolt of the hero. *Other-monologism* is precarious in other ways: its Achilles' heel is "parasitism," the tendency to consider itself forever incomplete, and thus the temptation peculiar to it is to hand the whole of itself over to another (a horizontal-

---

[42] See the basic distinction in "Author and Hero in Aesthetic Activity," *A&A 90*, esp. 22–25.

[43] "Problema obosnovannogo pokoia (doklad M. M. Bakhtina)" [July 1924], in *MMB kak filosof 92*, 234–36. This essay, cast in sacrificial rhetoric, deals with the genres of prayer, ritual, repentance, and hope as peculiarly *singular* dialogic forms requiring the orientation toward a transcendent Third as addressee. Bakhtin exemplifies the "chasm between self and other" as "the cross for myself and happiness for others" (235).

ization of life's relations). Literary selves built in this environment often suffer from an excess of materialism or naturalism, as well as from a deficiency of personal voice. If the crisis associated with I-monologism is a revolt of the hero, then characteristic for other-monologism is a crisis of the author.

At this point the outline of Gogotishvili's analysis becomes suggestively clear—and although she does not take her thesis this far, one is tempted to provide a capstone. The closeted, obsessive, rebellious Raskolnikov is trapped in the vortex of an I-monologism, whereas the grotesque, generous Gargantua and Pantagruel (at least as Bakhtin reads those giants) approach the irresponsible fantasy of other-monologism. As anchors at either end of this spectrum, Bakhtin's twinned enthusiasm for these two fantastical authors, Dostoevsky and Rabelais, makes good sense. Might not this spectrum suggest another way out of the harsh judgment that Natalia Reed, Fridman, Kariakin, and others have passed on Bakhtin's overly benevolent polyphonic readings—which, in their opinion, turn Dostoevsky into an armchair parlor game, a talk show where there is nothing at stake but words? Looked at not as a routine operating procedure for dialogue but as only one extreme, intrinsically unstable pole, polyphonic consciousness can begin to answer for the most exaggerated states of loneliness, anger, crisis. The pathology Bakhtin exiles from his interpretations is thus invited back home—and properly so. For if polyphony does provide some heroes with multiple options and does lead some sinners to grace, most of the time, we would probably agree, Dostoevsky's world is manifestly not experienced as a free or friendly place for the driven, ungrateful individuals residing in it. Its psychological norm is a "lonely 'I-for-myself'" forever tensing toward its environment, making of everything a task and taking nothing as a gift.

Gogotishvili does not explicitly locate, along this spectrum, Bakhtin's two "incompatible" monographs on those literary masters. (Although, to strengthen her separation thesis, she does ignore the "carnivalization" chapter in the revised Dostoevsky book.) She emphasizes, however, that this spectrum is not static but multi-planar and dynamic. Distance is always being collapsed and then reestablished between the two extremes, within literary history and within a single text as well. "Strivings toward the monologic," of both the carnival and the polyphonic sort, switch direction, prove each other inadequate, break each other down, liberate each other. Each new resolution occurs on a higher plane and with adjustments unforeseen in earlier epochs.

Here Gogotishvili displays some of the positivistic (Hegelian) faith in linear histories we sense operating in Bakhtin's chronotope essay. She hypothesizes that Bakhtin's two pioneering monographs (the lost study of Goethe is not discussed) can be linked in the following way. Rabelais broke down the "I"-dominated monologism of the Middle Ages, which had been idealistic and vertical. But his success inevitably encouraged various "other"-dominated monologisms to proliferate on the ruins (materialism, a worship of matter for its own sake, a restriction of life to its horizontal dimension). This domination by other-monologism was overcome only by the advent of Dostoevsky's polyphony, rooted in the idea-person and the word: it was carnival's necessary corrective and antidote.[44] But the lessons of matter were not forgotten nor were the gains of earlier idealistic stages cast aside. If there were no vertical axes in Dostoevsky's polyphonic world, there would be nothing around which the heroes could construct a dialogue (126).

In this connection, Gogotishvili refers us to the refinements of the carnival idea that Bakhtin provided in his 1941–44 text, "Additions and Changes to *Rabelais*" (published for the first time in 1992, together with the "Variants and Invariants" essay).[45] In those notes Bakhtin himself investigates the intersection of polyphonic and carnivalistic principles at close range and on the basis of individual texts. Dostoevsky's carnival side, reduced to a dot or a line, is represented in Bakhtin's readings by the novelistic threshold: this boundary is at work in the ambivalence of Zosima's bow to Mitya Karamazov, in Raskolnikov's paralyzing visual contact across doorjambs, and in the increased sense of potential mystery at precisely those points where one should be saying one's final, departing, finalizing word (153). (In supplementing himself with these notes,

---

[44] Thus does Gogotishvili explain how polyphony reestablished the "I/other" balance and corrected the "parasitism" of other-dominated monologism: "Challenging the 'pure' form of monologism of the opposite tendency (at the time this was a *body-monologism* [*telesnyi monologizm*]), Dostoevsky reestablishes a vertical picture of the world [i. e., cross-sections marked by *coexistence* and *interaction*], but no longer in its static variant [i.e., as in Dante] but incorporating also the temporal factor . . . If Rabelais surmounted the bodily loneliness of medieval man, then Dostoevsky surmounted the body totalitarianism of naturalistic, biological, sociopolitical ideas, counterposing to them the newly reborn idea of the inner 'I-for-myself'. . . . But the inner 'I-for-myself' in Dostoevsky is different than it was in the Middle Ages and different than it was for the Romantics—who, according to Bakhtin, were the first in modern times to open up the inner infinity of the subject against the background of the infinity of the external world as opened up by Rabelais. Dostoevsky strives to overcome the loneliness of the inner 'I,' severed both from the 'spiritual' value of the vertical and from its 'clan body' [*rodovoe telo*]." Unlike earlier attempts at synthesis, however, Dostoevsky gives his heroes full-bodied personalities, not only a body and a soul but also a spirit [*dukh*] of their own, a private "I" that can be a "thou" to others and a site of dialogue. This restricts his own authorial prerogatives, that is, it creates the ground for polyphony: "All the author's coalitions (either with the reader or with the hero) have fallen apart," and thus the hero is available for autonomous, moral co-being with other "I's" (126).

[45] M. M. Bakhtin, "Dopolneniia i izmeneniia k Rable" [written 1941–44], *Voprosy filosofii*, no. 1 (1992): 134–64. Further page references given in text.

we might add, Bakhtin addresses those critics who charge him with ignoring "silent dialogue" in his treatment of Dostoevsky.) A carnival sense of death—that is, a disregard for death—is shown to animate even as grim a murder mystery as *Crime and Punishment*. "Raskolnikov's room," Bakhtin writes, "is a coffin, in which Raskolnikov passes through a phase of death in order to be reborn as a renewed man. . . . But it is characteristic that life and death here are given exclusively on the internal plane, they touch only the soul, physical death does not threaten any of the major heroes, the battle between life and death on the earthly plane is altogether absent; the heroes live in an absolutely safe world" (146). That there is something "safe" about Dostoevsky's metaphysical dilemmas, which touch "only" the soul, might strike us as a strange postscript to the unanswerable, ultimate questions that constitute the "heroes" of a polyphonic novel. It is a curiously moving comment to come out of the darkest and most dangerous years of the Second World War, where bodies were so terribly under threat—and was motivated, perhaps, by Bakhtin's nostalgia for the pure idea-battles still possible in a pre-Stalinist world.

Gogotishvili's hypothesis—that Bakhtin intended carnival and polyphony as alternating literary principles that condition each other along a historical continuum—is borne out by archival fragments from the Saransk period now being brought to light in the *Collected Works*. In one notebook entry, Bakhtin remarks that the carnival worldview in Dostoevsky can no longer be naively joyful, affirmative, or externalized as it was in Rabelais; it cannot forget the lessons of its own epoch. "The psychologization of the material-bodily *lower stratum* in Dostoevsky," Bakhtin jotted down. "In place of the sexual organ and buttocks we have sin, the sensuous thought, corruption, crime, double thoughts, inner cynicism; the sanctity of the great sinner (a fusion of high and low, of face and buttocks; going in circles; the devil as Ivan wrong side out; the problem of the double)."[46] Judging by the several surviving plans, Bakhtin had in mind a much greater "darkening" of Dostoevsky (and precisely along the carnival seam) than in fact occurred in the revision; the working plans

---

[46] The fragment continues: "The carnival foundation of Smerdyakov's image: the coupling of a sinner with a holy fool (a saint) . . . the ambivalent nature of Smerdiashchaia's ["Stinking Liza's"] image, stinking sanctity, stinking death and resurrection. The carnival nature of the parricide problem in the novel: Grushenka as the prostitute saint (who, incidentally, seduces-saves Alyosha—'The Onion'); Zosima, the stinking saint. . . . Every room in Dostoevsky . . . is a chunk of the public square (a chunk of hell or heaven, a chunk of Golgotha, a chunk of carnival square), where they crucify or torture, tear the Tsar-jester to pieces." "K istorii tipa (zhanrovoi raznovidnosti) romana Dostoevskogo" [undated notebook, 1940s–1960s], in *MMB: ss 5 (96)*, 42–44, esp. 42–43.

are as full of the coarse violence of carnival as the Rabelais book was indifferent to it.

For Gogotishvili, a textologist thoroughly familiar with the notebooks for both the Rabelais and Dostoevsky projects, crucial to any objective rehabilitation of carnival are Bakhtin's attempts to make laughter more nuanced and responsible. As a corollary, "seriousness" emerges as less one-sided and monologic, less a term of abuse. "According to Bakhtin, not every seriousness leads to terror," she emphasizes (129). Or rather, "official seriousness" is bad—but not because it is ordered or hierarchical per se. It is bad because it intimidates. "Unofficial seriousness," on the other hand, is fully positive, expressed in human compassion for suffering and weakness (135). In general, seriousness is not a vice except where it refuses to accept *stanovlenie* ["becoming" or coming into being], that is, when it overinvests in the eternity of things. The polar opposite of carnival laughter is not seriousness but stasis and terror.

It is important to note that Gogotishvili, like other Russian moral philosophers who have taken up Bakhtin, distances herself (and her subject) from any implication that carnival behavior *on its own terms* is a value in Dostoevsky—or a pleasure for Bakhtin. She categorically denies that amoralism, voyeurism, or carnival license is ever celebrated by Bakhtin in the scenarios he selects to illustrate his principles (despite Bakhtin's several indications to the contrary; in his inflated affection for such nasty little menippea as "Bobok," for example). In her view, laughter serves Bakhtin solely to restore a balance to "personalistic dualism." Carnival does not need (although it does not necessarily reject) a Christian scaffolding in order to fulfill a moral function. Even in its secular guise, it is the opposite of what Isupov, Ryklin, and others of the "demonic/Stalinist" school presume it to be. Along with Makhlin, Gogotishvili insists that Bakhtin urges us toward laughter to replenish our inner "I," not to lose it on the public square. There is no need to choose between carnival and polyphony, two of the sturdiest principles in Bakhtin's world. Properly grasped, they can highlight each other's shortcomings and provide energy for literary evolution.

Let us now sum up the fortunes of carnival. The three main lines of its rethinking—as sacralized ritual, as demonized or Stalinized allegory, and then the more neutral attempts to see it as an analytic device in literary history—are evidence indeed of Bakhtin's "philosophical gift for broadening out problems." What scholars still dispute is Bakhtin's own personal investment in carnival and laughter as part of a survivor's philosophy. Why was he so devoted to the idea? In the light of this chapter, and the accumulating weight of memoiristic testimony, two reasons might be offered: one cognitive, the other sociopsychological. Neither is dependent on Stalinism for its coherence or validity. First, we cultivate laughter as a route to knowledge. This was Bakhtin's point at his dissertation defense: you laugh, you cease to be afraid, you can then investigate, and there is no surer path to a self-confident humanism and control over one's resources, both inner and outer, than this. Second and more pressingly autobiographical is the relationship between regret, disappointment, anger, and laughter. Anger is always ridiculous to the party that is not angry, and Bakhtin was too proud to wish to appear ridiculous. When disillusioned he would be silent—or recommend laughter. Such options are absolutely in keeping with everything we know about his personality and relations with the world: respectful, distanced, dignified, apolitical to the extent this was possible, nonresponsive to criticism, ungoadable, and honorable in the old-fashioned, condescending sense that he expected little self-control or discipline from others but large amounts of it from himself. Under stress, words explicate and thus obligate; laughter (a much more private and impenetrable reflex) can confound and liberate.

In closing, we might attempt a balance among these richly contradictory evaluations of carnival energy by returning to the thoughtful centennial essay by I. N. Fridman, "Carnival in Isolation," on which the Introduction to this study opened.[47] Fridman attaches carnival (as does Gogotishvili) in a complex weave to its apparent opposite, polyphony—and more generally, to the "I-thou" relation that Bakhtin celebrates in dialogue. But he imparts a darker cast to the whole, tying it more tightly to the pressures of Soviet ideology. He interprets both polyphony and carnival in light of the major realignments in Bakhtin's thought—and in Soviet politics—at the end of the 1920s. The dynamics of polyphony, he suggests, reflect Bakhtin's waxing utopian hopes for what openness alone could do to keep creativity and consciousness alive. The quality of "completion" [*zavershenie*]—previously valued as full of grace, lovingly bestowed, pragmatically necessary in order that personality function properly and that a work of art emerge in our disorderly world—is reinterpreted as "closure" or "enclosedness" [*zamknutost'*]. It becomes a destructive force that behaves like "a robber on the high road," stealing up on us and attacking from behind (85). This shift strikes Fridman as fatal, not just for Bakhtinian aesthetics but for any aesthetics; for in his view, once "aesthetic pleasure" and "catharsis" have been exiled from the work of art, the boundary between life's processes and art's products cannot be sustained. According to Bakhtin's new understanding, ideas and forms

---

[47] I. N. Fridman, "Karnaval v odinochku," *Voprosy filosofii*, no. 12 (1994): 79–98. Further page references given in text. A similar trajectory is suggested in Morson and Emerson, *Creation of a Prosaics*, part 1, ch. 2.

(along with their human carriers) do not naturally desire consummation or resolution. Thus heroes, readers, and authors are never taken down off the rack. The instability and psychic distress that accumulates in such a model eventually triggers the move from polyphony to carnival. For if the polyphonic image is "a 'world symposium' headed by an insane Chairman whose sole concern is that dialogue never end" (86)—Fridman's unkind paraphrase—then the only way Bakhtin can avoid this travestied extreme is to wrap the whole dialogic process in an anesthetizing utopian envelope. Within that envelope, the "second life" of the mind in dialogue is like the laughing holiday, deeply authentic but suspended in both space and time.

According to Fridman, Bakhtin's polyphony and his carnival are equally utopian constructs. If the Dostoevsky book creates out of that novelist's world a personalist utopia, then the Rabelais book is its mirror opposite, a hymn to the *rodovoe* [clan-based] body (86). The two are connected, Fridman suggests, in the new fourth chapter on genre in *Problems of Dostoevsky's Poetics*, through Bakhtin's eccentric concept of "genre memory" (87). This "memory of the genre" is really a sort of "fore-memory" [*pra-pamiat'*] that combines elements of a collective preconscious with prerogatives of the conscious individual. Its one determining characteristic is that it seems to remember only what everyone else forgets. Bakhtin avoids the (consciously acknowledged) classics in the art of the novel "like a danger zone"; when he invokes genuine carnival forms, he lets it be known that any attempt to incorporate them into literature must reduce and distort them almost beyond recognition. For this reason, Fridman is reluctant to call Bakhtin an aesthetician at all. "The subject of Bakhtin's aesthetic theory," he writes, "its authentic substrate, are the peripheral zones lying on the threshold, on the border that divides art from pre- or supra-art, anything but art itself. . . . [Both the dialogic novel and the model of carnival] provide a definition of art—but only in the specific Bakhtinian sense of 'delineating the limits' of something, and even so, not from within but from 'without'" (88).

Fridman's comments lead us to the edge of that most fraught area in which Bakhtin has been rethought, the theme of our next chapter, *vnenakhodimost'* [outsideness]. The term refers both to the cardinal value Bakhtin placed on external perspective, as well as to Bakhtin's own multiple identity as literary scholar, culturologist, and ethical philosopher, outside each discipline and native to none. With their competing methodologies and different validating logics, are these various professions eroded when combined in his person? If so, is this a blessing or a misfortune? For however much we might sympathize with Bakhtin's antipathy toward "official thinking" [*ofitsial'shchina, ofitsioz*], there is much to recommend professionalism. An internal consistency of argument, an obligation to assess what others have researched and registered, a consensus over basic terms, an agreement as to what constitutes a misuse of evidence, the modest placement of oneself within an established language: in the best of worlds these are virtues that professional insidership can foster. Even in the worst of worlds, the Soviet Union circa 1930–50, the cohesiveness of intellectual tradition and a sense of shared texts was what had kept Russian philological scholarship alive.

Bakhtin, however, did not seek to be an insider to things. In places he rivals Leo Tolstoy in his reluctance to join, endorse, or build on (with any degree of appreciation) a definition that precedes his own. And in matters of art, as it was for Tolstoy so it is for Bakhtin: art is not primarily a matter of pleasure, beauty, perfect proportion, or disinterested play but the site of another, more essential task—knowledge of the self through communicative exchange. Beauty and aesthetic pleasure might even be said to get in the way. In the next chapter, and from a somewhat different angle, we will revisit this conceptual realignment in Bakhtin's thought that took place in the late twenties. The guides here will be, among others, Natalia Bonetskaia and Konstantin Isupov—who, in Fridman's spirit, ask whether *form itself* possesses the resources to survive the pressures Bakhtin applies to it. The role form plays in other paradigms of the creative process is occupied in Bakhtin's scheme by an assortment of more vulnerable and porous matter: speech genres, voice zones, loopholes, participatory outsideness, aesthetic love. Can Bakhtin's mature aesthetic, derived from Kant, from the theory of relativity, from biofeedback models and the example of Christ, steeped in Goethe and Schelling, ever achieve the minimum disinterestedness, attention to details and to wholes, and respect for configuration that we have come to expect from a theory of art?

CHAPTER 5

Внеходимость:
"Outsideness" as the Ethical Dimension of Art
(Bakhtin and the Aesthetic Moment)

AMONG the more remarkable aspects of Bakhtin's present fame as mentor to the humanities is the ease with which he has shed his strictly *artistic* dimension. That Bakhtin was not a conventionally "academic" literary scholar is now readily acknowledged. But his own casual remark that literary studies were a "parasitical profession" can hardly be taken at face value. After all, his major life's work centered around Dostoevsky, Rabelais, Goethe, the novel—and for twenty-five years as teacher and professor, he delivered spellbinding lectures on all periods and genres of world literature. Perhaps ironically, the literary aspect of his legacy has been assimilated, reduced to cliché, subjected to the sober criticism of specialists—and thus become canonical and, after a fashion, invisible. Disputatious attention has shifted to Bakhtin's "first philosophy," to the worldview that preceded those provocative readings and the god-terms that might tie them together.

This chapter focuses on Russian considerations of one problematic node at this higher level of abstraction: Bakhtin's insistence on *vnenakhodimost'*, the necessary "outsideness" of one person in relation to another. "In the realm of culture, outsideness is the most powerful lever [*rychag*] of understanding," Bakhtin wrote in his *Novy mir* letter of 1970.[1] But the theme had been sounded fifty years before, in his earliest philosophical writings, where Bakhtin replaced the principle of transcendence [*preodolenie*], so important to Kantian ethics, with the more modest, interactive, horizontally oriented ideas of mutual "surplus" [*izbytok*] and "supplementarity."[2] Russian scholars who have worked on this idea (Volkova, Makhlin, Gogotishvili, Bonetskaia) properly see it as the common denominator between Bakhtin's ethics and his aesthetics; it is also the

---

[1] For the 1970 *Novy mir* letter, see Bakhtin, "Response to a Question from *Novy mir*," *SpG*, 7 (translation adjusted).

[2] For a centennial discussion of the "logic of outsideness" as it contributes to a unified field of literature-and-life studies and to postmodernist attacks on logocentrism as well, see M. O. Gorobinskii (Ekaterinburg), "Dialogika M. Bakhtina: Logika vnenakhodimosti i printsip dopolnitel'nosti v iskusstve i zhizni," in *MMB i gum mysh (II)* 95, 29–32.

concept most often held responsible for Bakhtin's negligent attitude toward traditional aesthetic concerns. The neglect is indeed there. Bakhtin's theory of art frets little over prescriptive rules, directives, or the particular "artistic" challenge of symmetry and harmony (these technical
matters, apparently, are taken for granted). A work of art must meet the
same criteria that govern every other creative event in Bakhtin's world. It
must be singular (that is, nonsystematizable and unique); answerable
("signed" by its author or beneficiary, responsible); "participatory" (oriented toward another consciousness, response-worthy), and it must be
undertaken in a spirit of "aesthetic love." The enabling condition for all
these attributes is outsideness.

BELATEDLY FINDING A PLACE FOR THE VERY EARLY BAKHTIN

At the turn of the 1990s, when Bakhtin's philosophical manuscripts were
still a novelty and Russian specialists were making strenuous efforts to
acquaint the lay public with their curious content, the publishing house
Znanie [Knowledge] published in its popular-scholarly series three pam-
phlets on the early aesthetic thought of Mikhail Bakhtin.[3] All presumed
familiarity with Bakhtin's later, more famous ideas and catchwords—and
were designed, in part, to forestall a further banalization of these ideas by
providing an account of their genesis. Each represents a different critical
approach to its material and to its Russian (soon to be ex-Soviet) reader-
ship. The first of these, a pioneering pamphlet by Vitaly Makhlin, was a
dissident document, written with the public-spirited impatience that
marked the late glasnost years. As a professor of philosophy appalled at
the party-minded, homogenized condition of his discipline under Soviet
rule (and grateful for the groundbreaking Western work on Bakhtin),
Makhlin drives home those aspects of Bakhtin's early life and thought
that most emphasize his subject's personal outsideness, solitude, and
nonacceptance of official ideology.

As Makhlin reminds his glasnost-age audience, even in the relatively
free 1920s, Bakhtin, with his non-Hegelian and nonmaterialist views,
could only find himself increasingly marginalized as an aesthetician (21–
23). But even against the background of classical aesthetics, his founda-

---

[3] The first pamphlet, by V. L. Makhlin, "Mikhail Bakhtin: Filosofiia postupka," appeared
in the Znanie series "Filosofiia i zhizn'," no. 6 (1990): 63 pp. [text, excerpts from Bakhtin,
and a glossary of terms]; the second, by E. V. Volkova, "Estetika M. M. Bakhtina," was
published later that year in the series "Estetika," no. 12 (1990): 63 pp.; and the third,
coauthored by V. L. Makhlin, A. E. Makhov, and I. V. Peshkov, "Ritorika postupka M.
Bakhtina," appeared in the series "Ritorika," no. 9 (1991): 41 pp. Further page references
given consecutively in text.

tional ideas on art did not easily distribute themselves among the familiar rubrics of the true, the good, and the beautiful. In Bakhtin's view, art was an *active co-creation of images* that served to link an individual person "responsively" to an immediate reality. As such, it posited a sort of "aesthetic activism" that was wholly new for the Russian intelligentsial tradition, which tended to overlook benign, pragmatic interactions among real people in favor of utopian projections or abrupt discontinuities. Makhlin suggests that Bakhtin, in recoiling from that tradition, set a standard for independent thought that the Russian critic of the 1990s, so given to inversions and extreme negations, would do well to heed. "So far our criticism of the past has proceeded monologically," Makhlin concludes (27), "and even our rejection of Stalinism has been realized in the well-known genre of 'final judges,' people who in Dostoevsky's time were most often the socialists and today are their antipodes, their opponent-doubles." In a paradox he will later richly develop, Makhlin suggests that Bakhtin, by being such an outsider to the terms laid down and approved by his own time, reached a higher and freer degree of answerability.

Elena Volkova's contribution to this "Bakhtin cluster," appearing six months later in the Znanie series *Aesthetics*, is less hortatory and more straightforwardly descriptive. Unlike Makhlin, who sees an overall continuity in Bakhtin's thought and holds contemporary readers (with their bad habits) accountable for not grasping it, Volkova admits of some internal tension in Bakhtin and thus some legitimate confusion. She opens her discussion of "aesthetic outsideness" with a disclaimer. "At first glance," she notes, "the principle of outsideness might seem contradictory" to Bakhtin's central concepts of dialogue, the responsible deed, participatory thinking. After all, "does not being located 'outside' mean total aloofness, nonparticipation, indifference, complacent neutrality, residence on Mount Olympus from which one can gaze down on the flickering little figures of other people? That this is not the case, the following will demonstrate" (19).

Volkova anticipates her reader's objections step by step. "Being outside" does not mean isolation, security, or abstraction for the self. The healthy self is highly vulnerable and wholly involved in others, she hastens to explain, only it does not pretend (in the name of empathy or devotion) to duplicate their particular space or time; it enters another's worldview and then, with a memory of that other horizon, returns to its own place. It must return, because only by that act does it regain its distinctive excess, or surplus, of vision vis-à-vis the other. And only by reclaiming my unique outside position, by once again being in a position to see what you cannot see, can I render you an absolute service—which will be valuable to you as a supplement regardless of the energy, kindness, or creative intelligence that accompanies it. (It is worth noting that Bakhtin's vision of outsideness is wonderfully nonelitist, nonjudgmental, and open to all, whatever our gifts or inclination. He does not stipulate that we do the other party any positive *good*, only that we assume an outside position toward that party. Even the laziest and most passive outsider can always help me out by letting me know what is happening behind my head; in my laziest, most passive, most testy and unengaged moods I can render outsiders at least that much of a service.)

But why, Volkova asks, does this outsideness possess *aesthetic* potential? Because, she explains, only "a position 'outside' provides the possibility of 'finalizing' an event," and the act of finalizing or consummating, *zavershenie*, is the most crucial aesthetic moment. In our daily interactions with others we bestow partially finalizing images all the time: by passing judgment, picking up our end of a joint task, tendering congratulations (or a complaint), telling a story with a well-defined end. But these gestures are often one-sided, opportunistic, governed by our transient moods or needs. Others are rarely valuable to us in their whole selves, but only in that aspect of them turned toward us and attachable to our desires or our task at hand. "It is not easy to see a person as a whole [*tselestno*] in everyday life," is how Volkova paraphrases Bakhtin on this point (22); in the process of seeking out another's face, "we must pass through a stage of arbitrariness and grimaces." We must also work to overcome our own random reactions to that face. Only occasionally in life are we required, by the nature of the relation, to take the necessary time to conceive a psychological whole, worry about its every angle, linger over it and grasp sufficiently the logic of its parts so that this human entity can be released into its own time and space—and still cohere.

In Bakhtin, Volkova emphasizes, "the nature of artistic finalization by means of outsideness" (23) is realized in a nonformalist way. What matters is "not so much the artist's work with the material and with the form dictated by material" as it is the finalization, or at least the stabilization, of an *evaluative position*. Bakhtin believed that even in such realms as music, architecture, or abstract design, the artist senses a potential human consciousness and strives to delineate it and serve it. As he emphasizes in "Author and Hero," artistic visualization of whatever sort works within two parameters created by the artist at the outset: a spatial world with its evaluative center in a living body and a temporal world with its evaluative center in a soul (190). To be sure, various genres, styles, and media require that authors practice different degrees of outsideness; "the quality of the author's horizon may be more or less stable." But an author always enjoys some surplus of vision vis-à-vis another potential consciousness in a work of art; this is what makes art a "self-other" relation. It is the responsivity and high refinement of this spatial surplus that sets the category of art apart from the rest of our harried lives.

Compared to Makhlin, then, Volkova's treatment of "outsideness" is relatively apolitical; it is also only tangentially related to literature and raises its questions almost entirely in the realm of ethical philosophy. Her focus is apt, for Bakhtin's originary scenarios allot only a secondary role to words. Polemicizing with the Russian Formalists, Bakhtin even states outright that "the author's creative consciousness is not a language consciousness" ("A&H," in *A&A*, 194). In this early text, creative activity is perceived as closer to a "sculpting" one. The artist's work always takes place on the boundary between one self and another, and consists in "giving a form to inner life *from outside*, from another consciousness . . . To find an essential approach to life from outside—this is the task an artist must accomplish" (101, 191).

Variations on this immensely difficult task recur throughout Bakhtin's fifty years of researching the nature of art. Sculpture and images of the body dominate the early writings (how we "feel" embodiment differently from an inner and an outer perspective). With the advent of his own "language consciousness," Bakhtin began to examine words, too, for insiderly and outsiderly qualities. Interestingly, his first full-scale published study, on Dostoevsky's prose, turned out to be an extreme case—for *vnenakhodimost'* is maximally intense and fastidious in polyphonic writing. As Bakhtin reconfirmed in 1961, the polyphonic novelist's willingness to assume an outside position toward fully (and at times even aggressively) "alive" material is "an activity of a higher quality. It surmounts not the resistance of dead material, but the resistance of another's consciousness, another's truth . . . A creator re-creates the logic of the subject but does not create that logic or violate it."[4] With its exaggerated respect for the inviolability and autonomy of the created character, polyphony indeed presents a great formal challenge to a literary author. However, the overall gesture that Bakhtin recommends here—an ousting of one's self to some outer, and thus more privileged, position from which to then *look in*—is part of the larger and prior "battle against interiority" that dominated philosophical debates during Bakhtin's Belarussian and Leningrad years.

Natalia Bonetskaia provides a context for this debate in a 1993 essay entitled "Bakhtin and the Traditions of Russian Philosophy."[5] She sees in Bakhtin's model of self-other relations a significant departure from the

---

[4] Bakhtin, "Toward a Reworking of the Dostoevsky Book," in *PDP*, 285–86.

[5] N. K. Bonetskaia, "M. M. Bakhtin i traditsii russkoi filosofii," *Voprosy filosofii*, no. 1 (1993): 83–93.

widespread presumption (which is erroneously attributed to Kant) that knowledge, being limited to personal experience, could never adequately or reliably be extracted from another person's soul. Information, it was assumed, could be gathered solely "from the inside out," that is, by self-observation. Bakhtin rejects that position utterly. He insists that it is precisely our own selves that we cannot know, since the human psyche is set up to work "from the outside in"—that is, to encounter and come to know truths *from others*. By so insisting, Bakhtin separates his "philosophical anthropology" from the mainstream teachings of Russian Orthodox philosophers (Soloviev, Lossky, Frank, Florensky) which, although not hostile to individual personality, tend to locate ultimate grace in scenarios of collective coming together and harmony, in *vseedinstvo* and *sobornost'* [all-unity and communality]. For Bakhtin, in contrast, what grace there is must be found in *drugost'* and *inakovost'* (otherness and "otherwise-ness"); an ideal coming together is always predicated on subsequent departure and vigorous differentiation. (Hence, we might add in support of Bonetskaia's thesis, Bakhtin's attempt in his early writings to amend the misleading biblical precept: "Love thy neighbor as thyself." We do not have categories for self-love, Bakhtin argues. Even when I pose in the mirror, it is the other's reaction to my image that I impersonate; I fantasize that the face I see, smiling with delight, is not merely a reflection of my own foolishly grinning self but is some other person looking back at me—which is to say that most of the time we do not know with any certainty what we think about ourselves, but we do know that we wish to be looked at, loved, stimulated, and changed *by others*. Thus the real challenge is to love thy neighbor as that other, *as thy neighbor.*) In a crucial but problematic move, Bakhtin will come to link outsideness with the question of form—which, in his opinion, can be applied or "bestowed" solely from without.

Several large advantages come with this position, of which we might note two. The first has to do with the individual author in the context of a tradition. As suggested at several points in this study, the Russian sense of tradition is absorptive and inclusive; it is less likely to become anxious over influence than it is to recruit, admire, and canonize predecessors. In keeping with this spirit, Bakhtin's insistence on the outsideness of creating artists vis-à-vis their heroes and their chosen artistic genre permits those artists to add constructively to the dialogue rather than to displace or obliterate it. It liberates the artist from the burdensome mandate to create continually new content and forms, and thus from the need to destroy tradition in order to find one's own voice. One's own voice is guaranteed by one's position, which is, by definition, uniquely new. (A recent comparison of Bakhtin's aesthetics with that of Georg Simmel emphasizes this point; unlike the German philosopher, Bakhtin could revere established styles and "sanctify tradition" while sacrificing nothing of the individual creative self.)[6]

Second, by insisting that even the most complex aggregate is formless when viewed from *within* the event, Bakhtin makes a minimum of two active consciousnesses absolutely necessary for aesthetic awareness. Such plenitude might well seem ludicrous to an orthodox Formalist (say, Viktor Shklovsky), for in a structuralizing approach to art, the parts of a literary work are viewed as relatively inert and remain in their assigned places, equally identifiable from whatever perspective one chooses. But Bakhtin understood the nature of aesthetic material differently. It always contains potentially unruly relationships and unpenetrable matter. This understanding of artistic form is grounded in his tripartite model of the self, introduced at the end of chapter 4 and now ready for elaboration: the self's division into an "I-for-myself" and a two-sided "I-for-the-other"/"the-other-for-me."[7]

The latter two linked self-other categories generate, in Bakhtin's terminology, a "soul," *dusha*. They alone have any real hardness or edge to them, any finalization of form—and thus any ability to share a language and to communicate. The "I-for-myself," permeated by what Bakhtin calls *dukh*, or "spirit," is inchoate and fluid, without an articulate consummating voice of its own. It knows, with its inner sense of paths not taken and potentials not realized, that any of its fixed surfaces or completed acts perceived by others could have been different (either better or worse); it is thus unable to rest securely on any accomplishment. Security in time and space is granted to us by other people, who inevitably see us as more stable and accomplished than we can ever see ourselves. The "I-for-myself" receives whatever forms it has at its disposal—its store of images and verbal cues—from others. It can filter, domesticate, integrate, and dispute those cues, but it is unable to form a fixed image out of its own inherent or primordial materials.

It is important to note that Bakhtin's model of mind acknowledges no equivalent of a Freudian id with autonomous, nonnegotiable, and presumably universal demands or drives. Nor does the Bakhtinian self admit

---

[6] See P. N. Vorokhov (Saransk), "M. M. Bakhtin i G. Zimmel'," in *MMB i gum mysh I (95)*, 150–52. Although Simmel and Bakhtin both advocate an interactive relationship between life and artistic form, Vorokhov sees this divergence: "For Simmel it is axiomatic that the author-creator resides wholly in the form that he or she created. Thus the major condition for the creation of new form, of a new artwork, is the obligatory destruction of the old form. Bakhtin, however, throughout the entirety of his career insisted on the primary outsideness of the author in relation to the hero and of the creator in relation to form. For that reason the destruction of old form was by no means necessary, for the author does not reside in it but rather comes upon it as a task. This permitted Bakhtin to sanctify style and tradition. For Simmel, both are obstacles to creativity" (152).

[7] See chapter 4 of the present study, pp. 198–201; see also "A&H," in *A&A 90*, 22–25.

the grip of a superego that the conscious self must accommodate through submission, guilt, or fear. Such hypothetical structures provide the conscious self with impossibly tempting "alibis for existence," others to blame. Whereas the fluid "I-for-myself" does indeed realize or stabilize itself solely in categories that originate in a world external to it, all the same, it has considerable negotiating power and reasonably full awareness as it reacts to pressures and influences. As we saw in chapter 3, such awareness need bring no particular blessings. ("Consciousness," Bakhtin wrote shrewdly, "is much more terrifying than any unconscious complexes"[8]). But Bakhtin would insist that the mind is equipped to deal adequately, even creatively, with this terror. A healthy self, in order to maximize its choices and thus reduce its impotence in the world, will always strive to expose itself to a multiplicity of inputs and perspectives from the outside, that is, it will strive toward a "novelized" state.

In Bakhtin's original metaphor, then, the "I-for-the-other" and "the other-for-me" (that which produces a soul) is not really a configuration of words. It is a product of space and perspective, parameters that literally "mold" another's image from the outside and leave palpable, almost sculptural results. Despite the theological resonances, then, for Bakhtin *dusha* is more an aesthetic category than a religious, ethical, or psychological one. Our soul is the shape of consummated surfaces and deeds; it is concerned with those mechanisms that permit selves to *appear* to one another. It does not ask whether this image is pleasing, moral, just, or productive. "The soul is spirit the way it looks from outside, in the other," Bakhtin writes; in an audacious corollary, he presumes that looking at another person is by its very nature a generous activity, welcomed by both sides. "The aesthetic interpretation and organization of the outer body and its correlative world is a *gift* bestowed on the hero from another consciousness" ("A&H," in *A&A*, 100). Anyone who bestows form on us in this way—whether kindly or unkindly—increases our repertory of choices and responses and is thus a benefactor, an author, and a participant in aesthetic activity.

As we shall see, in Bakhtin's subsequent variations on the authoring idea, the nature of this "gift" changes. Form-bearing outsideness turns out to have its own rules of behavior, which coincide neither with "aesthetic consummation" nor with the demands of "aesthetic distance." In fact Bakhtin's reformulation of those two traditional criteria for art becomes quite spectacular. Initially the artist is portrayed as "outsider" in an engaged but still businesslike way, the way a sculptor must be professionally outside a block of marble. Throughout the 1920s and into the

---

[8] "Toward a Reworking of the Dostoevsky Book" (1961), in *PDP*, 288.

1930s, however, Bakhtin's idea of form becomes ever more interactive, dynamic, open-ended. And precisely because the "formed material" is increasingly granted the right (indeed, almost the mandate) to *resist* being shaped by its author—precisely because it is so "alive"—the "formal question" has inevitably been conflated with the ethical in debates over Bakhtin's legacy.

A lucid examination of the point where ethics and aesthetics are conjoined in Bakhtin's early thought has been provided by the American scholar Deborah Haynes, in her monograph entitled, somewhat too narrowly, *Bakhtin and the Visual Arts.*[9] Her concern is Bakhtin before 1925, before his attention was seized by the potentials of language and his ideas still cast in spatial metaphors. (Thus her choice of title; a welcome focus, for Bakhtin's early writings have long deserved nonretrospective treatment outside the gravitational pull of the more famous word-based dialogism to come. One recent [1991] Moscow State University dissertation on Bakhtin's aesthetics was even so bold as to divide all of Bakhtin's thought into two periods: up through 1924 and then from 1924 to 1970.[10]) Haynes opens her study by placing Bakhtin's early ideas among prominent aestheticians (largely German) at the turn of the century, all of whom Bakhtin had studied and most of whom, in a woefully telegraphic way, he refuted. He argues against the neo-Kantians for their normative moral imperative; against expressivists such as Theodor Lipps for their reductivist understanding of empathy; against impressivists such as Alois Riegl or Eduard Hanslick for the exaggerated role they assigned to *Kunstwollen*, or the "will to form"; against Russian Formalists for their mechanistic materialist aesthetics; and against theorists of "art as play" (for example, Karl Groos) for underestimating the indispensable role of the other in artistic production. There are nevertheless some important points of convergence. Similar to Kant, Bakhtin designates "the aesthetic" as that overlapping place where cognitive concerns (open, free, impersonal, systematic) and ethical concerns (closed, duty-laden, personal) can be brought together. The "intuitive unity" of those two flanking realms during aesthetic activity is one major reason for literary art's intoxicating appeal, for it alone enables us to participate in alternative worlds where human images are real and viable but not burdened with real-life obligations or consequences. Bakhtin differs from his continental predecessors, however, by insisting that the unique individual consciousness and its concrete relations with other persons is that one obligatory

[9] Deborah J. Haynes, *Bakhtin and the Visual Arts* (Cambridge: Cambridge University Press, 1995), esp. chs. 1, 2, 4. Further page references given in text.

[10] Elena Anatolievna Bogatyreva, "Estetika v filosofskoi sisteme M. M. Bakhtina," avtoreferat, Moscow State University, 1991, esp. 2.

fulcrum around which aesthetic value must be organized. He also insists that the aesthetic moment is not (as Kant and later the Formalists suggest) "autonomous" or exceptional in human experience—nor is it, as in Romantic or Symbolist parlance, an eruption of inspiration or frenzy into our otherwise humdrum noncreative lives. On the contrary, Bakhtin felt that a proper understanding of the aesthetic task would reveal it to be a paradigm for all other (even the most humdrum) human tasks.

Such an ambitious aestheticization of life—realized not by making life less ethically responsible but by making art, in some vaguely defined way, more so—radically changed the meaning of "art for art's sake," especially as that debate had developed among Decadents and Symbolists toward the end of the last century. As Haynes points out, attempts to reduce art to mere sovereignty in its own realm, with little more at stake than a pursuit of perfect form, creative freedom for the artist, and sensuous intuition, were perceived by Bakhtin as indications of a serious crisis, "an attempt by artists simply to try to surpass art" (36). Against this sort of escapism, with its reliance on hedonism or scandal to produce the new and with its tiresome rhetoric of the End, Bakhtin opposed the philosophy of the individual conscious act or deed [*postupok*]. As Haynes sums up Bakhtin's position, this act is always unprecedented, always productive of further acts, and inevitably incurs some further obligation ("the morally responsible deed expresses the nonaccidental, nonarbitrary character of a given life" [55]). Only by means of my own act can I hope to become an *author* in my life and make of that life something resembling a work of art.

Let us expand on Haynes's discussion, drawing on Bakhtin's reminiscences, details from the early essays, the example of his own life, and some Russian work that postdates her study. First, we should note some consequences of Bakhtin's postulate that there must be an outside perspective for any aesthetic event to occur. For in matters of art, the boundary between two conscious positions was the only firm boundary Bakhtin drew. Unlike the Russian Formalists—with their polemically clear-cut (but in practice rather arbitrary) distinction between "everyday life" [*byt*] and "literariness" [*literaturnost'*]—and unlike the Freudian theorists with their opposition between "real experience" and that foggy, quasi-conscious triumvirate of dreams, fantasy, and illicit impulses to art, Bakhtin believed that aesthetic relations were both an ongoing, everyday activity and a healthy, conscious, structuring one.[11] In his view, aesthetic

---

[11] I draw here, with considerable compression and some alterations, on chapter 5, "Psychology: Authoring a Self," from Morson and Emerson, *Creation of a Prosaics*, esp. 188–89.

or art-generating activity is distinguished from other activity in our everyday lives (practical tasks, business, dreams, games, and fantasy) by one overwhelming factor: the presence of a spectator, an outsider. What characterizes both the practical, goal-related projections of our inner life and our fully impractical fantasy worlds is not, Bakhtin would argue, their degrees of "reality" (for fantasy feels plenty real; that is why we engage in it) but rather an exclusively "inner self-sensation," the absence of an "outward expressed quality" to the self ("A&H," in *A&A*, 67). Fantasy-sensations can only "imagine"; they cannot "impart an image" to anything because they do not require the presence of a genuine other consciousness. Being inner, they are unable to consummate or finalize the primary actor, which is the "I-for-myself." And for Bakhtin, art requires above all a second self who perceives the creation *as* art, that is, as a finalized object viewed from the outside. There must be someone exercising a surplus of vision with respect to the event. In this regard, of course, artistic creators and their audiences are functionally indistinguishable, in that both must remain outside their heroes' event in space and in time. So important is this shared status of outsideness that Bakhtin frequently combines the author with the spectator or contemplator into a single composite term, *avtor/sozertsatel'*.

The ethical and the aesthetic, although separate spheres, are indispensable to each other, and their interaction can help us resolve some of life's most intolerable questions. To escape being a mere random occurrence in life, to what sort of continuity should I aspire? How do I get outside of my life—with its pain, indignity, missed opportunity, crimped perspective—so as to shape it into something I can live with, that is, shape it as I might shape an artistic creation? Bakhtin's response to such questions is again in the spirit of the Stoics and Epicureans who thought so deeply on the proper place of the transient body. Most of us, Bakhtin intimates, should not risk the exhibitionist-outsider's route to life-as-lived-art, the path of an Oscar Wilde, Baudelaire, Rimbaud, Mayakovsky. Although those great poet-rebels left a magnificent literary testament, in Bakhtin's judgment it is unrealistic to assume that flamboyant or outrageous behavior in itself will make us freely creative or more "aesthetically informed." "Outsideness" in the Romantic or Decadent sense—where the artist is ranked above and apart from others, tragically misunderstood, devoted to the "idea of integral or 'total' creation" in a life constructed largely in an alternative world—was for Bakhtin symptomatic of a *crisis* in authorship, not its triumphant realization. For under such conditions "one is unable to humble oneself to the status of a toiler, unable to determine one's own place in the event of being through others, to place oneself on a par with others" ("A&H," in *A&A*, 203). As with Dostoevsky's travesty of the Underground Man, rebellion and isolation in the would-be creator is more likely to lead to repetition and intensified bondage than to originality or autonomy.

The artist, then, gains little by a stance of alienation. Artists are servitors, and they serve the larger world by providing models for "organizing relationships." The dynamic here was explicated in a programmatic 1993 essay on Bakhtin's theory of art, which identifies six axes along which Bakhtinian aesthetics "organizes consciousness": among inner selves, from self to other, from other to self, from self to another's creation, from self to its own created object, and, finally, among others for others. The author intimates that Bakhtin's dialogic model for joining art to life is simply not compatible with those aesthetic attitudes now so familiar in the modern world: rejection, estrangement, *confrontation*. On the contrary, the very mechanics of this model are predicated on acquiescence and assimilation: "Art as a complex means of human adaptation to the world has as its goal a special sort of ordering of phenomena on the micro-level, that is, on the level where the inner spiritual life of a person flows, his or her psychic reality. . . . In art, a person assimilates reality and comes to control it by making sense out of it through images."[12]

And so Bakhtin counsels us to come to terms—and thereby become authors. For him, an aesthetic attitude is an "answerable" one: by accepting the world, we heighten our responsiveness to real others from our outside position in their worlds and thus participate in a maximal number of relationships—in short, we *reconcile* ourselves to dialogue. But assuming that such a conciliatory relation is honestly possible, to what, precisely, are we answerable? Does there exist a normative ethical or aesthetic model, a standard for the Good and the Beautiful against which I must measure my act—or are there other continuities and types of rootedness? Unsurprisingly, Bakhtin, singer of the grotesque body and the sprawling novel, makes no special plea for the True and the Beautiful. But perhaps surprisingly, he also seems indifferent to the details (and certainly to any enforcement) of the Good. He insists that we are answerable not to a law of proportion or to a theoretical moral imperative, but only to our own unique "act-taking I."

Here the problems begin in earnest. For given the fact of the tripartite self, the virtue assumed to be inherent in multiple perspectives, and the value everywhere placed on proliferation and on a departure from the site of one's last residence, how can an "I" be expected to cohere? This question fascinated the young Bakhtin. The coherence of culture, he appears to have believed, takes care of itself (here non-Russians can only wonder,

[12] V. I. Samokhvalova, "Soznanie kak dialogicheskoe otnoshenie," in *MMB kak filosof 92*, 190–205, esp. 201.

again, at the awesome, identity-bestowing hold of Russian culture on its communicants). One might even say that we recognize culture as such by its interrelatedness and cohesiveness, qualities that appear to be in place without any special effort from each of us. But how is an *individual human whole* possible, since persons must participate in fragmented projects and are subjected daily to so many pressures beyond their control? Against the grain of his generation, Bakhtin dismissed both the abstract and the intuitivist solutions to the problem of unity within a self. In their place, inspired by a motley and still underdocumented set of philosophies, he devised a concrete, cautiously interactive model that we recognize, in retrospect, as a rudimentary preverbal form of dialogue.[13]

The basic components of the model are *dan* and *zadan*, Russian equivalents of Kant's *gegeben* and *aufgegeben* as reworked by the Marburg neo-Kantian Hermann Cohen (in Cohen's formulation, what is "given"—the world I wake up to—versus "what is posited by me as a task"). Life presents us with givens [*dannost'*]: formless disasters, undeserved illness, mindless revolution, unexpected good luck. In lived experience, as a rule, we do not come upon already existent unities or wholes. What makes me whole—Bakhtin might say, the only thing that can make me whole—is a *response*. It is rarely within an individual's power to initiate or guarantee a unity of content in the world at large (at least in no world Bakhtin ever knew). But by being actively outside of and different from that world, it is always within my power to initiate a whole in myself by stringing together, through my active volition, a series of responsive acts that are marked as mine. Integrity by means of response is infinitely more difficult

---

[13] Kant, Schelling, Buber, and Cassirer are among the sources of Bakhtin's philosophy. In their recent contributions to a "darker" image of their subject, Makhlin, Isupov, and the Minsk scholar Tatyana Shchitsova have argued that Bakhtin's thought—with its passionately literary imagination, its refusal to aestheticize or psychologize sin by making it a general human condition rather than a concrete act, and its ranking of reality over mere possibility within a Christian ethics—closely parallels the writings of Kierkegaard. Shchitsova argues further that this influence (or confluence) has been enriched by the discrepancies in the German translations on which Bakhtin relied but surely "read through." In an essay on Kierkegaard and the hermeneutics of sin, Makhlin makes a strong case for Bakhtin's kindred resistance to the externalization of sin as a "given": sin cannot be metaphysicized or psychologized, Makhlin concludes, for sin is not a science, sin is my mistake. It can be addressed only by becoming itself the object of address, an object of uttered speech and communication. In his entry, Isupov sees in Kierkegaard's meditations what he has come to see, obsessively, in Bakhtin's work: the disappearance, or death, of the real other. See T. V. Shchitsova, "K ontologii chelovecheskogo bytiia (Kirkegor i Bakhtin)," *DKKh, no. 3 (95)*: 34–42, followed by an annotated translation by Shchitsova into Russian of selections from the "Concluding Unscientific Postscript" (1846) to "Philosophical Fragments." For Makhlin and Isupov, see V. L. Makhlin, "Germenevtika grekha," 53–68, and K. G. Isupov, "Odinochestvo v Drugom (S. K'erkegor naedine s soboi)," 69–77, both in T. V. Shchitsova, ed., *K'erkegor i sovremennost'* (Minsk: RivshiGo, 1996).

to achieve than integrity through consistency of content or through a refusal to engage.

Bakhtin laid down the groundwork for this aesthetics—personalist, responsive rather than referential, profoundly "non-postmodernist"—in the very early 1920s. His writings from that period all counsel, as the surest route to self-mastery, the slow acculturation and incorporation of others (or rather, of others' worldviews and words) on "micro-levels" of consciousness. Outer reality is to be overcome by an inner generosity and by a curiosity for juxtaposing, within the mind, as many perspectives as possible. (As we saw in chapter 3, this eager internalization of alien viewpoints has been read by some as polyphony's singular indulgence and as a central reason why Bakhtin can extract from Dostoevsky's very dark art such hopeful and friendly principles.) In 1974, a year before his death and after all the horrors of his century, Bakhtin reiterated this basic truth in his final essay, loosely concerned with a methodology for the humanities. Our consciousness can rest, and perhaps even triumph, only as an *aesthetic* consciousness, he reaffirmed. "Meaning [*smysl*, or the sense of a thing in context] cannot (and does not wish to) change physical, material, or other phenomena," he wrote. "It cannot act as a material force. And it does not need to: it is itself stronger than any force."[14] Can we agree with Bakhtin that the contextualized meaning of a thing is stronger and more satisfying than a material force? How "aesthetic" can the ethical moment be allowed to become?

OUTSIDENESS: WHAT IT IS AND IS NOT

In considerations of Bakhtin's first and final writings, which appeared so belatedly, certain confusions about *vnenakhodimost'* have proved to be routine. Four recurring problem spots demand our attention.

First, that Bakhtin believes in openness, unfinalizability, and dispersal does not mean he rejects the idea of *wholes*. Rather, the contrary is true. Were the world really only disjointed fragments, we would not trust our individual selves to exit into it. But trust is only part of the answer. The other part is psychology of art. This moment is deceptive in Bakhtin— and repeats, along another axis, the confusion between a "philosophy of relativism" and a "theory of relativity" that was noted in chapter 3. It is precisely because unfinalizability and malleability are inherent in living personalities, in everyday events, and in time-space parameters that the achievement (not the acknowledgment, not the discovery, but precisely the achievement) of a whole is so indispensable—and so laden with obli-

---

[14] "Toward a Methodology for the Human Sciences," *SpG*, 165 (translation adjusted).

gation. The whole of something can only be seen from a position that is outside of it in space and after it in time. But since a whole can be variously realized from an infinite number of angles (and each of these realizations will be fully recognized as such only by its own "finalizer"), a sense of wholeness is always "bestowed," not merely decreed or revealed. It looks different, and differently perfected, to each person who beholds it. Human beings are form-bestowing creatures. It is part of our nature to crave to finalize. This craving, according to Bakhtin, is the aesthetic instinct.

As Volkova emphasizes in her chapter on "Outsideness and Dialogue,"[15] the aesthetic phase in any reaction is always the final and culminating one. "Before reacting aesthetically," she asserts, "the author reacts cognitively, ethically, psychologically, socially, philosophically—and only then finalizes the world artistically and aesthetically" (17). This final move, although conditioned by all the others, is the fullest and purest. "If values in the world are confused and mixed," Volkova writes, "then in art they receive their definitive place thanks to the wholeness of the hero (even a potential hero) and to the creative context of the author" (18). In her role as explicator and professional philosopher, however, Volkova tends to underestimate the sheer difficulty of the human task Bakhtin calls on us to accomplish. It is only through that difficulty, I suggest, that Bakhtin's thought finds its ultimate coherence.

As is the case with genuine dialogue, to create a persuasive whole takes a great deal of sustained work. A successful author must constantly return to the same site, be drawn to the consciousness that is being shaped there, cultivate dependencies and vulnerabilities in his own self that then risk going unsatisfied, undergo what often seems like arduous and futile training to master the creative medium (wood, marble, musical tones, words). This labor knows some highly compressed moments—the fantastically efficient energy of inspiration and intuition—as well as the slower time of trial and error. We are driven to spend this time and do not regret the expenditure. But because of the intense and time-consuming nature of the drive, for most of our daily interactions we cannot, as a rule, afford to be too profligate in our creation of wholes. We fully commit to creating them only in love and in art.

Thus Bakhtin discusses those two states, making art and creating love, under a single rubric. (Matvei Kagan and Hermann Cohen were the immediate sources for Bakhtin's concept of "aesthetic love," to which we will return below). In both activities, we suspend the usual open-ended state of the world—with its promise of disorder, apprehension, unreliability, betrayal, unexpectedness, slack—and are persuaded that form,

[15] E. V. Volkova, "Estetika M. M. Bakhtina," in Znanie series "Estetika," no. 12 (1990).

contour, proportion, and coincidence have a natural, effortless justification that "speaks for itself." In this special sense, a beloved person is a work of art; that is, regardless of local errors in behavior or judgment, the parts of that person fit together and cause delight. (Although no creative poet himself, Bakhtin comes closest here to understanding the function and addictive appeal of a Muse.) The image of such a beloved person can be said to resemble the potential personality that is always, in Bakhtin's view, at least a shadow presence in the work of art (and in the well-governed life): a radiant personal image of the sort that had prompted Dostoevsky to say that if forced to choose, he would "remain with Christ rather than with the truth." Each of these quasi-fictional, quasi-real images is understood so thoroughly and from so many different, subtly nuanced points of view, and has been called up in conversation over such a lengthy stretch of time, that it is pardoned in advance for whatever it might do. For just this reason, Bakhtin properly divined, there is no experience more galling than to witness the "deserved shaming of a person beloved by me"—because lovers see wholes, and the rest of the world, as is its right, sees only isolated, single-sided acts.[16] It is not surprising that in Bakhtin's earliest writings, where the question of aesthetic finalization is first discussed, we find his most excruciating comments on love.[17]

Let us now reformulate this sequence of psychological moves, so important to Bakhtin's concept of human "becoming," in language less technical than Bakhtin and his neo-Kantian colleagues were wont to use. The psychology here is not as sentimental or counterintuitive as it might seem—and practicing fiction writers will confirm its overall logic. Once we have put in the necessary work to bestow a whole image on another personality, however tentative or provisional that working whole, we have some assurance that further energy spent in its direction will not dissipate without trace. We find it first comfortable, and then compelling, to formulate words and actions in its "zone"; we welcome its responses; we begin to trust its "integrity" sufficiently to risk interacting intimately with it and investing ourselves in it. The integrity can be that of a Desdemona

---

[16] "Toward a Philosophy of the Act," 62: "When I contemplate a picture showing the destruction and completely justified disgrace of a person I love, then this picture will be quite different from the one I see when the person destroyed is of no interest to me from the standpoint of value. And this will occur not because I am trying to justify [the beloved] contrary to sense and justice . . . the picture may be just and realistic in its content." Since every individual gazing at a given object perceives that object as oriented uniquely in time and space, such agony on behalf of a beloved "is not a biased, subjective distortion of seeing" but *reality itself*; "the architectonic of seeing does not affect the content/sense aspect of the event."

[17] For a preliminary statement and the relevant portions of Bakhtin's texts, see Caryl Emerson, "Solov'ev, the Late Tolstoi, and the Early Bakhtin on the Problem of Shame and Love," *Slavic Review* 50, no. 3 (Fall 1991): 663–71, esp. 663–65.

or of a Iago; virtue is not the issue here. What matters is a convincing human whole. And I know that another's personality has become a whole when, from my perspective, this personality ceases to need *only me*—only the questions I ask of it or the trajectory I impose on it—and declines to obey my fantasies of it without a murmur; in short, when it emerges as open and able to devise needs of its own. Only by thus risking ourselves with another's open personality, by "filling it in" with deeds of proffered commitment where there was once only fantasy, does a bridge of reciprocal influence become possible. Once laid down, this bridge can lead to a broadening of vocabularies on both sides and eventually to genuine learning and change.

Why are we so inclined to author, and how can we improve our authoring skills? Given the rate and depth of disillusionment in the world, it follows that if I wish my self to be healthy, I must seek to be finalized by as many *different* people as possible. Each of them, in orienting toward my zone, projects for me a potentially new and integral "I" that can be internalized, evaluated, drawn on, and, where necessary, even donned in whole cloth. Where no one orients toward us, Bakhtin counsels, we must not turn, for there will be no tools for living in that place. As Lev Vygotsky, the great Soviet developmental psychologist, remarked regarding optimal learning environments for a child, people interact most productively not with their documentable past experience but with a "zone of proximal development"—that aura of competence and curiosity that accompanies the taking on of tasks when outside help has been made available and the inner self feels itself securely equipped with the proper "psychic tools."[18]

For this reason, Bakhtin—loner, survivor, human ecologist—would recommend that I not seek out people *just like myself* for the sake of security or identity. It narrows my scope and thus is too much of a risk; should I change or the environment change, I might become extinct. (Here, as elsewhere, Bakhtin is not one to pick up on a cry of despair, abandonment, humiliation. That the persecuted might need the reassurance of a group would strike this aristocratic proponent of dialogue as quite futile.) Any instinctive clustering of like with like threatens to reduce my "I" and its potential languages to a miserable dot. Those who surround themselves with "insiders"—in heritage, experience, appearance, tastes, attitudes toward the world—are on a rigidifying and impoverishing road. In contrast, the personality that welcomes provisional finalization by a huge and diversified array of "authors" will command

[18] The Vygotsky-Bakhtin connection is receiving a great deal of attention in post-Soviet scholarship. For the basics, see Morson and Emerson, *Mikhail Bakhtin: Creation of a Prosaics*, 205–14.

optimal literacy. It feels at home in a variety of zones; it has many languages at its disposal and can learn new ones without trauma. From its perspective, the world appears an invitingly open, flexible, unthreatening, and unfinalized place.

For this reason, an indispensable stage in human "becoming" is a leap of trust. I must take it on faith that if I go forth, I will not be ignored or destroyed by you. This gesture is without guarantees or fixed parameters and thus it resembles an act of grace. In everyday life, we are driven to risk this act only under conditions of love. ("Historical life begins with love," Matvei Kagan wrote in the early 1920s. "The goal itself is transcendental. Saying that we strive to realize our goal makes sense only when we know and accept that life is not indifferent to us. . . . Who knows whether the struggle for perfection and purification would exist in the face of indifference to love?"[19]) True love, like every other trustworthy thing, must be tendered from an outside zone, and thus its origins are always partly in the dark. But as Bakhtin argues repeatedly in his essay "Author and Hero" (doubtless inspired by his own constantly tormented leg), any notion of empathy based on duplicative innerness, that is, on "experiencing another's suffering as one's own," will be anesthetizing, "pathological," an "infection with another's suffering and nothing more," a gratuitous "cry of pain" and thus a doubling of the suffering in the world. What is called for in the presence of another's love or pain is not identification with it but a creative outsiderly response to it, "a word of consolation or an act of assistance" (26).

In art, the starting point for activity is somewhat different from that of love, but the task and goal are the same. We must work at our creation until it embodies a viably "whole" consciousness—one with its own inner logic, worldview, habits, mental and physical reflexes, contours that are not arbitrary—in a word, a consciousness that (were it to spend as much time on us as we on it) potentially could love us back. Viable images are sufficiently integral to be released into their own time and space, and survive. Any other relationship to one's creation, Bakhtin insists, is "secondhand," passive, parasitic, and will fail to bring out the dynamic potential of the hero. No less important, authors, deprived of this potential feedback from their viably whole creations, will find their own creative imagination stunted. Thus an "inner merging" cannot be the "ultimate goal of aesthetic activity" ("A&H," in *A&A*, 26). Aesthetic activity begins only with "the author's loving removal from the field of the hero's life" (14). In Bakhtin's own eloquent summary of his position: "The author is the bearer and sustainer of the intently active

---

[19] Matvei Kagan, "On the Pace of History," cited in Brian Poole, "Rol' M. I. Kagana," *B sb III 97*, 167 (see ch. 3 n. 35).

unity of a consummated whole . . . This whole is in principle incapable of being given to us from within the hero, insofar as we identify ourselves with the hero and experience his life from within him. The hero cannot live by this whole; he cannot be guided by it in his own lived experiences and actions, for it is a whole that descends on him—it is bestowed on him as a gift—from another creative consciousness: from the creative consciousness of an author" (12).

Such an authoring scenario, with its theological resonances and intimations of grace, brings us to a second paradoxical area in Bakhtin's thinking about outsideness: the "I-Thou" relation. Perceived as a strength of German-Jewish thought, this special category of dialogue was widely discussed (in both its religious and secular variants) by European philosophers throughout the 1910s and 1920s: Georg Simmel, Ferdinand Ebner, Hermann Cohen, Franz Rosenzweig, and, most famously, Martin Buber. It reached Bakhtin in provincial Nevel and later in Petrograd through his close friend Matvei Kagan, who repatriated to revolutionary Russia in 1918.[20] By the 1990s seven decades of ban had lifted and Russian scholars were free to investigate the fundamental sources for Bakhtin's philosophy of "I-Thou-We" relations in the larger European context.[21] Of spe-

[20] Kagan studied for eight years in Germany (Leipzig, Marburg, and Berlin) from 1910 to 1918. As Poole relates, Kagan, always more politically active than Bakhtin, had been arrested in St. Petersburg after the 1905 Revolution. To escape the exclusionary quota system for Jews in Russian universities he repaired to Germany, but in 1913 German universities began to set quotas against Russians (i.e., against Jews). Paul Natorp made a special plea to admit the highly promising Kagan to Marburg above quota. The effect of Kagan's voracious and varied academic experience on the sedentary, semi-invalided Bakhtin was enormous, Poole has demonstrated. As he writes in "Rol' M. I. Kagana,": "If we compare the list of seminars Kagan attended . . . we discover that Kagan probably sat in the living rooms of a large part of the authors cited in Bakhtin's early works ("Author and Hero," etc.): not just Cohen, Cassirer, and Natorp, but also Volkelt, Hamman, Alois Riehl, the eminent Wilhelm Wundt, Georg Misch—author of the history of autobiography Bakhtin profited from immensely—and Georg Simmel himself" (171).

[21] In 1995 Makhlin published a textbook on I-Thou relations (V. L. Makhlin, *Ya i Drugoi (istoki filosofii 'dialoga' XX veka)*, ed. K. G. Isupov [St. Petersburg: PKhGI, 1995]). In his foreword he outlines his larger purpose in publishing these "materials for a graduate seminar" (six lectures): although the "decentration" of the logocentric subject has long been a priority in Western philosophy, Makhlin notes, Russia's shackled past and her current whirlwind liberation prepared her poorly for receiving this project. "As a whole, our native philosophy (idealistic as well as 'materialist') did not go beyond the bounds of the Fichtean-Hegelian identity of I = I, neither in its 'atheistic' (Soviet) nor its 'religious' variant. The sorry consequences of this we see in contemporary attempts to break through to a new philosophy and new thinking from inside what might be called post-Soviet postmodernism" (3). Makhlin updated the book as *Ya i drugoi: K istorii dialogicheskogo printsipa v filosofii XX v.* (Moscow: Labirint, 1997). See also A. B. Demidov, "The Foundations of a Philosophy of Communication and Dialogue," which places Bakhtin's thought in the context of I-Thou-We categories elaborated by Karl Jaspers, Martin Buber, Semyon Frank, and the

cial interest, of course, has been Bakhtin's relationship to Buber, a philosopher he greatly admired. Comparative study of the two thinkers was facilitated by new editions and translations (in 1989, the final segment of *Die Frage an den Einzelnen* appeared in Russian, and in 1993, *Ich und Du*).[22] Initial studies have suggested, however, that although broad symmetries exist between the two philosophers, their approach to *das Zwischenmenschliche* is not the same.[23]

The local Bakhtin-Buber debates provide another window into the macrodynamics and stress lines of the Russian Bakhtin industry. One dissimilarity between the two thinkers was raised (crudely, for disreputable reasons, but with provocative results) by the arch-nationalist Vadim Kozhinov, in his contentious 1992 essay entitled "Bakhtin and His Readers: Ruminations and in Part Reminiscences."[24] In one of the field's more peculiar East-West overlays, Kozhinov drew for support on an American lay student of Russian philosophy, Clinton Gardner, founder and director of the Transnational Vladimir Solovyov Society, whose essay "Between East and West: Rediscovering the Gifts of the Russian Spirit" was translated into Russian and published in Moscow in 1993.[25] Reviewing Gard-

Austrian-American sociologist of intersubjectivity, Alfred Schutz. Interestingly, in this company Bakhtin as philosopher begins to seem excessively "literary"—since his I-Thou formulations are developed largely in connection with the Dostoevsky book. See A. B. Demidov, "Osnovopolozheniia filosofii kommunikatsii i dialoga," *DKKh, no. 4 (95)*: 5–35.

[22] See E. A. Kurnosikova (Saransk), "Problema 'Ya-Ty' v zerkale refleksii (A. [*sic*] Buber—M. Bakhtin)," in *MMB i gum mysh I (95)*, 170–72. She remarks that the Buber revival was part of the general postcommunist inquiry into collectivism as a special sort of tragic solitude, with the I-Thou relation understood as a possible way out of the impasse between the discredited Soviet option and uncomforting Western "individualism."

[23] For an early survey of the congruencies, see Nina Perlina, "Mikhail Bakhtin and Martin Buber: Problems of Dialogic Imagination," *Studies in Twentieth Century Literature* 9, no. 1 (Fall 1984): 13–28. Brian Poole is of the opinion, however, that the differences are more significant. "Martin Buber," Poole writes in "Rol' M. I. Kagana," "lies at one end of a spectrum of Jewish intellectuals, less philosophically trained (see his correspondence with Rozenzweig, Cohen's student) and Cohen himself on the other. . . . The opposition between these thinkers runs through all issues, from the question of subjectivism through the reception of the mystic literature of Eastern Russian Jews to the question of Zionism. We should hold on to this context" (168).

[24] Vadim Kozhinov, "Bakhtin i ego chitateli: Razmyshleniia i otchasti vospominaniia," *Moskva* (July 1992): 143–51, esp. 150.

[25] Clinton C. Gardner, "Between East and West: Rediscovering the Gifts of the Russian Spirit" (RR 2, Box 20, Norwich, Vt., 1991); in Russian, Klinton Gardner, *Mezhdu Vostokom i Zapadom: Vozrozhdenie darov russkoi dushi* (Moscow, 1993). In the English version, see esp. 30–32, "Our Four Speech Orientations" ("Imperative or Vocative Speech: Toward Future Time"): "We hear the vocative in the words of anybody who cares for us, addressing us as thou. . . . A person who is starved for such speech cannot discover who he or she is and therefore cannot speak his or her own imperatives. Decadence is the inability of one generation to communicate imperatives to the next. All education, therefore, which is not simply technical, aims to create and maintain imperatives. This future-creating speech pre-

ner's work and scarcely containing his delight that this nonacademic author appeared not beholden to the untrustworthy cosmopolitan forces controlling American educational institutions, Kozhinov sums up Gardner's position in this way: "Bakhtin's and Buber's views on dialogue do not coincide. Buber's formula says: 'Becoming an I, I say Thou.' *On the contrary*, Bakhtin's dialogism holds that 'My I becomes an I only when others turn to me in the capacity of a Thou.' Bakhtin, in opposition to Buber, presumed that an 'I' was simply impossible, its existence was unthinkable without a 'thou,' without an 'other.'" Kozhinov then concludes in his own voice: "So Buber's 'position' ('Becoming an I, I say Thou') is in no way compatible with the concept of *authentic* dialogue, a fully weighted doctrine created by Bakhtin—who relied for support on the whole of Russian spiritual development" (151). At stake, clearly, was the inherent "Russianness" of the Bakhtinian model of dialogue, which (according to Kozhinov) begins humbly, with an effaced "I" expressed largely in the other's need of me, with addressivity itself. Unlike dialogue in materialist, individualistic, acquisition-oriented Western cultures (including, of course, the Judaic), which Kozhinov considers to be in thrall to punitive laws and to self-righteous legal subjects, Russian dialogism could never *begin* with an "I."

Two panelists at the 1995 centennial conference delivered papers devoted to Bakhtin and Buber, and Kozhinov's aggressive distinction was much on their minds. Mikhail Girshman, in his contribution to the debate, specifically cited and refuted the Gardner-Kozhinov position, arguing that Buber's teaching indeed resembles Bakhtin's in this matter of the timing of selves. "For both Bakhtin and Buber, the becoming of the 'I' and the becoming of the 'Thou' are in principle simultaneous—and this is true of personalities as well as of peoples and of the human race."[26] But Girshman then remarked on two areas where Bakhtin and Buber genuinely diverge. The first concerns the relative urgency, in each model, of vertical versus horizontal modes of communion. Whereas Buber emphasizes "the originary, 'androgynous' unity of one human being with another, turned toward the eternal Thou, toward God," Bakhtin, in contrast, "confirms the originary separateness and singularity of each human personality" and then leaves any turning toward an eternal or unitary Being vague and negotiable. Within a Bakhtinian universe, it appears,

---

cedes and determines all the others. Until we sense this orientation, and feel overwhelmed by it, we never really begin anything new in our lives" (31).

[26] M. Girshman (Donets State University, Ukraine), "M. Bakhtin i M. Buber o khudozhestvennom proizvedenii," *Proceedings of the Seventh International Bakhtin Conference*, Moscow, 26–30 June 1995, Book 1, 11–15, esp. 13. In successive reworkings of the debate over Kozhinov among Russian students of *dialogovedenie* [dialogue studies], Girshman's position has been upheld.

dialogue *must* be primary—not because there is necessarily love or compatibility in that universe but because all participants are equally unprivileged: "unity, plurality, and uniqueness are equally indigenous in each human personality, realized in an answerable act on the border and before the person of a unique other." Recast in terms of this chapter, then, dialogue, according to Bakhtin, is always "outside" any potential whole, more likely to remain isolated for longer and expected to sustain itself in the absence of transcendental guarantees. Bakhtin's world is by far the lonelier, less easily connected place. In a probable allusion to Buber's image of the one "Thou" who cannot become an "It"—the resident of an eternal present, the Interlocutor who, once encountered, permits us to experience what is authentic and real beyond a concretely given time and space—Girshman suggests that Bakhtin will not so easily release dialogue (even of the divine sort) from history or from memory.

Girshman notes a second area of divergence as well: the role of the I-Thou relation as embedded in the work of art. Whereas Buber concentrates on the artist's "communion with the artistic image and on the artwork" as a created, completed whole, for Bakhtin "more important is the communion, the dialogue *within* the artwork." Bakhtin investigates not only the higher spiritual functions of dialogue but also (and perhaps even more) the arduous, fastidious "objectivized forms" necessary for realizing it in everyday interaction: "forms that exist not within a person and not outside a person but among people." Being objectivized, these forms can be transferred from life to art and manipulated in good conscience on the flatter, more controlled planes of literary creation. In this sense, Girshman intimates, Bakhtin remains a Formalist; but since the forms that concern him are so "alive," he enjoys neither the security of a Russian Formalist working with literary devices nor the faith in an autonomous divine image that inspires Martin Buber.

These intuitions—dark on Bakhtin, rosier on Buber—were reinforced in subsequent juxtapositions of the two thinkers. During the 1995 Bakhtin readings in Saransk, the Izhevsk scholar V. L. Krutkin argued that Bakhtin and Buber might indeed share a "responsive paradigm," but the nature of the response is fundamentally different for each.[27] The "value center of Buber's dialogics is many 'thous' united into a community" and grounded in an "absolute Thou," for only in this way can "thous" be saved from becoming "its"; Bakhtin, by investing all value in the concrete individual other, leaves the "I" unrooted and solely a place of potentials. Thus "Bakhtin's 'I' lives only in the future, it has no present," Krutkin asserts. "And the other also does not coincide with itself; it also

---

[27] V. L. Krutkin (Izhevsk), "'Ya' i 'ty' (Bakhtin i Buber o dialoge)," *MMB i gum mysl II* (95), 86–88. Further page references given in text.

lives not in the realm of the essentially existing [*sushchee*] but in the realm of obligation [*dolzhnoe*]" (87). At the end of the present chapter, we will return to this unsettling pattern of reciprocal negation as it has been explicated, mournfully, by Konstantin Isupov—here as elsewhere, the first to see the darkest side of every Bakhtinian idea.

In the second centennial paper devoted to the "Bakhtin-Buber" theme, P. S. Gurevich pursued a more profound difference.[28] Of the two thinkers, he argues, Buber observes a more "traditional understanding of dialogue as emotional connections among people" (with good reason does Bakhtin, in his essay on the chronotope, refer to Buber alongside the Romantic Schelling and the phenomenologist Max Scheler). Buber's contribution to nineteenth-century thought was to reorient this rather conventional, emotionally grounded dialogue toward religion, "to see in dialogue not only a drawing close to the truth but also the salvation of a human being" (28). Despite the exceptionally broad scope Buber gives to dialogue—between people, between human life and nature, between material life and the spiritual spheres—"a secular and humanistic understanding of the problem remained alien" to him. Two important results obtain, according to Gurevich. First, Buber "underestimates the dangers of monologism"(30). Since for him dialogue is *dannost'*—a given and a ground rather than a problem—his anxiety is other than Bakhtin's, for whom dialogue is a task. This task requires continual, intense, and tension-filled effort merely to keep the territory open, even if no content is ever resolved on it. Second, Buber's God is indeed an approachable personality—but still an "absolute" one, an autonomous whole regardless of who turns to Him. And for Bakhtin? For him dialogue is a "problem field," not just a "drawing together of voices." Bakhtin's image of God can only be inferred from his extant writings. "Buber is a religious thinker," Gurevich asserts (20). But can the opposite be claimed of his friendly other, "can it be said of Bakhtin that he is an advocate of [wholly] secular thinking?"

With this question we get to the core of the I-Thou debates, and to the degree, quality, and potential security provided by the "outsideness" so crucial to Bakhtin's dialogism. For it is fair to say that notwithstanding all the accusations raised against dialogue and polyphony in chapter 3— that it robs the "I," that it raids the "other," that it is smug, solipsistic, logos-centric, that it makes Dostoevsky incalculably less frightening than that great writer intended himself to be—the dialogic principle, as Bakhtin espouses it, takes very little for granted. Dialogue is by no means a

---

[28] P. S. Gurevich, "M. Buber i M. Bakhtin: Intellektual'naia kontroverza," *Proceedings of the Seventh International Bakhtin Conference*, Book 1, 25–30. Further page references given in text.

safe or secure relation. Yes, a "thou" is always potentially there, but it is exceptionally fragile; the "I" must create it (and be created by it) in a simultaneously mutual gesture, over and over again, and it comes with no special authority or promise of constancy. Since perfect timing among selves is so very unlikely and our need of one another so capricious, imbalance is the norm. No absolute or autonomous presence can be presumed to exist at any point along the boundary. To achieve Bakhtin's desired state of "participatory autonomy," interpersonal trust is required. And a climate of trust is infinitely more difficult to sustain than a climate of faith, to which one can heroically cling—consider God's servant Job— even when manifestly betrayed.

Let us step back for a moment from contemporary Russian debates and return to the early 1920s, keeping in mind Makhlin's comments on Bakhtin, Kierkegaard, and sin. Where is the watershed that divides Buber's thought (on one side) from Hermann Cohen's, Matvei Kagan's, and Bakhtin's on the other? According to Brian Poole, our best chronicler of Bakhtin's "Marburg period":

> [Thus should we understand] the rejection of metaphysics, which not only stands in contrast to Buber's neoromantic dialogism, but also explains the logical possibility of the coexistence of rationalism and ethical idealism in Cohen's religious thinking . . . : God is the axis of man's relation to his fellow man *for the sake of the fellow man*. Cohen (followed by Kagan and Bakhtin) repeatedly denies the metaphysical immortality of individual man, and for obvious reasons. (For the Marburg school, immortality is a cultural phenomenon.) Positing a transcendental atonement or "answerability" for our sins (like the proleptic gesture serving as an introduction to Rousseau's *Confessions*) would actually sublate the historical and social quality of ethics, nullifying the dialogic environment. . . . There is no such thing, says Cohen (and Kagan in his Russian adaptation of this passage [from *Die Religion der Vernunft*]), as a sin before God. Sin and retribution must apply to and are fulfilled before the other by the doer of the deed.[29]

Poole's reading of the Marburg school is highly suggestive for these discussions of the I-Thou relation. As a surrogate for God—a God who can forgive, absolve, resolve—Bakhtin's "dialogic environment" is most precarious. For that reason it must strike many as wholly unsatisfying. Just as there is no originary sin in Bakhtin's scenarios (again we should note his overall indifference to origins), so is there no unconditional redemption; no community of believers stands ready to invite an individual inside once and for all or to promise absolution to the repentant. In

---

[29] Personal communication from Brian Poole to the author from Marburg, 19 March 1994.

Bakhtin's understanding of human nature, people are not innately disposed to worship and do not need to be "saved." People need, and want, to be considered interesting. If found inadequate, they want to be changed. Self-esteem is *natural,* and when I sense a deficiency of it in myself I will seek to strengthen others surrounding me so they might more readily refract that strength back on my person. (How remarkable, really, that this luminously healthy philosopher was drawn to Dostoevsky.) And it is characteristic of Bakhtin, renegade Formalist, that when he does posit an "ideal third party" toward whom we instinctively orient our utterances (what he calls the *nadadresat,* or "superaddressee," that stabilizing reference point which supplements any I-Thou relation), "God" is but one option among many functionally similar possibilities. As Bakhtin writes,

> the author of an utterance [in addition to addressing the actual second person in any exchange] presupposes, with a greater or lesser awareness, a higher *superaddressee* (a third), whose absolutely just responsive understanding is presumed, either in some metaphysical distance or in distant historical time (the loophole addressee). In various ages and with various understandings of the world, this superaddressee and its ideally true responsive understanding assume various ideological expression (God, absolute truth, the judgment of dispassionate human conscience, the people, the court of history, science, and so forth).[30]

This third party, Bakhtin continues, "is not any mystical or metaphysical being"—although for some it might be expressed as such. The superaddressee is a "constitutive aspect of the whole utterance" and thus will always reveal itself under impartial analysis. This formal positing of some perfectly sympathetic listener, such as we meet in love and in art, might be seen as Bakhtin's equivalent of the Kantian "as if"—except that in this instance we are seeking not empirical laws, which stand a chance of remaining in place from one minute to the next, but everyday interlocutors, who do not.

In a 1995 essay on the influence of the Marburg school on Bakhtin's philosophy, Brian Poole expands on this secular, de-theorized understanding of interhuman communion that requires neither absorption into a whole nor the "survival"/resurrection of the individual.[31] The unrelentingly positive attitude toward the *future* in Bakhtin's philosophy (and his belief that individuals continue their "historically significant" lives far

[30] Bakhtin, "The Problem of the Text in Linguistics, Philology, and the Human Sciences," *SpG,* 126 (translation slightly adjusted). Further page references given in text.

[31] Brian Poole, "Nazad k Kaganu," *DKKh, no. 1 (95):* 38–48. See also the neighboring entry by M. I. Kagan, "Paul Natorp i krizis kul'tury," 49–54, and a lengthy fragment of Kagan's translation of Natorp's *Sozial-Idealismus* (1920), 55–126.

into the future) is wholly consonant with the teachings of Cohen, Paul Natorp, and Kagan. Poole argues that the influence of these neo-Kantian thinkers becomes stronger—not weaker, as is usually assumed—in the dialogic and then carnivalesque phases of Bakhtin's thought in the 1920s and 1930s. The capstone of this influence is the huge lost *Bildungsroman* book, of which only fragments on Goethe survived. The Marburg school espoused a profound Old Testament understanding of eternal life, viewing it not as a personal possession but as something more cultural and genealogical; it is this notion of collectivity, *not* the self-effacing collectivism of Marxism, that comes to inspire Bakhtin's paradoxical carnival optimism during the darkest years of Stalinism.

The I-Thou relation that Bakhtin endorses, then, does not prepare us for eternal salvation. It cannot even promise us a local consummation—after which we might lay down our burdens and rest. God is a *possibility* in this relation, but not a necessity. Dialogue can unfold under the aegis of a third—but this third party is more a medium of communication, more a climate of trust, than it is an anchored communicant with a fixed moral perspective and repertory of answers. Thus, one might argue, Buber's "eternal Thou" or "absolute Thou" has no equivalent in Bakhtin's thought. And this basal distinction between the two thinkers—which Kozhinov suspects, Girshman and Gurevich elaborate, and Brian Poole confirms—should counsel us to consider more circumspectly the whole question of Bakhtin's allegiance to an anthropocentric or theistic view of humanity. Is Bakhtin a "secular thinker" as opposed to a religious one, as Gurevich asks? More probably, Bakhtin is attempting to break down this binary opposition as well. He considered the "material aesthetics" of the Formalists flawed because it could not take into account the moral orientation of consciousness—and because it degraded everyday life [*byt*] to the status of formless irritation. ("Pure everyday life is a fiction," Bakhtin wrote near the end of his life, "a product of the intellect. Human life is always shaped and this shaping is always ritualistic, even if only 'aesthetically' so.")[32] But the vertical, metaphysical route to moral awareness that marks both Kant and Buber was also not entirely congenial to Bakhtin, who always preferred to work from the bottom up and out to the sides, starting with the obligations that accrue in a "chamber scenario." Duplicating, perhaps, his own (increasingly needful and immobile) life experience, he begins with two people who sit facing one another in a room, permanently outside each other but obliged to fulfill each other. There is no greater challenge in the world. Resembling in this regard Leo Tolstoy, Bakhtin was apprehensive about any ethical problem not approached on

---

[32] "From Notes Made in 1970–71," in *SpG*, 154.

an everyday, homely scale—for the grand, abstract formulation always urges us toward evasion and passivity. We can ignore problems that we cannot see, dilemmas that do not arise from our own daily situatedness. We feel justified in doing so, because we see no way to solve them. And we see none because the problem itself has been designed in no-man's time and space.

Gurevich's observations open up a third area where Bakhtin's concept of "creative outsideness" finds itself in august company: its relation to Kantian aesthetics. As an aesthetician, Bakhtin remained throughout his life more responsive to the concerns and questions posed by Kant—and later by the Russian Formalists—than to the aesthetic theories of Symbolists, Futurists, Natural School critics, or Marxists. When he disagreed, it was largely with the quality, degree of "interestedness," and overall purpose of the aesthetic whole that the Kantians and Formalists espoused—and which, in his scheme, an author must be perpetually *outside of* in order to bestow. The Kantian connection is now receiving considerable attention from Russian scholars as part of a vigorous interest in Bakhtin as a pre-Bolshevik ethical philosopher.[33] We will enter this huge and learned realm in pursuit of a single accessible motif: the Kantian component in Bakhtin's concept of "aesthetic love." What does Kant contribute to that attractive idea?

Kantianism was the reigning philosophical movement in Petrograd University during Bakhtin's undergraduate years, and as a double major in philosophy and classics, he absorbed from his famous professors frameworks that lasted him a lifetime. As we have seen, in imitation of the Third Critique, Bakhtin locates the aesthetic moment midway between cognition (knowledge) and ethical activity (active desire). Again like Kant, he assigns to aesthetic judgment the task of interrelating those two realms. But as his thought developed, Bakhtin came to subscribe neither to Kant's definition of judgment as "the faculty of thinking the particular as contained in the universal" nor to his definition of art as a "purposive whole without specific purpose." Bakhtin was also unwilling to measure aesthetic pleasure by the subjective satisfaction we experience when we successfully place an artwork in the orderly scheme of nature (nature in

---

[33] See, for lucid introductions in English, James M. Holquist and Katerina Clark, "The Influence of Kant in the Early Work of M. M. Bakhtin," in *Literary Theory and Criticism: Festschrift Presented to René Wellek in Honor of His Eightieth Birthday*, part 1, "Theory," ed. Joseph P. Strelka (Bern: Peter Lang, 1984), 299–313; and more recently, Michael F. Bernard-Donals, *Mikhail Bakhtin: Between Phenomenology and Marxism* (Cambridge: Cambridge University Press, 1994), esp. ch. 2, "Neo-Kantianism and Bakhtin's Phenomenology."

general is not a category of much importance to the superbly verbal and urban Bakhtin).[34] Any "placement" of a singular phenomenon within a larger preexistent unity was suspect to Bakhtin, because in his view this move tends to put too high a premium on sameness and on the drowsy securities of the inside.

In fact, *unity*—as the word is usually understood in logic, analytic philosophy, and art—cannot be an ultimate criterion for Bakhtin's aesthetics. In "Toward a Philosophy of the Act," Bakhtin even recommends that "the very word *unity* [*edinstvo*] be discarded as overly theoretized," since what is required for understanding is "not unity but uniqueness [*edinstvennost'*]" (37). "One can even establish a certain inverse proportion between theoretical unity and actual uniqueness or singularity," Bakhtin writes in that early essay. "The closer one moves to theoretical unity (constancy in respect to content or a recurring identicalness), the poorer and more universal is the actual uniqueness; the whole matter is reduced to a unity of content, and the ultimate unity proves to be an empty, only potential content, identical with itself" (39). Judged from within, uniqueness promises isolation, loneliness, and a sense of abandonment. The virtues of singularity can be appreciated solely from the outside.

Bakhtin's complicated debt to Kant and his departures from neo-Kantianism underlie all the writings of the early 1920s, where individuation and separation from system are so closely tied to the aesthetic project. The nature of this debate was made clearer in 1993, with the publication of a set of seminar notes by Lev Pumpiansky, fellow study circle member and precocious scholar, based on Bakhtin's 1924–25 Leningrad lectures on Kant, Bergson, and religious philosophy.[35] In one of these lectures—actually, Bakhtin's response to a paper read by Mikhail Tubiansky on the

---

[34] A dialogue under these conditions would occur not between two personalities, but—if the word *dialogue* still applied at all—between our cognitive faculties and the teleologically informed natural world. For suggestive differences between Bakhtin and the Symbolists in this regard, see James West, "Ivanov's Theory of Knowledge: Kant and Neo-Kantianism," in Robert Louis Jackson and Lowry Nelson, Jr., eds., *Vyacheslav Ivanov: Poet, Critic, and Philosopher* (New Haven, Conn.: Yale Center for International and Area Studies, 1986), 313–25.

[35] "[Lektsiia M. M. Bakhtina]," 1924–25, ed. and annotated by N. I. Nikolaev, in *MMB kak filosof 92*, 236–52. In the second lecture Bakhtin divulged what for him was so convincing about *un*systemic philosophizing: "In it, natural consciousness wants to be singular" (239). As he elaborates further, there are three reasons why nonsystemic philosophizing is plausible and valid: first, the imaging capacity [*obraznost'*] inherent in the thought process itself; second, revelation [*otkrovenie*]; and then the remarkable third reason, "reality [*real'nost'*] as the ultimate instance for verifying philosophical views" (238). Further page numbers given in text.

role of miracle and Revelation in religion—we come across this curious and revealing passage:

> Saint Augustine against the Donatists subjected inner experience to a considerably more rigorous critique than does psychoanalysis. "I believe; Lord, help me in mine unbelief" finds in inner experience just what psychoanalysis finds. Help is needed not for the object of faith but for the purity of faith itself. Revelation is characterized not by help but by personality, which *wants* to reveal itself; the most important moment in Revelation is the moment of the personal. . . . A personal relationship to a personal God—this is the sign of religion, but this is also the special difficulty of religion, thanks to which there can arise a distinctive fear of religion and of Revelation, a fear of personal orientation, the wish to orient oneself in a single object-based world, within a single meaning, free from the risk of falling into sin; . . . [the temptation here is] to answer not from oneself, not personally, but to answer in a unified consciousness, to answer systemically as an ethical, moral, etc., subject; this is an attempt to perform an event with only one participant . . . the Incarnation itself destroyed the unity of the Kantian personality. (246)

In sum, the "Kantian personality," as Bakhtin conceived it, does not provide sufficient ground for personal answerability (individuation) and thus for creativity. As he argues in "Toward a Philosophy of the Act," the unity of the "actual, answerable, act-performing consciousness" cannot be grasped as a "principle, a right, an internally consistent law"; for creative unity is of a different order. It is more accurately characterized "by the word *faithfulness* [*vernost'*, being true to], the way the word is used in reference to love and marriage, except that love here should not be understood from the standpoint of a psychologically passive consciousness" (38). In this delicate gesture, redolent of Erich Fromm's famous advice in *The Art of Loving* (that we attend too much to the heady state of "falling in love" and "being loved," too little to the difficult, active state of "standing in love" and being a lover),[36] Bakhtin relates uniqueness to fidelity—and both those qualities to the active, task-oriented energy that is the starting point of art. Or as he writes in his several paragraphs toward a theory of love in "Toward a Philosophy of the Act": "Lovelessness, indifference, will never be able to generate sufficient power to slow down and linger intently over an object, to hold and sculpt every detail and particular in it, however minute. Only love is capable of being aesthetically productive" (64).

---

[36] Erich Fromm, *The Art of Loving: An Inquiry into the Nature of Love* (New York: Harper and Row, 1956), ch. 1: "Is Love an Art?" esp. 4.

In her 1990 pamphlet,[37] Volkova devotes an entire section ("Bakhtin's 'aesthetic love' and Kantian 'disinterestedness'") to this contrast between the "loving affection" recommended by Hermann Cohen, Matvei Kagan, Bakhtin, and—at the other pole—the sterner, more dispassionate criterion for art posited by Kant. She finds their methods different but the desired results surprisingly the same. The goal of both is to *free up a situation* (from necessity, utility, the distortions of an urgent need), and thus both value the cognitive over the sensual. Aesthetic love, in Bakhtin's usage, appears to have no sexual component—which, pressing as it must toward fusion, always puts "outsideness" at risk ("the sexual factor is not capable of seeing the body as a finished, well-defined artistic entity," Volkova notes sensibly; "[sexuality] is wholly concerned with what the body promises me" [35]). She also stresses that a loving relation in art does not exclude negative or hostile reactions. An evil character can be lovingly drawn. But for Bakhtin, "hatred and love are present in the aesthetic act in unequal parts" (36). To be wholly indifferent or hostile to something will mean simply not to see it, for we will turn away; under such conditions, no boundaries can be drawn and no form will emerge. "Only love can be aesthetically productive, because in its presence it is impossible to draw too close to the hero, impossible to fuse with him, but at the same time impossible to distance oneself entirely" (36).

In Volkova's redaction, "aesthetic love" recalls not so much a work of art as it does a hopeless but sweet affair of the heart: conducted from afar, superhumanly patient, forever being interrupted and then reestablished with no lost credit, in the best of times sustained by intense reciprocal interest but in barren times no less giving of itself. In this sense, Kant's criteria for making and receiving works of art as "disinterested, purposive wholes" indeed overlaps with Bakhtin's. But more precise parallels between the two thinkers on this question of aesthetic love can be found in the realm of ethics rather than aesthetics. In his "Metaphysical Foundations of Morals," Kant discusses the relationship between duty, happiness, moral worth, and the biblical command to love our neighbor.[38] "To secure one's own happiness is a duty, at least indirectly," Kant writes. "For discontent with one's condition under pressure of many anxieties and amidst unsatisfied wants might easily become a great temptation to transgression from duty." He counsels us to promote our happiness "not from inclination but from duty": "Undoubtedly, it is in this manner that we are to understand those passages of the Scripture in which we are

[37] E. V. Volkova, "Estetika M. M. Bakhtina," in Znanie series "Estetika," no. 12 (1990).

[38] "Metaphysical Foundations of Morals" (1785), in Carl J. Friedrich, ed., *The Philosophy of Kant: Immanuel Kant's Moral and Political Writings* (New York: The Modern Library, 1949), 140–208, esp. 146–47. Translation corrected.

commanded to love our neighbor, even our enemy. For love, as an affection, cannot be commanded, but beneficence for duty's sake can be, even though we are not impelled to such kindness by an inclination, and may even be repelled by a natural and unconquerable aversion. This is *practical* love and not *pathological*. It is a love originating in the will and not in the inclination of sentiment; in principles of action, not of sentimental sympathy" (147).

To recast Kant's thought in Bakhtinian terms, "pathological love" is indeed a product of "sentimental sympathy." Like all sentimentalisms, it relies on inclination, spontaneous inner identification, and a fusion of horizons for the personalities concerned. Such acts of love, which feel good and into which we fall, cannot acquire true moral worth, which is achieved only when we "promote our happiness not from inclination but from duty." Duty—*dolzhnoe, dolzhenstvovanie, Sollen*, "the ought"—is a central concept for both Kant and Bakhtin, and there is nothing dry or passive about it. It insists on a gesture initiated by the lover "regardless"; the lover remains outside, with no promise of a reciprocating response. We are duty-bound to act in this loving way, note, not out of any ascetic virtue or despotic morality; this duty is simply *practical*, or, as Bakhtin would say, productive (not just reflective) of love.

Under these conditions, what becomes secondary in artistic consciousness is the desire to possess, the fear that time will run out, a reverence before the artwork that approaches the sublime, a passionate fascination with form. None of those reactions is as fundamental to the enterprise of aesthetic love, and of artistic creativity, as is attentive, long-term, active benevolence. At this point, however, matters simplify somewhat for the Kantian artist and Kantian contemplator of art. Those adepts will not fail to recognize the aesthetically beautiful as a symbol of the morally good.

Bakhtin has a harsher Muse. She promises only outsideness, ongoing dialogue, and responsibility. In contemplating the anxieties of authorship, Bakhtin appears to have worried little about beauty, craftsmanship, the influence of precursors, or the immediate reception of the artifact. What he did intuit, while thinking about the love relation as apprenticeship for art, were anxieties lower and closer to home: The remark he makes in "Toward a Philosophy of the Act," for example, that to witness the *deserved* shaming of a person one loves is among life's most agonizing experiences (*TPA*, 62). Or these remarks on love during a time of violence, contained in the 1943 notebooks:

Only love can see and delineate the inner freedom of the object. It [i.e., love] is still serious, but it wants to smile; this smile and joy, continually defeating seriousness, defeating a threat in the tone. . . . Love fondles and caresses boundaries; the boundaries take on new meaning. Love does not speak about an object in its absence, but speaks about it with it itself present. The word-as-violence presumes an absent and silent object, one that neither hears nor answers . . . [But] the word wants to exert an influence from the outside, wants to define from the outside. The world is stewing in its own juice; what is essential is a constant inflowing from the outside, from other worlds [*iz mirov inykh*].[39]

Only "lovingly interested attention" from without can generate sufficient power to *see* something in the world, and this seeing creates love, which creates value: "'I love him not because he is good, but he is good because I love him'" (*TPA*, 64).

In all these scenarios the most difficult work I face is creating a self whose integrity I can stand behind, which I can love and respect. Only then will I seek no "alibis." (Echoing Kant's precept that "to secure one's happiness is a *duty*," Bakhtin must have surmised early on that to dislike oneself chronically does not prepare one for repentance or conversion but simply becomes a habit, a way out of answering for acts.) In an overwhelming tribute to art, Bakhtin made the creation of just such a desirable, uniquely answerable "I" the central test of an aesthetic approach to the world. For this reason, his theory of art lies at the heart of every other task; for this reason, too, it seems forever poised to become something else. As Deborah Haynes writes in her introduction to *Bakhtin and the Visual Arts*: "Most aesthetic theories are concerned with the category of beauty, which is visible both in nature and art, yet invisible in moral and intellectual activity. Some give priority to the aesthetic object or work of art. Others privilege the perceiving subject, the viewer who looks and experiences. . . . Bakhtin brings us back to the aesthetics of the creative process itself, back to the activity of the artist or author who creates" (4).

There is a final area in Bakhtin's thought where "outsideness" is an unavoidable yet paradoxical value. This is the nature of the boundary [*granitsa*] itself. As we have seen, Bakhtin is wholeheartedly positive about boundaries, thresholds, delineations, delimitations, drawing them wherever possible and as often as possible: between life and art, between one consciousness and another, between one person's language and another. He advises us to draw a line, cross it, and then consider what we can offer the far side from our new perspective. Apparently he did not fear that this constant pressure to differentiate, to redraw the boundary so that ever more minuscule points of disagreement can be registered upon it, might in fact work to blunt communication rather than to vivify it. He certainly

[39] The fragment, dated 12 October 1943, is known by its first line: "Rhetoric, to the extent of its falseness, strives to evoke terror or hope." In *MMB: ss 5 (96)*, 63–70, esp. 66.

did not worry (at least in his theoretical musings) that we might kill one another across a boundary. In the natural order of things, he felt, world-views or "voices" become increasingly receptive, articulate, and accessible in the process of becoming more personalized and nuanced. But is this dynamic in fact a natural one? Or put another way: What is the primary work of a boundary? To divide, define, protect, defend, wall off, or connect?

With this question we confront a Bakhtinian utopia to match the utopian dream of the semioticians with its universe of recodable signs. For Bakhtin believed that separation and connection happen simultaneously, in a complementary way, without contradictory aims and without threat of abandonment or assault.[40] As he asserts at the end of "Author and Hero," when this benevolent interactive situation does *not* obtain we are in an abnormal state, a "crisis of authorship" (203). As soon as confidence in our right to "outsideness" is shaken and external perspective is no longer considered essential,

> lived life tends to recoil and hide deep inside itself, tends to withdraw into its own inner infinitude, is *afraid of boundaries*, strives to dissolve them, for it has no faith in the essentialness and kindness of the power that gives form from outside; any viewpoint from outside is refused. And, in the process, the *culture of boundaries* (the necessary condition for a confident and deep style) becomes impossible . . . all creative energies withdraw from the boundaries,

[40] Not surprisingly, these sentiments from the master's mouth are rejected by theorists on the neo-Marxist Bakhtinian Left. In an essay entitled "Boundaries versus Binaries," Graham Pechey, among the more eloquent of these critics, elaborates a "radical politics of the boundary" whose dialectic continually displaces and rediscovers "a militant 'outsideness.'" According to Pechey, Bakhtin is an anti-philosopher who mocks "all synthesizing and homogenizing projects whatever." Pechey would not approve the accommodationist, neo-humanist Bakhtin now in favor among post-Soviet Russians. Preferring to associate Bakhtin with the "revolt of the colonized" in the spirit of Gramsci, Frantz Fanon, and Paolo Freire, Pechey concludes: "[Those three liberationist thinkers] are doing for the margins what Western Marxism sought to do for the revolutionary process in the metropolis—tracking the oppressor and exploiter down the latter's last outposts in culture and in consciousness, inventing new ways of activating the self-articulation of the oppressed . . It is a profound irony of our postmodern era that these genuine correlatives of Bakhtin's thought should both be found in the southern half of the American continent: while the liberal academics of that continent's aggressive northern *imperium* produce and reproduce themselves as intellectuals in misreadings of his work, Bakhtin himself lives in the fighting, praying, dialogizing, carnivalizing thinkers of the continental body's trangressive lower half." See Graham Pechey, "Boundaries versus Binaries: Bakhtin in/against the History of Ideas," *Radical Philosophy* 54 (Spring 1990): 23–31, esp. 25, 30. Recently, Pechey has produced superb work on Bakhtin's early ethical thought. See his "Eternity and Modernity: Bakhtin and the Epistemological Sublime," in *Theoria* 81/82 (October 1993): 61–85, and in the premiere issue (1998) of *Dialogism* (Sheffield, England), "Philosophy and Theology in 'Aesthetic Activity,'" 57–73.

leaving them to the mercies of fate. Aesthetic culture is a culture of boundaries and hence presupposes that life is enveloped by a warm atmosphere of deepest trust. ("A&H," in *A&A*, 203)

We now turn to one troublesome boundary in Bakhtin's thought that has proved highly resistant to satisfactory resolution: that between life and art.

Bakhtin counsels us to integrate the real-life deed with the aesthetically shaped word. But so vague is he on this important point that even his beloved, parodically double-voiced word has been turned against him affectionately by his own devoted students. In the third of the Znanie booklets on Bakhtin (1991)—a whimsical coauthored project entitled "Bakhtin's Rhetoric of the Act: Reminiscences of the Future or Predictions of the Past?"—the question of words versus deeds is addressed in a carnivalized genre, modeled after a mock-Soviet "roundtable discussion," the nineteenth-century journalistic feuilleton, and the ancient genre of "Dialogues in the Kingdom of the Dead."[41] The discussants rejoice that Bakhtin is being celebrated for his notion of the responsible deed—but how much of this is rhetoric (in the debased as well as the classical, oratorical sense of that word)?

"At present, half the scholarly world is making a career off Bakhtin," one participant notes, hinting at a practical and highly profitable link between art and life, between rhetoric and action; "in the West, Bakhtin has become a messiah for the humanities" (4). The simpleton at the table agrees: in Russia, "the deed has been completely replaced by the word, goods have been replaced by a promise of goods, money by the possibility of receiving 40 percent of what is due you after three years. That's glasnost for you, indeed. I don't know how it was in the beginning—but in the end, all that will probably remain is the Word" (5). The critics then ask whether literary culture really helps us to shape responsible personalities. Citing Robert Musil (his famous retort that world literature is one monstrous shop where people can walk in and purchase pride, jealousy, love, despair), one participant insists that culture, both high and low, simply gets in the way of a responsible life. True to its menippean spirit, "Bakhtin's Rhetoric of the Act" ends on a note of cheerful resignation and nonresolution (41):

> *Peshkov*: So we have two intact worlds here: the worlds of freedom and of necessity, of possibility and of reality, of word and of deed. To construct out of these two worlds a single kingdom—the kingdom of a human being—can be accomplished only by the word, by speech, by communion.

[41] V. L. Makhlin, A. E. Makhov, and I. V. Peshkov, "Ritorika postupka M. Bakhtina," in Znanie series "Ritorika," no. 9 (1991).

Makhov: Well, all right, we could have realized that without Bakhtin's help. Now let's try to live."

Do Bakhtin's own texts provide more serious guidance on this matter of art and life in each other's service?

Bakhtin devoted his tiny maiden publication from 1919, "Art and Answerability," to just this boundary. Its seven short paragraphs—wedged between two sentimental poems and an essay by Kagan on "Art, Life, and Love" in the September 19 issue of "Den' iskusstva" [Day of art], the newsletter of the Nevel' Union of Workers of Art and an eclectic, rather avant-garde affair[42]—can be reduced to a series of self-limiting cautionary statements. Art is not life, but neither is art mere lofty inspiration. Poetry is guilty before the "vulgar prose of life" (although the nature of that guilt is not spelled out); a life that is frivolous and unexacting will be rewarded with a sterile art (notwithstanding massive evidence to the contrary among artists of genius). We must beware of the desire of art and life to lighten each other's burdens by dispensing with each other—for although it might be "easier to create without answering for life and easier to live without any consideration for art," such a solution is both unethical and aesthetically barren. And then comes Bakhtin's concluding sentence: "Art and life are not one, but they must become united in myself—in the unity of my answerability."[43]

What in the world does this final sentence mean? For we are not speaking here of two personalities, each unique but still structured in a similar way, who might negotiate their coming together on the basis of a common language. Art and life, Bakhtin insists, are different substances. What, then, is the nature of the boundary that separates these two realms, and through what chemistry can two such disparate entities come together and "unite" in me? Clearly the obligation on both sides is of a different order than either the "purposive wholes without specific purpose" recommended by Kant or the device-driven "literariness" of the Formalists. In what medium is this unity expressed? To what higher value must it answer? Unpacking this tiny essay of Bakhtin's has proved exceptionally difficult.

In the later, more leisurely essay on authors and heroes, the life-art boundary performs a variety of duties. At one level it is simply a site.

---

[42] A facsimile of this eight-page, 19 September 1919 issue of "Den' iskusstva" is reproduced as an appendix in *Nevel'skii sbornik*, no. 1 (Sankt-Peterburg: Akropol', 1996). The journal also contains reviews of activities of the Bakhtin circle reported in "Molot" for 1918–20, including discussion sessions by Pumpiansky and Bakhtin on such topics as God and socialism, religion, and the meaning of love (147–58).

[43] Bakhtin, *Art and Answerability*, in *A&A 90*, 1–2. Further page references to "Author and Hero in Aesthetic Activity" given in text.

Although each of us is outside every other person, that outsideness can be turned to creative purpose in varying degrees. What makes us specifically artist-authors is not so much the artifact we produce as it is *how we act* on that interpersonal boundary. Attitude is all: the extent to which we attempt to see in other human beings "that which they cannot see in themselves, while remaining in ourselves and living our own lives in earnest" ("A&H," in *A&A*, 190). To become an author is to achieve this balance. "The artist is, in fact, someone who knows how to be active outside lived life," Bakhtin writes (190–91): "someone who not only partakes in life from within (practical, social, political, moral, religious life) and understands it from within, but someone who also loves it from without—loves life where it does not exist for itself, where it is turned outside itself and is in need of a self-activity that is located outside it and is active independently of meaning. The divinity of the artist consists in his partaking of the supreme outsideness."

Bakhtin suspects—and rightly so—that in the alternative worlds of art, which we bring into existence from without, it is considerably easier for us to act consistently and lovingly than in the real world of life, "which exists for itself." Art, in this sense, is an important practice zone, an environment where good habits might be efficiently acquired and reflexes tested. But in addition to the art-life boundary as test site for moral behavior, there is also an "artifact" component to Bakhtin's concern. The art-life boundary is a dividing line between *types of form*.

The topic became central to Bakhtin early in his career, by 1924. That year marks a watershed in Bakhtin's thought, the end of the "manuscript" period of philosophical speculations and the beginning of his concentration on the literary word. During that year Bakhtin prepared for publication a philosophical treatise in response to the Formalists. Entitled "The Problem of Content, Material, and Form in Verbal Art," it contains a final section on "The Problem of Form." Since the essay's delayed publication in 1975, separated by a half-century from its original interlocutors, this section has proved more problematic than its author could have foreseen.

THE PROBLEM OF FORM

Just as Bakhtin's biography can be viewed through the lens of his paradoxical attitude toward revolution (positive and "permanent" during carnival, negative and oppressive in prosaic reality), so might Bakhtin's paradoxical relationship to form be situated at the center of all that confounds us in his theory of art. Within his thought as a whole, the role of aesthetic form is vexed. As we have seen, Bakhtin as theorist has little to say about traditional aesthetic markers: perfection of shape or rhythm, the sense we receive from certain objects that we are in the presence of a clarity and proportion sufficiently stable to serve us as a standard, the whole world of norms and codes. What captures his passionate interest is always "the activity of the artist or author who creates." But let us now, in this penultimate section, shift our attention to the *receiving* rather than the creating end.

What are the dynamics of aesthetic response? This ancient question has no single answer, but most schools of thought would concur that we delight in aesthetic form and are energized by it when we feel ourselves resonating alongside it, when we contemplate it at the proper "aesthetic distance" and, if only briefly, align ourselves with it. Similar emotional needs are satisfied in us, I would argue, when we succeed in finding, if only for a moment, a compatible code. We embrace such a code enthusiastically because it clarifies our options, permits us to concentrate our energies, to suspend our questions and doubts, to fit in and relax. In our best "coded" moments we do not feel trapped or silenced. We feel realized. Finalization in this sense is a loophole out of everyday shapeless life—almost as Bakhtinian carnival and the polyphonic word, by wholly different routes, can be a loophole. Its benefits are pointedly not to be found in the rigors of independent judgment or individuation. We do not need to answer back, nor are we driven to supplement an idea or impression with something new of our own. Energy and bliss are released in us when we contemplate something finished and closed, something *not* in need of our dialogic input. This bliss will not last long; but aesthetic form, like laughter and inspiration itself, need only be answerable—as our chapter title suggests—for the "aesthetic moment."

That Bakhtin has a problem with form, thus defined, is easy to ascertain from the most familiar texts of his middle period. In the 1930s he dismisses epic, lyric, drama—in fact every genre with any fixed literary form or slot in a hierarchy—as carriers of unfreedom.[44] Later he speaks out categorically against semiotics and codes. Although Bakhtin does trim back his ecstasy at carnival disorder and has excellent things to say about the constraints and conventions of "speech genres," by the end of his life he nevertheless had come to link lyric poetry, epic, drama, the authoritative word, Structuralism, signs and codes in a loose bundle that had something of the feel of a prison about it.

Is this one-way trajectory the only way to read Bakhtin on form? Russian students of his thought appear to be divided on this question—and again, a familiar spectrum stretches out, from kindly sympathy to unholy

---

[44] See, for example, Bakhtin, "Discourse in the Novel," in *DI*, 286–88; 296–98 ("The poet is a poet insofar as he accepts the idea of a unitary and singular language and a unitary, monologically sealed-off utterance. . . . To achieve this, the poet strips the word of others' intentions. . . . Everywhere there is only one face—the linguistic face of the author.")

suspicion. Some have attempted to understand the evolution of his aesthetics in an integrated spirit; others (along the lines of those critics who so savaged dialogue and carnival) are committed to pursuing, to its bitter and unpalatable end, the ethical implications of Bakhtin's near-fatal passion for opening up fixed things. Before sampling contributions at each of these poles, however, we might recall the major points of Bakhtin's programmatic 1924 statement on the "Problem of Form."[45] In the process, the argument made at the beginning of this chapter, as well as our excursus on aesthetic love, will be revisited from a somewhat different perspective. We will seek out that moment when the *force of form* (as something preexistent, autonomous, striving toward consummation, as that force which works upon us but not yet in dialogic partnership with us) becomes a "problem." For there is a threshold in Bakhtin's thought, albeit muted and tentative, where form (or the activity of a "form-shaping consciousness") ceases to be a prerogative and a blessing for the creating artist to bestow and becomes instead a burden for the receiving, or created, personality to assume.

As we have seen, the early Bakhtin follows Kant in granting to aesthetic form an exalted mediating function. Intuitively unifying the cognitive and ethical spheres, entities constructed in this aesthetic "middle space" can partake of the best of both worlds: ideas have real people attached to them but these personalities are created from without—as a *vymysel*, or fiction—and thus are "free." They live in a world comprehended by an integrated vision. For this reason the author, as the bestower of form, can be, in Bakhtin's happy phrase, "axiologically tranquil."[46] Created heroes inside a text, of course, are more likely to be apprehensive and restless; they experience their lives in an ethical dimension bonded to consequences that are real for them. But their authors are calm, confident, disinterested, and always outside.

Even from this external position, however, form is not something that authors simply "apply" to material. Rhythm, rhyme, harmony, symmetry—these factors are all too active, Bakhtin insists, too intense to be understood as mere devices imposed on inert or passive verbal matter. The proper question for the aesthetician is not how to exile content so as to isolate form, but rather how form becomes part of content. Form is not a material trace, not merely a nick on some preexistent surface. It is

[45] Bakhtin, "The Problem of Content, Material, and Form in Verbal Art," trans. Kenneth Brostrom, in *A&A*, 257–325, esp. 303–18, "The Problem of Form" (translation liberally adjusted). Subsequent page references are to this volume.

[46] On aesthetic, ethical, and cognitive events, on the crisis in authorship that occurs when a bestower of aesthetic form gravitates too fully toward the ethical real-life world and thus loses outsideness and tranquillity, and on the inherent "kindness" of aesthetic activity, see "A&H," in *A&A*, 21–22, 205–7, 277–80.

the projection of energy from an agent. Thus it inevitably reflects an evaluating, value-bearing attitude; it has a cutting edge, a consciousness, a forward momentum, and it serves the ego. "In form *I find myself*," Bakhtin writes; "I feel intensely my own movement creating an object" (304). If cognition does not need a creator at all and ethical action is judged by the good it brings about in the world, then the impulse to form is always a striving to create and consummate—and in my own individual name. *What* I create is conditioned by content.

But content, Bakhtin is at pains to stress, is a delicate beast. By nature passive, receptive, a bit restless, it lies there in expectation, waiting to be shaped and loved. I must be active and fastidiously accurate in adding form to content or else it will rebel, become unruly, slip back into the more stable realms of the purely cognitive or purely ethical—where it will shed either its personality or its tranquillity. The task of form (and here Bakhtin refers specifically to the lyric as an exemplary genre) is to *detach and isolate content*—not, we should note, in order to neutralize it morally or drain it of its pathos, but to release it from dependency, enable it to relax, free it from any craven expectation of a response. Blessed with form, "a prayer no longer needs the God who could hear it, a complaint no longer needs help, repentance no longer needs forgiveness" (306, 308). In short, form detaches and isolates content so that consummation [*zavershenie*] can occur. At this stage in Bakhtin's thinking about aesthetics, then, a closed, consummated, self-sufficient whole is the goal of art. Any cognitive moment that is not integrated or consummated will be sensed as a *durnoi prozaizm* [a wretched prosaism] or a *nerastvorennyi prozaizm* [an undissolved prosaism] (282, 285). These references to prosiness are not marks of openness or freedom. They are indications of the failure of art.

Here as always the taxonomist, Bakhtin distinguishes between two types of aesthetic form. The first and simpler type is "compositional": how verbal masses are organized, what devices an author might employ to subdivide the material or move it mechanically around (chapters in a novel, the division of a play into acts, the format and layout of dialogues, the repeating rhyme scheme of a poetic stanza). Compositional form is important but apparently unproblematic. In composing, the competent artist is stern and merciless toward his material—"the poet casts away words, forms, expressions without pity, and he selects only a few; . . . fragments of marble fly from under the chisel." No matter how violent and exclusionary its genesis, however, the aesthetic result—if successful— will be "kind, accepting, enriching, optimistic" (279). For artistic success ultimately depends on a second type of form beyond the merely compositional: the "architectonic."

Architectonic energy arranges parts into a whole. It is thus the polar opposite of inertia and always brings into being a more internally complex living entity. This organism is dynamic, intuitive, grateful to be given life. Contemplating such a whole, we ourselves become kind: we have no desire to abolish things or push them away, "we recognize everything and remember everything" (279). (Such kindness and tolerance does not come upon us so naturally in merely cognitive states, Bakhtin intimates. Could this be what Dostoevsky had in mind when he remarked, "Beauty will save the world"?) Bakhtin speaks here of the "emotionally willed intensity of form"—its efficient, "tightly wound-up quality," as in a wound-up spring (266)—but this tension is never angry, aggressive, or disruptive. Unlike cognition and (we might add) unlike many of our everyday ethical responses to the world, architectonic form succeeds only when it is kind and merciful. It creates an aesthetic whole that does not divide, reject, or choose; it invites all inside, with *dobrota* and *blagostnost'* [kindness and generosity of spirit] (281).

In varying degrees, compositional and architectonic forms in literature draw on the same arsenal of formal aspects: the attributes and building blocks of verbal art. Bakhtin lists five such blocks: (1) the word's "sounding or musical" element; (2) its referential meaning; (3) its verbal connections with other words; (4) its "intonational/psychological/emotional" layer, permeated with the values and moods of the speaker; and (5) the "sense of the word's activeness," by which he means the feeling of "inner directiveness" or purposefulness that we experience when we give birth to a "meaningful sound" (310). From a later, more dialogic and novel-centered perspective, what is remarkable about this list, surely, is its overwhelmingly oral quality, its concentration in the speaking or singing "I" regardless of who might be listening and poised for response. The glory of language, it appears, is simply to produce it and to feel good by expressing yourself in it. "Form" relies on itself alone: it is the "acting soul and body" (312) of a creator [*tvorets*], who produces aesthetic unity by embracing content from an outside position and consummating it. In poetry, Bakhtin remarks, all five formal aspects of the word tend to be subsumed by the first aspect, the euphonic or "sounding" side of things, which is always the dominant. Sounds must work their magic on the ear first of all, if the work of the poem is to succeed.

What can be said at this point about Bakhtin on aesthetic form? It is a loving, self-sufficient, orally delivered poetic performance. And as such it is one of those gentle miracles that occur so often in his work: a creative principle that is entirely "I" or ego-centered, but not in a selfish way; it is kindly, energetic, open to the hypothetical other, but still risks nothing and remains thoroughly in control itself. The material it shapes desires that shaping hand. (Again, Bakhtin has little tolerance for personal anxiety: I can incorporate your formlessness and shape it in a friendly, non-possessive way; *you will like it.*) The other offers no violence or resistance to my creating self or its form-bearing activity, and my self, in turn, has no anger or bitterness to spend on defacing the other. Bakhtin does not resolve the potential tension between self and other; here, as elsewhere, he simply ignores it.

Crucial to the process is the mesmerizing, perhaps even incantational *sound* of form. It creates a community in which every participant can become an author—because a poem occurs not when it is written but when it is articulated. Intonation is that middle space between the bestower and the receiver of form, where the blessings of creativity can be felt by author and perceiver alike. In general, Bakhtin intimates, in order to experience form, seeing or hearing is not enough; we must rearticulate it ourselves, summoning for this activity the whole of our "creating inner organism" (315). Involuntarily one recalls Bakhtin's septuagenarian voice on the Duvakin tapes at the centennial, reciting with his phenomenal memory and in several languages a torrent of beloved poetic sounds.

Bakhtin ends his chapter on "The Problem of Form" with a discussion of form in the lyric versus form in the novel. Reading this 1924 essay retroactively—that is, aware that forty years of writing on the novel are to follow in Bakhtin's life, whereas lyric form will be abandoned—we sense the approaching divide. What happens to aesthetic form in what Bakhtin calls the "larger prosaic verbal wholes"? His remarks in this concluding section seem uncontroversial, almost banal. In works such as novels, he writes, "the phoneme [with its base in intonation and articulation] yields to the grapheme [the written word]" (314). The involvement or "attachment" to form that is characteristic of the "creating, inner organism" in the lyric mode becomes minimal.[47] That special energy which in poetry could be released only through co-articulating and co-hearing is now replaced, in "large verbal wholes," with "an intense, evaluating, remembering activity," with "emotional memory" (316). To be sure, the creator of a novel still organizes content, isolates it, bestows form upon it "as a gift"—but the dominant of the artwork has shifted. It has ceased to be the rearticulation of the uttered word at any given moment and has become *consciousness over time* as expressed in graphemes. Bakhtin ends his essay on the "Problem of Content, Material, and Form" at this point. But the most interesting problems are just beginning. Since novels contain multiple personalities, masses of time, and are written to

---

[47] "The significance of the creating, inner organism is not the same in all kinds of poetry," Bakhtin writes at this crucial juncture in the evolution of his thought. "It is maximal in the lyric, where the body, generating the sound from within itself and sensing the unity of its own productive tension [*napriazhenie*], is drawn into form; in the novel this attachment of the inner organism to form [*priobshchennost' forme vnutrennego organizma*] is minimal" (314).

be realized silently rather than recited aloud, some means must be devised under these new conditions to approximate that elusive intuition of "wholeness" and gratitude that a successful architectonics bestows upon the producers and receivers of poetry. In the "larger prosaic verbal wholes," we are led to believe, this aim is achieved if we respect the wholeness of evolving heroes alongside the wholeness of their author.

This shift to novelistic prose invites a new definition of the functions of form. Form is not just imposed from above by a creator to bring peace to restless content (what most of us would recognize as the "aesthetic moment"); form can now be registered as pressure from *another peer consciousness*—as a destabilization, a second presence, a question, a challenge. In fact 1924 is pretty much the last time that "axiological tranquillity" and "artistic consummation" are invoked by Bakhtin as special virtues bestowed by form. Novelistic form comes to be valued for the potency and degree of openness it can tolerate, for its power to stimulate. The authoring "I" no longer coexperiences and consummates; now it supplements and stirs up.

From this point on, the stages in Bakhtin's thinking are well known. His trademark terrain—first the polyphonic, then the dialogic, then the heteroglot, ultimately the carnivalesque—is progressively redefined as the site not of genesis or consummation but of *exchange* (or better, of interchange); novelistic words are scraped clean of starting points and become instead inspired way stations, intersections that do not let us "rest in art" but rather encourage us to look around restlessly, listening for the next voice. Gary Saul Morson is correct to credit Bakhtin as the inspiration for his wonderful idea of "sideshadowing"—that attitude toward time which sees it as a field, not a point, and thereby restores to life the "possibility of possibility."[48] Just such a spirit of multiple opportunities and still unshaped options is the essence of the mature Bakhtin's understanding of form.

Lest this all seem too loose and strange, two reminders are in order. First, we must not forget that Bakhtin, raised on German Romanticism, was drawn throughout his life to Schelling's idea of the responsive, creative "organism" endowed with inner resources that could transcend mere environmental constraints. The Schellingian "organism" represented a *union* of nature with the human spirit, not a fatal struggle of one against the other. It is also worth noting that the debate between these two worldviews, cast as a confrontation between the romantic Lamarck and the positivist Darwin, was profound among Russian poets of the

---

[48] Gary Saul Morson, *Narrative and Freedom: The Shadows of Time* (New Haven, Conn.: Yale University Press, 1994), esp. ch. 4, "Sideshadowing."

1920s and the early 1930s.[49] In this connection we might entertain a related notion: that in the famous dichotomy between form and content, "messiness" or "shapelessness" can become, under certain conditions, a category of content rather than of form.[50] One such site and set of circumstances is the organism. The "content" of blood, ganglia, glandular secretions can be formless and flowing, but these organs are nevertheless dynamic systems (blood cannot flow anywhere in the body and still sustain the organism). Form can, and must, regulate such "messiness." But more accurate here than the idea of "shaping," with its inspiration in the sculptural arts, is the idea of a "monitoring" activity that optimizes, tunes up, flushes out. Although at no time can the whole organism be stopped and fixed permanently in place (and continue to live), this monitor exerts a vital influence as a "finitizer" and "finalizer" of content. To invoke familiar Kantian rubrics, form here fulfills a regulatory rather than a constitutive function.

As with the dynamic processes of the body, so with Bakhtin's understanding of the "force of form" in the polyphonic and dialogic novel. Precision and control are abundantly present—but this shaping, constraining energy is registered as feedback rather than as structure and thus has multiple agents or "authors." The above analogy with liquid organs and life processes must be qualified in one respect, however. In the early 1920s Bakhtin criticized the popular organicist Bergsonian view that "the world was only a flow of changes," a fact supposedly hidden from us by our spatialized intellect.[51] In Bakhtin's view, *Lebensphilosophie* was too psychologized, too interiorized and tied to a single consciousness, and for this reason overly theoretized even in its attempt to exit from the straitjacket of reason into a more flexible intuitivism. Bakhtin believed that life's events simply could not be cognized as "inner flow"—and not because we are in the bad habit of spatializing time but because an event,

---

[49] In an elegant article on Mandelstam's position in the debate between anti-positivist Lamarckians and Darwinians in the Soviet 1920s (a debate of which Bakhtin was doubtless aware), Boris Gasparov discusses how such a Schellingian understanding of the "organism" was for some poets a force that gifted artists could oppose to an encroaching "Iron Age." See Boris Gasparov, "The Iron Age of the 1930s (The Centennial Return in Mandelstam)," trans. John Henrikson, in Stephanie Sandler, ed., *Rereading Russian Poetry* (New Haven, Conn.: Yale University Press, 1999): 78–103.

[50] I thank my father, David Geppert, for this notion of shapelessness as a category of content rather than form—and for decades of stimulating debate over a thinker he never dreamed he would have to take so seriously, for so long.

[51] Bakhtin's critique of Bergson's intuitivism comes in the form of incidental commentary on Nikolai Lossky's 1922 *Intuitivnaia filosofiia Bergsona* (itself a mixed evaluation), tucked into his unfinished essay, "K filosofii postupka." See *Toward a Philosophy of the Act*, 13, 21; for an interpretation, see Morson and Emerson, *Creation of a Prosaics*, 176–79.

to be given form and fixed in our consciousness at all, requires input from another outside person. As he writes apropos of polyphony in *Problems of Dostoevsky's Poetics*: "It is one thing to be active in relation to a dead thing, to voiceless material that can be molded and formed as one wishes, and another thing to be active in relation to someone else's living, autonomous consciousness" (285). Here is the "social" or interpersonal threshold below which Bakhtin could not fall and that kept his Romanticist metaphysics in check. With this criterion of outside consciousness, however, form ceases to serve what most of us would recognize as an aesthetic function and begins to serve an ethical or even a philosophical-cognitive function. As the singular authoring "I" yields to each surrounding "thou," the ideal of tranquil beauty gives way to equal rights of access, multiplicity, and interruption.

For all the reasons we know, this shift from centering to de-centering was a methodology well suited to resist the closing noose of Stalinism. But it was not especially well suited to close readings, to respect for symbolic or fatidic patterning in a work of art, to formal poetic structures, or to the dynamics of the creative process as viewed from inside a creator's head. To the extent that "prosaic" or dialogic readings shortchange these values, one could argue, they are inadequate as *literary* commentary. (It is of some moment, I believe, that we cannot imagine Bakhtin as a poet or primary creator, possessed by a desire to "get it right": he is not selfish enough and he does not exile others' voices soon enough; *re-voicing* excites him too fully.) Form has become a passage.

THE LOGIC OF AESTHETIC FORM AND "CONSUMMATION AS A TYPE OF DYING"

Debates over Bakhtin's understanding of form recall the debates over dialogism and carnival; indeed, they are intertwined. Bakhtin's supporters claim, however, that these routine complaints simply misconstrue Bakhtin's intent.[52] Dialogue is not wholly open nor at the disposal of any random speaker; carnival is not trivial; consummation need not be a defensive or definitive closing down. Bakhtin intended these to be coopera-

---

[52] As Vladimir Turbin has argued in defense of his mentor's maximally trustful scenario, the personalist task of the author—to "impart an artistically consummating shape" to a work of art—is much too delicate a procedure to be grasped by those "seduced by the mirage of such self-sufficient mechanizations as device-material, material-device." What the seduced Formalist fails to see is that "consummation [*zavershenie*] is not the same as completion [*okonchanie*] at the level of simple plot" (Vladimir Turbin, "U istokov sotsiologicheskoi poetiki [M. M. Bakhtin v polemike s formal'noi shkoloi]," *MMB kak filosof* 92, 46; subsequent quotes on 47, 45–46).

tive, not competitive, categories. As Matvei Kagan put the case, with the bucolic diction common to Bakhtin's circle, in a 1922 paper on the dual strivings of art: "Art is life's holiday, a holiday that is necessary to life, a holiday of giftedness by means of life. . . . After all, for art, the holiday of life is not a trivial or idle matter [*Ved' prazdnik zhizni dlia iskusstva— delo ne prazdnoe*]."[53]

The quaintly ecstatic tone of Kagan's fusion of carnival, life, and art provides a useful foil and contrast to this final section. Two melancholic explications will be juxtaposed from the centennial year 1995, written with the benefit of Bakhtin's entire intellectual trajectory in view. The first treatment is sympathetic, confirming and extending the conclusions we reached in our reading of "The Problem of Form"; the other is more speculative and direly pessimistic. Both find highly problematic the benevolent synthesis that Bakhtin and Kagan found so natural and argued with such conviction at the beginning of their careers as philosophers.

Natalia Bonetskaia opens her 1995 essay, "Bakhtin's Aesthetics as the Logic of Form," with a paradox: Bakhtin's work as a whole defies classification and contains contradictory theses, yet we sense in it an intuitive unity.[54] This unity must be sought not in his postulates, however, but in his concept of aesthetic form—which is persuasive largely to the extent that it is itself an evolving, dynamic category, much as Bakhtin's most favored image of the literary hero is dynamic and the product of an observable evolutionary process. Bonetskaia surveys the major works of the 1920s and 1930s (from "Toward a Philosophy of the Act" to *Rabelais*) in an effort to reveal the indwelling logic of Bakhtin's sense of form.

She detects in Bakhtin's early thought a bold challenge to aesthetics as it had been formalized by the turn of the century. In this essay she emphasizes not the Kantian connection she had previously researched but the aesthetic systems elaborated by neo-Romantic theorists and the poets of Russian Symbolism. In that later body of thought, the artist was seen as a tragic personality, a seer whose vision could never be adequately recorded; authorship (the bestowal of form) was understood as an activity that inevitably entailed constraint and the paralysis of inspiration (52). In muted dialogue with such luminaries as Simmel, Nietzsche, and Alexander Blok, Bakhtin was taking on the most vexed question confronting aesthetics in his day: how to devise a philosophy that would transcend what had come to be called the "tragedy of creativity" (55). Charac-

---

[53] M. I. Kagan, "Dva stremleniia iskusstva (forma i soderzhanie; bespredmetnost' i siuzhetnost')," *Filosofskie nauki*, no. 1 (1995): 47–61, esp. 60.

[54] N. K. Bonetskaia, "Estetika M. Bakhtina kak logika formy," in *Bakhtinologiia*, 51–60. Further page references given in text.

teristically he cast the question as a task, that of giving a shape and an image to "spirit" [*dukh*]. (Bakhtin's terminology here could have been acquired from the phenomenologist Max Scheler, one generation his senior, for whom *Geist* was the intuited—but as yet unembodied—unity of an individual personality prior to its realization in a concrete act.) For classical aesthetics, such as the theories of Hegel or Schelling, embodiment in art was not an insurmountable problem. Expression was good, possible, free. But on the far side of Symbolism, where art had inherited the territory vacated by religious faith, the problem had become immense. "Bakhtin seized on the most difficult task of all: to resolve the question of shaping that which in principle cannot be shaped, of imaging that which is fundamentally unimageable, of consummating the infinite" (53). The resolution of this task required the work of an entire life.

In his earliest thinking about the problem, Bonetskaia notes, Bakhtin saw aesthetic form "not as a communicative *event* but [on the contrary] as its sole stable aspect, as that single thing that could impart a [fixed] quality to the event and overcome its dynamism" (54). Form is "the only carrier of determinedness." In "Author and Hero," Bakhtin concentrates on abstract notions of "body" and "soul" and on musical and sculptural form, because in such contexts the recipients of form can be "absolutely passive." When the hero begins to "occupy a sense-laden [*osmyslennoe*] place in existence, however, he strives to confirm his position in terms of its meaning [for him] and thus to counterpose [that meaning] to the author's position" (55). With good reason does the sequence of literary forms examined in "Author and Hero" proceed from confession through lyric to romantic "type," for the task the hero must accomplish—and that is achieved, step by step, in those genres—is to outgrow the author's control over his consciousness. The point at which these early ruminations on aesthetics break off is of some import for Bonetskaia. She suggests that Bakhtin *abandoned* these essays, not just left them unfinished, because the next logical step, a genuine aestheticization of *dukh* [spirit], was simply unresolvable in terms of this initial progression.

In his book on Dostoevsky Bakhtin doubles back, starts over with new assumptions, and tries out a different approach to the problem of "shaping the unshapeable." Polyphony was his first attempt at a *formal* solution for "giving form to spirit," one that would guarantee (here Bonetskaia quotes Bakhtin) that "spirit could now be visualized in a way that only the soul and the body had been visualized before" (56). Bakhtin's means to this end was a "dialogic poetics." But the unfolding internal logic of *Problems of Dostoevsky's Art* made it clear beyond a doubt that this new starting point was separated by a veritable "chasm" from Bakhtin's earlier writings on aesthetics. The definition of "form as a boundary" no longer applied, because polyphonic form cannot finalize in the old way (56). In a fundamental revision of the form/spirit dichotomy, spirit comes to be associated with dialogic form itself—and "the form of novelistic dialogue does not deaden life because it is life itself: this is the culmination and major revelation of Bakhtin's aesthetics" (57). Bakhtin begins to speak of Dostoevsky's art as if it were interchangeable with unmediated life; recalling Martin Buber, "spirit" is now dissolved in form, and the whole sooner resembles a philosophy, a charged space, an orientation between two people than it does an artifact.

With its emphasis on the watershed of the late 1920s, this much of Bonetskaia's argument is familiar. What is striking, however, is her conclusion: that Bakhtin justified his mature conception of form—in its new, seemingly realistic guise of "art-for-life's-sake"—by a return to the great founders of classical aesthetics: to Schelling, Hegel, Goethe. She points out that for those thinkers, spirit could not ultimately be fit into any form at all: "Aesthetic perfection for the classical aestheticians meant going beyond the boundaries of form, it meant a substantive fusion of the work of art with life's primal energies" (57). If by this logic Hegel and Schelling could see in Romantic art the most highly perfected expression of form, "then for Bakhtin, aesthetic perfection was the 'realism in a higher sense' of Dostoevsky" (58). At this point we might recall the Duvakin interviews and Bakhtin's affectionate, enthusiastic reminiscence, one-half century after the fact, of many hours of discussions with his close friends Pumpiansky and Yudina in revolutionary Petrograd. In that Bolshevik decade, their topic was none other than Schelling's aesthetic theory— which, Bakhtin assured Duvakin in 1973, had always been "very dear to me."[55]

The accumulating frustrations and potentials of seeking artistic form within life's primal energy have their logical consummation in the study on Rabelais. Bonetskaia argues that carnival represents yet another approach on Bakhtin's part to the problem of form, one growing integrally out of the earlier dead ends. If form had been defined earlier as the aesthetic result of an interaction between author and hero, then the hazards of this dialogic definition were now avoided altogether, for "in Bakhtin's reading, Rabelais's novel contains neither hero nor author as personalities" (58). The heroes are "dissolved in the folk body," and the author (at least for the purposes of Bakhtin's analysis) "does not have his own individual voice . . . [he is] the mouthpiece of carnival, a passive medium for primordial carnival energies. Put another way, he is possessed by the carnival spirit." Thus in Bakhtin's aesthetic geography, spread over several decades, *dukh* is forced steadily downward. From its lofty aspira-

---

[55] "Razgovory s Bakhtinym: Mariia Veniaminovna Yudina" (interview no. 6), *Chelovek*, no. 6 (1994): 167.

tion to "consummate the infinite," it moves toward a polyphonic or "horizontal" regard for the immediate interlocutor, from there to the lower bodily stratum, and ultimately to the world below and beyond. "This is still spirituality," Bonetskaia assures us, "but a spirituality of the nether world."

The dark side of this trajectory will follow, but let us now sum up Bonetskaia's thesis. In her view Bakhtin, an immensely ambitious theorist, was preoccupied throughout his life with the potential of aesthetic form to *enable*—not merely to define or to reflect—the reality of life. In his early thought, aims are still modest: demarcation and formal consummation must precede any act of communication. As he increasingly broadens his scope, Bakhtin does not reject form but (on the contrary) posits ever more extravagant hopes for it, recruiting for this task the immortality and multidimensionality of the spoken word. And in his mature aesthetics, inspired by the Romantic dream of a fusion between artistic form and the natural elements, "he wants to grasp all of life's fullness by means of form" (59). But form, at least as explicated by the literary critic, must inevitably collapse under such "inner pressure exerted by life." At the far end of this itinerary, Rabelais's novelistic masterwork is treated as a "chunk of carnival existence," essentially as formless. Thus does the "logic of form" play itself out in Bakhtin's thought. It is itself "consummated," although in a possibly tragic key. "Life, in its striving to manifest itself in art and having found for itself an optimal form, proceeds to break down every kind of barrier that makes for aesthetic determinateness" (59).

Bonetskaia's closing note is conservative, an affirmation that life's openness and aesthetic form are, in principle, opposed. Bakhtin could only founder in his several attempts to combine the energies of both; what looks like a celebration of polyphonic and carnival dynamics is in fact the ancient familiar deadlock. In her reading, however, the cost of this failure is limited to a theoretical inconsistency, an aesthetics that does not cohere. The logic inherent in Bakhtin's thought does not in itself erode personality, diminish human potential, or facilitate evil. It can come as no surprise that Konstantin Isupov, familiar to us for his vision of the demonic at the heart of Bakhtin's carnivalesque, has also explored the grimmer implications of Bakhtinian outsideness. His 1995 essay, "The Death of the 'Other,'" accomplishes for dialogue what his earlier review of Losev on the Renaissance had achieved for carnival: an exposé of aesthetic love and its pretensions to creative Eros.[56] In the process, Isupov makes a case for Bakhtin's affinity with Thanatos. He suggests that the logic of Bakhtinian method—however much its author would like us to

---

[56] K. G. Isupov, "Smert' 'drugogo,'" in *Bakhtinologiia*, 103–16.

believe that it makes us free and our words immortal—in fact enslaves and kills us before our time. In Bakhtin's work, the opposition that matters is not between art and life but between art and death.

Isupov is weary of all those Russian philosophers and philosophizers—from Nikolai Fyodorov through the Symbolists and the revolutionary ecstaticians—who are obsessed with denying, transcending, or overcoming death. He wants a courageous exegesis of dying, one that looks at it straight into the light and without sentimentality, somewhat in the spirit, we might suppose, of epic bards like Homer or Leo Tolstoy. He finds such a dynamic at work in Bakhtin. We are confounded by Bakhtin's concept of "aesthetic outsideness," Isupov insists, not because it seems naive or benevolent but because it is simply too horrifying. To work properly, it requires death all around. Or, as Isupov puts it bluntly, "Bakhtin's golden key is an instrument for locking the doors on a living person" (109).

He arrives at this startling conclusion by the following route. Our difficulties with Bakhtin's early thought, Isupov argues, are owing to the curiously deceptive "space" of his critical word. On the one hand Bakhtin appears meandering and tentative in his exposition, open to others, conversational rather than rhetorical, always ready to be interrupted. But on the other hand he is "authoritative, like every creator of form": he establishes his dialogue with literary texts very much on his own terms and is so insinuatingly successful in his one-sided theses that we cannot now imagine Rabelais without carnival or the Formalists before the Bakhtin school's exegesis of them (104). "Bakhtin, like the heroes he describes in *Problems of Dostoevsky's Poetics*, is an *artist of the idea*." Isupov intends no compliments. Although a scholar and a critic, Bakhtin manipulates ideas with the artfulness of a primary creator.

What is the idea that Bakhtin instills in us with the personal stamp and skill of an artist? Time and again, in his thinking about art, Bakhtin brings a single god-term to bear on aesthetic matters: *be outside of it*. This universally accessible—and thus overwhelmingly democratic—mandate is almost all Bakhtin asks of the artist. Isupov contrasts Bakhtin's description of the poet's mission with Pushkin's. In Pushkin's elevating, elitist image of poetic creativity—say, in his poem "The Prophet"—mortals become poets when they are visited by a fiery angel, their hearts torn out and replaced by burning embers, when a "corpse in the wilderness comes back to life as a demigod." Bakhtin, however, is satisfied to "resolve the prerogative of the artist situationally": all that is required of the would-be poet is a surplus of vision (105). But even if we lay to one side the technical questions of craftsmanship and the quality of the artifact, if we are all artists merely because we are all "outside" and in a "consummating" capacity vis-à-vis others, how can we assure ourselves that the material we are shaping will stand still? To be fully consummated by another, one must have a perceivable outer crust. As Isupov sees the matter, in his writings on the subject Bakhtin lets it be known that this crust is death.

Isupov then examines the impress of Bakhtin's "spatial" prerequisite on our perception of mortality. Death, as an irreversible closing down of consciousness, cannot by definition be cognized from the inside: it exists only for others. Thus death is the single human condition for which outsideness is not only desirable but wholly essential: it enables the prototypical, perfect aesthetic object. Only *other people* can know that I am dead; if that fact is to be known at all, you must know it *for me* (or for the memory of my deceased self). Isupov pushes further, scenting another dimension to Bakhtin's bland and conciliatory pronouncements on this dark subject. Once actually dead, of course, I can no longer bestow an image nor can I "imagine" a thing. But while still alive I can, anxiously like every other mortal, imagine my own end. This ability to "anticipate my own death"—so closely tied to others' perception of me—could only have been learned through the experience of anticipating myself in the role of a surviving consciousness aware of others' death, and thus demonstrates to me that others must exist, that I am not alone (109).

Such a path to human community (in equal part commonsensical and macabre) has a larger significance for aesthetics. Isupov focuses on those passages in "Author and Hero" where individual death is specifically linked to artistic form—where, in Bakhtin's words, "one could even say that death is a form for consummating the personality aesthetically."[57] If we wish to treat the whole of the other, that person must be "dead for us, formally dead." Isupov refuses to read that troubling phrase metaphorically. He connects it with "the ancient intuition of form as a type of dying," concluding that "Bakhtin created an apophatic aesthetic of creative death" (110). But in itself, Isupov's conclusion does not take us much beyond the routine Romantic and Symbolist complaint that any artistic product is the graveyard of its originary inspiration. What really interests Isupov is not the aesthetic end of things—how Bakhtin utilizes the interactions of self and other to explain the dynamics of art—but the real-life, or rather real-death, dimensions of the model. What is the fate of this "aesthetically competent 'I,'" which is also the fate of every person outside of me as well, since each of our "I's" is other to someone else? To these questions Isupov responds:

> Why does Bakhtin say nary a word about the fate of the other, while this activity on behalf of aesthetic salvation and consummation is being completed? And why, too, do we learn nothing at all from Bakhtin's texts about

[57] Bakhtin, "A&H," in *A&A*, 131 (here and elsewhere, Liapunov translation adjusted and loosened).

the fate of the "I" in the role of the other? Where did the other disappear to? What has happened to the "I"? The answer, it seems to us, is roughly this. Bakhtin has nothing to say about the other because he no longer exists. He has died. He also has nothing to say about the "I" in its roles as an other, because that "I" also does not exist. . . . Bakhtin's aesthetics is an aesthetics of sacrificial self-slaughtering. . . . [There is no catharsis in this] aesthetic formal murder and sacrificial suicide-resurrection . . . . no one has an alibi in existence, good is evil, the demonic guffaw is a blessing, blasphemy and abuse is a prayer turned inside out. . . . But saddest of all: none of this makes any of it any easier. (111)

In Isupov's opinion this specter of a spreading death, where art is the natural end product of self-sacrifice and personalities are formalized only in memory, is Bakhtin's real legacy to moral philosophy. The aesthetic realm proves only a launching point, an arbitrary label for this larger interest. "In Bakhtin, the aesthetic formula of a resurrection-bearing death became possible with the transfer of the sense of Eros to the sense of Thanatos. . . . Bakhtin transformed death into a source of creative energy for Eros" (111, 112). In reasoning thus, we might surmise, Isupov identifies Bakhtin not so much with those clinical Freudian strivings of the psyche so commonplace for us today as with those neo-Romantic and Symbolist reworkings of the Tristan and Isolde plot that were a part of Bakhtin's youth in Petrograd. As Maurice Maeterlinck summed up the malaise in his celebrated turn-of-the-century account of the *Life of Bees*, "Most creatures have a vague belief that a very precarious hazard, a kind of transparent membrane, divides death from love, and that the profound idea of Nature demands that the giver of life should die at the moment of giving."[58]

Isupov ends his exegesis of Bakhtin's thought, as did Bonetskaia, on Rabelaisian laughter and the grotesque body. He sees Bakhtin's passion for carnival as a maximum test case, an exacerbation and apotheosis of all the death-bearing enthusiasms of the earlier texts. Carnival does not know Eros or any other form of intimate dialogic exchange, for Eros— and here Isupov completely endorses Bakhtin's ideas about love—resides only in "the personal effort of a responsibly acting 'I'." Like aesthetic love, Eros requires boundaries. It is tied to "individual personality and presupposes choice" (112); only "responsiveness in love slakes the thirst for death." In carnival-era Bakhtin, however, life goes fully on the defen-

---

[58] Maurice Maeterlinck, *The Life of the Bee*, trans. Alfred Sutro (London: George Allen, 1904), 252; as cited in Richard Taruskin, *Stravinsky and the Russian Traditions: A Biography of the Works Through "Mavra"* (Berkeley: University of California Press, 1996), 322. (Stravinsky used Maeterlinck's *Vie des abeilles* as the program for his Opus 3, "Scherzo fantastique" [1908].)

sive. "Death is triumphant in the book on Rabelais, death pregnant with birth [or birth pregnant with death], but in *Rabelais* there is no longer any word of love." Isupov does not divulge his own attitude toward this sinister dance. But he does fault Bakhtin for not foregrounding his mature aesthetics as a contribution to *ars moriendi*; if he had, what now seems like curiosities or inconsistencies in his work would have come together into a coherent whole and received the proper theoretical appreciation. "A philosopher-artist, Bakhtin offers us the opportunity to 'begin to feel' ourselves by means of 'formally dead others,' and steers us toward the idea of unfinalizably consummating death as a form of aesthetic freedom" (113).

Isupov's reading is grim fare. But it is hardly unexpected: Bakhtin's concept of form is being forced here through the same suspicious filter that in earlier chapters of this study revealed such troubling aspects of polyphony, dialogue, and the carnival grotesque. Isupov is not alone in detecting an aura of erasure and death in Bakhtin's mature sense of aesthetic form. Among Russians of the younger generation, the psychoanalytically oriented critic Aleksandr Etkind, in his 1996 collection of essays on the intellectual history of the Silver Age entitled *Sodom and Psyche*, presses Isupov's thesis even further.[59] "The traditional Russian understanding of love and death, similar to Dionysius, is reborn in the work of Mikhail Bakhtin," Etkind writes (244). In his view, Bakhtin's book on Rabelais, far from being old-fashioned or folklorish, contains "all the basic motifs of the Russian Moderne: the idea of eternal resurrection, the romantic ethos of de-individuation, the blurring and rubbing out of fundamental categories of rationality, the image of the androgyne"—in short, the standard self-obliterating and "dismembering" Dionysian complex as celebrated by Vladimir Soloviev and Vyacheslav Ivanov. Individuals become mere way stations, effaced and rendered formless; erotic processes become reversible, the grotesque body becomes bisexual. "The self-consciousness of the contemporary human being—the 'new bodily canon'—casts Bakhtin into despair," Etkind notes. Bakhtin vigorously resisted this new canon, with its (and Etkind quotes here from *Rabelais*) "completely ready-made, consummated, strictly delimited, enclosed, externally displayed, unmixed and individually expressive body"—and to this list Etkind adds, in his own voice, "a body that possesses a sexuality, either one or the other, that is either a subject or an object [but not both], that is either alive or not alive" (245). The new canon that Bakh-

---

[59] Aleksandr Etkind, *Sodom i psikheia: Ocherki intellektual'noi istorii Serebrianogo veka* (Moscow: ITs-Garant, 1996), ch. 4, "Kul'tura protiv prirody: psikhologiia russkogo moderna," 214–70. Further page references given in text. I thank Donald Fanger for alerting me to this intriguing text.

tin resists is defined precisely by the high value it places on a singular
choice among expressive options, on differentiation, on an authoritative
arrangement of parts, on a striving toward permanence—by all that is
traditionally meant by aesthetic form.

How persuasive is Isupov's thesis? Is Etkind a useful supplement to it,
and, overall, how sound is the charge that Bakhtin conflates aesthetic
form and death? As Isupov's somber centennial essay enters the next
round of Russian Bakhtin debates, its debt to Schopenhauer, Fyodorov,
Nikolai Lossky, Wilhelm Reich, and Sigmund Freud will doubtless be
explicated. (Alexandar Mihailovic, in his study of Bakhtin and Russian
Orthodoxy, offered the first non-Russian reading, bringing Isupov's essay
within the orbit of Russian religious imagery. As he noted astutely soon
after its publication: "According to Isupov, the sense in which every event
of reciprocated love is really a manifestation of a *Liebestod* is central to
many Orthodox conceptions of martyrdom and divinity that foreground
kenosis, or the emptying out of the self, a process that after all paradoxically posits the complete purging of consciousness as a prerequisite for
salvation.")[60] Several additional objections might be raised. They will also
serve to summarize the spectrum of opinions we have surveyed on the
topic of Bakhtin and form.

First, Isupov arguably oversimplifies and renders far too inelastic Bakhtin's understanding of "consummation." In some instances it is indeed a
"little death," in others it is the price of artistic form; but most of the
time consummation is no more than an unremarkable habit of our everyday perception. The tone of Bakhtin's own writing on this topic is considerably less melodramatic than Isupov's excerpts suggest. Bakhtin
repeatedly stresses that the ongoing incorporation of formalized and finalized *portions* of others—not the whole mortal crust—is a normal,
completely nonpathological reflex in each of us. Although we do seek to
leave as much trace of ourselves as we can in the souls of others whom
we care about, we are not structured to identify easily or often with *whole*
others, nor they with us. Bakhtin considers such identification unnecessary in any event; along with Anton Chekhov and Vladimir Nabokov, he is
one of very few Russian writers who presume the desire for a genuinely

---

[60] Alexandar Mihailovic, *Corporeal Words*, Introduction, 5–6. Mihailovic notes that Isupov's orientation, while indebted to Russian religious thought, is "very much that of a
Western critic"—at least "to the extent that Isupov views any breach of the individual
identity as a threat to its very existence" (6). Mihailovic notes that on this point Isupov
shares some ground with Western Marxist Bakhtin scholars: "In both instances the reaching
out from one subject to another (and indeed any penetrating of the membrane of individual
autonomy) is perceived as being potentially fatal to the self. . . . [but] the idea that identity
and self are nothing more than rigid templates of social constructedness or expressions of
ethnicity does not interest Bakhtin" (6–7).

private realm. Or as he puts the matter with some eloquence at the beginning of "Author and Hero":

> We are constantly and intently on the watch for reflections of our own life on the plane of other people's consciousness, and moreover not just reflections of particular moments of our life, but even reflections of the whole of it. . . . But all these moments or constituents of our life that we recognize or anticipate through the other . . . do not disrupt the unity of our own life—a life that is directed ahead of itself toward the event-to-come, a life that finds no rest within itself . . . If, however, these reflections do gain body in our life, as sometimes happens, they begin to act as "dead points," as obstructions of any accomplishment, and at times they may condense to the point where they deliver up to us a double of ourselves out of the night of our life. (16)

To satisfy what Isupov sees as Bakhtin's death-driven logic, we must read his texts *against* the spirit of such passages. A more sensible gloss on Thanatos was provided by Bakhtin himself, in his 1944 notes for additions and changes to the Rabelais project. "The arbitrariness, the insignificance of annihilation and death," Bakhtin writes. "There is nothing one can say about it; death is something transitory and in essence creates nothing, there is no basis for its absolutization; by absolutizing it, we turn nonexistence into perverse existence, absence into perverse presence; death is in time and temporal, for we know its actions only in the tiniest segment of time and space."[61]

In these comments we sense again that Stoic intonation of the Hellenistic philosophers who, in my hypothesis, most likely figured among the intellectual role models for Bakhtin. "Of human life duration is an instant, its substance is in flux," Marcus Aurelius wrote in his *Meditations*. Only philosophy could serve as a reliable escort along this route, and the proper philosophy consists in "keeping the daimon within free from outrage and harm, superior to pleasures and pains, doing nothing at random . . . . and in all things awaiting death with a cheerful mind."[62] With full justification, in fact, we might interpret the laughing carnival moment in Bakhtin as the Stoic moment: that philosophical stance required to protect us from outrage, pain, harm, and integrate us into a cosmos where annihilation and death are insignificant. Or as Bakhtin recasts this Stoic

---

[61] Bakhtin, "Dopolneniia i izmeneniia k <Rable,>" *Voprosy filosofii*, no. 1 (1992): 136.

[62] Marcus Aurelius, *Meditations*, 2.17, as cited in R. W. Sharples, *Stoics, Epicureans, and Sceptics: An Introduction to Hellenistic Philosophy* (London: Routledge, 1996), 132. Sharples ends his epilogue with another compatible sentiment, Diogenes's inscription at Oenoanda, where the teachings of Stoicism were preached as an "act of philanthropy": "for we have been set free from the empty fears that held us in their grip, and of pains we have excised the empty ones altogether, and compressed the natural ones into a very small compass" (133).

sentiment in his word-based ontology, "there is nothing to say about it"—and thus it is unworthy of our anxiety.

A second and more serious objection can be raised against Isupov's reading, however, beyond its immoderate tone and infusion of extremes. It will bring us round to one of the unifying themes of this chapter: the sophisticated dynamics of aesthetic love. Is Bakhtin's notion of Eros really so benign, so naive, so alien to possessiveness and decay, that Death—with its more selfish fears and appetites—can devour it completely? As we saw in chapter 3 regarding the much maligned category of dialogue, Bakhtin is not that easily charged with naiveté. Here, too, a strong counterargument can be mounted.

It is certainly true that in his discussions of love, Bakhtin dwells on its positive aspects. "The thirst to be loved, the consciousness of oneself, the seeing of oneself, the forming of oneself in the possible loving consciousness of another, the striving to turn the longed-for love of another into a force that impels and organizes my life": this is the primary energy that fuels "the anticipated image of myself" in my own mind and thus permits personal growth ("A&H," in *A&A*, 157). Bakhtin's temperament was always drawn to the *creating* aspects of the world, and (as we saw above) even about something as potentially interesting as death he had "nothing to say" because it is too accidental, not sufficiently productive of new value, not malleable enough by conscious means. The mortality of form—at least architectonic form—is a natural and unfrightening fact, since form is for him an outgrowth of personality and thus a precious, fragile, transitory gift.[63] But for all the exclusively positive sheen the

---

[63] Here an intriguing contrast can be drawn between Bakhtin and his elder brother in emigration, Nikolai. In 1928 four philosophical fragments by Nicolas Bakhtin were published in the Russian-language journal *Zveno* in Paris; these included ruminations on the physical senses—especially the most precious and underappreciated, the sense of touch; on the human body; and on the doomedness of form. The elder Bakhtin considered the impulse toward form to be fragile, "always tragic," locked in an unequal struggle with chaos, inevitably "more transitory than the material that was shaped by it," and, to the extent that it succeeded in walling off individuality from chaos and the Absolute, "the purest rejection of eternity." Judging by these fragments, which are devoted to the transient nature of form and the centrality of touching sensations and the body, Nikolai was of a more melancholic, less original turn of mind than his younger brother. Yet the parameters of their thought are remarkably compatible. Consider this *Zveno* segment on "The Wisdom of Touch": "The so-called 'higher senses' (vision and hearing), which we have developed in ourselves to the detriment of the 'lower,' are characterized above all by the fact that they permit, that they even require a certain distancing from the perceived object. Being isolated, severed, lying outside [*vnepolozhnost'*]—these are indications of what defines our place in the world and those feelings that have come to rule us. Between us and the world there is a flat and transparent chilliness. And unless we are under the power of hunger or of love, we do not want and are not able to touch, to grope for, to seize; we prefer to contemplate things passively. And things literally retreat from us, they become alien, ghostly. The world has lost

youthful Bakhtin casts over the services that "lovingly attentive form" performs for our psyche, it is important to separate this *illustration* of the dynamic of form from its essence.

Dialogue and aesthetic love are connected in Bakhtin's thought—but not, it could be argued, because we are necessarily made happier or more secure by their interconnection. Bakhtin was simply of the opinion that life's energy, its drive toward ever more precise articulation and differentiation, can be released solely in this way. Contra Isupov, this energy need not be understood as a drive toward death—nor, for that matter, toward pleasure or kindness. Bakhtin most certainly would have seen it as a drive toward knowledge. And as such, love (like the forward-striving dialogue that is its vehicle or like Oedipus recalling his encounter with the Sphinx) can be a manifest torment. In Bakhtin's philosophy, love's longing is almost wholly devoid of sentiment or sentimentality (and of lust there is not a trace); its pressure is expressed largely in cognitive terms.

Bakhtin never developed his thoughts on "loving form" into a coherent whole. Within the world's rich literature on philosophies of love, his ideas are not strikingly original. But there is a dignity and chasteness to his scattered comments on the topic that recommend them to our attention in connection with his theory of art. Recall how Bakhtin defines love (or rather, its absence): "Lovelessness, indifference, will never be able to generate sufficient power to slow down and *linger intently* over an object, to hold and sculpt every detail and particular in it." For this reason, "only love is capable of being aesthetically productive" (*TPA*, 64). Put another way, we will see in detail only those things we are driven to revisit. We return repeatedly to the site of love because it seems we have not yet quite gotten it right, that a little more "lingering"—Juliet to her Romeo on the balcony that first night—would permit us to grasp and retain the form, answer the nagging question, resolve the paradox. Consider how real love works. One of the reasons, surely, that love (toward an idea, an image, a person) is so innerly agonizing to its participants and so tediously irritating to watch from the outside is that no single piece of input between lovers is ever enough; new edges and complications are revealed in every new gesture, this fresh edge calls forth a supplementary adjustment or intonation, and each of these tiny variations is infinitely interesting to the partners, whereas those not implicated in the exchange are stupefied by its repetitive, non-information-bearing quality. To the

---

its sweet enfleshedness. 'Disinterested, pure, unwilled perception' has long been our official dogma in art and our natural inclination in life. Our wisdom has also become cold, perceptual. And we are proud of this" (122). See N. Bakhtin, "Chetyre fragmenta" (publikatsiia O. E. Osovskogo), *MMB i fil kul XX, 2 (91)*, 122–30; first published in *Zveno*, no. 3 (Paris, 1928): 133–38.

brute and uninvolved eye, love's "content" goes nowhere; but through this obsessive interest in sculpting the particulars, love itself is continually refreshed and refined in time. Such is its pure dialogic impulse—measured not by the moral worthiness of its plot nor even by the pleasure it brings, but by the plentifulness of its energy and its ability to slow down and sculpt. As Bakhtin shrewdly noted, to linger in this way takes strength and force of character.

Such an understanding of love and aesthetic form need not be naive or benevolent at all. It can easily be experienced as distracting, exhausting, insatiable. But it is always accretive, and it is driven to produce ever more fastidiously modified forms. It *must* be kinetic. So when Isupov, in an attempt to darken what strikes him as Bakhtin's overly innocent and translucent formulations, links the dialogic model of self-other relations with reciprocal sacrifice, with the emptying out of content, and ultimately with the undifferentiated inertia of death, his vision is at best a partial one.

Let us now consider the fate of outsideness and the ethical dimension of art through their permutations in this chapter—and in relation to part 2 of this study as a whole. The concepts of dialogue and carnival were well established in the canon (in fact they had been already well whipped in the backlash) before Bakhtin's early ideas on aesthetics became available. Over the past ten years a major task of Russian scholars, and increasingly of non-Russian scholars as well, has been to reconstruct the appropriate sequence of these value-concepts—architectonics, dialogue, carnival—in Bakhtin's developing thought. In the process, certain paradoxes have been clarified. Consummation is not finalization. Openness is fully compatible with a drive toward wholeness. The I-Thou relation is most interesting to Bakhtin as a formal dynamic designed to take place between two living people or within the aesthetic object (not between a human being and an Absolute), and he understands it as a process with no priorly fixed parts. Kantian "disinterestedness" in art would cause us to fall asleep on the job; art must have commerce with a person's soul [*dusha*], which cannot be created or uncovered by a Formalist device. And whereas wholeness might be a by-product of death, it does not depend on death to bring it about.

All these paradoxes have their origin in Bakhtin's subtle and problematic contemplation of aesthetic form. The authors of our final two centennial essays each chose to approach the problem genetically, beginning with "Toward a Philosophy of the Act" and ending with *Rabelais*; each was at pains to construct an integrated logic out of Bakhtin's successive phases and, at times, follies. Both conclude that the intellectual trajectory is bold, exciting, internally coherent, but that Bakhtin falls short of a comprehensive vision. All the same, Bonetskaia applauds his attempt, which she sees as a rebirth of that heroic Romantic impulse to define form so broadly that all of life's fullness can be encompassed by it. Isupov, at the other extreme, considers Bakhtin's aesthetics—and the increasingly vacated, immobilized forms it generates—to be a poorly disguised poetics of death. Neither investigates in detail what might well emerge as the focal point of future research into Bakhtin's philosophy: its absolute fearlessness as regards our mortality, its moral efficiency, and its unsentimental rendering of the tasks of love. For although it is true Bakhtin pays scant attention to the Grand Inquisitor's view of the world—a world responding solely to miracle, mystery, and authority—this neglect does not misread Dostoevsky. Bakhtin's entire ethics is permeated by the Elder Zosima's dictum of "active love": It is "labor and perseverance," an "entire science," and "a harsh and fearful thing compared with love in dreams."[64]

---

[64] Fyodor Dostoevsky, *The Brothers Karamazov*, trans. Richard Pevear and Larissa Volokhonsky (New York: Vintage, 1990), 58.

One Year Later: The Prospects for Bakhtin's инонаука [*inonauka*], or "Science in Some Other Way"

IN HIS final, unfinished essay, "On a Methodology for the Humanities," Bakhtin made a passing observation that touches a delicate chord in professionals who teach and write in those continually crisis-ridden disciplines. "The author, when creating his work, does not intend it for a literary scholar and does not presuppose a specific scholarly *understanding*," Bakhtin remarked; "he does not aim to create a collective of literary scholars. He does not invite literary scholars to his banquet table."[1] As the present study has demonstrated, Bakhtin's position on this matter is highly controversial. What justifies the special language and status claimed by experts in the *human* sciences? Who benefits from their services? When successful, whose truth or skills do they transmit? For teaching a novel or poem is not like teaching a foreign language or a theorem. Most primary creators would consider their works of art successful to the extent that intermediaries who "teach" or "research" them are not needed at all. Dostoevsky and Robert Frost wrote for ordinary questing human beings—not for a trained audience (in the way that mathematicians write for other mathematicians); what is more, artists and authors are jealous of that unmediated contact and consider it their due. But does that mean there is no banquet table at which the literary scholar is genuinely welcome? We return now, in this afterword, to questions raised at the end of the introduction to this study, and also to the juxtaposition of *explanation* and *understanding* that has structured so much of the debate over Bakhtin's legacy.

We might begin with the whimsical comment by Sergei Averintsev that serves as our epigram: Bakhtin should be enrolled not among the intellectuals but among the poets. Is Bakhtin himself best read as a sort of "poet"—or does he offer Russians and non-Russians alike a serious, professional alternative route to traditional academic scholarship on cultural texts, what in Bakhtin's homeland is called *filologiia* [philology]? Good astrophysics is international, so astrophysicists can compete with one another, move from lab to lab, be ranked for their scientific results. But do

---

[1] Bakhtin, "Toward a Methodology for the Human Sciences" (1974), *SpG*, 165.

national cultures so differ in the roles they consider legitimate for cultural criticism that any comparison among them is illusory?

Part of the problem is in the nature of the material. *Literaturovedenie*, the scholarly study of literature, is not a progressive science as is, say, physics or biology. In those latter fields Aristotle is a towering presence in the *history* of science, but he is not (as he is for the serious literary scholar) still an urgent, primary, untranscended source. But literary study, while not progressive, is also not wholly at the mercy of caprice, of change for the sake of change—as is, for example, the concept of "fashion" in clothing design, where change from one season to the next is unrelated to climate, comfort, attractiveness, or the shape and mobility of real bodies. Research into literary texts falls somewhere in between these two poles: it is accretive but not progressive, and its methodology is "falsifiable," although not in the manner of a scientific hypothesis. Most of us who profess in the humanities would agree that our research is "scientific" to the extent that it is innerly consistent, is aware of its method, communicates its findings in terms or categories that make some intuitive sense, and—excepting wildly deconstructionist practice—is compatible with the whole of a primary text and committed to the survival of that text, whether in or outside the canon. As we have seen, measured against this standard, Bakhtin's dialogic theory and criticism has seemed to many scholars in the humanities close to the outer limits of professionalism.

Four years after Bakhtin's death the Soviet journal *Literaturnoe obozrenie* raised these issues obliquely in a serialized forum on "The Tasks of Philology."[2] Among the scholars who participated are several who have played a prominent role in the present study, on various sides of the Bakhtin debates: Mikhail Gasparov, Yuri Lotman, Mikhail Girshman, Vadim Kozhinov. Each recommended a different interaction of aesthetics with ethics and proposed a different psychology for the legitimately researching mind. Bakhtin's "human science" has proved vulnerable at precisely the nodes examined in this forum; the most stimulating work now being done by the new generation of Bakhtin scholars addresses just these problematic areas.

Predictably, the most unsympathetic to a Bakhtinian worldview is Gasparov, whose contribution "Philology as Morality" (the title alone speaks volumes) closes down the forum. His position, in all its stubborn purity, is by now a familiar refrain. Philology arose as a method for deciphering ancient texts. Although applied to increasingly recent eras, philological

---

[2] Selections are taken from entries in "Zadachi filologii" [The tasks of philology], from the following three issues of *Literaturnoe obozrenie*: no. 3 (1979): 45–50 (for Kozhinov and Lotman); no. 4 (1979): 26–28 (for Girshman); and no. 10 (1979): 26–27 (for Gasparov). References in the text are made to the journal issue number for the year 1979, followed by the page number.

science nevertheless must always value *distance*. It must, Gasparov argues, because "human thinking is egocentric; in the people of other epochs we easily see what is similar to ourselves and often do not notice what is dissimilar." If not trained to do otherwise, we tend to collapse everything into our own experience and call the core of that experience "eternal." Philological training is moral because it instructs us that "there are no eternal values, only temporary ones" (no. 10: 26): "Philology is difficult not because it requires that we study alien systems of values, but because it commands us to put aside for a time our own system of values. To read all the books that Pushkin read or could have read is difficult, but possible; to forget (even for a while) all the books that Pushkin did not read but that we have read is immeasurably harder. . . . When we take into our hands one of the classics, we avoid asking ourselves the simplest question: for whom was it written? Because we know the simplest answer: not for us" (26–27).

Gasparov believes in the closed communication loop, associating it with privacy, personal dignity, the rights of authors to their own time and place. In a fastidious reaction against excessive reader-response criticism, he sympathizes with people "who feel uncomfortable reading, or even looking at, the published letters of Pushkin, Chekhov, or Mayakovsky, 'because they were not, after all, addressed to me'" (27). He even recommends that "this same sense of moral awkwardness, of one's own inappropriate obtrusiveness, be present in a philologist when he opens *Eugene Onegin*, *The Cherry Orchard*, or "A Cloud in Trousers"; one redeems this obtrusiveness only by renouncing one's own self and dissolving oneself in one's lofty interlocutor" (27). And thus, although the opening entry in the forum was entitled "Trust toward the Word" (*Doverie k slovu*), Gasparov would prefer "that philology begin not with trust but with distrust toward the word":

> We trust only the words of our own individual language, whereas the words of an alien language we first and foremost experience as if they corresponded precisely to our own. . . . Yuri Lotman, in his contribution to this discussion, said that philology is moral to the extent that it teaches us not to be seduced by easy paths of thought. I would supplement that. What is moral in philology is not only its path but its goal: it trains a person away from spiritual egocentrism. (It is probably the case that all forms of art teach a person how to be self-affirming and all sciences teach us how not to put on airs or be carried away.) (27)

Thus does Gasparov—joining E. D. Hirsch and other American critics who have argued for a distinction between "objective interpretation" and mere criticism—confine scholarly "dialogue" to acts of reclamation and serving the text to an unqualified reverence before it. To Bakhtin's remark about literary scholars not being invited to a poets' banquet, Gasparov would answer that academics should not pretend to be poets. They have no place feasting alongside primary authors and their untutored, spontaneous primary readers. Professional philology is a humbling and abstemious pursuit whose joys are other.

Before parting company with Gasparov, who has played such an important watchdog's role in the present study, it might be helpful to consolidate his reservations in a final analogy. One of the commentators on the Moscow centennial pointed out that of the 103 papers delivered at the conference, the vast majority "could be grouped, however strange it seems, under three rubrics organized in roughly the same way: 'Bakhtin and philosopher so-and-so,' 'Bakhtin and writer so-and-so,' 'Bakhtin and the problem of . . . ' "[3] This is true: for literary professionals and comparativists, binary juxtaposition (however it risks reducing both parties) is an exceedingly attractive approach to a complex biographical subject. But not all entities can be juxtaposed. Among the parlor games we play in this realm, therefore, it might be instructive to consider those "Bakhtin and x" themes that, for all the goodwill in the world, would never get off the ground. One such topic is "Bakhtin and competitive sports."

Why is this such a non-starter, a non-topic? Not because Bakhtin was missing one leg and moved around with a crutch. Rather, as Gasparov would grasp intuitively, it is because "competition" under pressure, the reality of winning and losing within a fixed time frame filled with precise moves or performances that cannot be rescinded, is alien to a primary commitment to dialogue as Bakhtin understood it. We should not be misled by his fondness for metaphors of "struggle." Bakhtinian struggle knows no stopwatch, fouls, or final innings. It is open-ended and unarmed, one big unwinnable, unlosable war of words. "Living in dialogue" encourages its participants, above all, to cultivate individually crafted horizons, standards of behavior, personal potentials—so that no matter what might happen to us in a given encounter, some response can be forthcoming that is still marked with one's own dignity of personality. Responsive aesthetics and aesthetic love rush to the site of a disappointment and assure the sufferer that a context can be found that will explain and justify the outcome (such, indeed, is the meaning of Bakhtin's "great time"). The same dynamic underlies Bakhtin's unsettling notion, jotted down near the end of his life, that even a word known to be false is not absolutely false, for it "always presupposes an instance that will understand and justify it, even if in the form: 'anyone *in my position* would

---

[3] V. V. Zdol'nikov (Vitebsk), "Bol'she sud'by i vysshe veka svoego . . . (vpechatleniia ot Mezhdunarodnoi konferentsii v Moskve)," in *DKKh, no. 3 (95)*: 140–52, esp.143.

have lied, too.'"[4] If, in short, serious game playing requires a single set of rules then Bakhtin would prefer not to play, because for him every act has its own place and gives rise to a new act that can dispute that place. As we read in Bakhtin's notes for revising the Dostoevsky book, not even catastrophe is allowed to finalize, resolve, or trigger a catharsis.[5] We do not win or lose; we renegotiate.

And Gasparov would say, as regards philological scholarship but perhaps regarding our everyday lives as well, that it is bad spiritual training to believe that you cannot lose. People who compete—that is, who agree to play with a single, conventionally acknowledged set of rules that produces one winner—are likely to be good losers. They must learn to be or they could not continue to be players, and because they want to win and are not too embarrassed (or too proud) to enter competitions, they know how to respond to losing. To be sure, not all victories and defeats are lone affairs. In its best-played moments, a team sport manifests a complementarity between communal and individual impulses that can approximate idealized dialogue. But because the ends are fixed, there will be a winner. The losers of the game are sad not to have measured up, but the best of them are not angry, nostalgic, or stubbornly bent on reinterpreting the terms. They spend that energy on perfecting their skills. In addition to being good practical losers, then, successful competitive game players also tend to become efficient learners.

The paradox that emerges here surely must be among the most intriguing in dialogism's arsenal. It is possible to become more rigid, vain, unforgiving, proud, closed down to new information and—most damaging of all—noncooperative with the world when we persist in believing that this world is forever open to negotiation. It blunts our sense of form. We do not know when to stop, when to acknowledge limited benefits and losses, and thus when to begin reconciling ourselves to them (the loss of an idea, a person, a match, a tournament). Agree to accept rules, codes, norms, fixed results, and one is better prepared for the next encounter, where again we will come up against operating procedures not of our own making and accidents of performance not for us to shape. We will be disappointed not to win these competitive encounters as well, but—and here is the payoff—disappointment, too, remains "within the rules." One has lost *only that one thing*, not the entire, fatally integrated

---

[4] Bakhtin, "The Problem of the Text," in *SpG*, 127.

[5] "The problem of catastrophe. Catastrophe is not finalization. It is the culmination, in collision and struggle, of points of view . . . Catastrophe does not give these points of view resolution, but on the contrary reveals their incapability of resolution under earthly conditions . . . By its very essence it is denied even elements of catharsis" ("Toward a Reworking of the Dostoevsky Book," *PDP*, 298).

mind or body. The psyche of a person on the losing side might be sadder, but it is arguably freer, stronger, and more humble than the dialogically embedded one. It moves on with more grace. Good game players—people who are competitive rather than dialogic by nature—sense the logic and virtue of this economy. The psychological self-discipline produced by such training is also more professional, which would be Gasparov's immediate point. Strength and humility, that is, solid training combined with a willingness to serve on someone else's terms, are, in his view, the marks of a philologist.

In his entry for the "Tasks of Philology" forum, a short piece entitled "That Difficult Text . . . ," Yuri Lotman does indeed advise philologists to "avoid the easy way," as Gasparov properly recalled (no. 3: 47). But Lotman is less flinty than Gasparov on this question of permissible scholarly dialogue and more willing to grant the critic some independence of thought and creative method. This method need not be considered wholly self-serving or reductive. (Significantly, in an appreciative 1996 tribute to Lotman, Gasparov commends that great semiotician for the sort of quantitative precision—the human being as a "phoneme, composed of differential signs" and "intersecting cultural codes"—that had long ceased to be definitive for Lotman's mature thought on the nature of personality.[6]) Lotman asks if philology has the right to claim scientific integrity along the lines of mathematics, physics, or biology—and affirms that it does. "The ancient task of philology is explanation, the deciphering of a text, the revelation of its meaning," he writes. This is a task "burdened with the most significant difficulties"—but these difficulties are resolvable, or at least fully approachable, by researchers of honest intent and sound training. This is the case because coming to know a text or a personality is not to know only one thing; every culturally valuable text is a "multilayered system in which an understanding of one layer does not guarantee penetration into the meaning of the others." Successes as well as errors are local, falsifiable, rectifiable as the functions and genre of each text are painstakingly reconstructed. To devise ever more sophisticated means of deciphering these systems is the philologist's task, and—although today's researcher is inevitably an outsider, both "alien" and "later" to the material at hand—trustworthy decoding is possible and provisional hypotheses can be coordinated and cross-checked. Stratification is not by its very nature mortifying. Thus the project of devising and applying, from the far end, one's own deciphering mechanisms is not in itself a fraudulent activity or an abuse of dialogue; it is unavoidably part of any reclamation project. In the depth and breadth of its reclama-

[6] M. L. Gasparov, "Lotman i marksizm," *Novoe literaturnoe obozrenie*, no. 19 (1996): 7–13, esp. 12.

tions, Lotman numbers the Russian philological tradition among the most responsible, thorough, and patient in the world.

Lotman is concerned, however, that the standards of training in Soviet educational institutions have become lax. Especially unwelcome, he remarks, is recent evidence pointing toward an alleviated or "relieved" philology, which produces "academic work often not devoid of acute observations and often interesting, but always subjective and purely 'a matter of taste,' a 'reading into' the text without relying on any linguistic, historical, or cultural erudition, posing as scholarly analysis" (48). We sense in these lines the apprehension Lotman felt when Bakhtin's concept of carnival laughter was applied—even by an academician of Dmitri Likhachev's irreproachable standing—to the worldview of medieval Russia, infinitely alien to Rabelais's France. The "stratification" method is saved from oversimplifying the world only by its filigree of complex intersecting strands, and by the enormous caution exercised by the philologist. For Lotman, any lightening of this task is dangerous, because "easy paths are not only false, they are immoral." Thus he shares Gasparov's anxieties about, if not his strictures against, scholars who employ an overly active creative imagination.

At the other end of the spectrum from Gasparov is Vadim Kozhinov, founding Bakhtinian. His contribution to the forum, "The Word and the Art of the Word," opens by examining the inevitable *drama* in every utterance. What makes the criticism of literature so confoundingly attractive and so difficult, he suggests, is that "the literary scholar, before beginning to investigate an artistic phenomenon, cannot fail to have been 'an object of the unmediated action' of art," that is, once under its spell and sway (no. 3: 46). How is one to remember that "primary" feel and at the same time gain the distance to research it responsibly? As Bakhtin had demonstrated a half-century ago, the "material aesthetics" of the Formalists will not suffice as a guide—although, Kozhinov adds, "it is sad to see how this hopelessly outdated approach to the study of the art of the word continues even today to define the work of many literary scholars." Philologists should investigate not only the word (in a Formalist spirit) but the *art of the word*, which involves acts of understanding as well as acts of explication. Formalist approaches can always confirm technique (although they risk confirming the researcher's technique rather than that of the primary artist); such approaches are helpless, however, to define the feel of a style. In Bakhtin's spirit, Kozhinov urges literary professionals to study the artistic *forms* of the word. He must presume, of course, that such study will be undertaken with all the modesty, erudition, and self-discipline that Gasparov and Lotman fear is in decay.

Our final exemplary entry from this forum, by Mikhail Girshman, is an attempt to achieve a Bakhtinian synthesis among these warring extremes.

It succeeds, I believe, largely because Girshman—who entitled his essay "The Foundation of Understanding"—locates himself on the boundary between an "understanding" that links or personalizes events and an "explication" that dissociates or depersonalizes them. As we saw in the preceding chapter, Girshman, fifteen years later at the Bakhtin centennial, would argue that the I-Thou relation in Bakhtin differs from Buber's formulation in its insistence on a separateness right up to (and including) the boundary between two speaking voices; also, he contended, in contrast to Buber, Bakhtin believed that the most exciting quarrels and dialogues take place not among competing interpreters or even among real-world readers but within the artwork itself, between authors and their fictional heroes. Thus the dialogue that matters is already self-contained, structured into the text, *philological*—even in the strict definition of that term. Although Girshman does not commit himself to this extent, he intimates that other lesser quarrels—ones that take place between you and me, or the ones going on in the forum where his comments appear—can be ignored (as Bakhtin indeed magisterially ignored them).

Girshman takes it as a given that "philology teaches understanding" (no. 4: 26). But who understands whom and from whose point of view? How are we to explain that the classic images of Hamlet and Oedipus speak to so many different cultures over so many generations? Anticipating Gasparov's objections and invoking an ancient defense of poetry, Girshman acknowledges that "the artist, to be sure, could not foresee all our questions and all the particularities of our perception. But certain fundamental particulars he not only foresaw but fixed in place in the wholeness of the artwork, in a special *artistic* positing of questions" that allows human problems to be at once both historically concrete and universal. Again, Girshman intimates that it is not human beings and their real-life worlds that make this miracle possible—and thus a real-life forum of scholars, such as this one in *Literaturnoe obozrenie*, will never resolve the questions it poses and may never even get a full-scale dialogue off the ground. But such inexplicable dialogues will occur, and repeatedly, inside art. This phenomenon is art's defining feature. If each new reader of *Hamlet* can claim to be, after a fashion, its new author, then such a claim is true "only to the extent that this new reader has found not only and not so much himself in Shakespeare as he has found Shakespeare in himself. In any case, it is only on the boundaries between these two human contents, at the points where they meet, intersect, and reveal a deep kinship, that the genuine life of the literary work takes place . . . Philology, maximally facilitating this encounter, helps to realize in practice this penetrability of the human personality" (27).

Girshman's insights provide "foundations for understanding"—but are they sufficient guidelines for *nauka*, for scholarship? Among those most sensitive to Bakhtin's embattled "scientific" status has been Sergei Averintsev, to whom Bakhtin himself referred in a rare, self-reflexive moment. In his "On a Methodology for the Humanities," making the case for contextual meanings against mere formal definitions, Bakhtin cited in his own defense the following quotation, which he identified as Averintsev's: "We must recognize that symbology is not an unscientific [*nenauchnaia*] but a *differently scientific* [*inonauchnaia*] form of knowledge, one that has its own internal laws and criteria for precision" (160). Bakhtin had come across the passage, it turns out, in Averintsev's entry on the "artistic symbol" in volume 6 of the Soviet *Short Literary Encyclopedia* (1972). That exceptionally informative little essay on symbology is also a thoughtful inquiry into the extent and degree of precision possible—and desirable—in the humanities.[7]

Averintsev's discussion everywhere recalls categories precious to Bakhtin. What, he asks, is the difference between a symbol and a sign [*znak*]? (Averintsev suggests, to the possible distress of the semioticians, that polysemy is a hindrance to the sign—overloading its circuits, as it were, making it difficult to load and unload—but a blessing to the symbol, which lives best when it is maximally full [826].) The meaning of a symbol, we read, "is not given, but posited"; thus "its sense cannot be 'explicated' or reduced to a monosemantic logical formula. It can only be 'clarified' and correlated with subsequent symbolic linkages" (827). Can a symbol be assimilated to the exact sciences? At this point Averintsev develops his distinctions between *nauka, anti-nauka, nenauka,* and *inonauka* [science, anti-science, nonscience, and "science in some other way"]. The symbol is most definitely knowledge but a dialogic form of it. "Its sense can be realized only within human acts of communion, within human dialogue"; that is, *how* each of us understands a symbol is itself an act of self-analysis. "Whereas things allow us to do no more than look at them, a symbol 'looks' back at us as well" (828).

Averintsev is by no means blind to the dangers that confront students of symbology. These include false and vague interpretation, a premature enclosure of meaning, subjective judgment, inadequate scholarly modesty, esoteric and unverifiable procedures. They are, of course, the dangers and torments of dialogue itself. But although the symbol itself is ancient, Averintsev reminds us, symbology is a young science. What seems like mystery today will eventually find its appropriate methodology.

No wonder this routine encyclopedia entry caught Bakhtin's attention, for in it Averintsev defends *avant la lettre* Bakhtin's own notion of *ino-*

---

[7] S. S. Averintsev, "SIMVOL khudozhestvennyi," entry in *Kratkaia literaturnaia entsiklopediia*, vol. 6 (Moscow, 1972), 826–31. Further column references are included in text.

nauka, that relative newcomer on the philological scene. We recall Averintsev's 1988 retrospective essay on Bakhtin's body of work: "His works are not a depository of ready scholarly results that can be mechanically 'applied,' but something other [*inoe*] and greater: a source of mental energy" (256).

As of 1996, what might be said of the potential directions for this "mental energy," the product of Bakhtin's "science in some other way"? It is interesting—and a little sad—that Averintsev, who by mid-decade had relocated to Vienna, remarked (according to Vitaly Makhlin) that "the time had come to fall silent for a while about Mikhail Bakhtin." His gentler temperament was unsuited to the turf wars of the Bakhtin industry, which showed no signs of calming down or slacking off. Judging by material in press, as well as by projects circulating but not yet published, where is Bakhtinistics headed? I speculate that a Bakhtin for the twenty-first century is likely to have an impact on three fields of inquiry.

The first, fueled by the Vygotsky centennial in 1995 and an accompanying surge of interest in developmental psychology, is the practice and theory of pedagogy. In the Russian lands the academic discipline of pedagogy (and the related field of children's literature) has traditionally enjoyed high intellectual status—much higher than in the West, where "teachers' colleges" are granted second-class intellectual credentials and raising children is considered more a matter of loving nurture than of scientific inquiry. In the 1980s the eminent philosopher of consciousness Vladimir Bibler, author of *Mikhail Mikhailovich Bakhtin or the Poetics of Culture* (1991), devised a curriculum for primary and middle-school students based on the principle of a "dialogue of cultures."[8] Intended to fill the methodological void following the collapse of communist pedagogical controls, this course of study would expose young children to successive incompatible worlds—in time and across geographical space—and encourage them not to resolve these worlds nor replace one by the other. For, as Bibler remarked, culture is not progressive; it is best understood as a drama in non-Euclidian space, as a "tragedy of tragedies, when the variegated global surfaces of dramatic action and catharsis are sharply angled one into the other (like in a Chinese dice puzzle or brainteaser)."[9] Only by teaching in this way, he claims, will the old ideal of an "educated

---

[8] As with many of his generation in the post-perestroika period, Bibler is enthusiastic about the philosophical anthropology of the youthful Marx and its pedagogical implications; see Vladimir Bibler, *Samostoianie cheloveka* [The coming-to-individuality of the human being] (Kemerovo: ALEF, 1993). For a summary of Bibler's project, see I. E. Berliand, "Shkola dialoga kul'tur," in *DKKh, nos. 2–3 (93):* 201–5.

[9] V. S. Bibler, "Kul'tura. Dialog kul'tur (opyt opredeleniia)," *Voprosy filosofii*, no. 6 (1989): 31–42, esp. 34, 36.

person" (one who lives merely by the latest scientific truth) be replaced by the far more desirable and flexible ideal of a "person of culture." People of culture are more than mere scholars or activists; they must be able to hold in focus, but at the same time hold in suspension, many incompatible and unresolvable truth principles.

On the ruins of the centralized Soviet curriculum, Bibler's tolerant and vaguely pluralistic message, as well as other experiments undertaken in Bakhtin's name, have temporarily inspired new pedagogical models. But teachers must be retrained before students can be set free, and Russian schoolteachers have proved as reluctant as any guild to abandon their expertise during a chaotic time. Of special interest in this project are the mass of Saransk-era "certification" documents now emerging from the local archives—curricula, class notes, lesson plans, oral legends—that attest to Bakhtin's professional concern, even during the politically most harassed years, for a renewed "culture of the teacher," not only of the student.[10] Several papers at the October 1995 Saransk readings were devoted to such topics as "dialogism in pedagogical culture" and "dialogue in the professional coming-to-maturity of a teacher's personality."[11] More ambitious plans for "the teacher in dialogue with culture" were outlined at the Krasnoyarsk Bakhtin centennial lectures, sponsored by the city's libraries. Rejecting the notion of (uppercase) Culture as an accumulation of static, preshaped content, one author urged teachers to transmit information to their students solely as a form of dynamic energy: not the "what" or even the "how" of a cultural event but predominantly the *why*. Why do some events cohere, "come together" into conceptual wholes and remain in cultural memory, whereas others do not?[12]

Should such "dialogic" curricula genuinely catch on by the new millenium, we can be certain they will be subject to the same criticisms—and give rise to the same anxieties—that we saw so amply reflected in the

[10] See, for example, Bakhtin's notes on teaching Russian-language stylistics to high school pupils in Savelevo and Kimry during the war years (1942–45), in *MMB: ss 5 (96)*, 141–56.

[11] See, for example, E. G. Osovskii (Saransk), "Dialogizm M. M. Bakhtina i pedagogicheskaia kul'tura uchitelia," and L. I. Oreshkina (Saransk), "Dialog v professional'nom stanovlenii lichnosti uchitelia," in *MMB i gum mysh I (95)*, 183–85, 181–83. In the latter précis Bakhtin is quoted as an advocate for slowing down: books, even textbooks, are difficult; never count on a rapid run-through; every text must be examined not only for content but also for its inherent methodology; what must be taught is the "logic of the given science" (182).

[12] See the précis by S. V. Ermakov, "Uchitel' v dialoge s kul'turoi," in *Proceedings for the Krasnoyarsk Museum Biennale in Honor of the Bakhtin Centennial*, "M. M. Bakhtin i sovremennye gumanitarnye praktiki," ed. A. G. Glinskaia (Krasnoyarsk, 1995), 80–82. At this juncture, of course, the mature work of Yuri Lotman is of enormous interest in connection with Bakhtin and Vygotsky (and perhaps a valuable "philological" corrective as well).

1979 forum on the tasks of philology. For skeptics will insist there is content in every culture, and in every humanities curriculum, that must be passed *down*, not across, and passed down intact, not debated or bartered. Does an unranked, accretive coexistence of values in each citizen's heart or mind necessarily promote civic virtue? Bibler's graduates, by temperament philosopher-kings, might be splendid creators and consumers of universal culture. But will they also be able to hold political office, draft legislation, further a just cause with stubborn conviction, negotiate what seems like an impossible difference, mold a consensus under noncrisis conditions?

Over the past decade the image of Bakhtin as pragmatist and Russian-style theorist of liberalism has won some distinguished converts among anti-foundationalist thinkers outside Russia. (In the American press, juxtapositions have been made between Bakhtin and George Herbert Mead, Richard Rorty, and John Rawls.) Some of this comparative work has begun to appear in translation in the Russian journals and will enter domestic academic debates alongside the revival of their own native liberal tradition.[13] It is too early to say whether a gradualist route to human rights can enter the Russian body politic "merely for the teaching of it"—or how quickly such a pedagogy can supplement Russia's one thousand years of largely authoritarian, maximalist, collectivist practice.

Now that heroic efforts to place "Bakhtin as a philosopher" have estab-

---

[13] See, for example, Don H. Bialostosky, "Dialogic, Pragmatic, and Hermeneutic Conversation: Bakhtin, Rorty, and Gadamer," in *Critical Studies* 1, no. 2 (1989): 107–19; translated by A. K. Vasiliev as "Razgovor: dialogika, pragmatika i germenevtika. Bakhtin, Rorti i Gadamer," in *Filosofskie nauki*, no. 1 (1995): 206–19. For a wide-ranging discussion of Bakhtin/Voloshinov, Vygotsky, Lotman, and (on the Western side) Marvin Minsky, Charles Sanders Peirce, and George Herbert Mead, see Francesco Loriggio, "Mind as Dialogue: The Bakhtin Circle and Pragmatist Psychology," in *Critical Studies* 2, no. 1/2 (1990): 91–110. Of special interest in Loriggio's discussion is the speculation that Mead would have found more in common with the mature Lotman than with any phase of Bakhtin's work (105); Bialostosky, for his part, properly aligns Bakhtin with Rorty's "edifying" philosophers (although not necessarily with their dread of institutionalization), noting that the practical outcome of a conversation—or for that matter even a reality check on it—is a secondary concern in both models. In a passage that could well serve as a motto in one of Bibler's new schools, Bialostosky writes: "Dialogics seeks neither agreement nor transcendence of differences but rather articulation of differences. Dialogics also finds in Rorty's image of epistemology a resemblance to its practice of characterizing others in its own terms, even if it does not claim that such characterizations can say what the other is *really doing*. . . . There is no dialogic guarantee that improved understanding of the other's ideas will leave us at ease with them or less estranged from their advocate. One does not feel at ease with a Raskolnikov or a Stavrogin once one gets to know him" (109). For a probing recent survey, see Carol Adlam, "In the Name of Bakhtin: Appropriation and Expropriation in Recent Russian and Western Bakhtin Studies," in Alistair Renfrew, ed., *Exploiting Bakhtin*, Strathclyde Modern Language Studies, New Series, no. 2 (1997): 75–90.

lished the basic contexts for his thought, a second influx of energy, I predict, will be registered in a return to literature. But the new work in this area will not resemble the old practice of the 1970s or 1980s: those endless, at times mindless applications of Bakhtinian catchwords (dialogue, chronotope, carnivalization, voice zone, the grotesque) to individual works that otherwise remain very much stuck in their prior grooves. Some scholars have begun to reconsider ignored seams between the Bakhtin school and its purported ideological foes (the Formalists, Hegelians, Symbolists). Magisterial textological work has been done on the Bakhtin archive in preparation for the *Collected Works*; a mass of minor, previously unknown material from Bakhtin's pen (that is, pencil) is expected to surface. Although nothing is likely to alter radically our image of Bakhtin, its reception will differ from the primary bulk of Bakhtin's writing in that we will now know, when it appears, where it belongs and what it modifies.

This filling in has already begun. The publication, in 1993, of Bakhtin's 1944 "Additions and Changes to *Rabelais*," with its lengthy commentary on several Shakespeare plays as well as its refinement of certain issues crudely handled in the published dissertation, promises a broader relevance of Bakhtin's thought to Renaissance studies. The *Bildungsroman* project, famously sacrificed for cigarette paper during the war years, has been almost entirely reconstituted in penultimate draft (seven hundred pages long); this text, annotated by Brian Poole and supplied with Bakhtin's extensive reading list of German sources, should reawaken interest in his contribution to that literary tradition and especially to the *Goethezeit*. And then there is the fate of Bakhtin's Dostoevsky. In the first volume of the *Collected Works* to appear (no. 5 [1940s–1960s]), a half-dozen fascinating fragments toward revising the Dostoevsky book are made available from various years, a great improvement on the single (albeit absorbing) text from 1961 that has long been in print (translated in *PDP*, 283–302). These notes vary from provocative, contentious, unsupported assertion—such as this entry from 1961: "Dostoevsky's heroes do not leave corpses. The image of the corpse (for example, Raskolnikov's or Ivan's) within Dostoevsky's world of visualization is not possible" (365)—to well-elaborated arguments, such as Bakhtin's comments from the early 1940s on the complex working of time, space, biological generation, and sequence in the Dostoevskian "scene."[14] Since several

---

[14] "The nature of the scene of an event in Dostoevsky," Bakhtin writes. "Feel out its traditional organization . . . He [Dostoevsky] could not work with big masses of time (biographical and historical): he never succeeded at a biographical novel, and none of his novels come together as a biographical novel, or a novel of generations, or a novel of [different] epochs. From such eccentric crisis-ridden infernal points you could never pull together a line of biographical or historical becoming. Usually a scene [in a novel] is the

scholars, most assiduously Yuri Kariakin, have regretted Bakhtin's indifference to precisely this "scenic" aspect of the novelist's art, these archival findings might refine the clichés and temper the critics. There are some remarkable lines. Clipped together with several pages on Flaubert is a fragment containing this comment: "We do not know what world we're living in. The novel wants to show us."[15]

This steady current of supplements to Bakhtin's life, especially in the areas of classroom practice and literary bibliography, have nourished hopes in those who see Bakhtin not only as literary scholar and theorist but also as the founder of a new, overarching *metaliteraturovedenie*—or even *metagumanitarnaia nauka* [metahumanities]. Bakhtin's most ardent apologists have long claimed for him this status. It is proper, these critics feel, that such a dialogic metadiscipline be lodged in one of the world's most tenacious nations of the book—and in a culture, moreover, undergoing an exhilarating transition out of tyranny into freedom, made wiser by its terrible experience, and never again to be taken in by naively monologic ideology now that it finds itself on the far side of communism, poststructuralism, and postmodernism.

One such proposal, "Bakhtin's Scholarly 'Testament' and the Problem of Metaliterary Study," was put forward by V. V. Kurilov at a Bakhtin centennial conference in September 1995 in the southern city of Rostov-on-Don (proceedings published in a tiny print run of thirty copies).[16] Its tone recalls the opening ceremonies at the Moscow centennial the preceding June: Bakhtin as both survivor of Stalinism and as pre-Bolshevik, whose biography is a bridge thrown over a nation's rudely interrupted intellectual heritage. Concentrating on the texts of the later years (1960s and 1970s), Kurilov emphasizes their links with the rich culture of the 1910s and 1920s—at which time, he insists, all the components for a

---

thickening of its ordinary way of life, a condensation of temporal life-process, conditioned by the pace and time of life; in D., [scenes] fall out of time, they are built on its explosions or collapses. One person dies and gives birth out of himself to an absolutely new other person, a person with no privileged connection to his own self; a continuation of the novel would be another novel about another hero, with another name." "Ritorika, v meru svoei lzhivosti," in *MMB: ss 5 (96)*, 64.

[15] "K stilistike romana" (1944–45?), in *MMB: ss 5 (96)*, 139.

[16] V. V. Kurilov, "Nauchnoe 'zaveshchanie' M. M. Bakhtina i problema metal-iteraturoveneniia," in N. V. Zababurova, ed., *M. M. Bakhtin i problemy sovremennogo gumanitarnogo znaniia (Materialy mezhvuzovskoi nauchnoi konferentsii. Rostov-na-Donu, 27 sentiabria 1995 goda)* (Rostov-na-Donu: Rostovskii gosudarstvennyi universitet, kafedra teorii i istorii mirovoi literatury, 1995), 3–9. As this book went to press, the pretensions of Bakhtinistics to a "special status" within the humanities was still being contested in leading Russian literary journals. For one answer in the negative, see V. Vakhrushev, "Bakh-tinovedenie—osobyi tip gumanitarnogo znaniia?" in *Voprosy literatury* (January–February 1997): 293–301.

metascience of literature had been in place in post-Silver Age Russia: history, theory, methodology, interrelations with linguistics, philosophy, society as a whole—plus a healthy tradition of self-criticism and self-correction (7). Then came the Stalinist night: literary studies abruptly began to be directed from the top down, with a single "social-engineering approach," and all natural development in the field came to an end (9). "The mission of today's population of Russian literary scholars is to restore the past glory of our national scholarship," Kurilov writes, and Bakhtin could be its patron saint. He would ascend definitively from unofficial to official. But how big, official, institutionalized, or explanatory can Bakhtin's ideas become before their spirit is lost?

Such postcentennial enthusiasms have a loose analogy in Bakhtin's own typology of single- and double-voiced words. Kurilov is amplifying, "stylizing" the legacy, developing it in the direction of its own acknowledged grain. But there is another highly interesting development in Bakhtin studies more akin to "active double-voicedness." It does not reject Bakhtin, not at all; fully conversant with, and converted to, the primary texts, it functions as a sort of affectionate parody from within the industry, working against the familiar bias of Bakhtin's writings. It is drawn to the loopholes, taboos, ignored or impoverished places in his thought rather than the manifoldly rich areas. One could argue that scholars of this latter turn of mind are working more in Bakhtin's own nonconformist spirit. Here belong those critics who fear Bakhtin's assimilation to pragmatic ethical theory because—however attractive this move might be in Western countries—all channels for honest moral thought in Russia had been destroyed by the Soviets, and thus, for the present, "the good and sensible" simply collapses into nihilism or hedonism.[17] Here also we find the first tentative attempts to examine frankly the utopian side of Bakhtin's culturology, which does not insist on God (or on any other primordial principle) and assumes infinite time, space, and resources for all meanings.[18] And here, finally, belong the "revisionist" critics who find dialogism useful in precisely those realms where Bakhtin himself chose to exclude it: in lyric poetry, epic, staged drama, the exact sciences, analytic philosophy, and in the psyche of the lonely or socially isolated self.

As mentioned in chapter 1, the Moscow centennial scheduled several

[17] See A. S. Frants (Ekaterinburg), "O dialoge morali i nravstvennosti," in *MMB i gum mysh I (95)*, 220–22.

[18] "What marvelous Bakhtinian culturological idealism!" concludes one Ekaterinburg scholar, after noting the modest social program that Bakhtinian thought demands of itself and its heavy reliance on preexistent "culture itself" as the alpha and omega of all human satisfaction. See L. A. Zaks, "'U mira est' smysl' (Dukhovnoe mirozdanie M. Bakhtina)," in *MMB i gum mysh II (95)*, 54–57.

panels of "poets for Bakhtin." Although no match for the vast novel-reading and philosophizing majority, a promising start was made and several study circles founded. In this afterword, with its leitmotif of the "human" versus the "hard" sciences, it suffices to mention only one additional expansion and revision of Bakhtin's categories, launched in the early 1990s by a group of gifted young Russian historians of science. Happily, an introduction to their work exists in English, including an interview with the prominent historian-philosophers Anatoly Akhutin and Vladimir Bibler.[19]

Their starting point is territory somewhat alien to Bakhtin as a theorist: the wages of real politics on the fate of the word. Specifically, they analyze the compensatory structures that emerge in a given society—and in an individual's psyche—that is compelled to live large stretches of time under oppressive or monologic conditions. Of special interest to these scholars is the small, informal, often illicit "dialogic community," the "backstreet circles" and "kitchen seminars" that always flourish during repressive regimes, where the lack of more general access to ideas or audience serves to compress and heighten an internal dialogism of thought. Or, as the interviewers expressed it, "perhaps in the solitude and silence of a closed society, one can hear the voices of a universal cultural community better than in the midst of an open society" (325). Akhutin makes the additional commonsensical observation that many serious thinkers and artists are "apparently asocial" or even completely solitary—not for rebellious or Romantic reasons but because the more deeply one is drawn into dialogue the broader does the circle of interlocutors become. And, in this regard, a reading room or study is more capacious than an actual social gathering. "The desire arises to become a lighthouse keeper or a country schoolteacher, a recluse or an anchorite" (384).

What is the nature of our private thought under such conditions? As historians of science and trained logicians, these scholars develop the implications of Bakhtin's *inoratsional'nost'* and *inologika* (a radically "otherwise," nonlinear, inclusionary approach to rationality and logic).[20] Specifi-

---

[19] A special edition of The Johns Hopkins University interdisciplinary journal *Configurations (A Journal of Literature, Science, and Technology)* (vol. 1, no. 3 [1993]) is devoted to this group. For the Bakhtin connection, see especially Daniel A. Alexandrov, "Introduction: Communities of Science and Culture in Russian Science Studies" (323–33) and Daniel Alexandrov and Anton Struchkov, "Bakhtin's Legacy and the History of Science and Culture: An Interview with Anatoli Akhutin and Vladimir Bibler" (335–86). Further page references given in text (translation slightly adjusted).

[20] For more on *inoratsional'nost'*, see G. L. Tul'chinskii, "Dvazhdy 'otstavshii' M. Bakhtin: Postupochnost' i inoratsional'nost' bytiia," in *MMB i fil kul XX, 1 (91)*, 54–61, esp. 58: "Traditional rationality reduces to the 'tekhne' of the ancients—the idea of an artificed and artificial transformation of reality. Rationality . . . is programmatic and goal-oriented; what is rational is what permits a goal to be achieved by optimal means. Reason, the realiza-

cally refuting Bakhtin's own categorization of the exact sciences as monologic, they would reopen debate over the distinction between humanistic and nonhumanistic (341). For if one considers the actual theoretical origins of science—the use made of the "personal philosophical letter" as a hard-science speech genre by seventeenth-century French scientists, for example—one discovers "real dialogue . . . in that sphere which Bakhtin himself regarded as definitely monologic" (347).

These revisionists push further. Not only is the lyric poet not monological, Bibler argues, but "quite the reverse. It is precisely where and when one is alone, in one's inner speech, that we are genuinely dialogic—and no escape is possible from this kind of dialogue. It is precisely here that one does not coincide with oneself, is not 'self-same' but 'located outside' oneself [*vnenakhodim*]. Dialogue in this case cannot be dispensed with. I have walked away and taken my dialogue with me. To put it another way: nowise can I escape from the 'dialogic inhesion' of my consciousness, thinking, understanding, simply because my opponent has moved into another room or left for good" (353). By another route, these scholars are affirming—for good or for ill—the authentically dialogic Raskolnikov, loner and misfit. Akhutin suggests that only a person who commands such a flexible, nondependent relation to the here and now of actual bodies can live fully in "the great time of culture" (384).

In sum, as a theorist of consciousness, these scholars claim, Bakhtin began with real-life time and space, people facing one another and located outside one another. He then analyzed their "encounters" by examining author-hero relations in literary texts—and eventually the internalization of that dialogue, which is the novelistic word. He chose not to begin with the more primary dialogic nature of thinking itself. But we need dialogue because of the way knowledge works, because of our natural cognitive bias toward our own experience and the necessity to resist that bias, not because dialogue makes us happier or more moral. Akhutin and Bibler conclude that by concentrating on the external, ethical virtues

---

tion of the idea, is primary over responsibility. Conscience, shame, sin, repentance are cast out as irrational. Such an understanding of rationality is fraught with pretendership, violence, with appeals to an inherent battle of contradictory forces or some other such 'dialectics' . . . Freedom is presented as the will to unfreedom [*kak volia k nevole*], as the acknowledged necessity of being structured into some goal-oriented program. But there is another tradition of rationality going back to the ancient 'Cosmos'—the idea of the harmonic wholeness of the world. This tradition is supplemented by the Eastern idea of 'Dao' as the Path of Truth in an integrated world. From this point of view, reason is secondary to an originary answerability . . . Reason is the means by which to recognize the measure and depth of this answerability. The world is not a battle of all against all, but the reciprocal supplementarity of unrepeatable individualities. Understanding is the path of freedom but not of will. Precisely in this way is Bakhtin 'rational in some other way' [*inoratsionalen*]."

of dialogism, Bakhtinians restrict the scope and force of their mentor's insights.

One unusually eloquent centennial summation recommends itself as a closing exhibit for the centennial year, for it is organized precisely around Bakhtin as a model for our mental processes. It has the added advantage of appearing in the provinces (Novosibirsk) and in the premiere issue of *Diskurs*, a journal founded in 1996 devoted to "communication, education, culture" and run by intellectuals of the undeniably New Guard. Its chief editor, Valery Tyupa, opened the journal with a Jubilee tribute entitled "Bakhtin as a Paradigm of Thinking"[21]—not as a paradigm of action, interaction, dialogue, but of *thinking*. His essay can remind us of the truly heroic distances traversed by the Russians who have reclaimed Bakhtin.

Tyupa urges us to ignore the fad and the boom and to take Bakhtin's paradigm with the utmost seriousness. From "Hegelianism to Derrida, not to mention neo-Kantianism, Neoplatonism, Marxism, existentialism, all the way up to God-seeking and demonology"—Bakhtin has been attached to them all. This profligacy is in part a result of the reluctance, on the part of Bakhtin's admirers, to systematize his thought. It has seemed inappropriate to this thinker; furthermore, Tyupa adds, "systematizers are rarely liked . . . [they] are accused of revisionism and epigonism at the same time" (10). But Bakhtin deserves this service, because his legacy lacks neither cohesion nor integrity. In honor of the centennial, Tyupa offers his own three-part "paradigm" to explain the dynamics of Bakhtin's thought—which turn out to be, much more ambitiously, the dynamics Bakhtin himself assumed are inherent in thinking in general.

The three parts of the paradigm are *personalism*, *eventness*, and *responsibility*. Each of these categories has its own image, antipode, and type of energy; each also generates a characteristic expectation. *Personalism* sets up an opposition between personality [*lichnost'*] and thing [*veshch'*]. A thing can be described technically and exhaustively, but a personality—since it possesses its own inner space—cannot; since anything that can be exhausted can be destroyed, things can be destroyed whereas personality, "in its wholeness, is unreproducible (unique) and indestructible (belongs to eternity)" (11). In like fashion, a thing can serve as a sign [*znak*] of another thing, but personality can never be a sign. Personality is an "absolute human value" and thus cannot be reduced or wholly represented.

---

[21] V. I. Tyupa, "Bakhtin kak paradigma myshleniia," in *Diskurs*, no. 1 (Novosibirsk: Nauka, 1996): 9–16. Further page references given in text. Tyupa, philosopher and literary critic, is author of a 1995 study entitled "Neotraditionalism or the Fourth Post-Symbolism."

Essential to Bakhtin's personalism, however, is that personality-essence and thing-essence are not antagonistic. The relationship is ambivalent and up to participants to determine. People can choose to treat one another as things; a thing, on occasion, can take on "its own little grain of quasi-personal mystery" (12). But the approaches are distinct, each producing its own data and trademark anxieties. As Bakhtin himself expressed it: "Both viewpoints are justified, but within certain methodologically recognized limits and without combining them. One cannot forbid a physician to work on cadavers on the grounds that his duty is to treat not dead but living people. Death-dealing analysis is quite justified within certain limits. The better a person understands the degree to which he is externally determined (his substantiality), the closer he comes to understanding and exercising his real freedom."[22]

The second part of Tyupa's paradigm, *eventness* [*sobytiinost'*], has three components, by now familiar to the readers of this study. There are event experiences of the "I," of the "other," and then "eventness" as a trait characteristic of thinking as a whole. "If personalism is the 'root system' of Bakhtin's paradigm of thinking and eventness its dominant productive principle ('the trunk'), . . . then the value-bearing 'crown' is responsibility" (13). The Russian word for responsibility [*otvetstvennost'*] implies both a literal "ability to respond," that is, "responsiveness," "answerability," as well as a more ethically burdened meaning. In both senses, Tyupa suggests, it is Bakhtin's "noncategorical imperative" that makes his thinking least akin to classical paradigms (14). Classical thinking was necessity laden. The twentieth-century reaction against this necessity has been free thinking (the most extreme example being deconstruction); but Bakhtin's resolution, Tyupa hastens to add, is at the opposite pole from that of a Barthes or a Derrida.

With Tyupa's comment in mind, we might remind ourselves that Bakhtin had no nervousness about language. He believed that the word, by definition, was adequate to the world's complexity. And, by definition, writers were craftsmen in control of the word. Authors were competent agents; whatever failures occurred were the result of individual lapses in patience, curiosity, energy, literacy, or talent on the part of that author. Words can be made to lie, of course, and Bakhtin was hardly naive about the power of rumor, slander, and the helplessness of historical fact before a timely or nourishing myth. But there is no sense in Bakhtin's work—as there is in the work of so many postmodernists, from Dostoevsky on—of the indwelling inadequacy of the word as such, no trace of that "underground" anxiety about narration and communication that breeds unanswerable crises of identity in modern texts. For the committed decon-

[22] Bakhtin, "From Notes Made in 1970–71," *SpG*, 139.

structionist, no language commands respect. For a disciple of Bakhtin, speakers and authors must believe in and respect *all* languages. If words fail to stick or fail to make sense, I have simply not listened attentively enough to them, not learned enough languages, not put in the required work over them.

Echoing Makhlin earlier, Tyupa concludes that Bakhtin can be called a "neo-traditionalist" in his attitude toward language, obligation, and self-other relations. To be traditional, it appears, means to move slowly and to be satisfied with small gains. Freedom for the "I" inevitably means self-delimitation in relation to an "other." Tyupa notes astutely that Bakhtin rarely reproaches personality or thinking processes for their inconsistency (that would be a "systems" complaint); "the most serious Bakhtinian reproach is always formulated, one way or another, as a reproach for irresponsibility" (14).

Tyupa's last point conceals a minefield of moral uncertainties. For Bakhtin asks that we combine two difficult, diverging qualities: responsiveness (which must be elastic) and obligation (which must be bound). The nature of "responsive obligation" has been one of the unresolvable themes of the present book. For Bakhtin, the phrase appears to mean obligation driven less by referential content than by one's own responding word. If I commit to it, then do it: a good deed, a term paper, a contract murder. If I address a word to you, then I stand by the utterance. When people or conditions change, I can alter those words by uttering new ones; but, being alive, I cannot ignore the fact that words have been uttered and someone might be waiting for a response. Bakhtin was very taken by Thomas Mann's image of hell as "an absolute lack of being heard."[23] And it was surely in light of that ethical dilemma that Bakhtin returned so often to this curious sentiment: that the only relief— he calls it a "gift"—we can offer those who love us, who find us oriented toward them in expectation and yet who crave aesthetic consummation, is our own death.

To work at all, Bakhtin's "responsibility" must presume a series of miraculous balances. There must be outsideness but not aloneness; a vulnerable openness to participation but at the same time autonomy and an indifference to critical assault or personal rejection; a full reserve of "aesthetic love" but combined with a willingness to be more lover than beloved. In Bakhtin's understanding of "response," I can never demand from another person the specific content I think I need. I can only sup-

---

[23] See Bakhtin, "The Problem of the Text" *SpG*, 126. The translator Vern W. McGee glosses this comment as follows: "In Mann's *Dr. Faustus*, the devil describes hell as 'every compassion, every grace, every sparing, every trace of consideration for the incredulous [crying out that this cannot be done; but] . . . it is done, it happens, and indeed without being called to any reckoning in words; in the soundless cellar, far down beneath God's hearing, and happens for all eternity" (130 n. 19).

plement whatever I have managed to elicit. As Bakhtin would have it, this is the dynamic that governs all fundamental human relations: the link between authors and heroes, the impulse to dialogue, the world's wisest novels, the most successful lives. Such a notion of answerability is not so much benevolent or naive—it is neither—as it is exceptionally difficult to live by. Nevertheless, Bakhtin would insist that creative thinking has no other route or option. In chapter 5 we remarked on Bakhtin's definition of architectonic form in his 1924 essay on aesthetics, a spiritually mature position that remained unaltered until the very end of his life. Form is tensed and intense, like a wound-up spring, but never angry or disruptive; it does not divide or reject; it is merciful; and regardless of the bitterness or desperation of its content, it turns toward the world with *dobrota* and *blagostnost'*, kindness and generosity of spirit.

It is tempting to end this study on a scene from the literary life of the supreme artist of the Russian word, a man on the brink of his bicentennial who shared with Bakhtin this understanding of creativity: Alexander Pushkin. No poetic genius was less naive or less encumbered. Nowhere in the Russian nineteenth century—an era increasingly given over to didactic pronouncement and literary prophecy—do we find so perfect a balance between art and moral judgment. ("An immoral work," Pushkin wrote in 1830, in a response to his critics designed never to be published, "is one whose aim or effect is to subvert the rules on which societal happiness or human dignity is based . . . but a joke inspired by heartfelt gaiety and a spontaneous play of the imagination can seem immoral only to those who have a childish or obscure notion of morality.")[24] One could argue, moreover, that no other poet in the Russian language made the idea of *blago-* [goodness, kindness, blessing] more central to more situations, both in the plots of his characters and in the destiny of the ideal poet. His texts are rich in *blagoslovenie, blagodarnost', blagorodstvo, blazhenstvo, blagodat'* [blessing, gratitude, nobility, bliss, grace]. During his final year, a time filled with intolerable personal tension and soon to culminate in the duel of honor that cost him his life, Pushkin published in his literary journal *Sovremennik* his review of a new French translation of *Dei doveri degli uomini* [On the duties of man], a memoir by his contemporary, the Italian dramatist Silvio Pellico.[25] When Bakhtin, in the early 1970s, pulled together his scattered thoughts on the problem of the

[24] "Refutations of Criticisms" [1830, unpublished notes], in Carl R. Proffer, ed. and trans., *The Critical Prose of Alexander Pushkin* (Bloomington: Indiana University Press, 1969), 114 (translation adjusted).

[25] "Novye knigi: Ob obiazannostiakh cheloveka (Sochinenie Sil'vio Pelliko)," in *Sovremennik* 3 (1836), repr. in *Sovremennik, literaturnyi zhurnal A. S. Pushkina 1836–1837: Izbrannye stranitsy* (Moscow: Sovetskaia Rossiia, 1988): 235–38, esp. 236–37. Translation in Proffer, *The Critical Prose of Alexander Pushkin*, 203–6.

text, he made reference to this review of Pushkin's in one laconic phrase: "Pushkin's well-known aphorism about lexicon and books."[26] Given the context, what might Bakhtin have had in mind?

Silvio Pellico had what we would call today a Dostoevskian, or even better a "Soviet," biography. Arrested as a suspected member of the Carbonari in 1820, he was sentenced to death, which was then commuted to ten years in some of the more ghastly dungeons of Europe. His rumination on *The Duties of Man*, published after his release, was such a humble, forgiving, and inspired confirmation of Christian faith that many European readers were confounded. As Pushkin wrote in his review, Pellico had revealed himself to be a *chelovek blagogoveniia*, a man of reverence.

> The astonishment was universal: people expected complaints saturated with bitterness—but instead they read touching meditations filled with clear tranquillity, love, and goodwill. But let us confess our own idle suspicion. Reading these notes, where no expression of impatience, reproach, or hatred ever slips out from under the pen of the unfortunate prisoner, we involuntarily presumed some hidden intention in this indestructible "benignness" [*blagosklonnost'*] toward everyone and everything; this temperance seemed to us an artificed thing. And while enthralled by the writer, we rebuked the man for insincerity.

Pushkin then rebukes his fellow readers for such suspicious reactions. He also calls to account a fellow critic who had claimed, in his review of the book, that *The Duties of Man* would have been read as a dry, dogmatic series of clichés were it not for the well-advertised suffering and dismal life experience that had preceded it. Pushkin resists the implication that eloquence, nobility of spirit, and giftedness need be tied to one's own fate or the conditions of the material world. (As Bakhtin would later make this point: "Freedom cannot change material existence (nor can it want to) . . . Creativity is always related to a change of meaning and cannot become naked material force.") "Does Silvio Pellico really stand in need of an excuse?" Pushkin asks of this radiantly affirmative book. And he answers in a passage that could only have been written by a person wholly confident in the power of language to come together with personality—and live forever. Here is Pushkin on Pellico's critics:

> *But that's not new, that's already been said*—this is one of the most common accusations of the critics. But everything has already been said, all concepts have been expressed and repeated in the course of centuries: so what? Does it follow that the human spirit no longer produces anything new? No, we will not begin to slander that spirit: the human mind is as inexhaustible in the *grasping* of concepts as language is inexhaustible in the *linking up* of

[26] Bakhtin, "The Problem of the Text," *SpG*, 124.

words. All words can be found in a dictionary; but the books that appear every minute are not repetitions of the dictionary. Taken separately, an *idea* can never offer anything new. But *ideas* can be varied and diverse to infinity.

The passage so partakes of Bakhtin's spirit that Averintsev might well be correct in assigning Bakhtin, that great singer of prose, to the ranks of the poets.